OVERCOMING DIFFICULT BEHAVIOUR

OVERCOMING DIFFICULT BEHAVIOUR:

a guide and sourcebook for helping people
with severe mental handicaps

JOHN L. PRESLAND

First published 1989

© **1989 BIMH Publications**

Published and distributed by: **BIMH Publications,**
Foley Industrial Park,
Stourport Road,
Kidderminster,
Worcs. DY11 7QG

ISBN 0 906054 67 2

Typeset by: Action Typesetting Limited, Imperial House, Russell Street, Gloucester GL1 1NE

Printed by: Birmingham Printers (1982) Ltd., Stratford Street North, Birmingham B11 1BY

Contents

Acknowledgements

Many people have, in one way or another, contributed to the content of this book. Teachers, psychologists, and others who work with people with severe mental handicaps have provided helpful information and understanding, either through conversation, through their writings, or by demonstrating their skills. When the first draft was submitted, a number of anonymous reviewers went through the text with fine-tooth combs and offered invaluable advice on how to improve it. My thanks to them all.

I thank also the staff of Wiltshire County Council Library Headquarters, who have been so helpful in obtaining relevant literature for me. I am grateful to the members of Wiltshire Local Education Authority for providing me with employment which has helped me to further my interest in this area – though they are not to blame for, and do not necessarily share, any opinions I have expressed.

Finally, I would like to thank Sylvia Newbould, who has the finest toothed comb in the world, for her extremely helpful editorial guidance, Anne Whelpton, for seeing the manuscript through the final stages, and BIMH Publications for providing me with the opportunity to write for a wider readership.

JLP

PART A

Introduction

Purpose

Matthew, now aged thirteen, has a profound mental handicap. He lives in a small social services home for children and young people with mental handicaps. He was admitted there at the age of six years when his parents, having struggled with the problems he presented until then, felt that they were no longer able to cope and that the effects on the lives of his brother and sister were no longer acceptable. Matthew attends a day special school for children with severe learning difficulties. He has attended special schools since the age of three, moving to the present one on admission to the social services home. He spends every other weekend at home with his family. The problems Matthew presents are much the same in all three settings.

Matthew is mobile and he understands very simple instructions, but he cannot talk, is only partly toilet trained, and feeds himself only with his fingers. Food is often regurgitated and chewed further, which is causing his teeth to decay. Left to himself, he shows different patterns of behaviour at different times. Sometimes he rocks backwards and forwards in a chair for up to twenty minutes at a time. On some days he bangs his head violently on the back of the chair while doing this. Occasionally he stops rocking and claps his hands repeatedly for a while. At other times he shows more interest in people and things around him; but then wanders round the room kicking adults or other children, or pulling other children's hair. At the moment these more mobile and aggressive behaviours are common, while the rocking and hand-clapping are less frequent.

Matthew sometimes does as he is asked and can then sometimes complete a very simple jigsaw with an enjoyment and efficiency that is surprising in view of his other behaviour and skills. More commonly, however, he shakes his head or walks away when asked to do something. If attempts are made to guide him physically he usually resists, often lashing out with his hands, or kicking or banging his own head violently against the nearest hard surface. He has several scars on his forehead where he has caused himself physical damage in this way.

Matthew is not a real person, but he illustrates a collection of behaviour problems which, individually, will be recognised by most people involved with children or adults with severe mental handicaps. These problems may occur singly in one person, or in a variety of combinations. Matthew, for illustrative purposes, is depicted as showing an unusually large number of difficulties, but such a combination is not impossible. Whatever the pattern of such behaviour problems they usually result in serious interference with helpful development in the person concerned and a great deal of stress for other people with mental handicaps and for those who seek to help them. Some of the problems may result in physical injury: to the person showing the behaviour; to other people with handicaps; or to staff and relatives who work with and care for them.

This book is intended as a guide which can be used to help with the problems shown by Matthew and many other people with severe mental handicaps. It is aimed primarily at two main groups of helpers:

> those who have some familiarity with behavioural techniques and use them in their work: which includes teachers, nurses, senior care staff, and some staff in adult training centres, social education centres, and other establishments for helping adults;

> those who offer training, advice, or help to daily users of the techniques: which includes clinical and educational psychologists, doctors, senior social workers with responsibility for training, lecturers in higher education and training establishments, and other professionals with sufficient training and experience for the purpose.

It is hoped, however, that the contents will interest anyone who lives or works with someone who has a severe mental handicap, including parents, other relatives, and volunteers. Accordingly, with the exception of Appendix 4, it is written in a way that assumes no previous knowledge of the techniques described.

Who should the guide help?

The guide is intended to enable help to be given to people of all ages who have severe mental handicaps. These are the 0.5 per cent or so of the whole population whose intellectual difficulties are so severe as to prevent them from leading independent lives when adults, though some can live on their own and take a job with few demands if they are provided with supervision and support. As children, they may need specific help with such activities as talking, feeding, and toileting; skills which are often assumed simply to arrive spontaneously in more able youngsters. Educationally, such children are usually referred to as pupils with severe learning difficulties. They usually attend special schools specifically designed for their needs, though there are occasional special schools which include such provision alongside provision for pupils with less severe difficulties. There are one or two instances of special classes for children with severe learning difficulties in mainstream schools; and a few such children are found in special school or mainstream school special classes for children with less severe difficulties − or even in ordinary classes in mainstream schools. As adults, they may attend adult training centres or social education centres, or they may be employed in sheltered workshops. Many live in mental handicap hospitals or special hostels in the community, despite the current trend towards community-based services. About 30 to 40 per cent are commonly reported to have significant problem behaviours.

Particular care has been taken *not* to exclude from the wide range of people covered:

those with *profound mental handicaps* (0.1 per cent of the total population), who have so many difficulties with everyday activities that they are usually totally dependent on others, or almost so;

those with *multiple handicaps* (difficult to quantify), who combine a severe mental handicap with at least one other severe handicap, such as paralysis or inco-ordination of the limbs, hearing loss, or visual difficulties; and

those with *autistic features,* who often have a similar range of difficulties in coping with everyday activities as people with severe mental handicaps, though some may have abilities within the normal range. Individuals described as having autistic features commonly: appear unaware of other people; will not look at faces; are limited in their use and understanding of language; repeat inappropriate actions, such as rocking or flapping their hands; and resist direction by others, often quite violently. Up to 15 per cent of children with severe mental handicaps have been reported to show such features.

As children, these three groups of people are often placed in "special care classes" within schools for children with severe learning difficulties. Some children who are autistic, however, attend special schools specifically for them. As adults, people in all three groups may attend a "special needs unit" in a hospital or in the community, though some adults with autistic features can cope in environments designed for the wider range of people with severe mental handicaps, and there is at least one specialised community for them in the UK.

Some confusion may arise because of the different systems of nomenclature that exist. For instance, the World Health Organisation differentiates severe mental handicap as defined here into "moderate mental handicap", "severe mental handicap", and "profound mental handicap". Despite my reluctance to use intelligence test scores as an aid to definition, the clearest way to describe the scope of this guide is to state that it refers primarily to people with "IQs" of about 50 and below. Having said that, most of the principles and many of the practices described apply to people generally, so there should be much that is relevant to people who are more able.

Why is help necessary?

A writer of a guide of this kind must first consider certain questions. Why do we speak of some people as "having behaviour problems"? Why do we regard particular behaviours as problems? What should we do about such problems? And for whose benefit? These questions lead to others that are more fundamental. What is the nature of our helping role with people who are severely mentally handicapped? What are we aiming to achieve? How do we reconcile the needs of this group with those of other people?

When seeking to help people with severe mental handicaps it is important to remember the following key principles.

They have the same value as anyone else in society, and their dignity should similarly be respected.

They are individuals all of whom have needs, wishes and rights which are just as important as those of people of the same age who are not handicapped.

They have a right to lead a decent life, as normal and full as possible. This includes as normal a living environment as possible and opportunities to participate in all social, creative, or recreational activities.

They should have as much independence as possible, including as much power to make decisions about their own lives as they can handle safely.

They should receive the same professional services as are available to others and also such special services as will allow their individual abilities and personalities to develop to the full.

They should be protected from exploitation, discrimination, abuse, and degrading treatment.

The kinds of behaviour problem dealt with in this guide seriously interfere with applying the above principles. It is extremely difficult for anyone to treat with dignity people whose hands and faces are covered with faeces which they have smeared on themselves. One of the most fundamental needs of life is sufficient nourishment, and this is adversely affected by such behaviour as refusing or regurgitating food. People may wish to go swimming but be afraid to get into the vehicle that will take them to the swimming baths. A normal living environment is hardly possible for someone who has to be kept away from others because of violent behaviour that is too dangerous to them. Engagement in social, creative, or recreational activities is precluded if someone is exclusively preoccupied with rocking backwards and forwards, repetitive hand-flapping, and other stereotyped behaviours. People cannot be allowed to be independent and make decisions about their own lives if they engage in serious self-mutilation as soon as they are released from control. Full development of abilities is greatly impaired if they refuse to cooperate with those who try to help them develop skills. Protection from exploitation and other evils ideally requires that they be helped to learn how to resist or avoid such hazards, and this is not possible if problem behaviour prevents cooperation in such learning.

It is important, also, to bear in mind that other people with severe mental handicaps, as well as those who are not handicapped, can have their needs, wishes, and rights interfered with by someone's problem behaviour. Violent behaviour may harm them, regurgitation may revolt them, and witnessing self-injurious behaviour may well distress them. Indeed, if they could express their feelings, they might say that having to put up with such things in their living environment was an affront to *their* dignity as human beings. Relatives and staff also have needs, wishes, and rights which must be taken into account. It is probable that they will be less likely to be really helpful to someone who defeats, demoralises, upsets, or injures them by dangerous or otherwise unacceptable behaviour.

While efforts to decrease behaviour problems in general are, therefore, in the interests of all concerned, it must be recognised that different people's interests may sometimes conflict. For instance, someone with a mental handicap living in a hostel may well think it preferable to refuse to get out of bed in the morning; but this may be extremely inconvenient for those who are trying to clean the bedroom and very discourteous to those who have prepared breakfast. How are priorities to be decided? Fortunately, most of the behaviour problems dealt with in this guide are clearly against everyone's interests; but from time to time readers may ask, "Why shouldn't they do that if they want to?". No general rules of guidance can be given here. The interests of the various people concerned must be carefully weighed in each case and the best possible balance found.

General features of behavioural approaches

The approaches recommended in this guide are based on theory and research findings on learning processes, particularly in people with mental handicaps, and their application to behaviour problems. These findings suggest that most behaviour is learned, whether it is appropriate or problem behaviour. Someone who has learned a particular problem behaviour can also learn *not* to engage in it and to engage in some appropriate behaviour instead. The learning can almost always be brought about by carefully planned changes in the person's environment.

Applying theory and research in this way is a major part of the behavioural approaches on which most of the suggestions in this book are based. These approaches focus primarily on what is observable in the behaviour of the person who is to be helped, rather than on what that person may be thinking, or feeling, or planning. This emphasis arises partly because people with mental handicaps are not very efficient at communicating what is going on inside; but also because approaches of this kind have more often been demonstrated to be effective than other methods in decreasing problem behaviours. There is some research which gives a scientific basis to more cognitive approaches to behaviour problems, and this has been incorporated into behavioural thinking, but hardly any of it has been conducted with people who are mentally handicapped.

People with severe mental handicaps cannot make all their own decisions reliably. The most handicapped of all cannot even express their needs and wishes. They rely on those responsible for them to discover what their needs and wishes are, guard their rights, and generally improve their care. For this reason most research and practice in helping them, particularly with their behaviour problems, has concentrated on helping these responsible people to decide what is to be done and how it is to be achieved. This guide is, therefore, couched largely in those terms, though the participation of people with severe mental handicaps is emphasised whenever possible. It is hoped that increasing knowledge will help such participation to become more prominent in the future.

A range of approaches which is rather neglected here is that which assumes medical causes and remedies for problem behaviours. Not being a doctor, I cannot advise competently on medical techniques in any detail. Medical factors certainly can be involved in the genesis of behaviour problems, and medical intervention can sometimes decrease problem behaviours. Some medically defined "syndromes" include particular behaviour problems as part of their definition. Moreover, team work between different professions can lead to combinations of medical and behavioural approaches which are more successful than either alone. Reference is, therefore, made throughout the text to medical factors and interventions which might be appropriate and which may indicate that advice or help from a medical practitioner should be sought.

Application of behavioural approaches requires a close focus on the problems they are attempting to solve. It is, therefore, very important to bear in mind that the person being helped has *many* needs − not just a need to decrease certain behavioural problems. All forms of intervention should be part of an overall life plan, which identifies needs from the person's point of view and requires services to be designed to meet those needs. Needs should be selected from a very broad range, embodying collectively all the key principles for helping people with severe mental handicaps listed earlier.

Expert advice

The extent to which readers apply unaided the approaches described in this guide will vary. It will be influenced by differing levels of experience and training. For detailed implementation with the most complex problems, those with daily responsibility for people with mental handicaps will usually need advice and/or help from a suitably trained psychologist, or some other professional specifically trained in behavioural approaches to problem behaviour. Readers with no previous familiarity with the techniques may wish to seek such help with *any* intervention.

Advice and/or help may also be needed from various professionals on more specific matters. The need for medical expertise has already been mentioned. It can provide information which is of use in designing interventions or excluding identifiable medical causes. Occupational therapists will have much to offer, particularly when there is a need to design apparatus or materials to help with an intervention. Physiotherapists, speech therapists, and dentists will have valuable contributions to make in specific instances. As mentioned earlier, all those trying to help someone with a mental handicap should be working together as a team.

Outline of contents

There are many ways in which a guide of this kind could have been written. In this case an attempt has been made to produce one of interest to readers with differing training, experiences, and attitudes.

The guide begins with Part B, which is a systematic account of the range of techniques available and the ways in which they can be implemented. Part C applies these techniques, in more specific detail, to particular ranges of problems. It offers an account of each group, explains why they are problems, gives such information on their origins as is likely to be helpful for practice, and provides a number of illustrative studies from the literature and/or from my own experience. Knowledge of the material in Part B is assumed.

Part D then looks at measures which are needed to ensure that the techniques are implemented in the most helpful way. These measures include: providing training in applying the techniques; organising the necessary human and other resources, support, and supervision for those employing the techniques; and taking precautions and devising procedures associated with ethics and the law.

There are four Appendices. Appendix 1 is an Action Record, suggested as a suitable format for keeping written records of the planning, implementation, and monitoring of action. Appendix 2 indicates sources of materials needed for applying some of the approaches described. Appendix 3 lists selected books, articles, and assessment schemes which I consulted. Appendix 4 contains notes and references on controversial issues. The book concludes with a bibliography of relevant books and journal articles which readers may find of interest.

References

This book is intended to be a practical guide. Reference in the text to other publications is, therefore, limited to those which provide further information that is directly usable in practice. An exception to this is in Part C, where references are given to the published case studies described so that readers may consult the original if they wish. Appendix 3 provides lists of references which may be helpful either as an aid to practice or as a way into the research or other literature. Appendix 4 offers a few references to support the position I have taken on various controversial issues. No attempt is made to provide a complete bibliography of all works consulted in preparing the guide. Such an enterprise would almost justify a separate publication.

PART B

A guide to action

SECTION 1. INTRODUCTION

Introduction

This section offers a step-by-step guide to dealing with difficult behaviour problems. The guidance is expanded further and illustrated in relation to *specific* behaviour problems in Part C.

Principles and concepts

·The guide is based on a set of concepts called the *ABC analysis,* often referred to also as *behavioural analysis* or *functional analysis.* The analysis starts from the assumption that a behaviour occurs largely because of the circumstances and events occurring around the same time. When investigating the causes of some kind of problem behaviour, therefore, it is necessary to look at what is happening immediately before and immediately after it occurs. The behaviour may be caused by either of these, or by the two in combination.

The following example illustrates this. Graham, a resident in a hospital ward, regularly kicks George, another resident. This may happen largely in response to George's accidentally bumping into Graham. It is also possible that, whenever Graham kicks George, a member of staff rushes up to tell Graham to leave George alone. If Graham likes the resulting attention he may repeat the kicking, either immediately or at another time, in order to attract attention again. A third possibility is that the accidental collision sets off the kicking, and the staff intervention makes it more likely to happen again.

The above events can be represented by the concepts *antecedent, behaviour,* and *consequence* − or *ABC.* These are defined as follows:

Antecedent – an event, object, or situation which has an influence on whether or not a particular behaviour occurs immediately or shortly afterwards. In the example, if George's colliding with Graham is an event which makes it more likely that Graham will kick him, then the collision is an antecedent for the kicking.

Behaviour – this is the action or actions for which an explanation is being sought. In the example, the behaviour is Graham's kicking.

Consequence – an event, object, or situation which occurs immediately or shortly after a particular behaviour and has an influence on whether or not that behaviour occurs again on a similar occasion in the future. In the example, if staff attention makes it more likely that Graham's kicking will be repeated, it is a consequence for that behaviour.

This sequence can be represented by the following diagram:

Antecedent ⟶ Behaviour ⟶ Consequence

| (for example, George bumps into Graham) | (for example, Graham kicks George) | (for example, staff member lectures Graham) |

If these events occur regularly, then Graham's kicking George is likely to become established as a regular response to collision with him.

In applying the above analysis to help resolve behaviour problems, some further concepts are helpful. Firstly, behaviour can be divided into *appropriate behaviour* and *problem behaviour*. These are defined as follows:

Appropriate behaviour – a behaviour which needs to increase (that is, occur more often). For instance, among many behaviours staff might want Graham to increase, they might ask him to watch George and move to avoid collisions, or to move away immediately after a collision, or to ask George to be more careful, since these are all relevant to overcoming the problem.

Problem behaviour – a behaviour which needs to decrease (that is, occur less often). Graham's kicking is an obvious example.

It is important to realise that the absence of an appropriate behaviour can itself be the problem; for instance, if a person does not speak to anybody, though capable of doing so.

Secondly, antecedents and consequences can make a behaviour either more likely to occur or less likely to occur. For instance, George colliding with Graham is an antecedent which makes Graham's kicking *more* likely to occur; but if George walked carefully round Graham instead, this antecedent would make the kicking *less* likely to occur. For consequences, technical terms are available to help make the distinction:

A *reinforcing consequence*, or *reinforcer*, makes the behaviour more likely to occur again, either immediately or in the future. When this happens the behaviour is said to have been *reinforced* and *reinforcement* to have taken place. It could be said, therefore, that attention from a staff member is a reinforcing consequence for Graham's kicking.

A *reducing consequence,* or *reducer,* makes the behaviour less likely to occur again. When this occurs the behaviour can be said to have been *reduced* and *reduction* to have taken place. If, for instance, Graham is made to sit ignored in a corner every time he kicks George, this might make him less likely to kick George again. The action, therefore, could be said to be a reducing consquence for that behaviour. (It should be noted that the terms *punishers, punished,* and *punishment* have been used more commonly for this set of concepts but, for the reasons outlined in Appendix 4, I would like to see these terms discarded.)

From principles to practice

The approaches in this guide assume that, if a problem behaviour occurs because of particular antecedents and consequences, it can be decreased by changing those influences. In addition, it assumes that the appropriate behaviour which should replace the problem behaviour can be increased by careful choice of antecedents and consequences. The approaches, therefore, aim to:

> *increase appropriate behaviours* by systematic use of antecedents and consequences which make them more likely to occur, and reinforcing consequences which make them more likely to occur again. As an antecedent, for instance, Graham could be asked to respond to collisions with George by asking him to be more careful and, when he did this, he could be congratulated as a reinforcing consequence. If these procedures were followed regularly, Graham should respond to George in a more acceptable way more often.

> *decrease problem behaviours* by systematic use of antecedents which make them less likely to occur, and reducing consequences which make them less likely to occur again. An antecedent for Graham could be to warn him in advance not to kick George, and a reducing consequence could be to make him sit ignored in a corner for a short while if he did. If these procedures were followed regularly, kicking should decrease.

The sequence of guidance

Though the specific approaches in this guide vary widely, they can be encompassed within a reasonably standard sequence of stages. These stages are described in the remaining sections of Part B, as follows.

Section 2. Problem behaviours are identified as well as appropriate behaviours which should replace them. These are defined very clearly and specifically.

Section 3. Priority behaviours for intervention are selected. Some may need to be divided into steps so that the person can achieve the target behaviour gradually.

Section 4. An accurate record is made of the occurrence of each of the behaviours selected in order to assess their frequency and severity. This provides a baseline which can be compared with later measures to show the extent of improvement.

Section 5. Before embarking on an intervention, the environmental events and circumstances (that is, the antecedents and consequences) which are fostering the problem behaviours are investigated.

Section 6. In the light of the findings in *Section 5*, decisions are made about what modifications of the environment (that is, of the antecedents and consequences) are needed to give the best chance of changing a person's behaviour in the directions wanted. This section covers changes in antecedents and consequences needed to *increase* appropriate behaviours.

Section 7. As in Section 6, decisions are made about modifying the environment to change a person's behaviour. This section covers any changes in antecedents and consequences needed to *decrease* problem behaviours.

Section 8. The modifications identified in Sections 6 and 7 are incorporated into a planned, systematic intervention programme.

Section 9. The programme is implemented and its effects measured.

Section 10. The results of the programme are evaluated. This may lead to a modified programme or a new programme to improve on the results. Alternatively it may lead to systematic fading out of the first programme in ways which will not result in a return of the problem behaviours.

Figure 1 illustrates the stages outlined and their inter-relationships.

Recording

A careful record should be kept of the planning, implementation, and outcome of each intervention programme. These records should be kept together and be readily accessible. Together they form what, in this book, is called an Action Record. There must be many possible ways of producing such a record. The scheme offered in this book can be purchased separately, full size, for individual use with people with mental handicaps. Its particular design is based on the following assumptions, which any alternative scheme should also take into account:

The forms should be simple to understand and use. To this end, each numbered form serves just one specific purpose at one particular stage of intervention.

It should be easy to find forms in the Action Record when reading about them in the text or in the instructions for the record itself. The forms are, therefore, numbered in the order in which they appear in the text and the instructions.

It should be easy to restore the forms to the correct order when, inevitably, they get mixed up. They are, therefore, numbered according to the order in which they will be used. All that is needed to restore them to order is to look at the number on the top right hand corner of each form and assemble them consecutively.

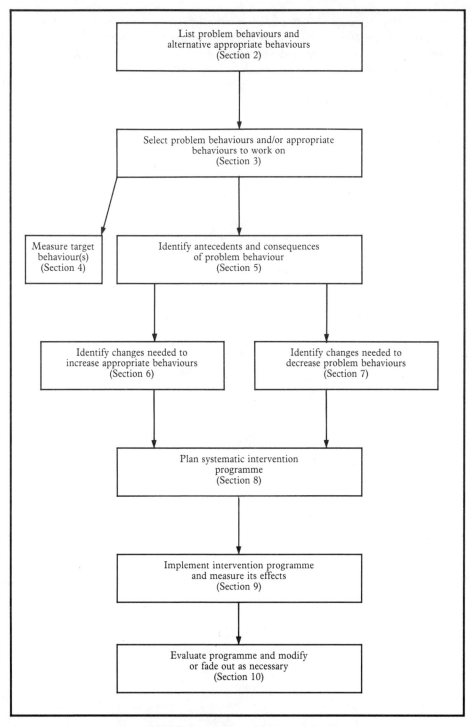

FIGURE 1. Stages in intervention

The numbering system should take account of variations in the combinations of forms used for different interventions. There is, therefore, a main set of forms numbered 1 to 12 which will be needed for every intervention, and additional and supplementary forms labelled, for instance, 12A, 12B, and 12C, which will also sometimes be needed at particular stages of an intervention. This system avoids confusing gaps in the numerical sequence which would otherwise occur when the extra forms are not required.

The complete Action Record suggested in this book is set out in Appendix 1, together with a brief guide to using it. Use of its constituent forms will be illustrated at intervals in the sections that follow. It should be borne in mind that, since the procedures which will need to be followed cannot be entirely predicted, the Action Record as set out in Appendix 1 cannot be used in a fixed routine. The precise combination of constituent forms will vary from one intervention to another. Permission is granted to copy some forms where duplicates are needed as explained at the beginning of the Action Record set. There should, however, always be a front sheet (Form 1) which identifies the person to whom the Record relates and lists all the forms that have been used (see Figure 2).

Name: _Rachel Robertson_   **ACTION RECORD FORM 1**

Date of birth: _12/3/1969_   **Contents of Action Record**

Group and/or establishment: _Ash Villa_

Completed by: _Mr. Perks_

Action by: _Direct care staff on ward_

Any special notes: _Rachel receives regular medication to control epilepsy. Frequency of seizures approx. 1 grand mal seizure per month._

List of Action Record Forms completed:

Form number	Date completed	Form number	Date completed
2	2/5/89	12A	1/7/89 - 8/7/89
3	2/5/89	12B	9/7/89
4	6/5/89 to 21/5/89		
5	14/5/89 - 26/5/89		
6	27/5/89		
6A	27/5/89 - 1/6/89		
7	1/6/89		
8	1/6/89		
9	1/6/89		
10	2/6/89 - 23/6/89		
11	24/6/89		
12	24/6/89		

FIGURE 2. Example of a partly completed Action Record Form 1 showing forms used in interventions to date

PART B

A guide to action

SECTION 2. DEFINING THE PROBLEM

Problem behaviours

Defining problem behaviours

Defining a problem as it affects the people involved and defining it in a way that may lead to an effective solution is not necessarily the same thing. Plainly, the latter is more helpful in the long run. Initially, however, there is something to be said for looking carefully at what is bothersome. If someone is showing "a behaviour problem", what exactly is that person doing? Why is it a problem? To whom?

It is suggested that, if someone is showing "a behaviour problem", the first step is to make a list of all the behaviours the person presents that are problems and need to decrease. These can be referred to as *problem behaviours.* Each of these behaviours should be described very specifically, so that anyone reading the list would know exactly what occurs.

Firstly, the precise actions should be specified. To say, for example, "Tom is aggressive" is too vague. "Tom hits Fred and Jane on their heads" is much clearer.

Secondly, the circumstances in which the actions occur should be noted. In deciding this it may be helpful to ask the following questions.

Where does it happen? Perhaps Tom hits Fred and Jane only in a particular room – or even only at a table.

When does it happen? It may, for instance, only occur late in the afternoon.

Are other events occurring regularly when it happens? For example, does it happen when Fred and Jane are receiving attention from some person with responsibility?

In whose presence does it happen? Perhaps it occurs only when a person with responsibility is there, or only when a particular person with responsibility is there. Or only when no such person is in view.

To record the circumstances in which "Tom hits Fred and Jane on their heads", the following information might be added: "when sitting at a table at any time when no specific activity is required of him and no person with responsibility appears to be looking".

It is important to give careful consideration to why a behaviour is identified as a problem. Sometimes this is because it is interfering with the needs of the person with a mental handicap who is displaying it. Perhaps the person would like to go for a walk without being held on to by someone else and, to achieve this, it is necessary to overcome the problem behaviour of rushing heedlessly into the road, ignoring all instructions to stop or come back. Sometimes, it is because it presents a problem for other people with mental handicaps in the same environment, for instance, if the person kicks them or pulls their hair. And sometimes the behaviour creates problems primarily for those with responsibility who may, for example, be attacked, or prevented from doing things that are important because of someone's excessive, attention-seeking behaviour.

These examples can all be legitimate reasons for regarding a behaviour as a problem. However, different people have different needs and interests. It is, therefore, necessary to consider how great a problem the behaviour is to each person concerned and to balance the needs of the one showing the behaviour against the needs of the others. To this end, as well as those with responsibility, the person exhibiting the problem behaviour and any other people with mental handicaps involved in the situation should be consulted about which behaviours need to be decreased, if they are able to discuss this in a meaningful way.

Recording problem behaviours

One way of recording the results of the above observation and thinking is to use Form 2 of the Action Record, as illustrated in Figure 3.

Appropriate behaviours

Defining appropriate behaviours

Sometimes, instead of a problem behaviour occurring that needs to be decreased, the difficulty is that certain kinds of behaviour are *not* occurring. For instance, Jenny may appear to understand that her father wants her to come to him, but may not do so. When thinking in terms of solutions rather than difficulties it can be useful to identify behaviours which should *increase*, so that the person concerned engages in these rather than in the problem behaviours. These various behaviours can be referred to as *appropriate behaviours*. A person may already be able to perform them but rarely does so, or may need to learn to perform them.

As with problem behaviours, a list should be made of any appropriate behaviours that are considered desirable for the person to develop. It might include:

Behaviours whose absence is a problem in itself. In the example, this would mean Jenny going to her father when called (as opposed to refusing to do so).

Behaviours incompatible with specific problem behaviours. If Tom works continuously on a jigsaw at a table, for instance, he cannot at the same time hit somebody else who is careful to stay on the other side of the room.

Name: TOM EVANS	ACTION RECORD FORM 2
Date of birth: 7-11-73	Problem behaviours
Completed by: MRS. CROWTHER	

What problem behaviours do you want to decrease in frequency?

Specific action involved	Circumstances of occurrence (places, times, events, people, etc.)
HITS FRED AND JANE ON THEIR HEADS	WHEN SITTING AT A TABLE AT ANY TIME, WHEN NO SPECIFIC ACTIVITY IS REQUIRED OF HIM AND NO PERSON WITH RESPONSIBILITY APPEARS TO BE LOOKING
STAYS WHERE HE IS OR WALKS AWAY	UNPREDICTABLY, WHEN SOMEONE WITH RESPONSIBILITY SAYS "COME HERE", IN THE CLASSROOM, WORKROOM OR HOSTEL
STRUGGLES WITH AND KICKS PERSON WITH RESPONSIBILITY	WHEN ANY PERSON WITH RESPONSIBILITY MAKES ANY ATTEMPT TO TAKE HIM TO THE TOILET
RUNS AWAY SCREAMING	WHEN ANYBODY WEARING A WHITE COAT COMES INTO THE SITTING ROOM OF HIS HOSTEL

FIGURE 3. Example of part of a completed Action Record Form 2
showing identification of problem behaviour

Behaviours which serve the same purpose as specific problem behaviours. If Tessa throws objects around dangerously for the purpose of attracting the attention of care staff, for instance, staff could attend to her for finding a duster and dusting some furniture instead.

Behaviours which are worth encouraging because they may make someone less likely to engage in problem behaviours. If, for instance, Tom learns to use an interesting new object or game, he might not wish to hit others even if they are within range. If he learns how to "sign" that he wants something to eat or drink, or some attention, he will not need to have a tantrum or engage in attention-seeking self-injurious behaviour to demonstrate his wishes.

As before, descriptions should be in terms of specific behaviours and they should specify the circumstances in which the behaviour ought to occur by asking questions of a similar type to those suggested for problem behaviours. Where possible, they should also state the standards to be reached. Thus the specific behaviour might be "Tom goes to person with responsibility", the circumstances "whenever he is asked to at any time or place and (almost) regardless of what he is doing", and the standards "within 5 seconds of being asked".

As with problem behaviours, wherever possible the person with a mental handicap, if able to communicate sufficiently, should be asked to help in the selection of appropriate behaviours to increase.

Recording
Recording can be carried out using Form 3 of the Action Record as illustrated in the example shown in Figure 4.

Further guidance on selecting appropriate behaviours
Identifying appropriate behaviours to encourage, as alternatives to problem behaviours, leads into the very large area of selecting tasks for learning and developmental progress generally. This cannot be covered in detail here. For fuller guidance, readers are referred to texts and assessment schemes such as those listed in Appendix 3.

In general, however, the process starts by establishing aims for a person with a mental handicap. Such aims might be, for instance, to help the person to become more independent, to engage in a greater variety of interesting and satisfying activities, to develop existing abilities to the full, and to relate better to other people. The kinds of learning required to achieve these aims are grouped under a number of main areas of functioning, such as movement, language, intellectual functioning, social skills, self-help, and play/leisure activities.

It is usual to foster learning and development within each of the areas relevant to the aims. Within each area, it is possible to identify sequences of specific learning tasks and to place these in order for teaching purposes. Thus, for play/leisure activities, one of the earliest items might be:

When a startling noise (eg, bell, rattle) is presented, blinks or otherwise responds in a way suggesting it has been noted within 5 seconds of its presentation.

At a later stage, the learning tasks might include items of increased level of difficulty, such as:

Name: TOM EVANS	ACTION RECORD FORM 3
Date of birth: 7-11-73	Appropriate behaviours
Completed by: MRS. CROWTHER	

What appropriate behaviours do you want to increase in frequency?

Specific actions required with standards	Circumstances in which required (places, times, events, people, etc.)
SITS AT A TABLE AND WORKS ON A JIGSAW FOR 5 MINUTES	ANYWHERE, AT ANY TIME WHEN NOT REQUIRED TO DO ANYTHING ELSE BY A PERSON WITH RESPONSIBILITY
GOES TO PERSON WITH RESPONSIBILITY WITHIN 5 SECONDS	WHEN A PERSON WITH RESPONSIBILITY SAYS "COME HERE" AT ANY TIME IN ANY PLACE
GOES WILLINGLY TO TOILET WITH A PERSON WITH RESPONSIBILITY	WHEN A PERSON WITH RESPONSIBILITY TAKES HIM BY THE HAND AND SAYS "TOILET" AT ANY TIME IN ANY PLACE
CONTINUES CURRENT ACTIVITY	WHEN ANYBODY WEARING A WHITE COAT COMES INTO THE SITTING ROOM OF HIS HOSTEL

FIGURE 4. Example of part of a completed Action Record Form 3 showing identification of appropriate alternative behaviours.

> When a large object (eg, rattle) is placed 6 to 9 inches from one hand, reaches for it within 5 seconds.

To provide for a wide range of ability, many such tasks can be arranged in a long series, culminating in items like:

> Plays draughts with another person with a mental handicap, following all the rules accurately and accordingly to planned purposes.

By completing checklists of such tasks, it is possible to identify those which it is most appropriate to teach a particular person at a particular time. A group of related items of similar difficulty level identified in this way is often referred to as a *goal*. An individual item, described specifically and unambiguously, is usually called an *objective*.

Within the play/leisure area, a goal for a particular person might be:

> Drawing shapes and simple pictures.

Objectives within this goal (adapted from work done by a teacher with a 10-year-old boy in the course of a workshop I organised) might include:

> Given paper and an easy-to-hold crayon, draws a roughly straight line on request.

> Given paper and an easy-to hold crayon, draws a roughly circular shape upon request.

> Given paper and an easy-to-hold crayon, draws a simple human figure on request.

> Given paper and an easy-to-hold crayon, draws a simple house on request.

Any one of these might, on investigation, prove to be the most suitable objective to teach at a particular time.

Careful teaching of almost any task, carefully selected as described, can make problem behaviours less likely to occur during learning time. However, many problem behaviours occur most often when nobody with responsibility is involved with the people presenting them. It is, therefore, important to select, where possible, some behaviours which will allow people to occupy themselves in appropriate ways when left alone. These behaviours will usually be ones used in play and leisure activities generally, and in acceptable exploration of the environment. If people are engaged and interested in activities of these kinds, then problem behaviours are less likely to occur. Ideally, a range of appropriate behaviours should be selected, so that they have some better alternative to problem behaviours whenever these are likely to occur. Identification of objectives within each of the areas of functioning relevant to the established aims for each person can help to achieve this.

PART B

A guide to action

SECTION 3. SELECTION AND FURTHER ANALYSIS OF APPROPRIATE AND PROBLEM BEHAVIOURS

Establishing priorities

If the lists recommended in Section 2 contain more than a very small number of behaviours, it will be difficult to work on them all at once. A decision will need to be made on which to deal with first. This might be just one behaviour to increase or decrease, or several. The person being helped should contribute as much as possible to this decision, according to ability.

It is difficult to offer specific guidelines here as each situation will be unique. However, a particular behaviour might be chosen as a priority for one or more of the following reasons.

It is the most troublesome − to the person showing the behaviour, to other people with mental handicaps, or to people with day-to-day responsibility.

It is easier to change than other listed behaviours − and quick results can be obtained which will encourage both the person with a mental handicap and the helper.

A change in his behaviour will be most helpful − to most of the people involved in the situation.

A change in this behaviour is likely to facilitate other changes − for instance, those who have responsibility would find it very difficult to work on any aspect of the behaviour of a person who regularly runs away from them, so changing the running away would be a priority.

A change in the behaviour is the most desirable objective ethically.

In general, it is more positive to *increase* appropriate behaviours than to work directly on *decreasing* problem behaviours. The former should, therefore, be given preference unless there is good reason for supposing that working directly on problem behaviours will be more effective.

For recording purposes, it is suggested that the behaviours chosen as priorities be underlined in the lists of problem and appropriate behaviours (see Figures 3 and 4).

Identifying behaviour chains

Sometimes, a priority problem behaviour is regularly preceded by other behaviours which are less problematic. If these earlier behaviours are stopped, a person may never reach the point at which the problem behaviour itself occurs. Sometimes, a regular chain of behaviours can be identified which culminate in the problem behaviour.

Continuing the example begun in Sections 1 and 2, Tom assaults others by hitting them on the head. He may lead up to it first by stopping his current activity and looking around, then moving away from it, then trying to take something away from Fred or Jane, then shouting at them, then pushing them, and then finally hitting one or both of them. If someone can intervene at the point when Tom stops his current activity, all the later behaviours might be averted.

All the behaviours in a chain can be listed in the same way as problem behaviours. A choice can then be made as to which shall be the object of intervention. This choice is then underlined and it becomes the priority behaviour for change.

Analysing priority behaviours

Once a priority behaviour has been identified, it is necessary to consider whether it can be worked on directly or whether it needs to be approached gradually. Where a gradual approach is needed, the behaviour changes required can be divided into a series of easy steps to be achieved in sequence. For example, Derek, who soils himself, struggles and kicks when a residential worker tries to train him to go to the toilet by leading him there. To begin with, therefore, the worker might first just get Derek to tolerate a hand on his arm. When that is achieved, she might get him to accept being led a short distance across the room, gradually increasing the distance until he is prepared to be taken to the toilet.

In other instances, the steps might be based on actions and standards, rather than on circumstances. For instance Nicola, who keeps taking off her clothes when she is supposed to be dressed, might first learn to keep one garment on, then two, and so on.

The component steps from this kind of analysis can be recorded in the same way as the original problem and appropriate behaviours, and the steps chosen to work on first underlined. For Derek, in the preceding example, a separate Form 2 from the Action Record might be completed as illustrated in Figure 5. As can be seen an extra code (i) has been added to the existing number so that it can be easily filed in the appropriate sequence. The alternative appropriate behaviour would be "Goes willingly with adult". This would be divided according to the same graded circumstances as the problem behaviour, and recorded similarly on a separate Form 3 of the Action Record.

An alternative appropriate behaviour sometimes requires further analysis because the child or adult needs to be taught how to perform it. In Section 2 an example was described of objectives selected for a 10-year-old boy. One of these was:

Given paper and an easy-to-hold crayon, draws a simple human figure on request.

Name: **Derek Tomlinson**   ACTION RECORD FORM 2

Date of birth: 15th June 1973   **Problem behaviours**

Completed by: M.S Terry

What problem behaviours do you want to decrease in frequency?

Specific action involved	Circumstances of occurrence (places, times, events, people, etc.)
Struggles and kicks	When an adult puts a hand on his arm and leads him 1 foot across the room, at any time in any place.
Struggles and kicks	When an adult says "Toilet", puts a hand on his arm and leads him 1 foot across the room, at any time in any place.
Struggles and kicks	When an adult says "Toilet", puts a hand on his arm and leads him 6 feet in the direction of the toilet, at any time in any place.
Struggles and kicks	When an adult says "Toilet", puts a hand on his arm and leads him all the way to the toilet.

FIGURE 5. Example of part of a completed Action Record Form 2, showing the component steps needed to change a specific behaviour

The teacher concerned analysed this task into steps, getting the boy to draw first a circle, then a straight line, then a circle with a straight line attached to it, then a head with facial features and hair, and finally a human figure with head and facial features, body, and stick arms and legs with feet and fingers. This could have been divided up further still, had it been necessary, so that, at one stage in the process, there could have been a sequence like:

. . . drawing two touching circular shapes to represent head and body . . .

. . . drawing two touching circular shapes to represent head and body with straight lines attached to body to represent arms and legs . . .

. . . drawing two touching circular shapes to represent head and body with straight lines attached to body to represent arms and legs and with eyes, nose and mouth . . .

A Form 3 would also be used for noting such a sequence.

PART B

A guide to action

SECTION 4. MEASURING THE PROBLEM

Purposes of measuring

It is helpful to obtain an accurate record of the extent of each behaviour to be changed before planning methods of changing it. People who have done this have commented that the procedure was helpful in that it aided objectivity, helped them focus more specifically on particular problems and assess them accurately, and gave a clearer picture of improvement.

One immediate purpose is to assess the severity of a problem behaviour in order to decide whether to plan an intervention programme and, if so, to decide how much time and effort should be put into overcoming the problem. It is sometimes found that the frequency of a problem behaviour is less than it was thought to be when judged subjectively.

Another purpose is to give a *baseline*, against which measures after intervention can be compared, so that an accurate determination of the amount of improvement can be made.

It is not uncommon, however, to carry out carefully planned interventions without prior measuring; and it is probably better to do that than not to plan systematically at all.

Measuring is also helpful for recording the occurrence of the appropriate behaviours which, it is hoped, will replace those that are problems. Sometimes, the appropriate behaviours alone might be measured – where the problem is non-compliance, for instance.

Types of measuring

There are two main methods of measurement in common use. One method, *event recording*, counts the number of occasions on which a behaviour occurs. The other, *time recording*, records the amount of time which the behaviour occupies. Each method has variations within it. Both methods will now be described and guidance given on which to use. The information is summarised in Figure 6.

Event recording

Nature of event recording

The simplest method of measurement is to count the number of times a behaviour occurs. This is called *event recording*. It should not be done from memory. Instead, each instance should be recorded immediately, perhaps by putting a mark on a piece of paper, or by any one of a variety of other devices. (Some suppliers offer a hand tally, for example, which can be pressed each time a behaviour occurs, and which then records the number of presses.) Recording should be carried out for a predetermined period, on a regular basis, and in the circumstances where the behaviour has to be changed. At the end of each period, the instances recorded should be totalled.

The process can be illustrated using Form 4 of the Action Record. One or more of the behaviours selected in Sections 2 and 3 are first written down, very specifically. A clear recording schedule is then devised and written down. This should state precisely what is to be counted, when the counting is to occur, the circumstances under which it is to occur, the duration of each counting period, and the way in which observations are to be committed to paper. When recording begins, the exact time and duration of each observation period should be written down, and each instance of the behaviour being counted should be noted as it occurs. At the end of the recording period, the number of occurrences should be counted, giving a total for that period.

An example is shown in Figure 7. It concerns Julie, a young woman who frequently bangs her head on the high back of a chair that has been specially adapted to enable her to sit upright despite poor back and head control. Though the head banging does her no apparent harm, there is concern that it might eventually do so or, if unchecked, that it may become more violent.

Recording the overall picture

It is useful to obtain an overall picture of the level of occurrence of the behaviour during this baseline period so that it can be compared with the level during a subsequent intervention programme. The average number of instances of the behaviour should therefore be calculated. In the example, the total number of occurrences over the six baseline observation periods was 250, so the average per observation period was $250 \div 6$ which is 41.7. During the subsequent intervention programme, the totals for the eight observation periods were 7, 3, 0, 2, 0, 5, 2 and 6, giving a total of 25 and an average of $25 \div 8$ which is 3.1 per observation period. This shows a dramatic decrease in banging of the head against the chair back.

An alternative method of recording is to draw a graph, and this is shown for the same data in Figure 8.

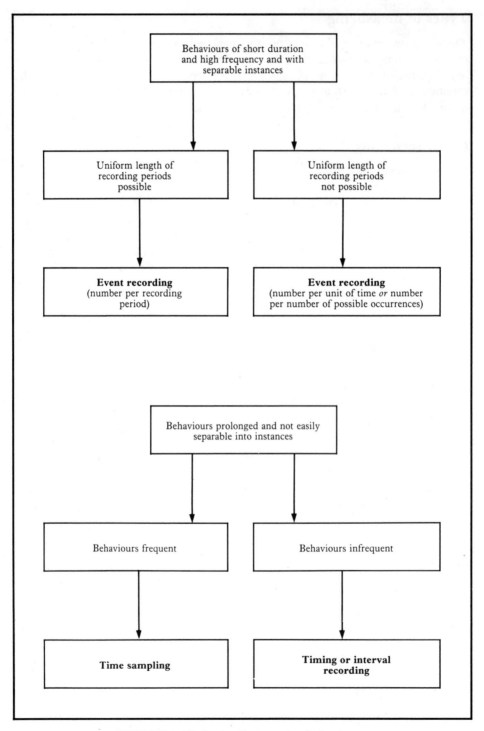

FIGURE 6. Methods of measuring behaviour

Name: _Julie Barnes_	ACTION RECORD FORM 4
Date of birth: _3/9/1966_	**Baseline measuring**
Completed by: _Mr. Peiks_	

Behaviour observed

On the ward, bangs her head against the chair back

Observation schedule
(state when, under what circumstances, for how long, what is observed, and what is to be recorded)

Between 10.15 & 10.45 each morning, on the ward, note each incident of head-banging

Records

Date and period of observation	Records of frequency or duration	Total for observation period
4th Apl. 86	~~HHH~~ ~~HHH~~ ~~HHH~~ ~~HHH~~ ~~HHH~~ I	26
5th Apl. 86	~~HHH~~ ~~HHH~~ ~~HHH~~ IIII	19
6th Apl. 86	~~HHH~~ ~~HHH~~ ~~HHH~~ ~~HHH~~ ~~HHH~~ ~~HHH~~ ~~HHH~~ ~~HHH~~ ~~HHH~~ ~~HHH~~ ~~HHH~~ ~~HHH~~ ~~HHH~~ ~~HHH~~ ~~HHH~~ I	76
7th Apl. 86	~~HHH~~ ~~HHH~~ ~~HHH~~ IIII	19
10th Apl. 86	~~HHH~~ ~~HHH~~ ~~HHH~~ ~~HHH~~ ~~HHH~~ ~~HHH~~ ~~HHH~~ ~~HHH~~ ~~HHH~~ I	46
11th Apl. 86	~~HHH~~ ~~HHH~~ ~~HHH~~ ~~HHH~~ ~~HHH~~ ~~HHH~~ ~~HHH~~ ~~HHH~~ ~~HHH~~ ~~HHH~~ ~~HHH~~ ~~HHH~~ IIII	64
	Total for 6 periods	250
	Average per period	41.7

**FIGURE 7. Example of part of a completed Action Record Form 4
showing the method of measuring using event recording**

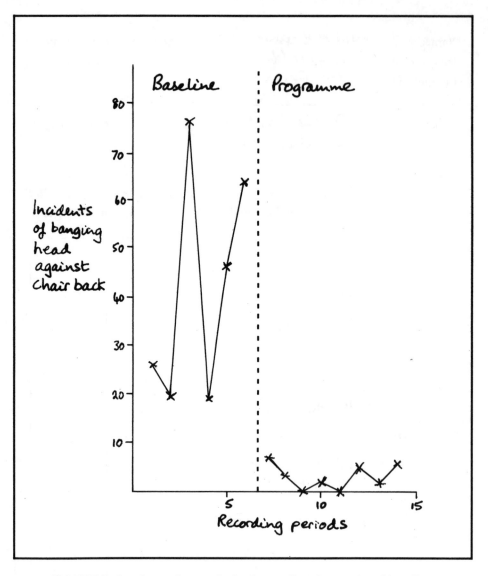

FIGURE 8. An alternative method of recording the results of baseline measuring of a behaviour using event recording

Suitability of behaviours

Event recording is the best and easiest method of measuring behaviours which occur in a consistent form, are of short duration, and take place often enough to make counting feasible, but not too often to make it impracticable. Examples of behaviours which can be recorded in this way are punching, kicking, refusing to comply with a single request, stealing food, and eating single items of rubbish. For some behaviours it is necessary to find a particular aspect to measure. Regurgitation of food, for instance, can be measured by counting each occasion that regurgitated material leaves the mouth or by counting the constrictions of the throat which occur during the process.

Timing and duration

Careful thought is needed for deciding the timing and duration of recording. Recording must be done at times of day when the behaviour usually occurs and when an intervention programme will subsequently take place. For very frequent behaviours, short periods of observation are sufficient; perhaps as little as five minutes, if that produces a total of useful size. These short observation periods can be planned as often as is feasible, but certainly at least once a day. For infrequent behaviours, on the other hand, longer periods of observation are needed. It may sometimes be necessary to make each period a whole day in order to obtain a measure sufficiently large to allow demonstration of a decrease when an intervention programme is subsequently introduced. Usually an average of five occurrences per period would be the minimum required, and 10 would be preferable. If a behaviour occurs less than five times a day on average, there is much to be said for having recording periods of two or more days each.

Variations of event recording

Sometimes, the procedures for event recording need to be altered to suit particular circumstances. If, for instance, it is not possible to have recording periods of uniform length, the totals for different periods cannot validly be compared with each other. It is then necessary to convert the results to, say, the number of occurrences per minute. In the workshop example of Julie, for instance, there was one 30-minute recording period in which she banged her head against the chair back 76 times. This number could be divided by 30 to give a rate per minute of approximately 2.5. This figure could then validly be compared with rates per minute similarly calculated from recording periods of other lengths, if these were unavoidable.

The likely design of the eventual intervention programme can have implications for measurement, though these will not necessarily be known at this stage. Some features, however, can often be forecast. With very severe self-injurious behaviour, for instance, any intervention programme must seek to prevent the behaviour occurring. If this is successful the behaviour itself cannot be counted but it may be possible to count the number of times the person makes a move towards it. Marie, for example, slaps her own face. If the programme involves the prevention of face-slapping by grabbing Marie's hand before it reaches her face, the number of times she moves her hand rapidly towards her face could be counted.

Another variation which anticipates programme design is of particular help when occasions for carrying out appropriate behaviours have to be specifically set up. If Terry is afraid of getting into cars, situations for doing this may need to be specially arranged. Periods of time are then not relevant. Instead the situation could be set up a fixed number of times each day, and the number of times Terry makes an appropriate response could be counted. If he is asked to get into a car on five occasions each day, the number of times he complies out of five should be recorded.

Time recording by time sampling

Nature and recording of time sampling

Time sampling is the most easily implemented method of measuring how much time is

Name: .... *James White*   **ACTION RECORD FORM 4**

Date of birth: .... *17 / 1 / 80* ....   **Baseline measuring**

Completed by: .... *Mrs. Fellows* ....

Behaviour observed

Rocking backwards and forwards

Observation schedule

(State when, under what circumstances, for how long, what is observed, and what is to be recorded)

Between 10.15 and 10.42 each morning, in the class-room observe James momentarily every three minutes.

Records *If he is rocking record R; if he isn't rocking, record N*

Date and period of observation	Records of frequency or duration	Total for observation period
	Moments 3 minutes apart	*Total Rs*
4th Apl 76	*R R R N R R N R R R*	*8*
5th Apl 76	*R N R R R R R R R R*	*9*

FIGURE 9. Example of part of a completed Action Record Form 4 showing the method of measuring using time sampling

occupied by a behaviour. It consists of determining, in advance, a series of particular moments at which a person is to be observed, observing at those moments, and noting on each occasion whether the person is or is not engaging in the behaviour to be measured. A timer (such as a kitchen timer) can be set to ring as a reminder, or a cassette recorder can be programmed to give a reminder at regular intervals. The *Dribble Control Box* (see Part C, Section 7) gives "bleeps" at pre-set intervals for a similar purpose.

As with event recording, the written record should include a clear description of the behaviour, a description of the observation schedule, the date and time of each observation period, records of behaviour made at the time of observation, and summary data. If James' stereotyped rocking were to be measured by this method, the record might take the form shown in Figure 9. Each total could, if preferred, be converted to a fraction, decimal, or percentage of the total number of observations: 8/10 and 9/10 respectively for fractions; .8 and .9 for decimals, and 80% and 90% respectively for percentages. As with event recording, an average total per observation period can be calculated, or a graph can be drawn.

Suitability of behaviours

Time sampling is best used to measure behaviours which are prolonged, and which cannot easily be split into equivalent, separate occurrences. Drooling is an obvious example. Stereotyped behaviours may also need this approach. Rocking backwards and forwards, for instance, often occurs too fast for individual "rocks" to be easily counted, so that event recording would be very difficult.

Duration and timing

As with event recording, time sampling needs to be carried out at times when the behaviour usually occurs and when an intervention programme will subsequently take place. The length and number of observations per recording period should enable an average baseline rate of at least five occurrences per recording period.

Other types of time recording

Some behaviours, though not easily separable into instances for counting, are not frequent enough to be measured effectively by time sampling. There are two other methods of time recording which may then be helpful, *interval recording* and *timing*.

Interval recording

The observation periods are divided into equal intervals, as for time sampling, but the observation is continuous. For each interval a record is kept of whether or not the behaviour observed occurred at all or did not occur at all. The total for each observation period is the number of intervals when the behaviour occurred, and this can be converted to a fraction, decimal, or percentage of the total number of intervals.

This method, however, is a very demanding way of recording, since it requires constant observation of behaviour and frequent attention to timing. Since it is most applicable to behaviours of low frequency, it requires these two kinds of vigilance to be maintained for long periods in order to record enough instances. It really requires an assistant who can concentrate specifically on the recording task. This method, therefore, should be considered only when no other method is available.

Timing

Using this method the total time for which the behaviour occurred during an observation period is measured directly. A stop-watch is used to measure the length of each spell of, say, rocking and this is then noted down, the results being totalled at the end of the recording period. Alternatively, a cumulative stop-watch which can be stopped and started without the hands returning to zero can be used. This automatically provides the total time at the end of the recording period without the need to add up the separate records.

This is another demanding method of measuring, and is therefore best used with behaviour which, though continuous when it occurs, does not occur very frequently. It is likely, therefore, that the recording period will need to be a day or more in length.

Further guidance on recording

Other recording methods can be used for specific purposes. Drooling, for instance, has been measured by weighing a bib at the beginning and end of a recording period to find the weight of saliva which has escaped from the mouth.

If it has been decided to measure more than one behaviour, it is possible to measure different behaviours at different times if this makes the process easier. The behaviours might be measured at different times of day, on alternate days, or even for alternate weeks or fortnights.

It is desirable, whenever possible, to involve people with mental handicaps in recording their own behaviour. Those who are more able might be able to make records of whether a behaviour has occurred or not, and perhaps may understand what simply expressed totals mean. Time sampling, for instance, has been carried out by young people with mental handicaps with the aid of a cassette recorder which gave a reminding "bleep" at predetermined intervals.

Whatever the method of measurement chosen, it is important to use it consistently so that any comparisons of behaviour before and after introduction of an intervention programme are valid. It is also wise to continue baseline recording for at least 10 recording periods, since smaller numbers run a greater risk of an overall measure which is not typical. This is particularly important where the behaviour is relatively infrequent, or where the frequency fluctuates wildly. Indeed, 10 periods may then not be enough.

PART B

A guide to action

SECTION 5. IDENTIFYING EXISTING INFLUENCES

The ABC approach

When problem and appropriate behaviours have been identified and measured, it is helpful to investigate what is causing them. A problem may have many causes, and these may stretch far back into the past and interact with each other in complex ways. It is doubtful whether it is ever possible to give a complete explanation for a problem which is absolutely certain to be valid. The approach taken in this guide is to seek information about causes which is likely to be directly relevant to planning an intervention programme. This involves looking for influences which are in the present rather than the past, since the past cannot be changed.

The ABC approach outlined in Section 1 is increasingly used for identifying the causes of a problem in advance of planning and intervention. It forms the basis of the suggestions made here. ABC, as already explained, stands for antecedents − behaviour − consequences. Antecedents have an advance effect on whether or not a behaviour occurs; while consequences occur after it and have an effect on whether it occurs again, either immediately or in the future.

It is important to realise that antecedents and consequences are more often *changes* in the environment rather than fixed features. The *removal* of some features can, therefore, be included in the definition. For example, Sarah may bang her head against the nursery wall every time another child takes a toy away from her. Removal of unwelcome control can also be a consequence. For instance, a nurse asks Joe, a hospital resident, to carry out an unwelcome task. Joe bangs his head on a wall and the nurse then stops her attempts to make him do as she wishes. This consequence would be expected to make the head-banging more likely to occur again.

Why identify antecedents and consequences?

If it is possible to discover what antecedents and consequences are making a problem behaviour more probable, that information can be used, when planning an intervention, in one or both of the following ways.

Antecedents and consequences that make a problem behaviour more likely to occur can be eliminated or lessened, in the hope that the problem behaviour will then decrease. If cuddling someone after an episode of head-banging is discontinued, for example, the head-banging may decrease.

Antecedents and consequences that make a problem behaviour more likely to occur might also be used to make an alternative *appropriate* behaviour more likely. For instance, Sarah bangs her head when a toy or other object is taken from her and then is cuddled. Instead, she could be cuddled for asking for the object back, or for indicating in some other way that she wants it returned. The cuddling consequence might then make this appropriate behaviour more likely to occur instead of the head-banging.

Possible antecedents of problem behaviours

It is best to start with no preconceptions. Anything *might* be making a problem behaviour more likely to occur. For instance, if Gary often has tantrums in a room with a blue door and is cuddled out of the tantrum each time, he may then have a tantrum every time he sees a blue door wherever it may be. Any blue door may signal to him that pleasant consequences can be obtained. Many antecedents, however, are more comprehensible from a common sense point of view.

In identifying antecedents of problem behaviours, some authors distinguish between: the *setting*, which refers to relatively stable features of the environment that make a particular range of behaviours more likely to occur; the *internal state* of the person concerned, which may also have a general predisposing influence; and *specific events*, which actually trigger off specific behaviours.

A setting may predispose people to engage in problem behaviour if:

they are in an environment where there are no interesting materials, activities, toys, games, or other features to hold their attention;

they are not getting attention from anybody;

something in the physical environment is irritating them;

somebody they dislike or fear is present.

An internal state may predispose people to engage in problem behaviour if, for example, they have a medical condition which is making the behaviour more likely to occur. There is evidence that pain, such as that caused by an ear infection, can lead to self-injurious behaviour, perhaps as an attempt to gain relief. Sometimes, medical *treatment* can contribute to people's behaviour problems, such as the use of medication to control epileptic fits which can affect their mood. The internal state can also be something relatively normal. It has been found, for instance, that just as in the general population, behaviour in some women with mental handicap can change for the worse just before menstruation.

Specific events that might trigger off problem behaviours in people with mental handicaps include the following:

being expected to work at something which is very difficult for them (the behaviour may then function as a means of escape);

being required to do something they don't want to do (again, the problem behaviour may be used for escape);

having something taken away from them by one of their fellows;

being assaulted by one of their fellows;

seeing others engage in problem behaviour.

Possible consequences of problem behaviour

Like antecedents that lead to problem behaviour, any consequence of a problem behaviour might make it more likely to occur again. Consequences which are known to reinforce problem behaviour include:

pleasant attention, such as cuddling, from an adult;

other kinds of attention, which most people do not find reinforcing but some individuals do, such as someone speaking in an angry tone;

attention from fellows;

noise, such as that resulting from head-banging or chair-throwing;

any kind of environmental change, regardless of its nature, just because it is interesting;

escape, such as when someone does not want to do what a person with responsibility requires, and avoids doing so by struggling violently. (This consequence in effect brings to an end an unwelcome antecedent, a process commonly referred to as *negative reinforcement*. This, however, is a highly confused concept which is best avoided.)

The escape consequence, however, is of particular help in understanding the nature of reinforcing consequences. The situation after someone has escaped from having to do something may not in itself be very welcome. Even so it is preferable to the situation that has been avoided, and thus it reinforces the behaviour which led to the escape. It can be stated as a generalisation that a consequence is reinforcing, not necessarily because of what it is, but more because it is preferable to what went before (that is, the antecedents).

Identification processes

The identification of antecedents and consequences might best be combined with measuring the problem behaviours. If it is too difficult to measure a behaviour and to note its antecedents and consequences at the same time, it may be wise to establish different times of day for the two processes, or to measure behaviour on one day and note its antecedents and consequences the next. If even that is too difficult, measuring of the problem behaviour could be carried out on its own until a baseline is completed. As many subsequent days as necessary could then be devoted to identifying the antecedents and consequences.

Sometimes, measuring the behaviour may in itself throw light on existing influences. In one recent study interval recording was used throughout the day with several young people with mental handicaps. This showed that, for two of the young people, the problem behaviours measured were occurring much more at some times of day than at others. This gave clues as to the people, activities, and events which might have been influencing the behaviour to occur.

For a more thorough identification process, each time a problem behaviour occurs, a note should be made of what is happening immediately or shortly before the occurrence and of what happens immediately or shortly afterwards. Descriptions should be as specific as possible. The written records could take various forms, but one possibility is provided by Form 5 of the Action Record, as illustrated in Figure 10. A separate Form 5 should be completed for each problem behaviour.

The recording process should continue until there are enough observations to show some sort of causal pattern, or to make it fairly clear that no regular pattern is going to emerge. Anything which occurs regularly shortly before the behaviour may be an antecedent making it more likely to occur; and anything which regularly occurs shortly afterwards may be a reinforcing consequence.

It does not necessarily follow that any single event observed is either an antecedent or a consequence. The things noted for Jonathan (see Figure 10) may have no influence on his wetting behaviour. If any one of them is noted a number of times, however, it is more likely to be relevant. Unfortunately, it cannot be assumed that an event which follows the behaviour rarely is *not* a reinforcing consequence. Once a behaviour is established, it can be maintained by only occasional reinforcement. In this situation the environmental features or changes which reinforce the behaviour may not often be observed. The procedures described here, therefore, suggest only some of the possibilities.

Medical investigation may reveal antecedents. As mentioned earlier in this Section, for instance, pain from an ear infection can lead to self-injurious behaviour. This antecedent, however, may not be evident without medical examination. It is harder to think of consequences that would be revealed by such investigation, but the possibility must remain open. Regular medical surveillance should be a routine part of the lives of people with mental handicaps. If it is not, and there is a sudden change in someone's behaviour, a medical investigation should be requested.

When conclusions are reached, they should be written down. For Jonathan, further observations along the lines illustrated might lead his parents to fill in Form 6 of the Action Record as shown in Figure 11. A separate Form 6 should be completed for each problem behaviour observed.

Name: Jonathan Barker

Date of birth: 5 - 4 - 78

Completed by: Steve Barker

ACTION RECORD FORM 5

Before and after a problem behaviour

Behaviour Jonathan wets his trousers and underpants at home between returning from school at 4.15 p.m. and having his evening meal at 6.30 p.m.

Occasion	What precedes	What follows
1	Mother said, "Do you want to go to the toilet?"	Mother took him to the bathroom, removed his trousers and underpants, washed and dried him, telling him at intervals that he was a naughty boy.
2	Favourite T.V. programme ended	Mother said, "I'm fed up with your wetting - you can stay wet", and went off to the kitchen.
3	Jonathan sitting watching T.V. on his own	Mother said, "Are you wet again? Well, I'm too busy to change you now".

FIGURE 10. Example of part of a completed Action Record Form 5 showing recording of events occurring before and after a problem behaviour

Name: _Jonathan Barker_

Date of birth: _5/4/1978_

Completed by: _Mrs. P. M. Barker_

ACTION RECORD FORM 6

**Existing patterns of
antecedents and consequences**

Behaviour _Jonathan wets his trousers and underpants
at home between returning from school at 4.15 pm and
having his evening meal at 6.30 pm._

Regular patterns of antecedents and consequences

We can't be sure of any regular antecedents for
Jonathan's wetting, but watching television might
be a setting antecedent. There were also two
occasions when he did it as soon as I asked him to
go to the toilet, so that might be a specific event
that makes him more likely to wet.

We're wondering if a possible reinforcing
consequence is our giving him attention,
because we either change him, or tell him
off, or both.

**FIGURE 11. Example of part of a completed Action Record Form 6 used to
suggest possible antecedents and consequences of a problem behaviour**

Identifying antecedents and consequences that discourage appropriate behaviour

Appropriate behaviours need to be increased, as well as problem behaviours decreased. There may be influences which are making an appropriate behaviour unlikely to occur. It is helpful to identify these. Though methods of discovery have not been studied extensively, the following ideas might be worth pursuing.

If an appropriate behaviour is *not* occurring, identifying any antecedents which are making it unlikely to occur is mainly a matter of speculation. It may be that the environment is bare, with few opportunities for appropriate behaviour; for example, there may be no activities, toys, or other features of interest. Or people may be asked to engage in appropriate behaviours which they perceive as being difficult or unpleasant. Or they may have a medical problem which causes them discomfort if they perform the behaviour. Listing the possibilities can be useful. Perhaps alteration of some of them (for example, introducing toys into a bare environment or replacing toys with more adult leisure activities to suit people's changing needs) may make appropriate behaviour more likely to occur.

If an appropriate behaviour occurs sometimes, though rarely, it may be possible to identify reducing consequences to account for this. For instance, when Paul completes an appropriate task for his teacher, the teacher may then stop attending to him, or may give him less attention than he had during the task. This may be a reducing consequence, making it less likely that Paul will complete the task on a later occasion. Alternatively, when Paul completes the task the teacher may ask him to repeat it for further practice. This could be a reducing consequence if he does not like doing it.

Consequences of this kind, which may reduce appropriate behaviour, can be observed and recorded in much the same way as recommended earlier for consequences of problem behaviours. Changing them might make the appropriate behaviour more likely to be repeated. For instance, if Paul completes a task this might be followed by continued attention from the teacher for a while, rather than an immediate withdrawal or lessening of it.

Medical investigation may also reveal consequences that discourage appropriate behaviour. For example, Sheila is found to have an anal fissure which the doctor thinks causes her pain after the normal passing of faeces. This pain is likely to act as a reducing consequence for appropriate toileting behaviour. Treatment of the medical condition to prevent the occurence of pain will make appropriate toileting behaviour more likely and will decrease the likelihood of the development of toileting problems.

In the Action Record, Form 5A can be used to record what happens on particular occasions, and Form 6 to write down conclusions. A separate Form 5A and Form 6 should be used for recording each behaviour.

Involving the person to be helped

Whenever someone with a mental handicap is able to communicate sufficiently, the processes that have so far been described should be supplemented by seeking the person's own view about what antecedents and consequences might be operating. For example, what does Bob think makes him engage in his problem behaviour? Which of these influences come before it, and which after it? What does Bob think stimulates him to engage in various appropriate behaviours, and what does he get out of them?

This involvement might be regarded as an extension, with those who are more able, of the communication process which is occurring with people with severe mental handicaps and behaviour problems generally. It has been argued that problem behaviours are themselves communication devices. They may represent requests for attention, information, affection, help, food, or play objects; or they may be intended to show that someone does not want to do something, or wants something to stop; or they may be attempts to share feelings such as distress, annoyance, pleasure, or humour.

The investigation procedures described in this Section could be seen as devices for obtaining the maximum information from personal communications with people with severe mental handicaps. It can then be used to help them to overcome their behaviour problems and to provide for their other individual needs.

PART B

A guide to action

SECTION 6. DECIDING ON CHANGES TO INCREASE APPROPRIATE BEHAVIOURS

Page

Appropriate behaviours as the priority

In planning intervention programmes preference should be given to increasing the appropriate behaviours which should replace existing problem behaviours. It is, therefore, best to seek first to identify any changes which can be made in the environment which will have that effect.

Using prior findings

The analysis of each problem behaviour and its present causes which has taken place up to this point may well suggest changes in antecedents and consequences which will help alter the behaviour in helpful directions. Carol, for example, a young woman who attends an adult training centre, shows problem behaviours because the work required of her is too unwelcome or too difficult. This antecedent might be changed for a new one, namely, presenting her with work of a different kind which she does not dislike. The new antecedent might then promote the more appropriate behaviour of participating in the work, and the problem behaviour may decrease as a result.

Turning to consequences, if it seems likely that attention from someone with responsibility is reinforcing a person's problem behaviour, care could be taken to withhold attention following the behaviour but to give it when the person is behaving appropriately. The attention is then being used to reinforce appropriate behaviour, which should therefore increase.

A different kind of consequence is escape from unwelcome control. Brian, for instance, who attends a school for children with severe learning difficulties, refuses to go into the classroom for a lesson. His teacher tries to guide him physically to do this but Brian struggles and the teacher then gives up and allows him to stay outside. Brian's struggling has been reinforced by escape from the teacher's guidance. However, this consequence could be used to reinforce appropriate behaviour – by continuing the guidance until Brian enters the classroom and allowing him to escape from it as soon as he has done so.

Advance investigation of why appropriate behaviours are failing to occur may also suggest helpful changes. If the environment is bare, introducing toys or other leisure activities may be an antecedent which will encourage appropriate activities with these materials. Potentially useful reinforcing consequences may also come to light. If a pupil is very slow to complete work tasks, it may be because completing the task results in the teacher's going away and attending to someone else. A promising change might then be to remain with the pupil and chat for a short time after completion of the task.

Other antecedents and consequences

The antecedents and consequences which are already occurring in the problem situation are far from being the only ones that could be used. The person trying to help may already be aware of others that would be likely to influence the behaviour of the person presenting a problem. If not, a method of discovering such possibilities and deciding which of them are most likely to be effective must be found. Some helpers may wish to investigate the possibilities thoroughly before planning an intervention programme, while others may prefer to try out a programme with some antecedents and consequences which look promising, but change the programme if it does not work. Whichever course is chosen a number of the most promising possibilities should be written down, and a decision made about which of these are thought most likely to be effective.

Welcome and unwelcome experiences

How can antecedents and consequences which will make appropriate behaviours more likely to occur be identified? Both are defined by their after-effects. They cannot, therefore, be identified for certain in advance. The only answer is to try to predict which experiences will have the required effects on behaviour. In order to do this it can be useful to identify:

> *experiences which the person appears to welcome;* for example, by active attempts to have or participate in them, immediate participation when they are presented, or engaging in them more than once;

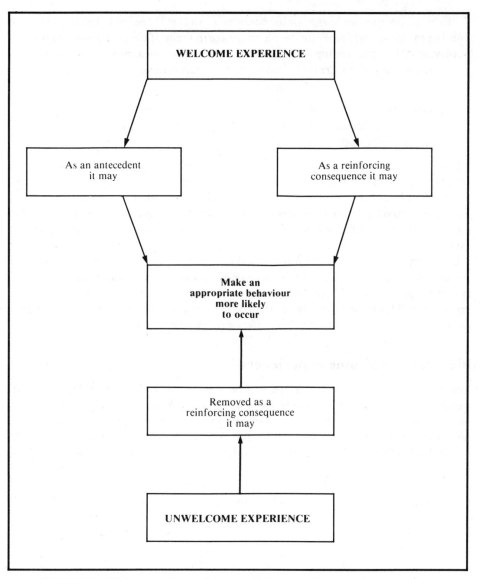

FIGURE 12. Welcome and unwelcome experiences and appropriate behaviour

experiences which the person appears to dislike or avoid; for example, by pushing something away, turning away, or making expressions of distaste.

For simplicity these will be referred to as *welcome experiences* and *unwelcome experiences* respectively.

Knowledge of which experiences are welcome and which are unwelcome to someone enables better predictions to be made of how far the experiences will help to make appropriate behaviours more likely to occur. The main possibilities, which are illustrated in Figure 12, are as follows.

Welcome activities can be appropriate behaviours. All that is needed to increase them is to provide opportunities for people to engage in them. If Claire is known to find playing with a spinning top a welcome experience, this is an appropriate behaviour which can easily be increased simply by the antecedent of providing a top and suitable circumstances for playing with it.

Welcome experiences can be directly usable as reinforcing consequences for appropriate behaviour. Thus, if Claire does as she is told by an adult her compliance might be reinforced by the opportunity to play with the top.

If an *experience is unwelcome, its removal can reinforce appropriate behaviour.* John is reluctant to put on his shoes. His parent might ask him to put them on, then physically prevent him from leaving the spot until he complies. As soon as the shoes are on, John is allowed to move away. This process, often referred to as *negative reinforcement,* can be useful if there is difficulty in effectively reinforcing a behaviour with welcome experiences.

It is recommended that, if planning an intervention programme for someone for whom antecedents and consequences likely to increase appropriate behaviour are not already apparent, procedures should be carried out to identify welcome and unwelcome experiences. This information should then be used to work out suitable antecedents and consequences. The rest of this section offers guidance on how this can be done.

Identifying welcome experiences

Many people with mental handicaps will be able to say what experiences they find welcome. Casual observation will identify a wider range. Anything people do voluntarily more than once can be regarded as welcome to them. For example, they may occupy themselves with some toys or leisure activities more frequently than others, or seek certain kinds of food, or look for praise or other attention from some people more than others. They may engage in some activities very frequently; even such activities as whirling round or making ritual finger gestures should be noted. They may actively seek activities that people with responsibility do for, or to, or with them; or may show by facial or other expressions, or by willing cooperation, that they look favourably upon them. Even problem behaviours should be noted since they presumably find engaging in them welcome, and this may be useful when deciding upon consequences.

It is important to remember that there can be marked individual differences. For instance, some people with mental handicaps find physical restraint an unwelcome experience, while others welcome it. Some like attention, while others prefer to be left alone.

Spontaneous observations about someone's welcome experiences should be written down as soon as possible after they are made. Each experience should be described as precisely as possible and there should be an equally specific account of the behaviours which showed it to be welcome. If necessary, the identification process can be made more systematic by listing a sizeable number of possible welcome experiences, presenting each a number of times, and making a written record of the reactions observed. The list should include things the person might like to do, eat, or have; as well as things done with, to, or for the person that are enjoyed. In this way it is usually possible to identify a number of welcome experiences. Form 6A from the Action Record is helpful for recording the information as illustrated in Figure 13.

It may also be helpful to establish degrees of preference between different welcome experiences. A selection of several experiences can be presented to see which the person chooses. Systems can, if necessary, be worked out for presenting the items in different combinations. A note is kept of the preferred item from each combination, and the process is continued until those preferred over all others become clear.

The process is likely to be more difficult for people with the most severe handicaps. It may be necessary to look for less obvious indications that an experience is welcome, such as curling of the toes, widening of the eyes, or stiffening of the body, which someone who knows them well feels able to interpret. The experiences presented will be more limited, often just simple sensory stimulation, such as the ringing of a bell, vibration from a mattress or hand-held device, flashing lights, stroking, tickling, cuddling, bouncing, or rocking. When people with responsibility cannot be providing such stimulation, it can be given by means of various devices: mobiles, which touch or are within easy reach; a radio or record player; a rubber animal which makes a noise when squashed; or small bells attached to parts of the body.

A systematic approach is of particular importance. A list could be made, for instance, of as many different ways as possible of presenting visual stimuli, auditory stimuli, smells, tastes, "feels", and sensations of movement. Longhorn (1988) provides some useful ideas. Each of these could then be presented for, say, two minutes each, and reactions noted. There is much to be said for having several "trials" for each item at different times of day, so that a potentially useful experience is not overlooked because of an atypical moment. It is also important not to jump too easily to conclusions about what kinds of stimulation are worth trying. For instance, bright lights have been shown to be very effective in stimulating many people with very poor vision, whereas the reverse might have been expected.

If there is difficulty in identifying which experiences someone finds welcome, it may be helpful to start by noting the person's reactions to particular experiences that are known to be liked. The same reactions should then be looked for in response to other experiences where there is less certainty. Stella, for example, takes food willingly, so it is probably a welcome experience for her. If her eyes widen and she goes very still when food is offered, these reactions might be looked for when other experiences are presented. If they occur, the experience they follow is probably welcome to her. Systematic written recording of such reactions could be helpful. The *Affective Communication Scale* (Coupe *et al.* 1985) is a helpful instrument which can be used for this purpose.

Identifying unwelcome experiences

As with welcome experiences, conversation and spontaneous observation can reveal a great deal about which experiences are unwelcome to which people. The results can be systematically recorded in much the same way. People may show that something is unwelcome in various ways. They may refuse to engage in a particular behaviour, or even run away when asked to do so. They may scowl or cry when something is done to them by someone with responsibility, or when something is taken away from them. They may show in various ways, such as crying or other "protest" noises, that they dislike being

Name:	Sally Singleton	ACTION RECORD FORM 6A
Date of birth:	3/8/1973	Welcome and unwelcome
Completed by:	Gill Preston	experiences

Experience	Reaction	Welcome or Unwelcome
Mr. A. rotates the wheelchair in which Sally sits	Sally laughs when it rotates. When Mr. A. comes near enough, she grabs his arm and puts it on the wheelchair.	Welcome
Mr. A. gives Sally a model car	Sally plays with the car for some time. If it falls to the ground she looks for it.	Welcome
Mr. A. plays his guitar	Sally goes still and her eyes widen	Welcome
When left alone Sally often rocks backwards and forwards in her wheelchair.	She continues the rocking for a long time	Welcome

FIGURE 13. Example of part of a completed Action Record Form 6A, used to identify possible welcome and unwelcome experiences

ignored or put on their own (or alternatively being given attention or being with other people). Again, more subtle indications have to be looked for in those with the most severe handicaps, when much depends upon the observer's familiarity with each person's facial expressions and bodily movements under varying circumstances.

It is doubtful whether identifying unwelcome experiences can be as systematic as identifying those that are welcome. It is certainly not reasonable to subject people to a battery of potentially unpleasant experiences just to see which they find unwelcome. With mildly unpleasant experiences, however, there is sometimes a case for presenting them systematically and noting reactions, usually when there is difficulty in identifying many welcome experiences likely to be useful in an intervention. Again, Form 6A could be used for recording purposes.

Changing antecedents to make appropriate behaviours more likely

Types of antecedent change
Section 5 described how any behaviour can be made more likely to occur by features of the environment (the setting), internal states, and specific events. Antecedent changes to make appropriate behaviours more likely will now be considered under those headings. It is important to bear in mind that the different approaches suggested overlap, and that some measures might be interpreted as examples of more than one of the approaches. This does not prevent the suggestions from being helpful in practice, however, if they are thought of as a variety of guidelines for selecting antecedents and consequences rather than as separate techniques. Every effort should be made to consult the people being helped whenever possible and to allow their views and wishes to be influential.

Changing the setting
Firstly, sources of discomfort or irritation in the environment need to be minimised. The temperature may need adjustment, the noise level may need to be reduced, or certain people may need to be kept out of the room or in a far corner.

Secondly, as high a level of welcome experiences as possible should be provided. Making television programmes available may be very effective for some people in some environments, and watching selected programmes with interest can be an appropriate behaviour. It should be noted, however, that this is *not* the same as people with responsibility switching on any television programme and then going away. Toys and/or other appropriate leisure materials should be provided. For instance, a large space with swings, slides, sand box, and jungle gym for climbing was found particularly helpful with some children with autistic features in one investigation; and a confined space with vinyl covered panels, slides, and stairs in another.

Provided individual capabilities are allowed for, a varied selection of activities is probably better than one or two. In educational situations, interesting learning tasks at an appropriate difficulty level need to be provided. In work situations, work which is enjoyed and which can be performed successfully is important.

Whatever the situation, people with responsibility need to interact with the people they are helping in welcome ways, such as talking to them, helping them to do things, sharing leisure activities with them, doing things for them, and accepting help from them. They should also try to encourage them to interact with the other people with mental handicaps who share their environment.

Changing internal states

Devices for changing internal states are many and various and include those already described under changing the setting. Maintaining a certain temperature in a room, for instance, might be important. The presence or absence of certain individuals might make a difference. A high level of welcome experiences should be helpful in maintaining interest and a sense of wellbeing. The main concern under this heading, however, is to bring improvements for individuals rather than to change the environment generally.

Medical measures of various kinds to reduce or eliminate pain and discomfort are obvious examples. Pain from an ear infection, for instance, is not very conducive to appropriate behaviour and can be cured. A physiotherapist can advise on comfortable positioning, so that discomfort does not distract someone with a physical handicap from appropriate behaviour.

Relaxation can also be beneficial and there is now a little evidence to indicate that training in muscular relaxation is possible with people with severe mental handicaps. This can help them engage in appropriate behaviours that they might otherwise avoid through fear, such as going on a bus. The technique usually requires verbal instruction beyond their understanding so that modifications may be needed, such as: physical guidance; provision of a model to imitate; or initial reinforcement of any small step towards relaxation, and then gradually requiring behaviour that is progressively closer to relaxation before reinforcement is delivered. One series of strategies used successfully with children with autistic features included guiding them to relax by various oral instructions, such as "Lie down", "Close your eyes" and "Pretend you are in bed where it is warm and comfortable", together with gentle manipulation of arms, legs, and neck. These instructions to relax were given while they were in lying, sitting, or standing positions, and they were praised for any behaviour that looked relaxed.

A more elaborate form of relaxation training (behavioural relaxation training or BRT) has recently been found to be effective with some adults with severe mental handicaps. It concentrates on aspects of relaxation which are clearly observable. The person sits in a comfortable chair, and the helper demonstrates first the unrelaxed, then the relaxed, state in each of a number of areas of the body. The person has to watch and then imitate the relaxed behaviour. The helper gives manual guidance where necessary and provides information on how successful the imitation has been. The relaxed behaviours to be imitated are:

an overall unrelaxed − and then relaxed posture;

quick breathing − and then slow breathing;

noisy − and then silent;

trunk fidgeting −˙and then trunk still;

head held tense or moving − and then leaning back and still;

eyes closed tight − and then lightly closed or open and still;

lips pressed tight together − and then relaxed;

throat swallowing or otherwise moving − and then still;

shoulders hunched – and then sloped and even;

fists tense – and then relaxed and open;

legs moving or tense – and then still;

feet moving – and then feet still.

Similar relaxing effects can be obtained in other ways. The presence of a familiar person, playing a game, and being tickled are examples of devices which have been used.

There are various ways of checking when someone has achieved a sufficiently relaxed state:

forehead should be smooth rather than furrowed or wrinkled;

eyes should be loosely closed;

neck should be smooth with veins and muscles hardly noticeable;

head should be tilted sideways or forwards;

arms should rest on chair arms, lap, or away from the body;

shoulders should be forward;

hands should be open, with palms up and resting on chair arm or lap;

legs should be apart, with knees outwards and no movement;

feet should be apart and resting on the heels with toes pointing outwards;

breathing should be slow and even.

Introducing specific events

Particularly important among antecedents to bring about appropriate behaviour is a range of devices for teaching those behaviours. Such devices may aim to teach people to engage in behaviours which they can already perform but do not, or they may need to teach new behaviours. Only a brief mention of such techniques is offered here. Readers are referred to other sources (Cunningham and Sloper, 1978; Kiernan, Jordan, and Saunders, 1978; Perkins, Taylor, and Capie, 1980 a and b; Presland, 1989a; Kiernan, 1981) for fuller information.

The most common techniques are:

Prompting through physical guidance. Initially, the helper moves the person's body or body parts in the ways required to perform the appropriate behaviour. This action is called a *physical prompt,* and the process *physical prompting.*

Modelling. The helper demonstrates the actions required and the person copies them. Additionally, prompting through physical guidance may be needed at first if the person does not imitate spontaneously.

Oral instruction. If the person has some understanding of language, the helper can use speech to explain what to do, at first using language at a simple comprehension level. This process is often referred to as *verbal prompting* or using a *verbal prompt.* Physical prompting may also be needed in the early stages.

Depending on the person's level of communicative ability, the process of oral instruction can become quite complex. In one study, for instance, a young woman with a mental handicap was verbally guided to identify feelings of "butterflies in my tummy", which commonly preceded her physically violent tantrums, so that she could bring herself under control before a tantrum occurred.

Another important range of antecedents involves engaging attention through welcome experiences. Provision of these as a normal part of the environment has already been mentioned. It is, however, important also to identify specific experiences for particular individuals, especially where the handicap is so severe that activity is largely restricted to watching. It has been found, for example, that people with very severe handicaps who engage in the repetitive and apparently meaningless movements known as stereotypies sometimes stop these to attend to simple sensory stimulation, such as the ringing of a bell, vibration, or a flashing light. Varying the kinds of stimulation given is likely to be desirable in most instances.

Antecedents that need to be used with more circumspection are *mildly* unwelcome experiences which are withdrawn when a specific appropriate behaviour occurs. If physical guidance is unwelcome, for example, it can be used to promote a particular appropriate behaviour, but withdrawn as soon as the person continues the behaviour without help.

Choosing antecedents

The range of possible antecedents is illustrated in Figure 14. To my knowledge there is no overall systematic procedure for deciding which to use to make appropriate behaviours more likely. Full knowledge of the person with a mental handicap should enable helpers to judge which antecedents are most likely to be effective with that person. Apart from this the only course is to embody some in an intervention programme and see what happens.

Changing consequences to make appropriate behaviours more likely

Categories of reinforcing consequences

Two main categories of reinforcing consequences can be distinguished. The preferred category is the use of welcome experiences following an appropriate behaviour. The other category, very much a second choice, requires presentation of an unwelcome experience as an antecedent. When the appropriate behaviour is carried out, this unwelcome experience is then removed, or the person allowed to escape from it.

The relationship of both of these categories of reinforcement to the overall process of selecting antecedents and consequences to increase appropriate behaviour is illustrated in Figure 14.

Using welcome experiences

Suitable welcome experiences may have been noted during the identification of existing antecedents and consequences in Section 5. It may thus have become apparent that a particular consequence regularly follows a problem behaviour and might therefore be reinforcing it. If this consequence can reinforce a problem behaviour, perhaps it can also reinforce an appropriate one. For instance, if Kathy is played with to distract her whenever she hits somebody, this may make it more likely that she will hit somebody in the future. Perhaps playing with her could, instead, be made a consequence of some appropriate behaviour towards another child, such as handing Pat a toy. Hopefully, using the consequence in this way will reinforce that appropriate behaviour.

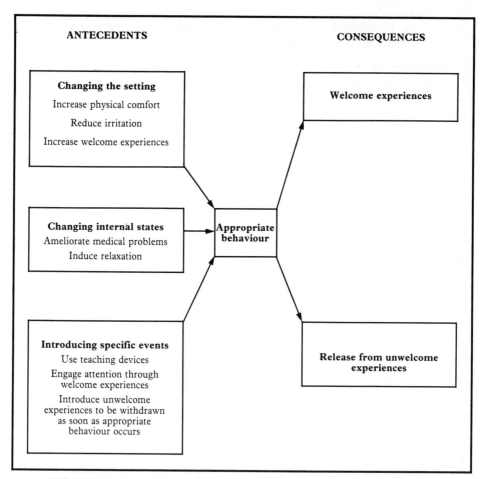

FIGURE 14. Antecedents and consequences likely to assist in increasing appropriate behaviour

Other potentially reinforcing consequences will have been identified as welcome experiences for particular individuals as described earlier in this Section. If people choose to occupy themselves with some objects more frequently than others, to seek certain kinds of food, or look for praise or other attention from some people more than from others, then access to one or more of these kinds of preferred experiences might be used as reinforcing consequences. As already noted, even such activities as whirling round or making ritual finger gestures may need to be considered as reinforcing consequences for people who do little else. As a general rule any behaviours that people engage in spontaneously more frequently than they engage in the appropriate behaviours required are likely to be suitable for use in reinforcing the appropriate behaviours.

Problem behaviours also can offer pointers to welcome experiences which may function as reinforcing consequences. In one investigation, for example, two children who engaged respectively in ritual patting of the leg and rubbing of the arm responded well to being patted on the leg and rubbed on the arm by the experimenter. Even being left alone can be reinforcing for some people, perhaps because it allows them to engage in a stereotyped behaviour undisturbed.

Using release from unwelcome experiences

If the procedures already described reveal no likely reinforcers, it may be necessary to identify unwelcome experiences, so that escape from them following an appropriate behaviour is likely to be a reinforcing consequence for that behaviour. An example of the use of release from an unwelcome experience was described in one study of a child with a very severe handicap. The only way that could be discovered of reinforcing an appropriate behaviour was to place an ice cube in the child's hand and remove it when the behaviour occurred.

Experiences which can be used in this way may have emerged from the identification of antecedents for promoting appropriate behaviours earlier in this Section.

Choosing consequences

Once possible reinforcing consequences have been identified, choices need to be made between them. Only limited knowledge is available as a guide. There is evidence, however, that reinforcing consequences are more effective if they have a direct (or functional) relationship to the behaviour they are intended to reinforce. Thus, if a person is to be reinforced for turning the pages of a book, a reinforcer which can be found under one of the pages turned is preferable to one that has to be handed over separately.

The effect of any reinforcer can wane if it is used repeatedly. It is, therefore, wise to select a range of reinforcers of different kinds rather than just a few very similar items, and to vary their use in order to maintain their effectiveness. It is preferable to use social events rather than food or toys where they are equally effective, since these occur more commonly as reinforcing consequences in everyday life and are therefore more likely to lead to maintenance and generalisation of any behaviour changes which occur.

Finally, a balance is required between what is most effective and what is most desirable from other points of view. Although, for some people, edible reinforcers are most effective, they may be undesirable because of the effects on their teeth or weight. Fortunately, for people with the most severe handicaps, various kinds of sensory stimulation, particularly vibration, are just as effective.

Escape from unwelcome experiences may have to be used as a reinforcing consequence if nothing else can be found.

Recording

A written record should be made of the antecedents and the consequences thought likely to increase a person's behaviour. The most promising of these should be underlined. Figure 15 illustrates this using Form 7 of the Action Record, using the example of an imaginary young woman in a sheltered workshop who cries and struggles when asked to approach a sewing machine.

Name: Yvonne Bailey ACTION RECORD FORM 7

Date of birth: 9 - 7 - 63 Influences which may increase an appropriate behaviour

Completed by: Sue Brown

Behaviour

When asked to go to the sewing machine, does so without crying or struggling

Antecedents

Play Yvonne's favourite music in the sewing room.

Mrs. Brown will walk to the sewing machine, then ask Yvonne to do the same.

Mrs. Brown will guide her, by gentle physical pressure, to walk towards the sewing machine, simultaneously engaging her in conversation about her favourite music.

Consequences

Yvonne will have an outing to the shops.

Yvonne can choose the next taped music to be played.

Yvonne will have a piece of chocolate.

Yvonne will be allowed to look at a picture book.

Mrs. Brown will stay with her for a while and talk with her.

FIGURE 15. Example of a completed Action Record Form 7 showing possible antecedents and consequences for increasing appopriate behaviour

PART B

A guide to action

SECTION 7. DECIDING ON CHANGES
TO DECREASE PROBLEM BEHAVIOURS

Introduction

It has already been suggested that, in planning intervention programmes to help overcome problem behaviours, preference should be given to increasing the appropriate behaviours which should replace them. In some instances, no procedures to decrease problem behaviours directly will be used until attempts based on increasing appropriate behaviours alone have been tried. It is, however, wise to give the matter thought at this stage, since methods of increasing appropriate behaviours can sometimes be seriously undermined by existing antecedents and consequences which are promoting the problem behaviour, such as presenting someone with a task that is too difficult and attending to the resulting problem behaviour.

   It is suggested, therefore, that the observation and recording procedure that will now be outlined should be carried out, though the findings will not necessarily be strongly represented in a first attempt at intervention.

Using prior findings

As was the case with identifying changes to increase appropriate behaviour in Section 6, the advance investigation of present causes recommended in Section 5 may well have suggested changes in antecedents and consequences which will be helpful. If, for instance, a child in a residential setting throws a tantrum when asked to wash up, and this is thought to be because of the difficulty of the washing up task, this antecedent can be changed so that the washing up task is simplified or some easier task presented instead. If head-banging occurs in the absence of toys, steps can be taken to ensure that toys are present. If a problem behaviour occurs every time a person sees a blue door, the door can be covered with paper or paint of a different colour.

Prior findings may also suggest changes in consequences. If attention is reinforcing a problem behaviour, care can be taken not to provide it while, or immediately after, the behaviour is occurring. Noise, as a reinforcing consequence of head-banging can be prevented by fitting a cushioning head-dress. If someone tries to avoid physical guidance by struggling, and this non-compliant behaviour is reinforced by escape, this consequence can be altered if the physical battle is not begun or if the person with responsibility makes sure of winning it. In this last situation, struggling is likely to result in even closer physical control, which might then act as a reducing consequence so that the non-compliant behaviour becomes less likely to occur in the future.

Investigation of why appropriate behaviours are failing to occur may also suggest helpful changes. If it looks as though someone refuses to engage in an important appropriate behaviour because it is presented in a way that is difficult or unpleasant, a modified form of presentation may be found which will make the non-compliant behaviour less likely to occur. In a work training situation, for instance, Peter refuses to attempt a task requiring him to insert and tighten six screws because it is difficult and tiring for him. Presentation of the task could be modified either by asking Peter to do just one or two of the screws and return to the rest later, or by asking him to screw each one in a little until he feels tired, returning to tighten them all later.

Potentially reducing consequences may also emerge. In an earlier example, a teacher stopped giving attention to a child on completion of a task, possibly making completion of tasks less likely in the future. Withdrawal of attention could, instead, be used as an immediate reducing consequence for some problem behaviour, such as throwing objects on the floor, and the behaviour might then decrease as a result.

Welcome and unwelcome experiences and problem behaviour

As explained in relation to appropriate behaviours in Section 6, knowledge of which experiences are welcome and which are unwelcome to someone can help in predicting their usefulness in changing behaviour.

The main possibilities for decreasing problem behaviour, as illustrated in Figure 16, are:

a *welcome activity,* which can be an antecedent for making a problem behaviour less likely to occur. If Angela, a young child, likes spinning a top, for example, then being allowed to do so may make her less likely to bang her head against a wall because she is fully occupied.

removal of a welcome experience, which can function as a reducing consequence for a problem behaviour. For instance, the top can be near to Angela for most of the time, but be removed every time she bangs her head on a wall.

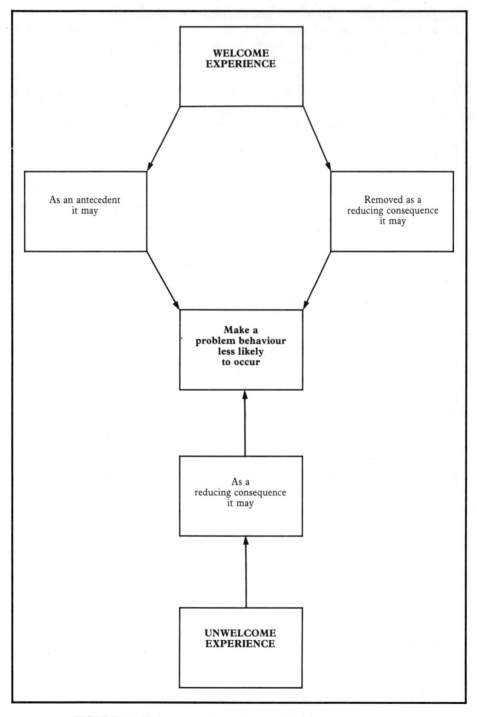

**FIGURE 16. Welcome and unwelcome experiences as a means
of decreasing problem behaviour**

an unwelcome experience, which can be directly usable as a reducing consequence for problem behaviour. If, for example, the sounding of a hooter is judged as unwelcome to Sam, who bangs his head on walls, then sounding it every time he engages in that problem behaviour may decrease it.

Welcome and unwelcome experiences will probably have been identified when seeking changes to increase appropriate behaviour. If not, then the procedures for doing so described in Section 6 will need to be carried out here. They should not, however, be carried to a more advanced stage with the aim of decreasing problem behaviour, and it is hard to think of circumstances in which it is justifiable to try out a range of clearly unpleasant experiences in order to determine which are unwelcome to a particular person with a mental handicap.

Changing antecedents to make problem behaviours less likely

Types of antecedent changes
Antecedent changes will be considered again here under the groups identified in Section 6: features of the setting; internal states; and specific events. As before, it is important to remember that the categories overlap and that this is a set of guidelines for selecting antecedents and consequences rather than clearly delineated techniques.

Changing the setting
The most helpful changes that can be made in the setting to make problem behaviours less likely to occur are much the same as those identified for making appropriate behaviours more likely in Section 6. Removal or minimisation of any source of discomfort or irritation is an obvious example, and provision of a high level of welcome experiences is another. If Bill, a man on a hospital ward, is busily engaged with a jigsaw puzzle, for instance, he is less likely to get up and hit someone. The best appropriate behaviours to substitute for problem behaviours are those which appear to be welcome. The required effect is more likely to be produced if the appropriate behaviours selected are incompatible with the problem behaviours. For instance, Bill would find it difficult to work on a jigsaw and hit someone on the other side of the room at the same time. Jigsaws, therefore, are just one example of a range of welcome leisure activities which should be made easily accessible.

Just as for increasing appropriate behaviours, appropriate learning or work tasks are most helpful for decreasing the likelihood of problem behaviours in education and work settings respectively. Finally, in all settings, there should be regular welcome interaction between people with responsibility and those for whom they are responsible. Any improvement in any of these directions should make problem behaviour less likely to occur.

Changing internal states
Again, there is little to add to the guidance given in Section 6, which suggested that changes in settings such as described above, and more direct approaches such as medical intervention and relaxation, might all be helpful. Ben, for example, is afraid of going to the toilet. Finding something that helps Ben to relax could make it less likely that he will cry or run away when faced with this situation.

For problem behaviours such as regurgitating food and chewing it again, which may be motivated by hunger, feeding a person to capacity will eliminate the feeling of hunger and so make the problem less likely to occur. This process is called *satiation*.

Changing specific events

Firstly, it is possible that various specific events or environmental features, that are making a particular problem behaviour more likely to occur, can be removed. For example, analysis of existing influences may have found that Michael, whenever he sees long black hair nearby, pulls it hard. If all people with long black hair wore a hat or put up their hair, the problem behaviour might well decrease.

Secondly, various methods of guiding someone to refrain from problem behaviour can be used. One way is to watch for early signs of problem behaviour and then say "No", or give a warning look, or physically guide the person concerned to engage in an alternative appropriate activity.

Other devices can take the form of helping someone to anticipate the consequences of a behaviour. There are two main ways of doing this. One is to make it clear that, if the problem behaviour occurs, it will *not* be reinforced. An example of this is to put a cover that deadens sound on the table top when somebody spends too much time in stereotyped banging of objects on the table. The assumption is that it is the noise that reinforces the banging behaviour, and removing the noise removes the reinforcing consequence. The cover on the table can then become an advance indication of the futility of the problem behaviour.

The other way is to indicate that, if a problem behaviour occurs, it will be followed by a reducing consequence. A verbal warning, such as a simple "No", may suffice once the person has learned that a reducing consequence will always follow the problem behaviour. Alternatively, a visible warning can be used. If Nigel, a child at home, is to be made to wash out his mouth with water as a reducing consequence for eating rubbish off the floor, for example, a beaker of water might be placed on view or a parent might "act" mouth-washing movements.

Choosing antecedents

The range of possible antecedents is illustrated in Figure 17, which represents both antecedents and consequences for decreasing problem behaviours. As with antecedents for appropriate behaviour, there is little established knowledge about how to select particular antecedents to use, and it must be left to the good sense of the person responsible.

Changing consequences to make problem behaviours less likely

Identifying and selecting consequences to reduce problem behaviours is no easy matter. A bewildering variety of procedures have been described in the literature, and the collection of concepts and terminology used to describe these is confusing (see Appendix 4). Though tempted to abandon them and substitute my own categories, I finally opted to use those which readers will encounter elsewhere in the literature. It is my hope that the concepts of welcome and unwelcome experience already described will help to clarify the nature and inter-relationship of these procedures. It should be realised that, once

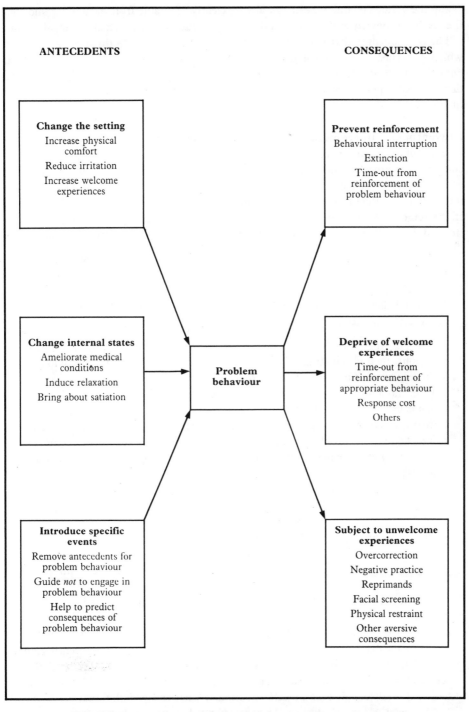

FIGURE 17. Possible antecedents and consequences for use in decreasing problem behaviours

again, the various techniques are not always clearly separable from each other and that the result is primarily a systematic guide for action, rather than an accurate classification.

The consequences that will now be described are grouped into three categories: one which aims just to prevent a problem behaviour from being reinforced; one which deprives the person temporarily of welcome experiences; and the third which employs direct use of experiences which are unwelcome. The range of possibilities is illustrated in Figure 17.

Preventing reinforcement of the problem behaviour

One way of preventing a problem behaviour from being reinforced is to stop it from being completed, a process called *behavioural interruption*. Another is to eliminate naturally occurring consequences which might be reinforcing it. If these consequences are removed during the behaviour or for a moment after it, the procedure is called *extinction*. If the removal is maintained for a specified period after the problem behaviour has stopped, it is called *time-out*. These three methods will now be described further.

Behavioural interruption. As soon as a problem behaviour occurs, someone with responsibility actively stops the person showing the behaviour from continuing with it and guides the person back to more acceptable, alternative behaviours. If the problem behaviour is not completed, there is little opportunity for it to be reinforced. This technique has also been called *positive interference*.

Extinction. If naturally occurring consequences are reinforcing a problem behaviour, then eliminating these may be sufficient in itself for the behaviour to occur less often. This is called *extinction*.

An example of extinction is the technique sometimes called *planned ignoring*, which is used when a problem behaviour is thought to be reinforced by attention. It involves determinedly giving no attention at all during and immediately after occurrence of the problem behaviour. It is important to realise that ignoring behaviour is not just a matter of not reacting. It can be very difficult to achieve and requires planned action, such as walking away, turning the head away, or pointedly attending to someone else.

Planned ignoring works only if attention is a welcome experience for the person showing the problem behaviour. Some people with mental handicaps avoid attention because it interferes, for instance, with stereotyped behaviours from which they apparently derive satisfaction. For them, ignoring is more likely to reinforce some kinds of problem behaviour and is, therefore, *not* the technique to use.

Sometimes, more specific measures are needed. For instance, there is a range of techniques called *sensory extinction*, in which naturally occurring sensory consequences of a problem behaviour are removed. For example, putting rubber gloves on the hands of people who scratch themselves severely, and apparently gain some kind of satisfaction from the physical sensation which results, eliminates this reinforcing consequence. Strictly speaking, this is an antecedent, like covering table tops for banging of objects mentioned earlier, since the change in the environment occurs in advance of the selected behaviour. However, it is possible to think of its *effect* as occurring afterwards, at least until the people concerned learn to anticipate it. Another procedure to which this last comment applies is *satiation,* which has also already been mentioned under antecedents because it is introduced in advance. In this situation people are allowed to eat to capacity so that behaviours thought to be motivated by hunger, such as regurgitating food and chewing it again, cannot be reinforced because there is no hunger to satisfy.

Time-out. If ignoring is continued for a specified period of time after the problem behaviour has stopped, the procedure is called *time-out,* or *time-out from reinforcement.* This denies the person showing the problem behaviour access, for that specified amount of time, to experiences which are thought to have been reinforcing the behaviour. This form of time-out is often called *non-exclusionary time-out.* If it is used with people with mental handicaps, the time period should be as brief as possible, at the most only a very few minutes.

Time-out, however, is more commonly used in a different form in situations where there is uncertainty as to what is reinforcing the problem behaviour. People showing problem behaviour are removed from the situation for a time, so that anything in that situation which might have been reinforcing their behaviour can no longer do so. They may have to sit alone, ignored and inactive, behind a screen for a specified period; or even in a separate room which has nothing of interest in it to act as a reinforcing consequence. This form of time-out is called *exclusion time-out, isolation time-out,* or *contingent isolation* to distinguish it from the non-exclusionary time-out previously described.

Since these early definitions were formulated, the use of the term "time-out" has been extended to procedures in which experiences which are reinforcing *appropriate* behaviours are withdrawn for a time. This variant does not necessarily prevent problem behaviour from being reinforced, and is therefore described under the "depriving" techniques that follow. Two new terms could be coined to highlight the distinction – *time-out from reinforcement of problem behaviour* and *time-out from reinforcement of appropriate behaviour.*

Depriving of welcome experiences

This group of reducing consequences overlaps with those included under preventing reinforcement of problem behaviour, since reinforcement is itself a welcome experience. Here, however, the deprivation is the essential element, rather than incidental. Furthermore, no claim is made that the experiences removed have been reinforcing the problem behaviour. The technique sometimes consists of withholding something very specific that is welcome and would otherwise have been available to the people showing the problem behaviour. In a situation, for instance, where young children usually gather together for a drink and a biscuit half way through the morning, any children who push their cups off the table are deprived of a biscuit, while all the other children receive one.

Two main forms of deprivation have their own technical labels. Where deprivation consists of withholding for a time experiences which have been reinforcing appropriate behaviours, the term *time-out* is used again. Where the welcome experience is something provided in advance which is then taken away a little at a time (one bit for each occurrence of the problem behaviour) the technique is known as *response cost.* These are further described and illustrated as follows.

Time-out. The forms of time-out relevant here are non-exclusionary. They depend on having a system for reinforcing any *appropriate* behaviours in operation at the time. When a problem behaviour occurs, the opportunity to obtain the reinforcing consequences is withdrawn for a predetermined period of time. This procedure, therefore, involves time-out from welcome experiences which have been reinforcing appropriate behaviours rather than the problem behaviour. It could be termed *time-out from reinforcement of appropriate behaviour.*

A simple example of this is to play music to reinforce abstaining from problem behaviour but to switch it off for a specified period every time the problem behaviour occurs. A more complex example is provided by a study in which a young man with a mental handicap in a further education situation was praised and given something to eat every 10 minutes if he worked without talking out loud or touching anybody. If he *did* engage in one of these problem behaviours, all his school materials were removed and he sat inactive and ignored at his desk for five minutes with no opportunity to gain reinforcement.

Response cost. Here, people are provided with something they welcome, and some of it is taken away every time they present a specific problem behaviour.

For example, a man resident in a hostel eats cigarette butts discarded by others. He could be given a pound, and 10p could be taken away every time he picked up a cigarette butt. Alternatively, he could be given 20 points, and one could be taken away for each instance of the behaviour; the remaining points each being exchangeable at a pre-arranged time for a fixed sum of money.

Subjecting to unwelcome experiences
Unwelcome experiences used directly as reducing consequences for problem behaviour can be divided into two categories. Firstly the person showing the behaviour can be made to do something unwelcome. Secondly, an unwelcome action can be carried out by the person with responsibility.

The first group includes the techniques called *overcorrection,* which involve actions which are appropriate or neutral, and *negative practice,* which requires performance of the problem behaviour itself. The second group includes actions that are sometimes referred to as *aversive consequences,* such as *reprimands, facial screening,* and a range of others with no common technical names. The various devices are further described as follows.

Overcorrection. Any actions which are unwelcome can be imposed as a regular consequence of a problem behaviour, ranging from requiring the person to sit still for a short period to making the person run up and down the room. It is sometimes necessary for the whole or parts of the person's body to be moved in the required ways by whoever is carrying out the programme. The label *overcorrection* is used because the actions required have to be carried out repeatedly for a continuous period of time and because they often in some way correct either the problem behaviour or its results. All the following categories of action have been used with this label although, as definitions vary, not all of them would necessarily be called overcorrection by everybody.

Restitution, which involves putting right to excess the effects of the problem behaviour. For instance, if a woman in an adult training centre pushes a table over, she might be required to put it back in its correct position and then dust it or wash it repeatedly until its condition is even better than it was before she overturned it.

Positive practice, in which the person with the problem behaviour is required to practise repeatedly a more appropriate behaviour which is an acceptable alternative but which the person considers unwelcome. The woman who pushes a table over, for example, might be required to sit at the table and carry out an appropriate task there, such as weaving or completing a jigsaw, provided that these tasks were unwelcome to her.

Restitution and positive practice combined. A man with the habit of drooling, for instance, might be asked to wipe his mouth with a tissue 50 times.

Functional movement training, in which actions are used that are not appropriate and do not correct the results of the problem behaviour. A woman who hits others, for example, might be required each time this problem behaviour occurs to raise her arms at right angles to her body, then above her head, and then down at her sides, each for 30 seconds, the whole sequence being repeated for several minutes. Using this technique the actions can involve the parts of the body that carry out the problem behaviour, as in the example, but sometimes they do not. For instance, arm movements have been used as a consequence for stereotyped head movements.

Negative practice. Here the consequence is having to repeatedly practise the problem behaviour itself. It is assumed that the problem behaviour will become an unwelcome experience, and therefore a reducing consequence for itself, as a result of this technique. For example, a man who spits might be required to spit into a sink repeatedly for 10 minutes or so and may, as a result, become less likely to spit spontaneously. Such a technique would be wholly inappropriate for seriously disruptive or dangerous behaviours and its range of usefulness is probably very limited. However, it may help in some instances.

Reprimands. This term includes such actions by a person with responsibility as saying "No", speaking angrily, and giving a stern look.

Facial screening. This consequence consists of placing a light cloth loosely over the face of the person showing the problem behaviour and keeping it there until about one minute after the problem behaviour stops. Alternatively, a blindfold can be used to cover the person's eyes for about the same length of time.

Physical restraint. The usual method of applying this technique is to prevent the person moving part or all of the body for a specified period (either mechanically or by physical holding) after each occurrence of a problem behaviour. The arms might be held tightly to both sides of the body, or the head might be held tightly between the palms of the person carrying out the intervention.

Other aversive consequences. A range of other unwelcome experiences that are likely to reduce problem behaviour because of their aversive properties include:

   imitating the problem behaviour; (In one piece of research, for example, the investigator imitated a girl's self-mutilating behaviour by hitting his own face and banging his own head on the floor though more carefully than the girl herself. This reduced the girl's self-mutilation.)

gently tapping the person's hand, arm, or back;

tickling (if an unwelcome experience);

spraying a water mist on the face for a second or two with a plant sprayer;

squirting an unpleasant-tasting liquid like lemon juice, or a hot-tasting sauce, into the mouth;

using ice to touch the skin or put in the mouth for two or three seconds;

making upleasant noises, such as a buzzer or shouting;

using unpleasant smells, such as vinegar or garlic;

employing more severe methods, such as shaking, slapping, cold baths, hair pulling, whiffs of ammonia, and electric shock.

The items in the last category are included for the sake of completeness rather than as recommended measures. They have sometimes been used where nothing else has been thought to be effective and they have been judged preferable to the effects of the problem behaviours, such as when someone habitually engages in severe self-injurious behaviour.

Choosing consequences

Little is known about how to discover which consequences are likely to be most effective for reducing any one person's particular problem behaviour. Again, good sense and a detailed knowledge of the person to be helped will need to be the main standby.

Effectiveness, however, is not the only consideration and every effort should be made to avoid the more aversive consequences if at all possible. To aid this, the various possibilities can be arranged in order of aversiveness and the least aversive tried first. Opinions will differ as to what the exact order should be. Possibly, for the main consequences considered in this book, it should be as follows, the least aversive being listed first:

planned ignoring;
sensory extinction;
behavioural interruption;
response cost;
non-exclusionary time-out;
other methods of depriving of welcome experiences;
reprimands;
facial screening;
isolation time-out;
water mist;
physical restraint;
overcorrection;
negative practice;

unpleasant noises;
unpleasant smells;
ice;
lemon juice;
severe methods, such as shaking, slapping, cold baths, hair pulling, whiffs of
ammonia, and electric shock.

If milder consequences are not effective, then a balance will need to be found between what is effective and what is acceptable to the person who is to carry out the intervention, to the person with the problem behaviour whose views should be sought whenever possible, to any relative or non-professional with a legitimate interest, to any senior staff with responsibility, and to relevant professional advisers. The last category should include an experienced psychologist, who should be consulted as a matter of routine whenever the more severe consequences are contemplated. If there is any fear of adverse effects because of medical conditions, then a medical opinion should also be sought before commencing any of the severe procedures.

In practice planned ignoring, as a mild consequence, should be the first to be considered. However, it is often difficult to implement, particularly because severe behaviour problems are often too worrying or dangerous to ignore. The most commonly used techniques, therefore, should probably be behavioural interruption, depriving of welcome experiences, and non-exclusionary time-out. Reprimands, facial screening, isolation time-out, physical restraint, overcorrection, and negative practice can be considered more or less in turn if any escalation is needed. Hopefully, anything beyond this level will not need to be considered.

Many people have reservations about using the most unwelcome experiences at all. Particularly careful thought is needed before doing so, as well as advice on avoiding possible physical danger to the person with the problem behaviour. Too much ammonia, for example, can damage the skin or the mucous membranes in the nose. If the person struggles so that the situation is not completely under control there can be a very slight risk of this occurring. Medical and psychological advice and monitoring is, therefore, essential if this or any similar consequence is to be contemplated.

Recording

A written record can be made of the antecedents and the consequences that are thought likely to decrease the frequency of the problem behaviour chosen for intervention. The most promising of these can then be underlined. An example, using Form 8 of the Action Record is illustrated in Figure 18. It is for an imaginary young man on a hospital ward whose problem behaviour is to bang his head hard on walls whenever he is left to his own devices.

Name: .... Alan Clarke ....   ACTION RECORD FORM 8

Date of birth: .... 21 / 3 / 1963 ....

Completed by: .... Jill Walters ....   Influences which may
decrease a problem behaviour

Behaviour

Bangs head hard on a wall in the ward.

Antecedents

Nurse will play 'draughts' with Alan.
Nurse will say "No banging" at intervals.
Nursing staff will keep Alan busy in
places away from walls.

Consequences

Alan will be made to stand in one place
holding his head still for 2 minutes.

Alan will have to sit in a room on his own
for five minutes.

Nurse will shout at Alan.

FIGURE 18. Example of a completed Action Record Form 8 showing possible
antecedents and consequences for use in decreasing problem behaviour

PART B

A guide to action

SECTION 8. PLANNING A FIRST ATTEMPT
TO OVERCOME THE PROBLEM

Planning an intervention programme

There is no way of being totally sure that any programme planned to change behaviour will have the predicted effect. Detailed planning should increase the chances of success, but the results of the programme need to be carefully monitored and it may be necessary to modify the initial programme or replace it by another. Several different attempts may sometimes be needed before an effective programme is devised, particularly for severe behaviour problems in people with profound handicaps. The following must, therefore, be regarded as planning for the first attempt.

The central feature of the programme is the systematic use of antecedents and consequences to change behaviour in the directions wanted. The following questions for planning can be identified:

What are the behaviours for which antecedents and consequences need to be supplied?

What antecedents and consequences are to be used?

How are the selected antecedents to be used?

How are the selected reinforcing consequences to be used?

How are the selected reducing consequences to be used?

What other features are needed in the programme?

At what precise times and in which places is the programme to be carried out?

How can the programme be introduced and the person with a mental handicap involved in its operation?

Each of these questions should be carefully thought out in the order presented. The specific planning decisions reached should then be written down. Further guidance for each question will now be offered.

What behaviours?

The behaviours requiring change should have been established before this stage, as described in, Sections 1 and 3.

What antecedents and consequences are to be used?

These should also have been determined before this stage, as described in Sections 6 and 7. The most helpful choice can vary, from one antecedent or consequence at the simplest, to relatively complex combinations of a number of each. For a first attempt, it is best to look for a small number of antecedents and consequences for increasing appropriate behaviours, perhaps supplemented by a small number for decreasing problem behaviours.

How are antecedents to be used?

Systematic use of antecedents

At first it is important to ensure that:

whenever a problem behaviour is expected to occur, antecedents which make it more likely to occur are absent, while those making it less likely to occur are present; (For example, Roger is liable to strike out with his fists when asked to carry out some activity. Antecedents to avoid may be giving him activities which are too difficult, and any annoying noises in his vicinity. Antecedents to encourage may be ensuring that he has an interesting activity, within his capabilities, to occupy him; and things in his environment to make him feel relaxed, such as his favourite music.)

whenever an appropriate behaviour is required, antecedents making it more likely to occur are present, while those making it less likely to occur are absent; (For example, Malcolm's showing a picture book to others has been selected as an alternative appropriate behaviour. Antecedents to make this appropriate behaviour more likely may be making him feel relaxed by talking to him quietly, and guiding him physically in showing the book. At the same time, it may be important to avoid such antecedents as loud noises, or sudden movements by people around him which have been found to distract him.)

whenever possible, there is more emphasis on using antecedents to promote appropriate behaviour than on using them to make problem behaviour less likely.

It is possible that some of the antecedents for making an appropriate behaviour more likely will quickly become redundant. Malcolm, who is required to show a book to another person may, for instance, soon do so without the physical guidance he needed at first. In this situation it is pointless to insist that he continues to accept such guidance, though it is important to remain ready to give it in case it becomes necessary again. For the most part, however, the planned antecedents should occur consistently until the whole programme is reviewed. Where they are allowed to lapse, it is best for this to be anticipated in advance, so that their absence is a planned part of the programme. In the example of Malcolm, for instance, the plan could be to tell or otherwise indicate to him that he should show the book, only providing physical guidance if he does not respond satisfactorily without it.

Difficulties

Some antecedents may present difficulties. Physical guidance, for instance, may be resisted. If so, then the guidance will need to be very firm. A school pupil who is made to sit down and carry out an activity at a table may struggle, scream, or hit out. If the teacher persists despite these protests, the pupil will often eventually comply and appear happy to do so. Such guidance, however, should not be attempted by a person who is not confident of being able to do it, since it is then likely to be either a failure or inconsistent.

It is important to ensure that antecedents to make problem behaviours less likely do not have a similar effect on appropriate behaviours. To take an extreme example, putting splints on Victoria's arms may be very effective in preventing her from scratching her face, but may also interfere with her participating in various leisure activities which should be encouraged.

Another danger to avoid is unwittingly reinforcing problem behaviours by the use of antecedents. If Andrew, who is reluctant to carry out his father's request, is repeatedly asked to do so, or is repeatedly reminded of what will happen if he does or if he does not, the resulting attention may reinforce his non-compliance. In these circumstances a brief reminder, repeated only once or twice on each separate occasion, is best. If this is not effective, an alternative antecedent should be sought.

How are reinforcers to be used?

Reinforcers and appropriate behaviours

Using reinforcing consequences for appropriate behaviours is preferable, wherever possible, to using reducing consequences for problem behaviours. The emphasis is then a positive one, focusing on the behaviour which is wanted. This is most straightforward when the problem is the absence of an appropriate behaviour. A suitable reinforcing consequence can then be arranged to follow every time the appropriate behaviour occurs spontaneously or can be made to occur by use of suitable antecedents. It should follow immediately upon the behaviour.

Sometimes, the appropriate behaviour wanted must occur continuously over a period rather than consisting of specific instances. An instructor in a work training situation, for instance, wants a trainee to continue trying to learn a particular skill, rather than wandering off to do something else after half-a-minute. To encourage this the instructor provides a reinforcing consequence as soon as the trainee has persevered for one minute. The instructor sets a timer, which rings after one minute has elapsed and gives the reinforcing consequence if the trainee behaves as required throughout that time. If the appropriate behaviour stops early, the timer is reset immediately for another minute. Alternatively, the instructor observes the trainee momentarily at precisely planned intervals, and provides a reinforcing consequence if the appropriate behaviour is in evidence at the time of looking. Suitable devices for reminding people to look at the planned times are described in Section 4.

Reinforcers and problem behaviours

When the problem is an unwanted behaviour that *is* occurring, it is best to use reinforcing consequences to increase appropriate behaviours as alternatives to the problem behaviour. There are two main approaches. One is to reinforce *any* behaviour other than the problem behaviour. The other is to reinforce selected *specific* appropriate behaviours.

> *Reinforcing any behaviour other than the problem behaviour.* This is called *differential reinforcement of other behaviour* (DRO). It involves providing a reinforcing consequence for a defined period of time during which the problem behaviour does *not* occur — that is, when any behaviour other than the problem behaviour is occurring. Again, a timer is helpful. The time period set should be of consistent length and relatively short initially, probably a maximum of 30 minutes. For people with very limited understanding or very high frequency problem behaviour, it may need to be as short as one minute or less.
>
> It is sometimes recommended that at first the time period should be the same as, or slightly less than, the average time between occurrences of the problem behaviour, as measured during the baseline (see Section 4). If, for instance, Jim bangs his head on the wall, on average, once every three minutes, he could be reinforced every time he refrains from this problem behaviour for, say, two-and-a-half minutes.
>
> An alternative procedure is to observe at set intervals and reinforce if the problem behaviour is *not* occurring at the time of observation. The meagre evidence available, however, suggests that this may be less effective.

> *Reinforcing specific appropriate behaviours.* Appropriate behaviours should already have been determined in Sections 2 and 3. The alternative behaviour that is to be encouraged in place of the problem behaviour can be selected in one of three ways, namely:
>
>> it can be *any* specific appropriate behaviour, which is known as *differential reinforcement of appropriate behaviour* (DRA)
>>
>> it can be a behaviour which, when it occurs, prevents occurrence of problem behaviour, which is known as *differential reinforcement of incompatible behaviour* (DRI); or,

it can be a behaviour which serves the same purpose as the problem behaviour, which is known as *differential reinforcement of equivalent behaviour* (DRE).

The second method is more likely to decrease the problem behaviour than the first. It is helpful, however, if the behaviour reinforced is appropriate in itself as well as incompatible with the problem behaviour. In other words, an attempt should be made to combine DRA and DRI. When this is not possible it may be necessary to settle for one or the other. DRE has been little used as yet, but it looks promising for decreasing some problem behaviours. Reinforcement should be provided regularly, as already described in relation to using reinforcing consequences for appropriate behaviour, whichever method is chosen.

Token systems

Sometimes it is difficult for supply reasons to provide reinforcing consequences as often as required. In this situation it can be helpful to use a *token system* in which the immediate reinforcer for an instance of appropriate behaviour is a gummed paper star, a slip of paper, a point, or some other item of little apparent value in itself. These items are stored, either by the person with the problem behaviour or by the person responsible for the intervention until, at a convenient time, they are exchanged for "real" consequences at a predetermined rate. A chart for displaying the number of reinforcers given by means of ticks or stars is useful to show the person how he or she is getting on.

A token system has the advantage that its reinforcing consequences are less likely to interfere with appropriate behaviours. For instance, if the immediate consequence of an appropriate behaviour is being allowed to play with a toy, a period of such play has to be allowed. This delays further performance of the appropriate behaviour which it is meant to reinforce. A token, however, can be received quickly and be followed by an immediate return to the appropriate behaviour. The system does, however, pre-suppose a certain level of understanding and it is unlikely to be appropriate for use with people with profound handicaps. Even people with less severe mental handicaps are likely to need training in how the system works before it can operate effectively.

Varying reinforcers

Sometimes a person may be reinforced by a particular consequence at one time but not at another. It is, therefore, helpful to have a variety of reinforcers available, so that there is always likely to be one that is effective. The choice of reinforcers should be built into the programme at the planning stage, rather than chopping and changing later. Once the programme has begun, it is best to apply it consistently, as planned, until it is decided to review it as a whole.

Where more primitive reinforcers are used, such as food and vibration, it is important *always* to accompany them with everyday social reinforcers, like praise. Through association with the more primitive reinforcers, these everyday consequences then often become reinforcing for people who were formerly unmoved by them. Their use prepares the way for changes that will be needed later when the programme is being phased out.

How are reducing consequences to be used?

Being cautious

Reducing consequences must be used circumspectly. They are appropriate only when reinforcing consequences are insufficient. When they are used, methods which cause less distress or annoyance should be considered before those which cause more. Indeed there is an argument for avoiding them altogether, until intervention programmes which use less alarming techniques have been tried and have failed.

Where any risk to safety is involved, however mild, careful watching must be pre-planned. If, for instance, it becomes necessary to put someone in a room alone for a period, it is essential to watch to ensure the person comes to no harm. If more severe methods are considered, it is important to have records to show that mild approaches have been tried first, and to consult with relatives, people in higher authority, and expert advisers before implementation. It is wise to have set procedures for these precautions and suggestions for this will be made in Part D.

Reduction and reinforcement

Reducing consequences should very rarely be the main element in a programme. The emphasis should almost always be on reinforcement, and reducing consequences should be seen as a way of either increasing the effect of the reinforcers, or of decreasing certain kinds of behaviour which prevent occurrence of the appropriate behaviours which need to be reinforced. For example, Kevin, who lives in a mental handicap hospital, struggles to get away every time a nurse tries to help him use a spoon to eat his food. His struggling interferes with learning to do so. If the food is taken away for half-a-minute every time Kevin struggles, and this eliminates the struggling, the spoon-feeding can then be more easily guided to occur. The reinforcing consequence of the food can then help to establish using a spoon in Kevin's repertoire of skills.

Even when the main emphasis in a programme has to be placed on reducing consequences, an appropriate behaviour should be borne in mind as an alternative to the problem behaviour that is to be reduced, and measures should be taken to encourage it. This should increase the chances of effectiveness of the reducing consequences. Figure 19 illustrates the differing levels of appropriateness of these differing patterns of intervention.

General principles for using reducing consequences

Once it has been decided to use a particular reducing consequence, the way in which it is to be used should be planned and written down. It is important to make the duration of the consequence an appropriate length. There is no reliable way of predicting this but, for most consequences, periods of a few seconds to a few minutes are sufficient and should be tried first. It is also important that, at first, the reducing consequence is applied every time the problem behaviour occurs and immediately it starts.

Sometimes, a planned reducing consequence can become reinforcing because of the particular way in which it is implemented, and care is needed to avoid this. In any procedure which uses a reducing consequence, it is important to minimise attention. Action and a short explanation is better than lengthy scolding, discussing, lecturing, coaxing, or persuading. If behaviours such as crying or tantrums follow the consequence, they should either be ignored or themselves be made the subject of a planned intervention programme. They should *not* be allowed to provide an escape route from the consequence, since this could also reinforce the problem behaviour.

Care must also be taken to ensure that a planned reducing consequence does not become reinforcing because a welcome experience follows immediately after it. If this

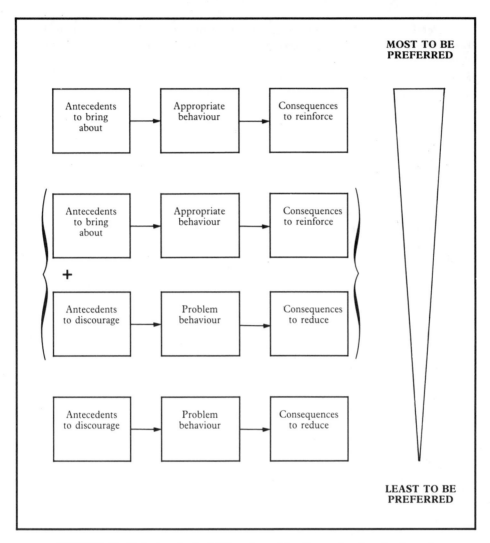

FIGURE 19. Relative desirability of combinations of antecedents and consequences

happens, the planned consequence can then become a signal that something more appealing is to follow, and this may override the reducing effects. For instance, Sue, who lives in a small residential setting, might be made to keep her hands in her lap for one minute every time she grabs food from someone else's plate. The residential worker might be tempted to praise her for keeping her hands there. Praising this, however, is unwise since it might make the whole procedure reinforce the problem behaviour.

Where relatively unusual reducing consequences are used, such as time-out or overcorrection, it is important to accompany them with words or gestures which indicate disapproval. These then become associated with the more unusual reducers and so often become reducing consequences themselves, where formerly they were ineffective. This is helpful when, later, steps are taken to discontinue an intervention programme.

A recently described technique might be considered when less intrusive methods have been unsuccessful because the problem behaviour is very infrequent or very hard to detect. It involves recreating the event in the place in which it occurred and then applying a reducing consequence. In one example a four-year-old boy with autistic behaviour, who stamped on people's feet, was repeatedly guided to bring his foot down on the foot of someone he had attacked in this way (though without sufficient force to hurt) and was, for each "stamp", immediately reprimanded loudly and made to stand still in a corner for one minute.

More detailed guidance

More detailed guidance on using the different varieties of reducing consequences identified in Section 7 now follows.

Behavioural interruption. Every time the problem behaviour begins, interrupt it immediately so that it cannot be reinforced, and guide the person back to a more acceptable behaviour in a brisk and unceremonious way.

Planned ignoring. This is the most commonly used technique, usually labelled *extinction*, where the reinforcing consequences thought to be maintaining a problem behaviour are not permitted. Whenever the specific problem behaviour to be changed occurs, determinedly ignore it by such devices as:

refusing to speak to the person showing the behaviour, or simply saying something like, 'I'm not taking notice of you while you scream', and then only once at the beginning;

avoiding eye contact, or looking in a different direction;

turning the whole body away;

walking away;

attending exclusively (and obviously) to another person who is behaving appropriately;

going into another room and closing the door;

going outside the building (or inside if the problem behaviour occurs outside);

asking other people including those with responsibility and those with mental handicaps to adopt similar ways of ignoring the problem behaviour – which may require training procedures, since it is not easy.

Consistency is particularly important with these procedures, since even occasional reinforcement of problem behaviour is sufficient to maintain it. Indeed, such *intermittent reinforcement* can be very powerful in maintaining a behaviour for a long time after reinforcement has ceased. There is an added danger – that intermittent reinforcement will be given selectively to the most alarming problem behaviours and it is these that will then increase.

It is important to persist in planned ignoring, even if the problem behaviour at first *increases* in frequency. This is not uncommon, but the technique can still be effective *after* the initial increase if it is continued consistently. If other attention-seeking behaviours occur, ignore them too.

Remember, when ignoring any problem behaviours, to give immediate, pleasant attention to any appropriate behaviours.

Sensory extinction. This process requires little operation, since the measures involved are usually taken in advance. For example, putting sponge rubber on a table top can prevent auditory reinforcement of stereotyped spoon-banging.

Satiation. This procedure is almost totally confined to overcoming eating problems and it does not have a general application. Description of its use is, therefore, delayed till Part C.

Isolation time-out. Time-out, or time-out from reinforcement to give the full name, is a term used for a variety of techniques. The most commonly used is often called *isolation time-out,* which involves removal for a short period of the person showing the problem behaviour from the environment in which the behaviour is occurring. It is assumed that something in that environment (probably attention) must be reinforcing the problem behaviour. Removal ensures that any such reinforcing consequence is eliminated. It is particularly important, therefore, that the procedure allows no reinforcement at all for the problem behaviour. The following steps are recommended.

Decide where the time-out place will be. It should be as uninteresting as possible, so that there is nothing in it to reinforce the problem behaviour. Ideally it should be a special room with nothing in it – no windows, or windows too high to look through, and concealed lighting and ventilation operated from outside. In practice, the available situation closest to this ideal will have to do. Sometimes, sitting in a corner of the ordinary room, facing the wall or behind a screen, is sufficient. It is important that the place chosen contains nothing to cause injury, and it must not be a frightening environment.

Decide how long time-out will last. One to five minutes is the usual range, with shorter times for young children or people with little understanding. Short times allow frequent repetition of the procedure if necessary and, therefore, faster learning.

Explain the rules of time-out (if the person showing the problem behaviour can understand them) – what behaviour will lead to it, where it will be, how long it will last, and what the person must do to be released from it.

Implement time-out immediately every time the problem behaviour occurs. Tell the person (according to the level of understanding) either what behaviour has led to it (for example, "That's hitting") or "No". Then tell the person to go to the time-out situation or take him or her there with minimal ceremony. In most cases do no more than state that the problem behaviour has occurred and that removal is to follow. If necessary, use the minimum force needed to get the person to the place of removal. For a young child, who can easily be picked up and carried ignoring all protests, removal by this method may be viable. For someone older, however, if physical resistance cannot be overcome without prolonged or dramatic struggles, it is best to seek some other method.

Remind the person of the rules for release, if these can be understood. Explain that release depends on the person behaving in a specified, appropriate way for the required length of time. Release must not be allowed while the original problem behaviour is continuing or if the person is screaming at release time. In this case screaming might be reinforced which could make the whole process reinforcing for the problem behaviour. Begin timing, therefore, when problem behaviour ceases and suspend it if the behaviour recommences.

Ensure that the prescribed rules are followed. Do not allow escape from the removal situation until the person has behaved as required for the prescribed period. If necessary, the door can be locked, though there should always be easy access and a means of observing what is happening to ensure that no harm ensues.

Allow a return to the ordinary situation without comment, as soon as the person has behaved appropriately for the time required. Then behave as though nothing has happened until the problem behaviour recurs.

These procedures are both particularly appropriate and particularly difficult to apply in public places, where problem behaviour can be very hard to ignore. Recommendations which have been made for use in a supermarket start with calmly taking someone showing the behaviour to stand in a corner till behaviour has been appropriate for, say, two minutes. If this cannot be managed, the person should be taken outside and the procedure carried out in some other suitable spot, as permitted by the weather. A car could be used for the time-out situation if available, the person implementing the procedures waiting outside for the prescribed period.

It is important to realise that these procedures are not appropriate for all problems and all circumstances. If removal allows escape from an unwelcome task which needs to be performed, or permits engagement in stereotyped behaviour, then it could reinforce problem behaviour instead of reducing it. A time-out situation must be unwelcome compared with the situation from which the person is removed. This will be more likely if the ordinary situation is made as welcome as possible.

Non-exclusionary time-out. This can take a variety of forms. For example, if planned ignoring is modified so that it continues, not just while the problem behaviour is occurring but for a fixed time after it has ceased, that is time-out. If the materials a person is engaged with are removed, so that there is no reinforcement for the problem behaviour from that activity, that is time-out. Or, if the person with responsibility leaves the room for a set period so that the behaviour is not reinforced by attention, that too is time-out. Yet another variation is to withdraw any reinforcement being provided for appropriate behaviours (such as music which plays only while the person is behaving appropriately) for a specific length of time when a problem behaviour occurs.

The general principles to follow in all these procedures are similar to those given for isolation time-out.

Response cost. Arrange for the person showing the problem behaviour to have a number of welcome items and remove a fixed amount of them as a consequence of each occurrence of the behaviour. For example, give the person a supply of sweets or one pence pieces. Remove one of these as a reducing consequence each time the problem behaviour occurs. It is important that the supply of items is sufficient to allow the consequence to occur *every* time. Alternatively, set up a token system using stars or ticks as explained earlier, and remove one of the tokens earned each time the problem behaviour occurs. Make sure that removal of the tokens does not reduce their effectiveness as reinforcers for their original purpose.

Other depriving techniques. Deprive the person of some welcome experience which would otherwise be provided, such as a chance to watch television, every time the specified problem behaviour occurs. Ignore protests or the resulting attention may reinforce the problem behaviour.

Overcorrection. A number of packages which make a person engage in unwelcome activities have been called overcorrection. Leading authorities have recently recommended that the term should be restricted to procedures which take the following form:

Every time the problem behaviour occurs, immediately say "No", and then state clearly to the person what has occurred; for example, "You hit Fred".

Select an 'overcorrection' behaviour. (See pages 72–73). There are varying accounts of the kinds of behaviour which qualify. For instance, procedures which do not use the same part of the body as the problem behaviour and do not correct its results are sometimes specifically excluded, yet they can be effective. For example, stereotyped head movements have been reduced by making a person engage in repetitive arm movements.

Decide on how long the overcorrection behaviour is to be carried out. Periods of 20 seconds have been found effective, but one minute upwards is more usual.

Make the person carry out the overcorrection behaviour immediately, for the prescribed period, every time the problem behaviour occurs. It should be carried out continuously, rapidly, and in a way which requires effort. Engineer this by verbal instructions and/or further guidance.

Use a procedure called *graduated guidance* to achieve this where necessary. This involves providing the minimum amount of force to make the person move as required, gradually decreasing this as long as the movement continues. If the movement stops or goes in the wrong direction, the force should be increased again, just sufficiently to correct this, and then gradually decreased once more. When resistance is no longer encountered, change to *partial graduated guidance*, in which the amount of physical contact used is less. For example, replace a hand hold with contact from a thumb and forefinger only. When no resistance is encountered to this, change to *shadowing*. Using this procedure keep one hand within an inch of the part of the person's body to be guided, following the movements but not actually touching the person. If the movements stop or go in the wrong direction instantly apply just as much physical guidance as required to restart or correct them.

To avoid reinforcement of problem behaviour, administer these procedures with as little personal attention as possible and do not allow the person to escape before doing what is required for the prescribed period. If this is not practicable, then overcorrection is not a good method to use.

Overcorrection always involves prolonged repetition of the unwelcome behaviour chosen. Sometimes, however, being made to do something unwelcome just once can be effective. There is no name for this technique.

Negative practice. This procedure involves repeated practice of the problem behaviour itself, in the hope that it will thereby become an unwelcome experience and therefore a reducing consequence for itself. The principles to follow are much the same as those given for overcorrection.

Reprimands. An authority in this field has recently made the following recommendations:

Ensure that the reprimand makes it clear what behaviour it relates to. Say, for example, "Stop kicking Fred". If it is likely to be helpful, also say what should be done instead; for example, "Stop kicking Fred and lay the table". There is sometimes some value in a brief explanation of why the behaviour is wrong. Say, for example, "Stop kicking Fred because it hurts him and *you* wouldn't like it". Take care, however, that this explanation is not so lengthy that it reinforces the problem behaviour with attention.

Deliver the reprimand in a deep tone of voice which makes the displeasure clear and sounds firm. It is important to avoid a whining tone or an increase in pitch at the end which makes it sound like a question. Sometimes, it is helpful to use a loud voice and to emphasise key words.

Accompany the reprimand with glaring, or looking continuously into the person's eyes with a fixed and serious expression. Sometimes, holding the person firmly by the upper arms or shoulders is helpful.

Get close to the person to deliver the reprimand.

Deliver the reprimand after EVERY instance of the problem behaviour, even if · behaviour has stopped before you are near enough to do so.

Use some other device immediately if the problem behaviour continues despite the reprimand, such as interruption, restraint, or overcorrection. The person may then be more likely to respond to reprimands alone on future occasions.

Physical restraint. The use of physical restraint was fully described in Section 7. The rules are very similar to those given for isolation time-out, namely: determine in advance the method of restraint to be used; decide how long it is to last; explain these matters to the person in advance if possible: implement the restraint every time the specified problem behaviour occurs; remind the person of the rules for release if these can be understood; and ensure that escape does not occur until appropriate behaviour has taken place for the time required.

In one study, physical restraint was used to increase the effectiveness of isolation time-out. A 17-year-old pupil in a special school engaged in almost continuous stereotyped hand and finger movements. Placing her in isolation time-out provided opportunities for her to continue these behaviours unhindered. A procedure was therefore introduced in which any movement during time-out was reprimanded and the pupil was held still for two minutes. Her stereotyped behaviour then decreased dramatically, both during time-out and in the classroom.

Facial screening and other aversive consequences. The least aversive unwelcome experiences do not require consideration beyond the descriptions already given in Section 7 and the general guidance offered earlier in this Section. It is my preference *not* to write further of the most aversive techniques, which have been mentioned mainly to indicate that they exist, since it is my hope that they will never need to be used. If they ever are considered, this must be under the guidance of qualified advisers experienced in their use and stringent consultation and other procedures should be followed. Part D will go further into the relevant legal and ethical procedures.

What other features are needed?

The foregoing pages have covered most of the essential features of a behaviour change programme. Any additional features should, however, be specifically written down. For instance, Mark is injuring himself deliberately. The various steps needed to protect him from harm, a cushioned helmet and soft furniture, must be noted together with the instructions for the intervention, even though they are more to make the programme possible than actually a part of it.

Medical action of various kinds may be needed as part of an intervention – and may sometimes be the *only* appropriate measure. If, for instance, a medical examination has indicated that Joan's self-scratching is due to a skin condition, prescribing something to relieve it may in itself solve the problem. In instances of incontinence of urine or faeces, however, although medical action may eliminate some physical cause, teaching techniques may also still be needed before the problem is fully solved. Three kinds of medical action which need more specific discussion will now be considered: medication; diet; and treatment for epilepsy.

Medication

Sometimes medication is recommended by a doctor to alter a person's behaviour directly, rather than to improve some identified medical problem that is affecting behaviour. The medication most commonly used for this purpose with people with mental handicaps is a group of drugs known as *major tranquillisers*, also known as *antipsychotic* or *neuroleptic drugs*. The best known of these are chlorpromazine (trade name *Largactil*), thioridazine (*Melleril*), and haloperidol (*Serenace* and *Haldol*), which have been used to control violent, self-injurious, and stereotyped behaviours and hyperactivity.

There are several problems in using the major tranquillisers with people with severe mental handicaps, of which readers should be aware.

It is difficult to predict who will benefit and from which drugs. The use of this medication seems to derive largely from its success with people with chronic schizophrenia and on opinions based on individual clinical work. Though there is some research basis for believing that these drugs are also effective with people with severe mental handicaps, it is limited.

The level of dosage required is hard to estimate. Inadequate doses can make behaviour problems worse and larger doses may have undesirable side-effects.

The drugs have a general sedative effect. They therefore decrease all behaviours, whether problem or appropriate. They can, as a result, interfere with learning, including learning to behave in more appropriate ways, as some but not all research studies have found. Sometimes, they decrease problem behaviours only by sending people to sleep.

They can have undesirable side-effects. These vary from drug to drug and from person to person, and commonly include sleepiness, drooling, involuntary stereotyped movements of the trunk and limbs, depression, constipation, low blood pressure, weight gain, and even fits. Sometimes, additional medication is required to counteract these problems. How far these side-effects can be avoided by careful selection of dosage level and subsequent monitoring is uncertain.

There can be quite severe withdrawal symptoms if the medication is stopped. These again include involuntary body movements and can also include behaviour problems which were not present before medication began. The seriousness of this problem is a matter of dispute.

More rarely, other medication is used. In most cases less is known about any effects, side-effects, and withdrawal symptoms which might occur.

Owing to the problems highlighted above, the use of medication to decrease problem behaviour in people with mental handicaps has increasingly caused alarm and run into severe criticism. Amid the clamour, it is possible that real benefits will be overlooked. It must be remembered that behavioural approaches do not succeed all the time either, and that unwanted results can sometimes accompany the improvements they produce. There is at least one research study where medication succeeded when a variety of behavioural approaches had failed. There are also studies which show that suppression of problem behaviour by medication can sometimes make it easier to use behavioural approaches to develop appropriate behaviours. These, in turn, can help to keep the problem behaviours at bay long-term and the medication can then be gradually reduced.

Where medication is to be used as part of an intervention, the people with daily responsibility need to be involved in the decision processes, so that there is appropriate coordination with measures they use in the everyday environment. They also need to help in the careful monitoring of the effects of the medication, since these are difficult to predict in advance. Daily observation is essential to ascertain the dosage at which positive effects occur, or adverse effects develop. Since the optimum dosage is often very difficult to determine in advance, medication is sometimes given in a very low dose at first and is then gradually increased until it is at its most effective or until unwanted side-effects occur. Drug-free periods may later be instituted to check whether medication is still necessary. These procedures also require monitoring.

The measuring techniques described in Section 4 can be used for these monitoring purposes but may need to be applied to behaviours additional to those which the medication is intended to change; for instance, where a drug improves behaviour but adversely affects learning.

Diet

Recently, there has been considerable interest in the use of exclusion diets to decrease problem behaviours. Helpful research with people with severe mental handicaps is virtually non-existent, but clinical studies have reported beneficial results from a meat-free diet, from a diet free from dairy products, from a reduction in caffeine intake, and from diets which have excluded artificial colourings, flavourings, preservatives, anti-oxidants, and naturally occurring salicylates. It is difficult to determine how far the changes are due to the diet and how far they result from changes in the behaviour of people with mental handicaps or those trying to help them because they believe an effective intervention is in progress. Ideally, an intervention of this kind should start with an *elimination diet*, which excludes *all* suspected foods, and these foods should then be reintroduced one by one, with careful monitoring of effects. It should then be possible to determine with more confidence whether any of these foods cause problem behaviours not caused by other foods. Careful liaison between doctors and others in contact with the person with a mental handicap is necessary for this monitoring to be effective in all settings used by the person.

Treatment for epilepsy

It is well known that people with severe mental handicap who also have epilepsy often show problem behaviours at the time of their seizures. It is quite common for them to behave in an anxious, irritable, or fearful manner immediately before a seizure, and some types of seizure involve involuntary behaviour that resembles violent and/or stereotyped behaviours, though these are rarely serious problems. Incontinence often occurs during seizures. If the seizures can be prevented medically, then these problem behaviours will not arise. A considerable range of medication can be used for this purpose.

Problem behaviours can also occur *between* seizures. Some people, for instance, become increasingly irritable for several days before a seizure. It is not clear whether this behaviour is part of the epileptic process, or whether the problem behaviour makes the seizures more likely to occur, or whether there are underlying neurological problems that bring about both seizures and problem behaviour. No conclusion can be reached, therefore, as to whether medical intervention for epilepsy would be helpful in overcoming problem behaviour in these people.

There are other behaviours, not clearly identifiable as seizures, which may or may not be epileptic in nature. These include sudden and inexplicable violent behaviour, sleep disturbance, incontinence of urine, and repetitive eye, hand, or mouth movements. Clues that they may be epileptic are feelings of sickness, discomfort, or anxiety beforehand, ill-coordinated movements, very brief duration (usually less than a minute), drowsiness afterwards, and an inability to remember later. Referral to a doctor may lead to use of medication to control the epilepsy and thus overcome the problem.

It is worth mentioning that seizures can also be simulated — to gain attention, for instance. The clues for identifying the epileptic phenomena described above are useful for distinguishing them from these simulations. A further clue is that someone having a seizure is unconscious and does not react to attempted restraint or to pain, as from a pinch; whereas someone simulating a seizure is likely to do so. If in doubt, a medical opinion should be obtained before deciding on any intervention procedures.

Epilepsy does not rule out behavioural interventions. These can decrease problem behaviour in people with epilepsy whether or not they are on medication. However, careful liaison between doctors and others is particularly important where epilepsy is involved, whether a behavioural intervention is in operation or not. Accurate records need to be kept of the frequency and duration of seizures, as well as precise descriptions of exactly what occurred on each occasion. The person's activities before and after the seizure should also be noted. These observations can help the doctor decide whether the behaviour is epileptic and, if so, what type of epilepsy is involved, so that appropriate medication can be prescribed. Once medication is begun, careful records must be kept of when it is given, the behavioural changes which occur, and any ill effects. Anti-epileptic drugs can have side-effects which interfere with behavioural approaches, and it is important to have information which relates their occurrence to measures of the behaviours to be changed. Doctors and others can then work together to coordinate the two approaches.

This discussion underlines the need for overall intervention programmes, planned jointly between members of the different professionals involved with the person with a mental handicap, using techniques that are carefully monitored.

What times and places?

The times and places when attempts to implement the intervention programme will be made should be determined, written down, and adhered to consistently. In coming to these decisions much depends on when and where the problem behaviours occur, on practicability of intervention procedures, and on the tolerance and endurance of all concerned.

If in doubt it is wise, initially, to operate the programme for a very short period each day in a particular situation. The results obtained from this will indicate whether it is likely to be worthwhile extending it to other situations and using it for longer periods.

How can the programme be introduced and the person with a mental handicap involved?

The more people with mental handicaps understand the purpose and structure of the programmes devised for them, the more they will be able to help in making them work. If they can understand sufficiently, therefore, they should be told exactly why their own programme is being implemented, exactly what behaviours are to occur and not to occur, and what the antecedents and consequences will be. Indeed, if feasible, they should help in planning and should decide on as much of the programme as possible themselves.

Involvement of people with mental handicaps in planning and implementing such programmes is not well-documented, but there are a few recorded instances in which they have made some use of antecedents and consequences to change their own behaviour. In one study, for instance, a young woman who had tantrums was trained to identify physical sensations which preceded them, to stop herself when she recognised one, and to record her success by putting a mark on a card. It has also been shown that people with mental handicaps can provide their own antecedents by learning verbal rules which they then repeat to themselves at appropriate times. Though this has not been demonstrated with people with severe behaviour problems, it is possible to envisage teaching some people to say, "I mustn't kick", and to repeat this to themselves when needed. This could even be extended to training them to carry out the actions that should follow from these statements by reinforcing them for doing so. This procedure is called *correspondence training*, because it increases the correspondence between what is said and what is done. For instance, Glenys, who gets angry and hits people when they do not do as she wants, might be encouraged to sit down instead. She could practise saying, "When I get cross I'll sit down". Before going into a situation where she is likely to become cross, she could be asked to repeat the statement. Then she could be observed, given feedback on whether or not she has done what she said, and reinforced if she has.

That people with mental handicaps can reinforce their own behaviour was shown in a study in which children were taught to put a coin on one square of a counting board every time they completed a worksheet. When a child's counting board was full, that child was allowed to choose a toy to play with. There is evidence that such self-reinforcement of appropriate behaviours can lead to a decrease in problem behaviour. Whether direct self-administration of consequences for serious problem behaviours is possible with people with severe mental handicaps has yet to be demonstrated.

The introduction to and involvement in an intervention programme of people with profound handicaps or those who do not communicate will inevitably be more limited. It may be necessary to implement the programme and allow them to grasp what is happening as they experience it. In some instances, however, if appropriate behaviours are prompted or modelled and the reinforcing consequences demonstrated at the same time, some advance understanding may be gained. Ingenious implementors of programmes may even devise ways of letting them know in advance what reducing consequences will follow their problem behaviours.

Recording

Form 9 from the Action Record can be used for writing a description of a planned intervention programme based on the above questions. A possible example is shown in Figure 20. This features Sandra, an imaginary 10-year-old girl with a profound handicap in school, though it could just as easily apply in other settings and, with modifications for age, to adults in a variety of environments.

Name: .... Sandra Smith ....   **ACTION RECORD FORM 9**

Date of birth: .... 11/4/1978 ....   **First intervention programme**

Completed by: .... Mr. Taylor ....

Note the following information in the order given

1. Precise behaviours to increase and/or decrease, including standards and circumstances.
2. Antecedents and/or consequences planned.
3. Precise ways in which antecedents are to be used.
4. Precise ways in which consequences are to be made conditional on occurrence of behaviours.
5. Any other features of the programme.
6. Precise times and places for operating the programme.
7. How the programme is to be introduced and the person showing the behaviour involved.

---

1. Increase "Rides a tricycle in the classroom at times when it doesn't interfere with other activities". (This is one of the few appropriate activities in which Sandra occasionally takes an interest.)

   Decrease "Scratches her face with her nails with sufficient force to draw blood at any time or place during the school day". I don't want this behaviour to occur at all, so in practice I'll work on "Moves either hand to within 12 inches of her face" whenever possible. (It won't do for mealtimes because I want her to feed herself, so I'll have to work directly on the scratching at those times.)

2. Taking the tricycle out of the cupboard, taking her to it, and inviting her to ride should be antecedents which make riding more likely. They should also be antecedents to make face-scratching less likely, because Sandra doesn't attempt it while riding. Praise and cuddles can be used as reinforcing consequences for tricycle riding and for periods free of face-scratching.

   I, or another member of staff, will hold her hands by her sides for 1 minute as a reducing consequence for attempts at face-scratching.

3. Whenever there is a free play period (quite often with this group of children who have very severe handicaps)

FIGURE 20. An example of a completed Action Record Form 9

the tricycle will be taken out of the cupboard and kept available for Sandra's use. She will be taken to it immediately and invited to ride. If she doesn't we'll try again after 3 minutes. If she does, but stops, we'll repeat the procedure after a 3-minute wait, unless she has already started to ride on her own initiative.

4. During free play periods, Sandra will be cuddled & praised each time she gets on the tricycle. When she is not on the tricycle at these times, she should be cuddled & praised whenever 1 minute passes without her hand coming within 12 inches of her face. A timer will be set for one minute and we will reinforce in these ways when it rings. If her hand comes within 12 inches of her face, the timer will be re-set for a new one-minute interval. During free play periods, whenever her hand comes within 12 inches of her face I, or another adult, will hold her hands by her sides for one minute.

5. At times other than free play periods, Sandra should wear a plastic splint on each arm designed to allow her to manipulate objects at a table but not to touch her face with her fingers. At mealtimes we will remove the splints and guide her carefully in feeding so that she is prevented from scratching her face.

6. The programme itself will be implemented only during free play periods, which are usually 3 times a day for about 20 minutes each, depending on the timing of other activities and how the children are responding to them.

7. No special introduction of the programme to the child, since she would not understand it.

showing the detail of a first attempt intervention programme

PART B

A guide to action

SECTION 9. IMPLEMENTING THE FIRST PROGRAMME AND MEASURING ITS EFFECTS

Consistency

An intervention programme should, ideally, be implemented exactly as planned and written down. However, implementation may immediately reveal unforeseen snags. It may prove more difficult than expected, for instance, to explain to a person with a mental handicap what behaviours are required or what behaviours must decrease. It may then be necessary to find a different way of communicating this, or even to substitute a behaviour which can be explained more easily. The person may show no response at all to antecedents and consequences that had looked promising, and so it may be necessary to change these. The standards for achieving a consequence may seem to have been set too high and so may need to be made less demanding.

Consistency is very important when implementing a programme. It is necessary, therefore, to be wary of changing the plan because of early difficulties like the ones outlined above. They may pass. On the other hand, if they are so problematic that they are thought virtually certain to make the programme ineffective, changes are advisable. It is best to try to make these early and then stick to the modified programme. What *must* be avoided if at all possible is chopping and changing every few days.

One possible exception to the consistency rule is where a person responds to particular reinforcing consequences on a few early occasions only. Indeed, the same might happen with antecedents. If this happens, the antecedents or consequences should be varied in order to maintain the appropriate behaviour. However, deliberate variation of antecedents and consequences should be planned in advance wherever possible, so that there is some kind of system about it and it is, in a sense, still consistent. It is also possible that, at any time, a particular antecedent or consequence which originally worked with a person will lose its effect, and replanning will then be necessary.

Monitoring progress

Ideally, the effects of the programme should be monitored by careful measurement. This should be carried out exactly as during the baseline measuring period, so that valid before-and-after comparison can be made. Preferably, measuring should be continued throughout the period of implementation, so that a full record of changes is obtained. The programme should generally be implemented for at least two weeks with measuring and measurements should be made for at least 10 recording periods before any revision of the programme is attempted. Form 10 of the Action Record provides for written recording, but need not be illustrated here since the process is the same as already illustrated in Section 4.

Ideal measuring procedures, however, are not always feasible, or even appropriate. Sometimes, the results of previous measuring and/or the detailed programme planning can indicate that the original measuring procedure is not particularly useful or that it is misleading. If so, a new period of baseline measuring should, ideally, be carried out before the programme is implemented. This, however, can make monumental demands on patience. Another possible problem is that beginning a programme may absorb so much time and attention that effective measuring is difficult to fit in. One partial solution here is to delay measuring until the programme is well-established. Hopefully, most people will be able to implement helpful measuring procedures; but it is worth repeating that, if not, it is probably better to carry out a carefully planned programme without measuring than not at all.

PART B

A guide to action

SECTION 10. SUBSEQUENT PLANNING AND IMPLEMENTATION

What should be done next?

Once an intervention programme has been implemented and its effects measured sufficiently, a decision must be made about what to do next. Firstly, an evaluation of the outcome of the programme should be made on the basis of the measures recorded. This is likely to be in the context of one of four broad classes of circumstances:

>   none of the changes wanted have occurred;

>   there have been very slight changes in the directions wanted;

>   the changes wanted have occurred sufficiently and there are no other changes which justify such detailed planning;

>   the changes wanted have been achieved sufficiently and a programme is needed to bring about further changes.

Guidance will now be offered for acting upon each of these outcomes, and Figure 21 provides a summary for quick reference. The person with a mental handicap should be involved in making the relevant decisions whenever possible.

If none of the changes wanted have occurred

Further action
There is no guarantee that an effective programme will result from the first attempt at planning and implementation. If there is no significant change, each element of the

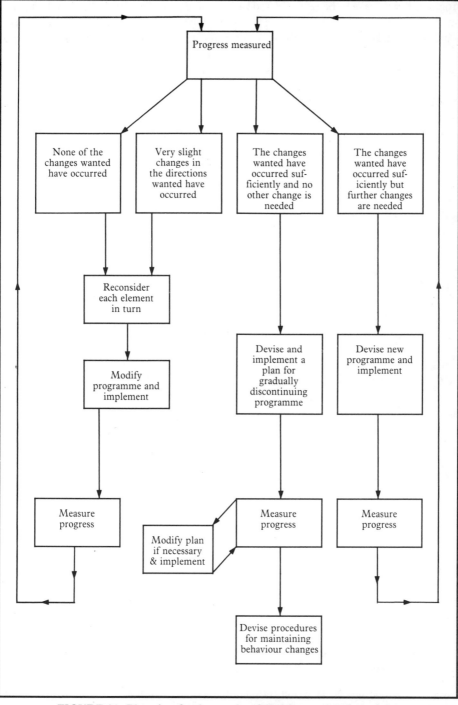

**FIGURE 21. Planning further action following evaluation of the
first intervention programme**

programme will have to be reconsidered in turn to see what modifications can be made, a modified or new programme planned, written down, and implemented, and measures of progress checked again. Sometimes, at this stage, there are second thoughts about what behaviours should be tackled first, or perhaps different or modified antecedents or consequences are needed. Maybe the standards of performance required of the person, or other aspects of the way consequences are used, need to be altered, or perhaps programme sessions need to be longer, or at different times.

Several new or modified programmes may need to be tried in turn before an effective one is found. A high proportion of first attempts do, however, achieve useful results, and where they do not, observations during implementation often give clues which enable a more successful second attempt.

It is always possible that a programme which is not effective initially will become so if continued for longer. The response of the person with a mental handicap may give clues to this. Otherwise, the person implementing the intervention will have to be guided by "hunches". If there is no change at all after about three weeks, however, it is unlikely that a suitable programme has been found.

Recording and evaluation
The Action Record offers possible formats for recording in its Forms 11 and 11a. Figure 22 illustrates the continuing story of Sandra, whose intervention programme for face-scratching was described in Section 8.

If the modified programme differs markedly from the original, it needs to be written out in full in the same format as used for the original programme. Form 11A makes provision for this. If this form were completed for Sandra's modified programme (rather than simply noting the modifications on Form 11), the description would be identical to the original programme, except that reinforcement for getting on the tricycle, and for one minute without attempting to scratch her face, would be a cuddle, praise, and a piece of apple.

Recording of progress during the modified or new programme would follow the same lines as illustrated for baseline measurement in Section 4. Form 11B could be used for this. The results would again be evaluated and a new decision made on what to do next. Form 11C would be used for this purpose as illustrated for Sandra in Figure 23.

If there are slight changes in the directions wanted

In this situation it may be decided to proceed in a way similar to that suggested for the situation when none of the changes wanted have occurred. However, there is probably a stronger case for continuing the original programme and measurement of progress for a longer period before making any changes. If it is decided to alter the programme, the modifications may not need to be so extensive.

If the changes wanted have occurred and there is no need for other changes

The recommendations made earlier for planning a first attempt at a programme were not intended to be complete, but were intended to maximise the chances of some initial change of behaviour in the desired direction. Having obtained such changes, it is unwise

Name: _Sandra Smith_

Date of birth: _11/4/1978_

Completed by: _Mr. Taylor._

ACTION RECORD FORM 11

Evaluating and modifying a programme

How far has the first intervention programme achieved its objectives?

Sandra attempts to scratch her face more or less as often as she did before the intervention.

Should the programme continue in its present form, or should a modified or new programme be designed, or should the programme be gradually faded out? If the programme is to be modified, what changes are needed?

The programme needs to be modified.

We suspect that cuddles and praise are not effective as reinforcing consequences. She is very fond of apples and we think pieces of apple might be used to accompany the cuddles and praise.

We might need a different reducing consequence as well, but we'll try changing the reinforcers alone first.

FIGURE 22. Example of completed Action Record Form 11 which shows the result of evaluation of a first intervention programme and suggested modifications

Name: Sandra Smith

Date of birth: 11/4/1978

Completed by: Mr. Taylor

ACTION RECORD FORM 11C

**Evaluating and modifying
a modified or new programme**

How far has the modified or new programme achieved its objectives?

Sandra's attempts at face-scratching decreased very rapidly with the modified programme. Within 2 weeks it had dropped to zero, and in the week since then it has occurred only once, and then she did it only very briefly and put her hands down to her side before we reached her.

Should the programme continue in its present form, or should a modified or new programme be designed, or should the programme be gradually faded out? If the programme is to be modified, what changes are needed?

The programme should be faded out gradually.

FIGURE 23. Example of completed Action Record Form 11C showing evaluation of a modified programme

just to withdraw the programme and return to previous management techniques, since the behaviour may then return to its former character.

On the other hand, though it may be wise to continue a programme for a further period to consolidate the improvements, it is not very often appropriate to continue it indefinitely to maintain the improvement because:

it is probably time-consuming, and the time may be needed for other purposes;

the person is usually behaving appropriately under contrived circumstances, whereas the need is for development of appropriate behaviour in a more normal situation; and,

the effectiveness of a programme can wear off, as though the person had become bored with it.

Devices for discontinuing programmes

The following devices for fading out programmes without losing behavioural improvements are suggested for use in combinations suitable for the particular person, problem, and situation. They are mostly dilutions of a "rigorous" programme. The techniques used become gradually less different from the handling which will occur when the programme has been discontinued. It is possible that if the programme is faded out in this way the person who originally showed the problem behaviour is less likely to distinguish between the presence and absence of the programme than if the programme were discontinued suddenly. The aim is for the person to behave appropriately regardless of whether the programme is present or absent. The steps to take are as follows.

Gradually modify any contrived antecedents used in the programme until they are no longer needed or are needed only to a 'normal' extent. This gradual elimination of a guiding procedure is known as *fading*.

To give an example, David, who lives in residential care, is required to sit down and do something at a table, instead of attacking someone. Karen, the residential care worker, could use physical prompting as an antecedent for bringing the behaviour about. She could do this by pushing David's body down into a chair and swinging his legs under the table. When this is working well, she might push him into the chair and just give his legs a slight push towards the required position. When David completes the movement himself, Karen could progress to just touching his leg to indicate the need to move it. At this stage a slight downward push might be sufficient to prompt David to carry out the sitting down part of the action himself, and then just a touch on the shoulder. Finally, just pointing at the chair may be all that is necessary.

Make increasing use of natural antecedents, that is, the kinds of instruction and guidance which are usually given to people. These might include requests for someone to do or not to do something, or gestures to indicate what is needed. Procedures may need to be built in for training a person to react to these more natural influences.

If someone ignores simple verbal instructions despite understanding them, for instance, it may be necessary to use physical prompting to train responding to a particular instruction. Once the response is established, the prompting can be gradually faded until compliance with instructions occurs without it. The same applies to training someone to imitate a model of the behaviour required.

It should be borne in mind that a successful response to one verbal instruction or to one model does not necessarily result in similar success with a different instruction or model. However, the more different instances the person is trained to respond to appropriately, the more likely it becomes that the training will generalise to new instruction and models.

Gradually decrease the frequency of reinforcement in an irregular sequence. To begin with, allow a few instances of the appropriate behaviour to occur without a reinforcing consequence, and then gradually increase the number of such omissions in an irregular sequence. Irregularity is important as it prevents the person from predicting when the reinforcing consequences are coming and so behaving appropriately only when they are expected.

Gradually increase the interval between the appropriate behaviour and the reinforcing consequence. A reinforcer that is initially given immediately after the appropriate behaviour is, instead, given after a short delay of, say, two seconds. The delay is then increased gradually to, say, five seconds, then ten seconds, then thirty seconds, and so on, repeating each stage several times before moving on.

Gradually reduce the amount (as opposed to the frequency) *of reinforcement* for appropriate behaviours *and/or reducing consequences* for problem behaviours. Gradually reduce the size of a drink of orange juice, for instance, until it is no more than a sip.

Teach other people to provide reinforcing consequences for a person's appropriate behaviours, in the hope that they will continue to do this when the programme is discontinued. This includes other people with mental handicaps if their abilities and characteristics allow. A simple programme involving antecedents and consequences to develop this helping behaviour in people with mental handicaps may be needed to teach them to carry it out.

Make increasing use of natural consequences. A smile, a word of praise, or some other pleasant attention is more likely to occur after the programme has been discontinued than the giving of, say, a plastic token exchangeable for sweets. Maintenance of the appropriate behaviour will be more likely if such natural reinforcing consequences are continued. The same applies to reducing consequences where a spontaneous frown or reprimand may well help to prevent recurrence of a problem behaviour.

Natural consequences, however, may not have been the main ones used in the programme, because the person showed little likelihood of responding to them. It was recommended earlier that more primitive reinforcers, like food, be regularly accompanied by more natural ones like praise, smiles, and cuddles, and more primitive reducing consequences, like temporary removal of food, by frowns and reprimands. In this way the natural consequences are likely to develop reinforcing and reducing effects respectively by their association with the primitive ones. The process of regularly using natural consequences should continue as the more primitive consequences are gradually faded out until, hopefully, natural consequences are all that are required to maintain the behaviour desired.

If natural consequences are inadequate, use additional consequences that are readily available. It is sometimes found that natural consequences are not sufficient to maintain appropriate behaviours on their own. In this situation the use of additional "surprise rewards" may help. Such rewards should be small and easily accessible. The helper could put on someone's favourite record, for instance, or the person could be allowed to operate a tape recorder.

Gradually increase variation in the procedures used. For example, vary the types of antecedents and consequences used, and the precise forms of behaviour reinforced.

Encourage the person with a mental handicap to seek natural reinforcing consequences. For example, encourage Carl to draw the attention of a person with responsibility to his appropriate behaviour.

Try to replace some kinds of consequences by antecedents. This applies particularly to reducing consequences. If, for instance, Pauline's throwing toys is regularly followed by removing the toys, she could be told "No" when she looks as though she might throw one. She may then come to associate "No" with the subsequent loss of the toys and so refrain from throwing. The reducing consequence will then be unnecessary.

The process for reinforcing consequences is more complex, since the associated antecedent (something like, "Be a good boy", perhaps) would need to be linked only with natural consequences like praise which were likely to occur long-term.

If at all possible involve the person with a mental handicap in devising and managing changes in the programme. Individual abilities and understanding vary, so different people will need to be involved in different ways. For example, some people might be asked to say how their behaviours could become even better, asked to choose their own preferred natural consequences, or helped to learn to make judgements for themselves as to whether their behaviour meets the criteria which have been used for dispensing consequences. Some can learn little guiding words, which the programme implementor used originally, and thus give themselves instructions as to how to carry out a particular kind of behaviour or what kind of behaviour to perform in a given situation. Such measures may possibly contribute to people's "self-discipline", as opposed to "imposed discipline", and so help to maintain behavioural improvements longer.

Maintaining the change

Very often, the above procedures will result in programmes merging into ordinary, day-to-day management. Sometimes, however, a time may come when a conscious decision is made to end a programme. In either case, it is still important to ensure that some of the general principles underlying programme construction are embedded in everyday management. This should minimise the chances of a person lapsing into the former problem behaviour.

Some or all of the following measures can be used to help to avoid the problem behaviour recurring.

Continue to give praise and pleasant attention for appropriate behaviours as often as possible. Try to develop and maintain a general attitude of looking for behaviours to be pleased about.

Continue to give occasional "surprise rewards" for specified behaviours, while not actually programming them.

Continue to praise and give "surprise rewards" to people with mental handicaps for providing natural antecedents and consequences which aid the development and maintenance of appropriate behaviour in each other.

Tell the person that special privileges will be provided for continued improved behaviour. Doing this will depend on the person having sufficient understanding. One way of explaining this to Gillian, for example, is to say that she has now become "so good" that her special programme is no longer necessary, but that special privileges or treats will sometimes be given as a surprise if her behaviour remains good. Also explain the rules about what will happen if she does not keep to the agreement. For instance, if she errs in a particular way, she will either lose the privileges for one week, or she might have to go back on the programme to earn them for a week, before returning to the "no programme" condition.

If, after discontinuing a programme, lapses into problem behaviour persist, recommence the original intervention programme or try a different one. A repeat, or some minor variation of the original, can sometimes lead to better maintenance of improved behaviour.

Recording and evaluation

Measures for fading out a programme can be implemented and evaluated before means of maintaining the changes are planned; or the two processes may be planned and evaluated as a unit. Forms 12, 12A, and 12B of the Action Record are designed to be used for either of these alternatives. The plans made are written down on Form 12, records of measuring behaviour during implementation described on Form 12A, and evaluation and further action noted on Form 12B. If methods of fading out the programme and maintaining the change are implemented separately, the forms are used once for each. The measuring and evaluation procedures and recording methods are essentially the same as for the original programme. However, the length of time required for measuring or, indeed, whether measuring is needed at all cannot be the subject of general guidance. Decisions on these matters will have to be made in the light of all the circumstances at the time.

To illustrate recording and evaluation, the intervention with Sandra is again helpful. It was previously decided to fade out her modified programme. Figure 24 describes plans which might be made for this using Form 12.

As the plans illustrated in Figure 23 are implemented, Sandra's behaviours can be measured in the same way as for the original programme, using Form 12A. Form 12B can then be used to evaluate progress, as shown in Figure 25.

Name: .... Sandra Smith ....   **ACTION RECORD FORM 12**

Date of birth: .... 11/4/78 ....   **Fading out a programme and/or maintaining the change**

Completed by: .... Mr. Taylor ....

Record the information relating to each of the following procedures in the order given.

1. How contrived antecedents are to be faded out.
2. How use of "natural" antecedents is to be increased.
3. How the amount, frequency and immediacy of contrived consequences is to be diminished.
4. How use of "natural" consequences is to be increased.
5. How variation in the procedures is to be increased.
6. Any other changes.
7. How the changes are to be introduced to the person and the person involved in decisions about the changes to be made.

---

1. We'll point to the tricycle instead of taking her to it. If necessary, we'll give her a gentle push in the right direction, but first try her without this each time. If she continues to go to the tricycle under these conditions for several days, we'll stop inviting her to do so, so that she can do it on her own initiative.

2. Pointing to the tricycle is perhaps more natural than taking her to it.

3. We'll occasionally leave out the apple, cuddles and praise for tricycle riding. If this doesn't decrease its frequency, we'll leave them out gradually more often, though in an unpredictable sequence. We'll also increase to 2 minutes the time for which Sandra must abstain from face-scratching to be reinforced. If the attempts remain more or less at zero for a few days, we'll increase it to 3 minutes. If all goes well, it can be increased more and more till its the whole of a free play period. After that, we'll leave out the reinforcement gradually, as for tricycle riding.

4. We'll try to fade out the use of apple as a reinforcer more quickly than the use of cuddles and praise.

5. Only as described above.

6. None.

7. No special introduction.

FIGURE 24. Example of completed Action Record Form 12 showing how a programme is to be gradually faded out while maintaining appropriate behaviour

Name: Sandra Smith	ACTION RECORD FORM 12B
Date of birth: 11/4/78	Evaluating and modifying
Completed by: Mr. Taylor	fading and/or maintenance procedures

How far have the procedures achieved their objectives?

Attempts at face-scratching are now very rare and Sandra nearly always stops them before any actual scratching occurs.

What further action is needed?

The fading out phase can now be regarded as completed. Procedures for maintaining the change now need to be determined and implemented.

FIGURE 25. Example of completed Action Record Form 12B used to evaluate the effectiveness of the completed programme

---

Name: .... Sandra Smith ....   **ACTION RECORD FORM 12**

Date of birth: ...... 11/4/78 ......   **Fading out a programme and/or maintaining the change**

Completed by: ...... Mr. Taylor ......

(i)

Record the information relating to each of the following procedures in the order given.

1. How contrived antecedents are to be faded out.
2. How use of "natural" antecedents is to be increased.
3. How the amount, frequency and immediacy of contrived consequences is to be diminished.
4. How use of "natural" consequences is to be increased.
5. How variation in the procedures is to be increased.
6. Any other changes.
7. How the changes are to be introduced to the person and the person involved in decisions about the changes to be made.

---

1. We'll occasionally point to the tricycle if she hasn't used it for a while.

2. Pointing is more natural than taking her to the tricycle.

3. We will continue to give cuddles and praise occasionally at times when Sandra is behaving appropriately, but not on any systematic basis. Pieces of apple will no longer be used. If face-scratching occurs to the extent of drawing blood, we will use the restraint procedure for attempts at it for a few days only. Hopefully, this will never be necessary.

4. Cuddles and praise occasionally are natural enough.

5. We'll encourage Sandra in a variety of alternative appropriate behaviours, though not necessarily on a systematic basis.

6. None.

7. No special introduction.

If the problem recurs to a serious extent, we'll return to the original programme or plan another one.

FIGURE 26. Example of completed Action Record Form 12 showing measures to be taken to maintain behaviour

If, as indicated for Sandra, it is considered appropriate to plan procedures for maintaining the behaviour changes that have occurred, the results can be written down on another Form 12 as illustrated in Figure 26.

If necessary, Forms 12A and 12B can be used for further measuring and evaluation.

If the changes wanted have occurred and further changes are needed

Using the same programme

If the behaviours to be worked on next are very similar to those which have already been the subject of a programme, it is often possible to use essentially the same programme again. For example, Mrs. Willis has worked on getting her son, Edward, to sit in an armchair without tantrums, and now wants him to sit up at a table in a similarly acquiescent fashion. The techniques used in the original programme may well be successful in bringing about this second behaviour change.

In Sandra's case, devices would be needed for extending the period of time in which she does not scratch her face beyond free play periods. The splints could be removed and procedures planned for influencing appropriate alternative behaviour by antecedents and consequences during other times of the day. The maintenance programme still being used during free play periods might be sufficient to achieve success at these other times. If not, something similar to the original intervention programme might be needed at these extended times, while continuing the maintenance procedures during free play periods. Another possibility is to extend the original intervention programme to other times *before* fading it out during free play. When success is achieved on a whole-day basis, the programme can then be faded out at all times simultaneously.

Using the same programme is particularly applicable where a major behavioural change has been divided into small steps and a programme implemented initially for the first step only. Someone who hits others, for instance, might first learn to stay away from them. The programme behaviour might then be extended to getting within a few yards of them without hitting them, then sitting next to them without hitting, and then interacting with them in simple ways without hitting. This process, in which behaviours that are progressively closer to what is desired are reinforced in sequence, is known as *shaping*.

Using a different programme

If the original programme is not suitable, a new programme can be devised for achieving new desired behavioural changes, or decreasing any new problem behaviours which may have arisen during the initial programme. Things learned about the person presenting the behaviour during the first programme can be of help in planning the new programme. For example, experience may indicate that less primitive consequences will be needed in the new programme, or that consequences need not be so large or so frequently delivered. Other features of the programme may need to be different because the person has become more manageable in some ways.

Where a completely new programme is devised, the measures already described for discontinuing the first programme without losing behavioural gains will need to be implemented.

Recording

Written recording of the new programme and the maintenance procedures necessary can be in the formats already described and illustrated for the original programme and the procedures following it.

Promoting transfer of learning between programmes

It is helpful to consider using devices for making it more likely that what is learned in one programme transfers to other learning tasks and other situations, so that further changes can be more easily and quickly obtained. Generalisation of this kind sometimes occurs spontaneously, but it is unwise to expect this. Appropriate devices can be incorporated into new programmes or into handling after programmes are terminated. The following suggestions can be helpful in aiding generalisation.

Gradually involve other people in the programme, who see the person with a mental handicap in various different situations.

Gradually implement the programme elsewhere, in an increasing variety of situations.

Think of ways of linking the different situations together. Is there, for instance, some conspicuous object in the room in which the original programme takes place, which the person can take when moving to a different room? Any similarity which can thus be engineered between the situations may aid transfer of behavioural improvement.

Provide reinforcement for new applications of what has been taught. If, for instance, Alice is taught to hug somebody that she formerly hit, reinforcing consequences could be provided if she then hugs another person that she might also have hit previously.

Find ways of reminding the person of the behaviours learned when they are appropriate in a different situation, and reinforce their performance.

Ask the person to promise to carry out the behaviour in a specified new situation. Afterwards ask if the person has done so, and reinforce both the accuracy of reporting and fulfilled promises. This is an extension of correspondence training, which was described in Section 8.

Making use of these suggestions in the example of Sandra, for instance, it might be possible to:

bring her parents into the classroom to help implement the programme;

extend the programme to work time, the midday break, and to home;

have a tricycle available at the midday break and at home;

praise and cuddle Sandra for rolling or throwing a large ball and climbing on the climbing frame, as well as for riding the tricycle;

draw Sandra's attention to the tricycle at the midday break and at home, and reinforce her for riding it.

These measures could be written down as part of the description of a new intervention programme for Sandra.

PART C

Specific problems

SECTION 1. INTRODUCTION

Structure of part C

Sections 2 to 9 of this part of the book each take a group of related problem behaviours and discuss their nature, causes, and incidence; apply the principles outlined in Part B and the findings from the research literature to make recommendations for intervention; and end with a selection of individual interventions, either from the literature or from my own work*. They do not necessarily have to be read at this point, though it is hoped that they will bring more of a real-life feeling to the reading than is possible with the more general account given in Part B. After digesting the general principles in Part B, readers can, if they prefer, proceed directly to Part D and wait until a problem arises before looking at the section of Part C that particularly applies to it.

My own work took place in the context of after-school workshops, which teachers attended for six weekly sessions. Each teacher was asked to select a pupil, plan and implement an intervention programme with that pupil, and report back on the results. The names used for the pupils in this book are fictitious, and certain other details have been altered to conceal their identities further.

Nor are the examples given at the end of each of Sections 2 to 9 essential to reading the rest of those Sections. They are referred to in the main text in sufficient detail to illustrate the points being made, but are then deliberately kept separate so that they can be read if and when required. Readers may prefer to look only at the examples that apply to their own type of setting (stated in the first paragraph of each) though the techniques described in one setting will often be usable elsewhere.

Reservations

Certain reservations are necessary when reading Sections 2 to 9. Firstly, the accounts have not been able to follow exactly all the stages of intervention set out in Part B. Relatively few published studies, for instance, describe investigation of existing antecedents and consequences prior to planning and intervention. After defining the problem, therefore, each section has to pay little more than lip service to that stage before passing on to planning intervention programmes. When it comes to action after the first attempt at an intervention, it has not been possible to do anything but refer to relevant individual cases in the Illustrative Studies sections. This is because many published studies, being primarily research rather than everyday practice, decided in advance on the procedures to be followed throughout. In practice, on the other hand, what happens after the first intervention attempt depends on the results of that intervention. Finally, it is virtually unknown for published studies to report any involvement of people with mental handicaps in the planning or implementation of programmes to change their behaviour. It is hoped, therefore, that the principles stated in Part B will be used, in practice, to fill in the gaps left by available examples.

Secondly, when reading the accounts of approaches to specific problems, it should be borne in mind that the research is, in some cases, quite small in quantity. Its nature has been much determined by the needs and interests of the people carrying it out. It cannot be assumed, therefore, that a technique which occurs frequently in the literature is necessarily of wide applicability, or that a technique which hardly appears at all is of limited value. Much of the research has additionally been carried out in the USA, sometimes in institutions away from the public eye. Techniques which have been used successfully under those circumstances are not necessarily acceptable elsewhere, either to the professionals concerned or to the public. The interventions described have, moreover, often been undertaken in quite specialised research situations, with plenty of manpower and helpful equipment and facilities. It may not always be possible to implement them in natural settings.

Thirdly, caution is needed in interpreting the examples. As already mentioned, since many were undertaken in research contexts their full course was often determined in advance, and there were adequate resources for carrying them out in an almost ideal way. Neither of these circumstances is likely to be found in practical everyday situations. The best examples from the literature have the advantage of describing interventions which have been implemented in the ways most likely to be effective. The examples from my own workshops may well be closer to what can usually be achieved in practice but, because of this, the interventions often have features which can be more easily criticised. It is heartening that, despite these limitations, the results were often most helpful; and heartening also to see just how well planned and executed some of the interventions were compared with many published ones, despite limited resources. However, there may well be problems and situations where more sophisticated interventions are required.

A fourth reservation is that the standard of reporting in published studies is extremely variable. Often it is not clear exactly what was done, and this makes generalisation from the examples difficult.

Sections 2 to 9 cover most of the severe behaviour problems commonly reported for people with severe mental handicaps. Readers must remember, however, that categories of human behaviour exist largely in the minds of the people categorising it. Grouping similar behaviours together is necessary to give structure to thinking and planning, but there is nothing absolute about it. Behaviours under one category in this book may, therefore, be found in a different category in other descriptions. Uncertainties in my own mind are noted in the text.

Behaviours *not* included in the main categories in Sections 2 to 9, because little is known about them, are dealt with more briefly in the following paragraphs of Section 1. Readers wanting more detail on the interventions described for them could follow-up the references listed in Appendix 3.

Behaviours not covered in detail

Hyperactivity

Of the problems not covered in the sections that follow, the most common is a collection of behaviours usually referred to as *hyperactivity*, or *overactivity*, or *hyperkinesis*. In one British mental handicap hospital, for instance, nurses rated about 20 per cent of the residents as showing "overactivity". In a study of all the people with mental handicaps born in a British city over a five-year period and still locatable later it was found that, at age 8 to 10 years, 40 per cent of boys and 19 per cent of girls with IQs below 50 were judged "hyperactive" and, even at age 22, the figures were 10 per cent and 6 per cent respectively (hyperactivity decreases with increased maturity). In another British study, in which the chief carer (usually the mother) of each of a representative sample of 200 children with severe mental handicaps aged from 0 to 16 years was interviewed, hyperactivity was noted as a problem in about 20 per cent. It is, therefore, puzzling that there has been almost no study of intervention procedures for decreasing hyperactivity in people with severe mental handicaps. Perhaps this is because it has been seen as a "normal" consequence of mental handicap, or perhaps far worse problems have captured most of the attention. It is interesting that some definitions of hyperactivity specifically *exclude* the diagnosis in someone who is mentally handicapped.

Progress in tackling the problems of hyperactivity is not helped by the lack of a clear definition of the term. In the first place the term itself is a misnomer, since various studies have shown that people labelled with it produce no more actual muscular output than is normal. Indeed, in some studies with the drug methylphenidate, improved behaviour has been accompanied by *increased* activity. The problem seems to be more in the quality of the behaviour than in its quantity. Hyperactive children certainly give the impression of hardly ever being still, since they commonly fidget, act impulsively, are easily distracted, and move frequently from one activity to another. They also often behave in disobedient, aggressive, or otherwise antisocial ways that make their movements particularly noticeable. Often they are demanding, irritable, and easily upset. However, there is no definitive set of behaviours for deciding whether a young person is or is not hyperactive. Indeed, the American Psychiatric Association now regards the main problem as an *attention deficit disorder* which can be accompanied by hyperactivity in some people. In their description, the hyperactivity component is distinguished by inordinate gross motor activity, such as excessive running, climbing, and fidgeting, inability to stay seated, and restlessness during sleep.

Stimulant drugs, such as dextroamphetamine (trade name *Dexedrine*) and methylphenidate (trade name *Ritalin*), have been found to have short-term beneficial effects with hyperactive children without mental handicaps. However, they have little long-term effect and can have a variety of undesirable side-effects. There is no convincing evidence that such drugs are of any help with this problem in people with severe mental handicaps, and they are very rarely used with this group. Where drugs are used with them to counteract such behaviours, they are usually major tranquillisers, such as chlorpromazine or thioridazine, which tend to decrease all behaviours, whether appropriate or problem, and these have already been described in Part B.

Dietary treatments have also been used to decrease the problem in children without mental handicaps but, despite a few convincing studies, these are still controversial. No research study of their use with people with mental handicaps has been located, though a recent clinical study reported success with a diet free of artificial colourings, flavourings, preservatives, antioxidants, and naturally occurring salicylates. The difficulty in interpreting such findings has been referred to in Part B.

Behavioural approaches have also been found effective in the short-term in decreasing hyperactivity in non-handicapped children, but there is little evidence of success with people with severe mental handicaps. However, some of the problems included under this term have been successfully tackled and these are covered in the sections that follow. Indeed, the problems of hyperactivity are most worrying when they include behaviours which can be categorised in other ways. One such category is *non-compliant behaviours*, covered in Section 2, where the description of Andrew, a 10-year-old boy with autistic features (Example 5) clearly includes hyperactivity. Andrew wandered all over the school, humming, running over furniture, licking objects, and crying. Attempts to influence his behaviour were met with struggling, screaming, and violent behaviour towards himself and others. The main focus of intervention, therefore, had to be on getting him to comply with adult directions. Another relevant category is *violent behaviours*, covered in Section 3. Here, seven-year-old Edgar (Example 1) could have been described as hyperactive, since he frequently left his seat, would leave the room if he could, and interfered with other children by shaking, slapping, pinching, and biting them. The main concern was his aggressive behaviours which were decreased when he was reinforced for staying in his seat and working (though a change in medication made it difficult to say whether the improvement was due to the intervention).

Out-of-seat behaviour is the main manifestation of hyperactive behaviour reported in the literature which is not specifically covered by any of the sections that follow. In Edgar's case, antecedent guidance and reinforcement of behaviour incompatible with the problem behaviour was the chosen package, as it was for some other children in my workshops. In one published study, brief physical restraint used as a reducing consequence was helpful with a group of children with mental handicaps, though in another this approach was unsuccessful because the restraint unexpectedly acted as a reinforcing consequence and the problem behaviour increased.

Sleeping problems

Sleeplessness is a problem which may be associated with hyperactivity, and has been reported as especially severe and frequent in children who have autistic features. A recent survey found it occurred in over one third of a sample of children under 15 years of age who had severe mental handicaps and autistic or psychotic characteristics. The main problems were waking at night and sleeping for an unusually short time. Both of these disturbed the sleep of other members of the family and had adverse effects on family functioning. Often the wakefulness was aggravated by other problem behaviours, such as self-injury, stereotyped movements, and noisy or aggressive behaviour.

The two published examples located concern disturbance of the family more than sleeplessness itself. The first example involved noisy distress when waking in a six-year-old boy with autistic features. His mother kept the level of protest down by sleeping with him and comforting him whenever he awoke. The intervention, which was successful, introduced a gradual series of changes. The mother first slept on a mattress beside the boy's bed and reached out to cuddle him when he woke; then she moved the mattress a few inches away and spoke to him and touched him without cuddling him; then she moved gradually further away and left out the touching; then she moved out of the bedroom and gradually further away, till she was able to sleep in her own bed and bedroom and just call briefly when he awoke.

In the second example, an 18-year-old girl with a profound mental handicap would sleep in bed for no more than half-an-hour, and then come downstairs and insist on sleeping the rest of the night on the settee with one of her parents next to her. If this was refused she would scream and bang her head with her wrist. If this did not result in parental submission she would bang her head on the corner of a wall, or bite her hand until it bled. Her parents always gave in eventually. The main features of the intervention were to insist that she stayed in her bedroom and to ignore all protest behaviour. Nursing staff from a day care unit stayed in the home to support the parents in this, and the problem was essentially solved within 10 nights. The picture is complicated by the use of chlorpromazine to prevent head-banging becoming too severe and lack of clarity about what effect the drug actually had.

Public masturbation

Masturbation, according to anecdotal reports, is relatively common among people with severe mental handicaps, especially in institutions. Yet references to it in the mental handicap literature are rare. Where it is mentioned it is usually as a problem which is to be decreased by use of reducing consequences such as restraint, squirts of lemon juice in the mouth, covering the person's face, and making the person engage in unwelcome activities, like running, washing hands and applying disinfectant to them, and repeatedly carrying out a sequence of specific hand movements (as in Example 6 in Section 5). Usually such measures are employed only if the behaviour occurs in public. Even so, such approaches seem harsh for this behaviour.

A more appropriate approach, at least as a first step, is to teach the person with mental handicap to masturbate only in private. A suitable private place must, therefore, be available, and the person's privacy there must be respected. A published example described an intervention with a 45-year-old man with a severe mental handicap in a sheltered workshop, who would often open his trousers, leave them undone for periods of time, and occasionally masturbate to orgasm. During the intervention, whenever he was seen opening his trousers, a member of staff would immediately make him zip them up and take him to a bathroom, telling him firmly that it was the only place to unzip his trousers. He was not allowed to re-emerge with unzipped trousers. No account has been located of teaching a person with a severe mental handicap how to masturbate. There is a possibility that it would constitute a legal offence, though prosecution is unlikely if it can be established that there is no indecent intention involved.

Another appropriately mild approach is to reinforce abstaining from public masturbation. This can be used in combination with teaching the person to go somewhere private. The 45-year-old man described in the previous paragraph for instance, was given a hug by a staff member every time he went 15 minutes without unzipping his trousers. In another study a six-year-old boy was given raisins at intervals if he was not playing with his penis when observed regularly by a houseparent. In another intervention, the opportunity to engage in stereotyped behaviour was used as the main reinforcing consequence. A 16-year-old boy with a severe mental handicap and a long history of rubbing his crotch in public was the subject of a classroom intervention. It was observed that, whenever he was given small objects, he repeatedly picked them up and dropped them into the other hand or switched them from one hand to the other. He liked doing this most of all with pieces of uncooked rice. He was, therefore, praised and allowed to engage in this "rice play" for 30 seconds whenever three minutes passed without his touching his genitals. After each rice play session he was also given a small portion of one of his favourite foods to eat. These procedures decreased masturbation to a very low level, which was maintained when the periods of abstaining required, and rice play allowed, were gradually lengthened.

Where antecedents and reinforcing consequences are insufficient, time-out may often be usable in a way that makes it a milder reducing consequence than some of those found in the literature. The six-year-old boy already mentioned, for instance, as well as being reinforced with raisins for abstaining, was sent to his bedroom whenever masturbation was observed until he had stopped playing with himself for two minutes.

For more detailed guidance, the general range of suggestions for stereotyped behaviours in Section 5 may be more appropriate; though such clearly purposeful behaviour does not fit the usual definition for that category. It should also be mentioned that cyproterone acetate (trade name *Androcur*) has occasionally been used to decrease public masturbation and other sexually motivated problem behaviours.

Stealing
Stealing is another problem little investigated in people with mental handicaps, though Section 6 on feeding problems includes stealing food. Reducing consequences have been used to decrease stealing behaviour. In one study, institutionalised adults who stole food were guided immediately to return the stolen item to its owner and then to go to a food display area, pick up another identical item, and give it to the victim. In another study coffee and conversation were used as reinforcing consequences for periods in which adults managed not to steal personal possessions in a dormitory. In a recent study, a

42-year-old woman with a mental handicap took part in group discussions based on ownership. These involved a series of antecedents and consequences which are not very easy to interpret within a behavioural framework.

A problem with stealing is that it is often a surreptitious activity. It is, therefore, difficult to ensure that appropriate reducing consequences follow every instance, or that reinforcement for a period of abstaining is not really reinforcement for evading detection. One response to this problem is to recreate the act by guiding the person through it and then applying reducing consequences. The only study of this kind located concerned a 17-year-old young woman whose mental handicap was only moderate, but whose difficulties were increased by total blindness. She stole and hid such items as biscuits, drinks, necklaces, and audiocassettes. She was rarely caught in the act. Whenever a stolen item was found it was put back where it belonged. The young woman was guided a number of times to pick it up, and was then reprimanded and made to stand still in a corner for one minute each time.

Stripping (or disrobing)
Removing clothes is a fairly common problem in institutionalised people with mental handicaps. In one British mental handicap hospital, nurses reported that 11 to 15 per cent of the adult population engaged in this activity. However, it features rarely in the intervention literature.

Intervention procedures known to me have most often taken the form of making the person engage in unwelcome activities as a reducing consequence, often accompanied by differential reinforcement of other behaviour. Example 9 in Section 5 describes how a young man with a severe mental handicap who ripped off garments was made, every time he did it, first to continue ripping the garment for 15 minutes and then to dress and undress repeatedly for another 15 minutes. Non-disruptive behaviours were reinforced. In another study, each time they stripped nude, two women with mental handicaps were made to dress in a collection of clothes additional to the few they usually wore. Wearing this collection, they then had to spend some time helping other residents in the institution improve their personal appearance, for example, by buttoning-up undone clothing, or putting on footwear that had come adrift. One of them was also taken for a walk in the grounds twice a day if she remained clothed for 30 minutes before the walk was due. A milder form of intervention has been described with a 12-year-old girl with a mental and physical handicap who kept removing her clothes in public places. This was overcome by ignoring the undressing and hugging her whenever no undressing had been attempted for five minutes.

Self-exposure (or exhibitionism)
Exposing genitals is another behaviour problem neglected in the literature. In one study a 52-year-old institutionalised man, with a profound handicap, learned not to unzip his trousers to expose his penis. This was achieved by observing him once every 10 minutes, hugging and praising him if his trousers were not unzipped but ignoring him if they were. In another study, time-out was used to stop a girl exposing herself to boys, though it was not clear if her mental handicap was severe.

Aggressive sexual behaviour
Though a rare occurrence, people with severe mental handicaps sometimes try to force

younger or weaker individuals to engage in sexual activity with them, or try to fondle others against their will. Such problems are almost totally ignored in the literature.

In one published account, a 14-year-old boy with a severe mental handicap, who forcibly held his brothers and sisters tightly while he rubbed his genitals against them, was admitted to a residential treatment centre. Here, he was subjected to time-out if he engaged in this behaviour. However, staff tried to anticipate the behaviour, and when it seemed likely to occur, would take him to his bedroom, tell him to masturbate there, and provide him with a large pillow to rub himself against. He soon found he could use this to produce an orgasm. He subsequently went to his bedroom to do this instead of annoying others. Later, similar procedures were successfully implemented at home.

Air swallowing (or aerophagia)

This is a rare problem behaviour in which air is swallowed, causing abnormal distension of the abdomen, excessive wind, and frequent belching. It can result in abnormal structural changes in the body, severe pain, and even death. Little is known about its incidence, causes, or treatment.

There is one report of a successful intervention with a 5-year-old girl with a profound mental handicap. After a number of unsuccessful approaches in a psychiatric hospital setting, air-swallowing was almost totally eliminated by a treatment package consisting of several different techniques. As soon as air-swallowing began, a hand-held device was used to produce 10 clicking sounds. The behaviour therapist then placed one hand over the girl's eyes so that she could not see anything, and used the thumb and forefinger of the other hand to block her nostrils. This was stopped when the air-swallowing ceased. It was argued that the "nose-pressing" was probably the effective part of the package, because it interfered with swallowing. If that was so, it could be interpreted as an example of behavioural interruption used as a reducing consequence.

Behaviours characteristic of depression

Depression in people with severe mental handicaps is another area that has been greatly neglected in the literature. Only one study of a behavioural approach has been located. In this, behaviours that led to a diagnosis of depression were tackled: speaking very little; complaining of physical illness; irritable behaviours; not keeping self neat and clean; making negative self-statements like "I can never do anything right"; speaking without tone, inflection, or accompanying gestures; avoiding eye contact; and delaying in responding to conversational approaches. The people being helped were guided to engage in more appropriate behaviours as alternatives to each of the problem behaviours, the guidance techniques including instructions and modelling associated with role-playing. Appropriate behaviour was reinforced with tokens exchangeable at the end of the session for food.

PART C

Specific problems

SECTION 2. NON-COMPLIANT BEHAVIOURS

Definition, causes, and incidence

Definition

In the literature, the term "non-compliance" is commonly used to mean failure to carry out an instruction within a reasonable period of time, varying from three to thirty seconds between different researchers. (Five seconds is most common.) A person showing a non-compliant behaviour may not respond at all, may respond only after unacceptable delay, or may respond with some other behaviour that was not requested. Non-compliant behaviour has also been referred to as *disobedient behaviour, negativistic behaviour, oppositional behaviour, and uncooperative behaviour.*

In this book the term *non-compliant behaviour* is used to refer to a person's failure to respond as required, within a reasonable time, to any clear indication that a particular behaviour should be carried out. A teacher may, for instance, push a brick along a table, then point to a child or to the child's hand, or may even physically move the child's hand on to the object. A compliant child would then push the brick along the table within, say, five seconds. A child who was not compliant might: do nothing; pick the brick up and hold it; say "No, I won't"; sweep the brick off the table; grab the teacher's hand or some object other than the brick; leave the table; knock the table over; scream; make stereotyped hand movements; attack someone; begin to self-injure; or carry out some other unwanted behaviour. Non-compliant behaviour, therefore, overlaps heavily with the categories of problem behaviour described in other sections. Where this is the case, the recommendations made in those sections will be appropriate for intervention purposes.

Also included in the non-compliant category is a person's failure to respond to instructions *not* to do something. However, such instructions are usually intended to prevent some problem behaviour, such as aggressive or stereotyped behaviour, and these are discussed, and recommendations made, in other sections.

Non-compliant behaviour, as understood here, needs to be distinguished from failure to understand or carry out specific tasks. A person with a severe mental handicap may be perfectly willing to comply, but may not understand what is wanted or may be unable to do what is required. In this situation teaching of the specific tasks involved is necessary and this will not be dealt with here.

Another distinction of some importance is between a person who has not grasped the notion of doing something because someone else requires it, and a person who is well aware of the need to comply but chooses not to do so. A choice not to may be made either because the person is poorly motivated to comply, or because the person derives positive satisfaction from *not* doing so – as in the testing-out behaviour common in non-handicapped pre-school children. These distinctions may not, however, be easy to make in practice, and both aspects will be covered here.

It is also sometimes difficult to distinguish between non-compliance and fearful avoidance (Section 8), particularly in people with mental handicaps who have not yet learnt to communicate their feelings clearly. Even people who are more advanced in this respect may pretend to be afraid in order to avoid complying with the wishes of others, as may young children *without* mental handicap.

Non-compliant behaviour can be specific or general. One person with a mental handicap may be generally compliant, but may refuse to perform one (or a few) particular action(s). Another may be non-compliant over a wider range of behaviours, but on a relatively small number of specific occasions. Yet another may show the problem most of the time, but be cooperative in relation to a few activities or on a few occasions. Or a person may never show any behaviour that is convincingly compliant.

Causes
There has been little direct investigation of the causes of non-compliance in people with mental handicaps. However, it may have much in common with the causes of similar behaviour in pre-school children who are not mentally handicapped, who comply with about 60 to 80 per cent of the commands and requests of their parents. With them it has been described as "a complex phenomenon in which constitutional and environmental variables interact". Thus children who are "fussy" in the first year of life tend, by the age of four, to resist physically any adult attempts to guide their behaviour, which might suggest some enduring temperamental characteristic. On the environmental side, a great deal of maternal criticism and restriction tends to result in verbal non-compliance (that is, saying "No, I won't"); whereas if mothers exert too much pressure and control for developmental progress their children tend to resist passively (that is, they just take no notice of adult efforts to direct their behaviour). Early pressure for *compliance* appears to increase non-compliance in some infants. There is evidence that vague or interrupted commands can lead to non-compliant behaviours and, if these occur regularly, such uncooperativeness can become a habit. Thus, various antecedents can bring about the behaviour. It is also likely that non-compliant behaviours often have reinforcing consequences, such as being able to carry on with a preferred activity because the adult gives in.

It seems likely that some people with mental handicaps do not comply because they have reached a stage of development at which they have not come to understand the notion of doing something at the direction of someone else. A certain amount of non-compliance is, however, normal at all stages of development and can be thought of as healthy progress towards independence. If people with severe mental handicaps are following a normal sequence of development it is to be expected that they will show a fair amount of direct and deliberately defiant behaviour early on, which will decrease as they mature, and that attempts to escape from the control of others will turn increasingly towards negotiation.

Incidence

Studies of the incidence of non-compliant behaviours are hard to locate, perhaps because they have not been clearly distinguished from other problem behaviours. However, in one study of the opinion of teachers working with children with severe mental handicaps, non-compliance was the most frequently identified behaviour problem, comprising 28 per cent of the total number of problems identified. In another study it was 16 per cent, though not the most frequent problem identified.

Why are they a problem?

There are several reasons why non-compliant behaviours in people with mental handicaps present problems. Firstly, it is important for people with mental handicaps to respond appropriately to directions for a range of purposes, including their own safety and their need for guidance in, and enjoyment of, learning. Secondly, the nature of a particular non-compliant behaviour may be a problem in itself, for example, if it takes an aggressive form. Thirdly, many of the techniques recommended in this book for overcoming behaviour problems can be implemented only if the people presenting the behaviour allow someone to direct them. Compliance, therefore, can be thought of as one of the most basic objectives in tackling both learning and behaviour problems.

Intervention techniques

Defining the problem

Examples of the precise kinds of description of the problem behaviour needed are:

> When given an indication within his understanding that he should engage in any action which is within his capabilities, Richard moves away from the nurse and does something different.

> When asked to come to her mother or father to have her shoelaces tied up, Michelle cries and struggles.

For action purposes, it is more important to define the appropriate behaviours with which the person is refusing to comply. For instance:

> When given an indication within his understanding that he should engage in any action which is within his capabilities, Richard performs that action within five seconds of receiving the indication.

> When asked to come to her mother or father to have her shoelaces tied up, Michelle comes within five seconds and accepts the shoelace tying without fuss.

Sometimes, where non-compliance is general, it may be possible to tackle all examples as though they were essentially *one* problem behaviour, and all compliant behaviours as though they were *one* appropriate behaviour. Thus, the behaviour defined for John, a 12-year-old boy with a severe mental handicap (see Example 4) was to comply with *any* instructions.

More commonly, however, a general pattern of non-compliance indicates a need to proceed in a series of steps. Thus Andrew (Example 5), a boy aged 10 with autistic features, did virtually nothing to adult direction and resisted violently any attempts to change this. He was required, as a first step, just to stay in his classroom for 10 minutes twice a day. Later, he was asked to participate in just one activity in the classroom as well, then two activities, and then eventually to try to learn new skills. For people with the most severe handicaps the steps towards compliance may need to be very small. Roger (Example 2), a 7-year-old boy who was blind, deaf, and spastic in all four limbs, was required only to move his head towards a source of air blowing into his face.

A useful rule to follow when faced with general non-compliance is to identify some simple action which the person can already perform, even though the person will not necessarily do it at anyone's direction. Getting the person to do so could be a first step towards compliance. Examples might be running round the room, or pushing a toy car along a table. In describing the behaviours precisely, it is best to include a very simple verbal instruction, even if the person will not understand it at first. An example of such a description is:

> When seated at a table with any residential worker, and the residential worker pushes a toy car about one foot along the table with a single arm movement and then points to the car and says "You do it", the child pushes the car at least six inches along the table using any arm movement within five seconds of the instruction.

As people with severe mental handicaps mature, it is important to move away from a conception of compliance as simply doing what they are told. Progress towards independent decision making needs to be encouraged, and they should be helped to develop skills that will enable them to negotiate with others when different people's needs and wishes conflict. The behaviours selected for teaching should reflect these changes. Little work of this kind with people with severe mental handicaps has yet been reported in the literature.

Measuring the problem

There is a danger, when measuring the incidence of non-compliant behaviours, of really counting the number of instructions given. It is best, therefore, to measure the *proportion* of occasions upon which a person complies or does not comply. Over a predetermined observation period, every instruction given can be noted, and a record made of whether the person complies or not. The final measure can then be the percentage of occasions on which compliance occurs.

For someone who hardly ever complies it is probably best for the first intervention programme to take place during specific sessions. It is then possible to require the person to carry out a particular action on a fixed number of occasions in each session. The measure might then be, say, the number of times out of 10 on which the person complies.

Identifying existing antecedents and consequences

It has been found that the nature or conditions of the instructions given can affect whether a person complies or not. Thus, a vague or interrupted instruction is less likely to be effective than a clear, direct one. In one study, adults with profound mental handicaps responded to instructions given in a loud voice, but not to those delivered in a softer one. Giving people time to comply may increase the likelihood of their doing so. There is also evidence that achieving eye contact in advance makes compliance with a spoken instruction more likely. With children who have autistic features careful guidance in a one-to-one situation has been found to evoke more compliance than a less structured situation in which one adult supervises the free play of four children.

The nature of the task required can also determine how effective it is as an antecedent. In one study, for instance, children with autistic features complied more often with a task at which they were successful than they did with a task at which they were not.

Naturally occurring consequences of non-compliant behaviours in people with mental handicaps have not been identified in the literature located. However, it seems likely that attention, or escape from demands, might reinforce such behaviours.

Changing antecedents and consequences for intervention programmes

Antecedents and consequences that are already occurring can either be changed or used more constructively. For instance, vague instructions can be replaced by clear ones; or consequences which reinforce non-compliant behaviours can be used for compliant behaviours instead.

Whether the antecedents and consequences used are natural or contrived, the first consideration is: how can they be used to increase the appropriate compliant behaviour? The most commonly used antecedents have been instructions, demonstration, and physical guidance. In Example 1, children with severe mental handicaps and autistic features were given an instruction, such as "Touch your nose". The teacher would then say "Do this", and would demonstrate the action. Physical guidance may sometimes be needed, if either the person does not understand the verbal instruction, or understands but does not follow the instruction voluntarily. Seven-year-old Roger (Example 2) was blind and deaf, thus making communication very difficult. To get him to move his head towards a draught of air, the teacher moved his head with her hands as part of the intervention procedure. Ernest (Example 3), a 12-year-old boy with a profound mental handicap, was required to sit at a table for a short while as a first step towards compliance, but he would run away rather than do it, and struggled and howled if anyone tried to make him. He was, therefore, determinedly held there despite his protests.

An antecedent-based technique which has only just appeared in the literature may be helpful when a person will comply with some instructions and requests but not others. It consists of preceding an instruction which is not likely to be followed with several others that are likely to be followed. For instance, in the only published account of the technique located, Bart, a man with a severe mental handicap living in an institution, did not comply with instructions like "Please put your lunch box away", "Please don't leave your lunch box on the table", and "Don't put your feet on the coffee table". Compliance with these instructions was increased by preceding them with a series of instructions with which he did usually comply, such as "Give me five", "Come here and give me a hug", and "Show me your notebook".

For some people with mental handicaps, obvious rewards will function as reinforcing consequences for appropriate behaviour. John, the 12-year-old boy with a severe mental handicap (Example 4), for instance, was awarded tokens for complying with any instruction in the classroom. The tokens were subsequently traded in for more tangible rewards. With other people the consequences may need to be of a less usual kind. Thus for Andrew, the 10-year-old boy with autistic features (Example 5), escape from adult restriction to be able to do more or less as he pleased (identified from prior study as a probable reinforcer) seemed the only available consequence for reinforcing his compliant behaviour – and was successful. For Ernest (Example 3) the same applied, though it was supplemented by a *Smartie*. Roger (Example 2), the seven-year-old boy with multiple handicaps, also presented a difficult problem since the only consequence that could be thought of involved subjecting him to an unwelcome experience (putting an ice-cube in his hand), so that escape from it could reinforce his compliant behaviour. In Example 6, 28-year-old Donald was reinforced by things to eat and drink, pats on the shoulder, and praise for complying with instructions *not* to perform a problem behaviour (flicking his hand at the wrist). In all these examples, a behaviour incompatible with non-compliance was being reinforced (differential reinforcement of incompatible behaviour or DRI).

Methods of increasing compliant behaviour may need to be supplemented by measures aimed directly at decreasing non-compliant behaviours. This is particularly true when the person with responsibility wants the person with a mental handicap to obey instructions *not* to do something. It might have been so with Sally, a 14-year-old girl with a severe mental handicap (Example 7), but the report does not say what, if anything, was said to her by way of instructions. It could quite well have been, "Don't take your plimsolls off". Her plimsolls were *sellotaped* to her feet to make them a little more difficult to remove, the difficulty acting as an antecedent making her less likely to attempt to remove them. Often, the same antecedent action by the person in charge can both increase the likelihood of compliant behaviours and decrease the likelihood of non-compliant behaviours – as when Ernest (Example 3) was held in his chair to ensure that he sat at a table and did not escape from adult demands.

Where more positive approaches are insufficient, there may be a need for reducing consequences for non-compliant behaviour. These should be as mild as possible. For instance, James (Example 8), aged 25 and multiply handicapped, was, as part of the intervention package, told "No" and made to sit in a chair for a short time (a "time-out" procedure) if he engaged in activities other than following an instruction to go to the toilet.

More intrusive methods are illustrated by Examples 9 and 10. In Example 9, with an eight-year-old girl with a severe mental handicap called Wilma, the reducing consequence was to make her engage in an unwelcome activity using an overcorrection procedure. Every time she failed to respond appropriately to the instruction, "Wilma, look at me", she was made to move her head to each of the positions up, down, and straight, and to maintain each one for 15 seconds, this continuing for five minutes. In Example 10, a 13-year-old girl with a profound mental handicap and autistic features, who avoided complying with training in self-help skills by lowering her torso to her legs, hand-flapping, and drawing her arms near her chest and tensing her entire body, had something unwelcome done to her as a consequence. Every time one of these behaviours occurred she was held still by the arms and legs for one minute.

An interesting reducing consequence was used with Bill (Example 11), a three-and-a-half-year-old boy with a severe mental handicap. He was given instructions and was physically prompted in carrying them out if he did not do so spontaneously. Forced engagement in the appropriate behaviour required, being unwelcome to Bill, was effectively used as a reducing consequence for non-compliant behaviour.

The illustrative studies that follow shortly indicate that techniques are rarely used singly in dealing with non-compliant behaviours. Reinforcement of compliant behaviours (differential reinforcement of incompatible behaviour or DRI) is virtually standard, but it is usually accompanied by antecedent devices or by reducing consequences for non-compliance. Roger, in Example 2 for instance, was taught to turn his head towards a stream of air by antecedent physical guidance and reinforcement by escape from an ice-cube in his hand. In Example 7 a 25-year-old man was reinforced by pats on the back and raisins when he complied with instructions but he was made to sit on a chair for a period as a reducing consequence when his response was non-compliant.

Subsequent action

Example 1 illustrates how compliant behaviours can be made to generalise from the situation in which they are learned to other situations. Children with severe mental handicaps and autistic features were taught compliant behaviours in a one-to-one situation, and other children were introduced gradually into the situation over a period while compliance training continued.

It cannot be assumed that a person who complies with one instruction will comply with another, though sometimes generalisation occurs between instructions that are very similar to each other. With some people, every instruction may need a separate intervention to begin with, though the chances of generalisation should increase as more instances are successfully covered. This seems to have occurred with Ernest (Example 3) who at first had only to sit in a chair, then tolerate an object on a table in front of him, then perform simple tasks with objects, eventually follow simple instructions, and later join in group activities and various kinds of play. Gradually he became more cooperative with adults generally.

Gradual fading out of intervention procedures so as not to lose improvements in compliant behaviour is illustrated by Example 8, in which a young man who was blind and deaf was reinforced for compliance with pats on the back and raisins. These were subsequently awarded only intermittently, and the raisins were finally eliminated.

Illustrative studies

Example 1 (Koegel and Rincover, 1974)

This study was carried out with eight children with severe mental handicaps and autistic features who were not acceptable in ordinary or special classes because of their self-stimulatory behaviours and minimal responsiveness to instruction. Their ages ranged from four to thirteen years. The intervention was carried out by a teacher and an assistant in a special classroom, at first on a one-to-one basis, and later with other children present. Measuring was undertaken by independent observers.

The children were required to make various verbal and non-verbal responses. Here, the non-verbal responses will be considered because they were closer to "compliance" as defined earlier. The teacher would give an instruction to a child and the child had to respond correctly within 10 seconds. The percentage of correct responses was calculated for both individual and group sessions, though the details are not altogether clear.

After a baseline period, which varied in length from child to child, an intervention programme was introduced without any reported advance study of antecedents and consequences. In daily 50-minute sessions, children were first taught the behaviours required on a one-to-one basis. Firstly, each child was taught eye-to-eye contact. The teacher said, "Look at me". Compliance was reinforced with food until the child looked at the teacher for a period of at least five seconds on 90 per cent of trials for three consecutive days. Then, imitation of a range of simple actions (such as hand-clapping and nose-touching) was taught, by physically prompting and reinforcing correct copying of the teacher's demonstration. The imitative skills thus developed were then used to prompt compliance with simple spoken instructions to carry out the actions which had been imitated, again using food reinforcement. The teacher would say, for instance, "Touch your nose", prompting by saying, "Do this", and demonstrating the action required. During this teaching disruptive behaviours were ignored, or the teacher shouted "No" or slapped the child briskly. When correct responses were obtained on 80 per cent of occasions, the child was taught new responses to spoken instructions in a group of two. When the 80 per cent level was reached in this situation the group size was increased to four, and the same criterion was used for a later change to a group of eight. During these last two phases, the frequency of reinforcement was reduced, first to once for every four correct responses, then once for every eight. Throughout these changes the teaching procedures were the same as in the individual session – physical prompting (until it was no longer necessary) and reinforcement.

The measured results are difficult to understand, and unnecessary to reproduce here, but seven of the eight children reached at least the 80 per cent correct level in a group of eight, and the remaining child made progress towards it.

Though this intervention taught the children to comply with instructions to carry out some rather pointless actions, and though it included slapping which cannot be recommended for use in this country, it is included here because it illustrates well the use of teaching procedures as antecedents for appropriate (that is, compliant) behaviours.

Example 2 (Alberto, Troutman, and Briggs, 1983)

Roger, a seven-year-old boy who was blind and profoundly deaf, had a spastic condition affecting all four limbs and no speech. He showed no consistent identifiable response to anything which impinged upon him. It is doubtful whether he would have had any notion of what another person wanted. The intervention was carried out in the classroom by a teacher and an aide. No measuring procedures are described.

Identifying some behaviour which Roger could perform was a considerable problem. However, since there was a consistent change in his rate of eye-blinking when air blew on his face, it was assumed he must be aware of the air in some way and might learn to respond to it. It was decided to try to get him to move his head towards the source of the air. No measuring procedures are reported.

In the intervention procedure, which was not preceded by any reported investigation in advance of existing antecedents and consequences, physical guidance was used to get Roger to make the head movement required. His teacher held his head so that it faced to one side, blew on his cheek and guided his head towards the source of the air until it was directed on to his lips. To make it more likely that he would eventually repeat the movement without physical guidance, possible reinforcing consequences for the head-turning were sought by exposing him systematically to a range of experiences. Since nothing positive emerged, it was decided to use escape from an unwelcome experience. Roger consistently removed his hand from an ice-cube placed in his palm. So, before the guiding procedure, an ice-cube was placed there. This was removed when the air was blowing on his lips. Gradually, the guidance was faded, by reducing the number of fingers used and the pressure involved, until Roger performed the movement on his own. Roger had, of course, learned to do only one small thing his teacher wanted, but it was a step on the road to compliance.

In this study, use of physical guidance as an antecedent to make an appropriate behaviour more likely to occur was combined with use of escape from an unwelcome experience as a reinforcing consequence for that behaviour. Since compliant and non-compliant behaviours cannot occur simultaneously, this intervention included differential reinforcement of incompatible behaviour (DRI).

Example 3

Ernest was a good-sized, 12-year-old boy with a profound mental handicap who lived in hospital. His gross movements were well coordinated. He had no speech, was able to understand a few commands, and was continent if taken to the toilet regularly. Ernest had severe difficulty in relating to others and avoided virtually all contact with other people, moving away fast at their approach and avoiding eye contact. A very large amount of his time was spent in one corner of the room where there was a shelf and an assortment of large barrels. He would climb about these with great concentration for long periods as long as no one else came near him, but he would not concentrate on any task which anybody else tried to set him. Ernest did, more or less, conform at meal times, presumably because of the incentive of food. Occasionally he was aggressive to other children, but was rarely aggressive to adults. The intervention with Ernest was carried out by his class teacher, Mr. L., in the classroom, with regular advice from me. No measuring procedures were attempted.

Careful thinking needed to precede planning of an intervention programme. Mr. L. identified his main aim as geting Ernest to relate to other people in a meaningful way. To begin with it was necessary to get Ernest to conform in one way or another to some demand, or at least to interact in some way. Getting him to sit in a chair for a short time was identified as a first step. It soon became clear that the antecedents to promote this behaviour would need to include physical compulsion. It was thought that sweets might possibly be used to reinforce sitting behaviour but that escape from adult control might be more potent.

The first intervention required Ernest to sit on a chair twice a day. It resulted in Ernest struggling, making crying sounds, and hitting Mr. L. and pulling his hair, though these aggressive behaviours were not very forceful. Mr. L. persisted, and eventually Ernest would give in and sit still for a moment, usually after about half-an-hour's protest. Further struggles then followed. Mr. L. continued each session until he felt Ernest had fully accepted that he had to remain seated. Ernest would then be released, given a sweet, and allowed to return to his shelf and barrels. Within weeks, he remained at the table without protest.

Over the next two years or so, Ernest was required to conform in gradually more demanding ways. Demonstration and physical guidance (and compulsion where necessary) were used to ensure compliance, and sweets and escape were used to provide the consequences. Firstly, Ernest was required to sit at a table and tolerate objects on it, instead of sweeping them off, as he did initially. Then he was required to put wooden cylinders in holes, put cubes in a cup, pick up a piece of string, and put beads in a bottle. Later, he had to follow simple instructions; for instance, he was told to pick up an object and give it to the teacher. Eventually, he was encouraged to play with a ball, play in a pool of water, sit in a circle during group instruction, and accept physical contact with other people. None of these steps was achieved easily, but eventually Ernest accepted physical guidance, followed simple instructions, and attempted a range of simple tasks with play objects.

It was interesting that, as his compliance increased, Ernest's behaviour towards people became more positive. He began to smile at his teacher and approach him for a cuddle, he chuckled when tickled, and he would approach somebody and take that person's hand to indicate that he wanted something.

In this series of interventions physical guidance (including compulsion) was the major antecedent for making compliant behaviours more likely to occur. Sweets and escape from the (initially) unwelcome experience of adult contact and control were reinforcing consequences for these behaviours (an example of differential reinforcement of incompatible behaviour, or DRI).

Example 4 (Barton, 1975)

John was a 12-year-old boy with a severe mental handicap who was resident in hospital. He was considered almost impossible to work with in school because of his non-compliant behaviours. The published account does not clearly specify the behaviours to be changed, nor fully describe the measures and procedures. However, during the baseline period, John was observed for 15 minutes each day at randomly chosen times and the 'percentage obedience' was calculated for each day.

After a baseline of 20 days, an intervention programme was begun without any reported advance investigation of antecedents and consequences. Compliance with any instruction was followed by an award of a token whenever this could be managed. The tokens were traded immediately for tangible rewards for the first few days so that John would realise their significance, but the trade-in was gradually delayed to the end of each two-hour classroom session. His "percentage obedience" over the 16 days of operation rose considerably above baseline level.

In this intervention a token system was used to reinforce appropriate behaviour. It was, therefore, an example of differential reinforcement of incompatible behaviour (DRI).

Example 5 (McKeown, 1978)

This study featured a 10-year-old boy with autistic features called Andrew, who would not cooperate with any learning procedure in his special day school. He wandered all over the school, humming, running, climbing on furniture, licking objects, and crying. If anyone approached him he ran away, and he kicked, bit, struggled, screamed, banged his head against the wall, and attacked other children if any attempt was made to interfere with these actions or engage him in others. The intervention was carried out in the classroom by the teacher and an assistant.

In designing the intervention, three main objectives were first identified: to get Andrew to stay in the classroom; to get him to do things in class; and to gain control over his temper tantrums. As a first step he was required to stay in the classroom for 10 minutes. No measuring procedures are described. Various possible reinforcing consequences for the behaviour required were considered, and it was decided that the only experience likely to be useful was freedom for Andrew to do as he liked. Since his deviant behaviour achieved this it was a reinforcing consequence for that behaviour, and it needed instead to be used to reinforce more appropriate behaviour.

The intervention required Andrew to stay in the classroom for 10 minutes at the beginning of each morning and each afternoon. A kitchen timer rang at the end of the period and he was then released, presumably if he had stayed in the classroom without undue fuss. After a week the time was increased to 20 minutes and he was also asked to do one specific thing, such as running round the room with the class in PE, or doing a simple puzzle at the beginning of the period. This continued for a third week, in which 30 minutes in the classroom were required. In the fourth week Andrew had to remain in the classroom for 40 minutes and he had to do specific things, with a 15-minute period of freedom within the classroom following each one. When this was successful, progressively more demands were made, until Andrew was able to participate most of the time and even learn to improve some skills. Throughout the programme tantrums were dealt with by making him sit in a corner of the classroom until he quietened down. He was never allowed to escape from doing something by having a tantrum (he would have to return to the task after this "time-out"), nor was he allowed to leave the classroom immediately after a tantrum or a time-out period. These procedures were successful very rapidly.

In this intervention, freedom from adult control was used as a reinforcing consequence for appropriate behaviours (differential reinforcement of incompatible behaviour or DRI). There was also a "time-out" procedure as a reducing consequence for certain kinds of non-compliant behaviour.

Example 6 (Weisberg, Passman, and Russell, 1973)
Donald was a 28-year-old young man with a profound mental handicap who was institutionalised and had no speech, made little response to instructions, and engaged in stereotyped flicking of the wrist. The intervention and its measurement was carried out by the researchers in a separate room.

The problem behaviour was defined as flicking of either hand at the wrist. This, of course, is an example of stereotyped behaviour rather than of non-compliant behaviour *per se*, but the alternative appropriate behaviours involved response to compliance training. Thus in the first experimental phase the alternative behaviour was to touch a cup within six seconds when the experimenter said, "Do this", and demonstrated cup-touching. In the second phase it was to refrain from hand-flicking for six seconds when the experimenter said "Do *not* do this", while shaking his head and imitating hand-flicking. There were five 30-minute sessions per week. The procedure was for the experimenter to act as just described, record whether compliance and hand-flicking each occurred during the next six seconds, wait for 12 seconds, and then repeat the procedure. The percentage of six-second periods during which each behaviour occurred was calculated.

The intervention and evaluation procedures were not preceded by any reported study of existing antecedents and consequences. They are too complex and confusing to be fully described here. However, for "Do this", intervention included: physically guiding Donald in various actions required; reinforcing compliance within six seconds with things to eat and drink, patting him on the shoulder, and saying, "Good"; and turning away of the experimenter's head when Donald did not respond correctly. Where necessary, small steps towards the action required were reinforced in sequence. For "Do *not* do this", refraining for six seconds was reinforced in the same way as for "Do this", while hand-flicking resulted in the experimenter's head being turned away. Touching the cup on request occurred at 100 per cent level immediately it was introduced (though after training on other actions), while hand-flicking fell from around 40 per cent to below 10 per cent within four sessions when the "Do *not* do this" procedure was introduced. In a later phase, the experimenter also said, "Do *not* shake your wrist", and the other antecedents were gradually faded out.

In this intervention, demonstration and physical guidance as antecedents and differential reinforcement of incompatible behaviour (DRI) as a consequence were used to increase the appropriate behaviour; while guiding gestures and differential reinforcement of other behaviour (DRO) (that is, any behaviour other than the problem behaviour) were used to increase compliance with instructions not to engage in the problem behaviour. Donald was being trained to comply with instructions not to do something. These instructions then acted as antecedents to decrease his problem behaviour. They would not have been effective *before* the training.

Example 7 (Orton, 1979)

Sally was a 14-year-old girl with a severe mental handicap who attended a behaviour modification unit at a hospital. The intervention programme was carried out in the unit by the staff there and at home by her mother.

Sally would not keep her shoes on, and the behaviour required was to do so, though it is not clear how this requirement was communicated to her. A baseline procedure (presumably in the unit) involved putting plimsolls on her feet 12 times during a four-hour period and recording how long they were kept on.

An intervention was introduced without any reported study of antecedents and consequences in advance. It began by *Sellotaping* the plimsolls to her feet to make them a little more difficult to remove. Praise and attention were given immediately after the plimsolls were put on, and for every three minutes they remained on. If Sally removed the plimsolls, no attention was given till the end of a 20-minute session, of which there were 12 per day. The same procedure was used at home, except that praise and attention were less systematically scheduled. During the first week, Sally kept the plimsolls on between two and four hours of the four hour session at the unit. During the baseline this behaviour had averaged three minutes, and the longest period had been 22 minutes.

The next week *Sellotape* was not used, and during the third week plimsolls were replaced by lightweight shoes. Sally was soon keeping her shoes on all day, and this was still the case a year later, even though the lightweight shoes had been replaced by more substantial ones.

In this intervention, *Sellotaping* the plimsolls was an antecedent to make the appropriate behaviour more likely, and the problem behaviour of taking them off less likely to occur. Praise and attention were used as reinforcing consequences for appropriate behaviour. Time-out by withdrawal of attention for a specific time was used as a reducing consequence for non-compliance.

Example 8 (Sininger and Yarnall, 1981)

James was a 25-year-old young man who was mentally handicapped, blind, deaf, and institutionalised. He indulged in self-injurious behaviour (the cause of his blindness), and this sometimes interfered with his compliance. The intervention and its measurement was carried out by the experiementers in the institution living room, with some later involvement by ward staff.

The behaviour required was defined as responding to a command in the living room within 10 seconds. During the baseline, James was given six commands (for example, "Go to the toilet") 10 times during each teaching session. For each session, a record was kept of whether he complied or not, and the percentage of times he did was calculated.

After a baseline of two sessions an intervention was initiated, without reported advance study of antecedents and consequences. James was given a command, physically guided to comply if necessary, and given pats on the back and raisins every time he did so correctly and rapidly. If he did not comply he was told "No" and was given the command again. If he engaged in another activity (such as self-injury or hitting the wall) he was told "No" and made to sit in a chair for approximately 10 seconds or until he calmed down. Records were kept of the number of incorrect responses, the number of correct responses using prompts, and the number of correct independent responses. From a baseline level of below 10 per cent, the number of correct independent responses rose to 53 per cent over five sessions. During a three-session return to baseline conditions, it dropped slightly.

At this stage a modified intervention procedure was introduced, in which reinforcement by pats and raisins was only intermittent. The percentage of correct responses climbed to over 80 per cent over five sessions and remained there for another four. The raisins were then eliminated and ward staff were involved in some of the sessions. Compliance continued at a high level. The improvement was maintained at follow-up eight weeks later.

This intervention featured physical guidance as an antecedent for appropriate (complying) behaviour which was reinforced by pats on the back and raisins (differential reinforcement of incompatible behaviour or DRI). Reducing consequences for non-compliant behaviour were being told "No" and having to sit on a chair – a time-out procedure.

Example 9 (Foxx, 1977)

Wilma was an eight-year-old girl with a mental handicap attending a day care programme. She was generally non-compliant to spoken instructions and showed erratic eye contact with adults. The intervention was carried out in a special room by therapists, who also recorded the results.

The intervention focused on an appropriate behaviour – defined as looking directly at the therapist's face within five seconds when the therapist said, "Wilma, look at me", and maintaining this for two seconds. During what was referred to as the baseline period, every time Wilma did this she was praised and given some cereal. Twenty trials were given five times a day by each of two therapists. A record was kept of whether or not

Wilma responded correctly at each trial, and the percentage of trials per day on which she complied was calculated.

After a seven-day baseline, an intervention commenced without any reported investigation of antecedents and consequences in advance. The same number of trials was used as for the baseline; and the same training procedure, except that failure to respond correctly was followed by a period of "functional movement training". In this procedure, Wilma had to move to her head to each of the positions up, down, or straight, and maintain each posture for 15 seconds. If she did not do it when told, she was physically guided. This continued for two minutes. Over three trials, compliance occurred in an average of almost 50 per cent of trials, whereas during the baseline it had been 32 per cent. The period of functional movement training was then increased to five minutes, and over 13 trials compliance averaged 89 per cent.

Subsequently, essentially the same intervention was carried out in the ordinary day care programme situation. Wilma rapidly increased her level of eye contact there, and the cereal and praise could soon be given intermittently and were eventually faded out, though the functional movement training continued to be used on those rare occasions when Wilma did not look when asked.

In this intervention, making Wilma engage in an unwelcome activity was used as a reducing consequence for non-compliant behaviour in a situation where reinforcing consequences for compliance were already in use and proving ineffective on their own. The successful procedure used was an example of overcorrection.

Example 10 (Tomporowski, 1983)
In this study a 13-year-old girl with a profound mental handicap and autistic features, who lived in a residential setting, was making no progress in self-help skills training sessions despite having previously learned basic toileting and dining skills and having also made some progress in dressing. She must have shown some degree of compliance in the past to have mastered such accomplishments, but was avoiding compliance with the training in progress by engaging in three main interfering behaviours: withdrawing from the trainer by lowering her torso to her legs; hand-flapping; and drawing her arms near her chest and tensing her entire body. The intervention programme was carried out in the residential living unit, and appeared to be implemented by the staff there, though there was help with recording from an independent observer.

The aim was to decrease the frequency of the three non-compliant behaviours described. During the baseline, daily 20-minute sessions were used in which prompting and reinforcement were given for behaviours successively closer to the self-help skills to be learned. The frequency of each of the three problem behaviours was recorded and converted to rates per minute. Also recorded were: the time required to complete each training trial of a particular self-help behaviour, the results being converted to an average time per trial for each session; and the number of attempts made by the girl to perform each task following prompting, the results being converted to the percentage of trials per session on which such attempts were made. Thus both problem and appropriate behaviours were measured.

After a baseline period of eight days an intervention programme was introduced. It was not preceded by any reported study in advance of existing antecedents and consequences. It involved two trainers. An immobilisation procedure was used every time one of the problem behaviours occurred. One adult held the girl's legs while another restrained her arms, and this continued for one minute. Appropriate attention to the self-help skill programme was followed by praise, physical contact, and something to eat. At first, the immobilisation technique met with extensive resistance from the girl and had to be applied repeatedly. Soon, however, progress was made. After 55 daily, 20-minute training sessions, the unwanted behaviours had ceased, whereas during the baseline each had occurred at up to 50 times per minute. Self-initiated self-help behaviour had been non-existent during the baseline, but during the intervention went steadily up to reach nearly 100 per cent. The duration of trials went down considerably, so that far more were completed during each session.

Once these high levels of performance were reached, one of the trainers moved gradually away, and the improvements were soon maintained without continued use of immobilisation.

In this intervention antecedents and reinforcing consequences were already in use for appropriate behaviour but not, on their own, very successfully. Subjecting the girl to the unwelcome experience of immobilisation as a reducing consequence for the problem behaviour was added, and improvement followed.

Example 11 (Russo, Cataldo, and Cushing, 1981)

Bill, a three-and-a-half-year-old boy with a severe mental handicap, was referred to a clinic for treatment of general non-compliance, tantrums, kicking and scratching of adults, and self-injurious head-banging. The intervention was carried out by a therapist in a special room, and independent observers recorded through a one-way mirror.

The behaviour to be increased in frequency was defined as an appropriate response within five seconds of a command. During the baseline period the therapist gave the instructions, "Come here", "Sit down", and, "Stand up". Each instruction was accompanied by a gesture (for instance, arms outstretched for "Come here") and was delivered five times during a 10-minute period, spaced out so that one instruction was given every 30 to 45 seconds. Bill had to respond correctly within five seconds, and criteria for correctness were laid down in advance. For instance, for "Come here", Bill had to move near enough to the therapist to be physically touched by him. Records were kept of whether or not the child complied with each instruction, and compliance for each period was measured as the percentage of instructions to which Bill responded correctly.

After a baseline of 10 sessions, an intervention was initiated without advance reported investigation of antecedents and consequences. There were several phases. First a "nagging" phase of six sessions, in which instructions were repeated several times at three-second intervals rather than being given just once. The next phase (of four sessions) involved following Bill's correct responses with pieces of food, physical contact such as a hug, and simple forms of praise, such as "Good boy". After another two sessions of "nagging", there were 14 sessions of a phase in which reinforcing consequences for correct responses were supplemented by physically prompting Bill in the correct response (for example, placing him in the chair) every time he failed to respond correctly within the five seconds, though *not* providing the reinforcers. During all except the last phase, average compliance never rose above 14 per cent, whereas during the last phase it averaged 78 per cent. As compliant behaviours increased fewer prompts were given, until none was necessary. Crying, self-injurious behaviours, and aggressive behaviours were also carefully defined and measured, and improvements followed a similar pattern.

In this intervention the crucial feature of the most successful intervention was making the child engage in the appropriate behaviour (an unwelcome experience) as a reducing consequence for non-compliant behaviours.

PART C

Specific problems

SECTION 3. VIOLENT BEHAVIOURS

Definition, causes, and incidence

Definition

This Section is concerned with almost any behaviour likely to be described as "violent" by an appreciable number of people.

Firstly, it includes aggressive acts towards other people, including kicking, hitting, biting, pinching, "strangling", scratching, pulling hair, pushing, bumping, butting, poking, pulling clothes, spitting, taking things away, name calling, and any kind of threatening behaviour. Secondly, it includes violent behaviour towards inanimate objects, such as pulling pictures from walls, kicking furniture, tearing things, breaking things, throwing things, sweeping things off surfaces, stamping on things, tipping things over, crushing things, and upturning things. Finally, it takes in behaviours which do not necessarily damage, or aim at damaging, anybody or anything, but are likely to be thought of as violent in character, such as screaming, fierce arm-waving, wild running, removing clothes angrily, shouting, thrashing about on the floor, crying noisily, slamming doors, and using abusive or obscene language. Often, a collection of these various kinds of violent behaviour occur together as a "tantrum", which may also include the kinds of problem behaviour dealt with in other sections of this book (for example, self-injurious, non-compliant, or stereotyped behaviours).

Causes

It seems likely that violent behaviours can be caused in various ways. Their frequent occurrence in specific syndromes which include mental handicap, such as the Lesch-Nyhan syndrome, Sanfilippo syndrome, and Klinefelter's syndrome, suggests that they can sometimes be due to physical disorders. However, the indications are that even in such instances the behaviours can be modified by environmental changes. Violent behaviour can also occur as a form of epileptic seizure, when it is usually so ill-coordinated as to be fairly easily manageable.

There is evidence that the occurrence of violent behaviours can be affected by both antecedents and consequences in ways typical of normal human learning. They have been shown, for instance, to be common in situations where adults are making demands on children with mental handicaps but rare where they are not. They are more likely to occur if a person is faced with a difficult task than if an easier task is presented.

Turning to consequences, there are a number of strands of evidence which suggest that violent behaviours can have effects which reinforce them. For example, violent behaviours often enable people to get their own way, and studies of interaction in families indicate that this makes the behaviours more likely to occur again. In one study young people with autistic features were given instructions at a rate decided on in advance, regardless of how they behaved. This meant that they were not allowed to use violent and other disruptive behaviours to escape from the demands. Those behaviours then decreased. It also seems likely that attention can reinforce violent behaviours.

Incidence

Violent behaviours are very common among people with mental handicaps. In one investigation, for instance, in which teachers were asked to identify the behaviour problems that concerned them, temper tantrums made up 17 per cent of the total and were exceeded only by non-compliance. Nurses in a mental handicap hospital, in another study, reported that 32 per cent of the residents showed "hostile irritability". A study of "aggressive conduct disorder" among all children with mental handicaps aged around 8 to 10 years who could be detected in a British city, found that 45 per cent of boys and 56 per cent of girls with IQ's below 50 showed this type of behaviour. When they were followed up at age 22, the figures were 25 per cent and 50 per cent respectively. Another study, which sampled the opinions of main carers (usually mothers) of children of 0 to 16 years with severe mental handicaps, found 25 per cent were reported as having temper tantrums and 21 per cent were reported to be aggressive.

Why are they a problem?

Violent behaviours are clearly a problem because they threaten health and property. They are also likely to lead to exclusion of the person who shows the behaviours from situations and activities that are open to other people. People with responsibility and others with mental handicaps may be constantly wary and fearful of someone who behaves in a violent way, and so may avoid and reject that person. This makes it more difficult for the person to relate to them in more satisfactory ways. Violent behaviours also, of course, disrupt almost any other activity.

Intervention techniques

Defining the problem

Defining the problem usually involves identifying clearly the precise violent behaviours which need to be decreased as well as some appropriate behaviours to increase, so that the person concerned can learn to engage in these instead of the violent behaviours. It is particularly helpful if the alternative behaviours are incompatible with the violent ones.

If, for instance, Mary is happily engrossed in playing with a toy, she cannot simultaneously attack somebody on the other side of the room. It is also helpful if the alternative behaviours chosen serve the same purpose as the violent ones. If Mary attacks other children in order to obtain a toy, she could learn instead to fetch a toy from a cupboard.

If careful thought is given to which behaviours to decrease and increase and to the situations in which those behaviours do, or should, take place, it ought not to be difficult to produce clear descriptions. Examples might be:

> When within two yards of Luke, Charlotte moves rapidly towards him, seizes a length of his hair, and pulls very hard until forced to release her grip.

> During a free-play time, Adam should find a toy, take it to Joanne and give it to her.

Measuring the problem

Once behaviours have been defined in this way their frequency during, say, regular half-hour observation periods can be measured and recorded. Some violent behaviours are, however, comparatively infrequent, in which case measuring all day may be necessary. Where they occur in continuous bursts, rather than as separate incidents, it is better to measure the *proportion of time* occupied by the behaviours rather than the number of occurrences.

Identifying existing antecedents and consequences

A wide range of antecedents and consequences can influence the occurence of violent behaviours, and it is wise to attempt to identify those which are maintaining the unwanted behaviour. Specific event antecedents which can make such behaviours more likely to occur include: demands made on someone to carry out a task which that person dislikes or finds difficult; an attack by another person; drinking coffee, for some people; and the removal or prevention of a welcome experience, such as playing with a favourite toy or running out of the room. The setting may also be relevant. There have, for instance, been records of boys with mental handicaps establishing and fighting over territory in a room, which is probably more likely if the room is small. A high noise level is another factor which can provoke violent behaviour.

Reinforcing consequences include: paying attention to the person showing the behaviour; giving something (such as a sweet) to quieten down the person concerned; or allowing the person to avoid an unwelcome task which would otherwise be required.

Changing antecedents and consequences for intervention programmes

It is possible that the antecedents and consequences that are making violent behaviour more likely to occur can be removed or used in more constructive ways. Perhaps a boy who fights over territory could, for instance, be given a corner of the room furnished with things he likes, to which he can retreat and from which others are banned. This action would change the antecedents for the behaviours. One study showed the effect of a person's general state as an antecedent; substituting decaffeinated coffee for ordinary coffee for adults with severe mental handicaps living in an institution resulted in a decrease in their aggressive outbursts. Consequences can be altered also; for example, by ignoring an aggressor and giving sympathetic attention to the victim. Additionally, or alternatively, new antecedents and consequences may need to be sought.

Though intervention programmes for violent behaviours have most commonly focused on the problem behaviours to be decreased, it is sometimes possible to concentrate entirely on alternative appropriate behaviours. Antecedents then consist of a range of devices for guiding a person in learning these behaviours. Reinforcing consequences can be provided for behaviours incompatible with violence (differential reinforcement of incompatible behaviour or DRI), for behaviours that serve the same purpose as violence (differential reinforcement of equivalent behaviour or DRE), or for any behaviours other than violent behaviours (differential reinforcement of other behaviour or DRO). DRI was used with seven-year-old Edgar (Example 1), who was taught to remain in his seat in the classroom more often, so that he was less likely to shake, slap, pinch, or bite other children. DRO was used to decrease assault, spitting, and tantrums in nine-year-old Mary (Example 2) when she was regularly reinforced for a defined period of time in which the undesirable behaviour did not occur. Prior study of reinforcing consequences following the problem behaviour may be helpful. If, for instance, a violent behaviour regularly achieves attention, attention might instead be used to reinforce alternative *appropriate* behaviours.

A range of techniques has been used to decrease directly the frequency of violent behaviours. Antecedents feature rarely, but an interesting, if vaguely described, example is that of Jane, a 20-year-old woman attending an adult training centre (Example 3). Using spoken instructions she was taught to spot various steps leading to her violent behaviour which had been identified during prior study of its antecedents, and to control them so that the stage of violent behaviour was not reached. It can be helpful, with some people with mental handicaps, to be more specific and to teach them to to engage in some pre-planned, non-violent activity before the violent behaviour starts. A simple version of this technique might be to say, "When you start to feel cross, come and tell me straight away". A more elaborate procedure was used with Danny, a 15-year-old boy with a visual handicap on the borderline of mental handicap (Example 4). He was taught, as part of his intervention programme, to sit in a comfortable chair, close his eyes, and breathe deeply in a slow, regular pattern whenever anxious behaviours, which had been identified as antecedents of aggressive behaviours, occurred. An interesting intervention with Joan, a 14-year old girl with autistic features (Example 5), decreased violent behaviours by changing her entire pattern of activity at the times when the problem was most marked, without identifying precisely which antecedents were relevant.

Interrupting a violent behaviour is a mild reducing consequence. This technique was used in a classroom with 19-year-old Tommy, who was severely mentally handicapped and blind (Example 6). Whenever one of several tantrum behaviours occurred, the teacher told him to stop, made him stand up, do one complete turn, sit down again, and continue working.

Removing reinforcing consequences is another mild form of reducing consequence which has been used for violent behaviours. It was very effective with a nine-year-old boy with a profound mental handicap and cerebral palsy (Example 7), whose throwing of toys and other objects was decreased by tying the objects played with to his wrist with a 12-inch string. Under these circumstances, when he threw the objects his behaviour was not reinforced by seeing them fly across the room, or by hearing them crash to the floor.

Applications of time-out are perhaps the most common reducing consequences described in the literature on violent behaviour. An illustration of this is the work with

Bertha (Example 8), an 8-year-old girl with a mental handicap in a special class. Every time she engaged in a "choke" or an "armwrap", she was placed in a small empty booth for three minutes. She was released only when she had remained there with no crying, yelling, or banging for fifteen seconds.

Overcorrection, which involves making a person do something unwelcome, has frequently been used as a reducing consequence for violent behaviours. Example 9 illustrates this. Here, Mary, a 21-year-old young woman with a profound mental handicap, who was also deaf-blind, was subjected every time she engaged in a violent behaviour to a procedure in which her arms were held, first at right angles to her body, then above her head, and then down at her side, each for 30 seconds. This sequence was repeated for a period of 10 or 20 minutes.

As a last resort, doing unwelcome things to a person showing violent behaviour might be considered as a consequence. George, a four-year-old boy with a mental handicap (Example 10), for instance, had water sprayed on to his face every time he bit or gouged another child. Studies in the USA have included putting unpleasant substances, like soap, in the mouth, but these techniques are unlikely to be acceptable in the UK.

The techniques described above can be combined in many ways if analysis of antecedents and consequences suggests it is appropriate. In a study of one 18-year-old with a severe mental handicap (Example 11), hitting, tearing, and throwing were ignored (extinction), while "on-task" behaviour was praised (DRI). Fiteeen-year-old Keith's aggressive and destructive behaviours (Example 12) were tackled by reinforcing appropriate behaviours with tokens that were exchangeable for more tangible rewards (DRI) and placing him in time-out in a separate room as a reducing consequence for aggressive behaviours.

Additional measures

Medication is sometimes prescribed to control violent behaviours, particularly in institutions. Major tranquillisers are the drugs most commonly used for this purpose (see Part B). Lithium carbonate (trade names *Camcolit, Lithicarb)* is a different kind of drug which has been shown to decrease aggressiveness in adults with mental handicaps, but it can cause the side effects of stomach-ache, headache, and tremor. Carbamazepine *(Tegretol)* is an anti-epileptic drug which has also been used to decrease aggressive behaviour, but its effectiveness is a matter of dispute.

Violent behaviour can sometimes occur as a form of epileptic seizure. If this is a possibility, medical advice should be sought to establish whether this is the case and to initiate any medical treatment that may be necessary. Such aggression is sometimes preceded by feelings of sickness, discomfort in the stomach, fearfulness, or anxiety. The behaviour hardly ever lasts longer than a minute and it is usually poorly coordinated, as though having no clear intention to harm. It can be accompanied by repeated, meaningless movements of various parts of the body, or by incontinence. The person may be drowsy or may fall asleep afterwards and does not remember the incident later. Any well-planned, coordinated, or sustained attack is exceedingly unlikely to be epileptic in nature. There is no evidence that problem behaviours shown by people with epilepsy *between* their seizures indicates any particular form of medical intervention. It can usually be tackled by behavioural techniques.

A meat-free diet has recently been reported to decrease aggressive behaviour in a clinical study, but research into *dietary intervention* with people who are severely mentally handicapped is virtually non-existent.

Many problems can arise in the *handling* of violent behaviours because people with responsibility fear that, in the end, they will not be able to avoid some serious injury occurring. It is important that they know, firstly, how to behave in ways that are least likely to provoke violent behaviours and, secondly, how to restrain the person presenting the behaviour in order to prevent injury either to that person or to others. There is little research evidence available to help, and the following suggestions are a summary of the guidance offered by a number of writers based on their own experiences.

To decrease the chances of violent behaviour, it is important that the people in charge behave as though they are confident and have everything under control, rather than as though they are expecting trouble. If it looks as though someone is about to erupt into violence, people with responsibility need to get into a position where they can deal with the behaviour, but without appearing threatening. Sitting down near the person (using slow movements), for instance, is less threatening than standing eyeball to eyeball. It is also wise to remove, as casually as possible, any potential weapons that may be nearby. Efforts should be made to engage the person in some acceptable, non-violent activity, even if it is only sitting down and relaxing. The person may need to be led quietly away from some source of irritation, or from others who might be harmed, perhaps even out of the room. If there is sufficient understanding, it is sometimes helpful to offer reassurance that the person will be helped not to lose control. All actions should be as "low key" as is compatible with effectiveness. Talking should be in a slow, soft voice, pitched somewhat lower than usual.

Sometimes, potential violence can be controlled at a distance by changing the environment suddenly and unexpectedly, so that the person is distracted. Examples of this are switching lights on and off, turning the television up to full volume, or "accidentally" dropping something like money and then retrieving it.

If, despite these efforts, violent behaviour does occur, it is important for the people in charge to remain calm enough to deal with it efficiently. It has been suggested that deep, slow breathing, and deliberate concentration on staying calm can be helpful; and that deliberate relaxation of muscles (which requires prior training – or at least practice) is helpful. With a cool head, it is often possible to restrain an angry person physically without harm to either party. If someone is held firmly, but without anger, for long enough that person will usually calm down and can then be safely released.

Methods of physical restraint are worth more detailed discussion. The first guideline is that, if the people with responsibility are uncertain of their ability to restrain a person successfully, they should do their best to delay the attempt until help is at hand. Rapid success in restraint is of great importance, since breaking free may be a reinforcing consequence for violent attempts to do so. Someone who is likely to behave violently should be taught quickly that effective restraint is an inevitable consequence of any behaviour that requires it.

There are dangers in describing precise methods of physical restraint in a guide of this kind. Firstly, accurate description is difficult. Secondly, what is written is not informed by knowledge of the sizes and strengths of the people concerned, who else is around, what else is in the room, and so on. Thirdly, there is considerable doubt about whether such things can be learned by reading. It is, therefore, strongly recommended that *practical* training be sought from someone with expert knowledge; someone involved, perhaps, in the training of psychiatric nurses or police personnel. If this is not possible, then moves should be practised with colleagues until they are clearly effective.

Before restraint is initiated try, if possible, to remove unobtrusively such potentially harmful items as wrist watches, spectacles, ties, and tie pins. Do not hold the person to be restrained by the head, throat, or fingers. If pressure has to be applied, it should not be to the throat, stomach, or chest but to the limbs, close to the joints to avoid fracturing. Avoid applying pressure to bare skin; cushion it with clothing. Talk calmly and reassuringly to the person who is being restrained as this may help the person feel less threatened and so be more easily and quickly calmed down.

The best policy for restraint is to involve several people who work as a team, according to some pre-arranged plan. Where violent behaviour is expected, each team member should have a whistle or some other device that can be used to summon the others quickly. Each person should restrain a particular part of the body.

The following ideas for restraint have been recommended by various authors. The first describes an example of two people working as a team. The others can all be used by one person in situations where individual action is required because restraint cannot be delayed until help is available. However, most of them can also be used in various combinations (for example, one team member using a "bear hug" while another grips the person's knees) to fit particular circumstances. To aid clarity in these complex descriptions they have all been based on interactions between Ann and Lynne, residential care workers, and Matthew, a large teenager with a severe mental handicap.

> Ann and Lynne can both approach Matthew at once, one on each side of him. Each grasps Matthew's wrist on her own side and then immediately his upper arm just above the elbow. Matthew's arms are then pulled behind his back. Ann and Lynne both place one foot behind Matthew's feet and pull him backwards towards the floor. Just short of the floor, Ann steps over Matthew and Lynne moves round him so that he can be placed on the floor on his front. One of them then sits on Matthew just above the knees to prevent him from kicking. It is claimed that this manoeuvre is painless and does not require brute strength. This two person method is particularly useful for restraining someone large like Matthew.

> Ann sits on Matthew's upper legs to prevent him from kicking.

> Lying across Matthew's hips and abdomen is a safe way for Ann to hold him down.

> Lynne uses a "bear hug" from behind to pin Matthew's arms to his body.

> A useful variation of the "bear hug" hold involves Lynne getting Matthew's arms crossed in front of his body, with his hands held firmly and low down.

> Lynne restrains Matthew's legs by gripping them together just above the knees.

> If Lynne needs to restrain Matthew's arms and legs simultaneously by combining or varying the last three methods, it is best done with Matthew and Lynne lying on the floor and Lynne's legs encircling his legs and crossed over in front of them.

One possible method Lynne could use to lower Matthew to the floor is described in the next idea.

Lynne faces Matthew, grasps his arms at the elbows, and pulls him towards her. She then gradually changes her grip and encircles him with her arms, still pulling him towards her. Then she moves to one side and places her nearest leg beside him. Keeping her foot firmly on the ground, Lynne pushes Matthew over her leg and lowers him and herself to the ground. She then quickly turns him on his face and lies across his trunk.

This starts in the same way as the last suggestion, but after encircling Matthew with her arms Lynne quickly gets behind him, still with her arms around him, and pushes him towards a nearby wall, where she leans on him and presses him to the wall.

Ann uses one hand to hold one of Matthew's wrists and to twist his arm slightly so that his elbow is away from his body, but his arm is still straight. She uses her other hand to grasp Matthew's upper arm and push it down so that he is bent low to near the ground. This puts him off balance and enables Ann to guide him, out of the room if necessary, to where there will be other people who can help her.

Ann and Lynne may also require *defensive manoeuvres*. The following devices have been recommended.

If Matthew is attempting to apply a stranglehold on Ann from behind, she should first tuck her chin in as close to her neck as possible. She can then place her hands in front of her face and push them out and slightly upward against Matthew's hands or arm. Or, she can grasp a single finger of each of Matthew's hands and pull outwards, bending his fingers backwards. She can then hold her arms out in front of her to keep Matthew as close as possible to her back until help arrives.

If the stranglehold is completed before the defensive action just described can be taken and Ann is in danger of injury, a sharp, but not excessive, jab of her elbow just below Matthew's chest may be the only useful option.

If Matthew attempts a stranglehold from the front, Ann should bend sharply forward from the waist. This will release his grip. During this manoeuvre, Ann should cross her wrists in front of her in case Matthew brings his knee up.

If Matthew attacks from the front and grasps Ann's hair or clothing, Ann should bring her arms together in front and in one rapid movement move them up and out. This should loosen Matthew's grip and push his arms away from Ann and out to his sides, where Ann can easily grasp them for purposes of restraint.

Another method of coping with pulling of hair and clothing, such as a scarf, is for Ann to grab Matthew's wrists and pull his hands towards her. She should hold on to this position, shout for help, and tell Matthew to let go.

If Matthew attempts to bite Ann she could grasp his hair firmly and hold his head still.

If Matthew attacks Ann with an object, she should shield herself with a chair or similar item and call for help. If no suitable shield is available, the recommended action differs according to whether the object Matthew has is blunt or sharp. If it is blunt it is best for Ann to close in quickly, grasp the object, and hold on tightly until help arrives. If it is a sharp object it is better for Ann to hold a large, thick piece of material with both hands at arms length, toreador fashion. Ann can use this to field blows. She can also attempt to smother the weapon with it and then grasp Matthew's wrists and hold on. If no material is available, Ann should deflect Matthew's blows with her forearm, and then grasp his wrists and hang on.

In any intervention to change violent behaviour, success may require methods that are more dramatic than usual, which may attract serious criticism. There should, therefore, always be careful advance consultation with parents or other relatives and careful recording of events. Appropriate procedures for this are suggested in Part D, Section 3.

Subsequent action
Example 12 includes a description of modifying a programme that was not very effective in order to improve results. A 15-year-old boy's aggressive and destructive behaviour in his residential unit was tackled by rewarding him for 15-minute periods of abstinence. When this had no significant effect it was supplemented by a "time-out" procedure and the problem behaviour was almost eliminated.

Example 11 illustrates the extension of an intervention programme to different settings. An 18-year-old young woman with a variety of aggressive behaviours was ignored when she displayed them and was reinforced for incompatible appropriate be-haviours. The procedure was introduced first in the art/music classroom, then later in the self-help classroom, and finally in the room used for lunch. Improvement in each setting occurred only when the programme was introduced there.

Example 5 shows how an intervention programme based on antecedent changes can be discontinued in very small steps without loss of improvement. The assaults of a 12-year-old girl with autistic features were decreased by altering her entire routine at times when the assaults occurred most often. The girl was then very gradually reintroduced to the original activities.

Example 4 shows how consequences in an intervention programme can be faded out gradually without loss of improvement. The aggressive and destructive behaviours shown by 15-year-old Danny were tackled by a complex pattern of interventions. These included a token reinforcement system in which he could earn 15 points a day for abstaining from the problem behaviour, and later exchange the points for short-term or long-term benefits. This was faded out by a gradual process in which the points were discontinued and Danny had to behave appropriately for progressively longer periods in order to gain reinforcement.

Illustrative studies

Example 1
Mrs. E., the teacher of seven-year-old Edgar, was involved in one of my workshops. Edgar, who was fully mobile, could understand only very simple language and had virtually no speech. He showed a variety of behaviour problems, of which aggressive

behaviour to other children was one. The intervention and measurement procedures were carried out in the classroom by Mrs. E.

Mrs. E. identified the problem behaviours to decrease: Edgar leaving his seat, leaving the room, and interfering physically with other children by shaking, slapping, pinching, and biting them. The appropriate behaviours which needed to replace these were: Edgar sitting still, listening to and looking at anyone speaking to him, and joining in activities with other children. Mrs. E. decided to start by working on increasing the time Edgar spent in his seat. He could not easily do this and simultaneously attack other children. During the baseline, the number of times Edgar left his seat during a set period each day (half an hour for four days, 20 minutes for the next eight days) was measured.

No study of existing antecedents and consequences was reported. The intervention programme began after the 12-day baseline. For approximately 10 minutes in the early part of each morning, Mrs. E. sat down with Edgar away from the other children, got him to look at her, and then explained that if he finished the task in front of him, remaining seated at the table, he would have a small sweet. The sweet was placed on the table where he could see it, not very far away from him. If the task was finished as required, Edgar was given the sweet immediately. However, if he threw the materials on the floor or ran away, no sweet was given. If he completed one task fairly rapidly, a second one would sometimes be given, in which case the programme would sometimes extend beyond 10 minutes.

The evaluation of this intervention was not very straightforward. During the intervention period measuring occurred only during programme times. As these varied from 7 to 12 minutes they were not comparable with baseline measures. However, during the baseline, the number of times Edgar left his seat averaged 5.25 per half-hour period during the first four days, ranging from 0 to 13 times; and 4.0 per 20-minute period, ranging from 0 to 6, during the last eight days. During six days of recording during the intervention, Edgar did not leave his seat at all. It was, in any case, clear to Mrs. E. that he was leaving his seat considerably less during programme times, and she felt there was some degree of improvement at other times. Unfortunately, there was another complication, in that Edgar's medication was changed during the baseline period. This step was intended to control his difficult behaviour, but resulted in Edgar first being very sleepy, and then having a variable degree of alertness. It is hard to say whether his improved behaviour was due to the medication, the programme, or both; or even, of course, some other cause.

Despite the uncertainties, this intervention does illustrate a way in which reinforcing consequences can be provided for a behaviour that is incompatible with the problem violent behaviour, a technique known as differential reinforcement of incompatible behaviour (DRI).

Example 2 (Luiselli and Slocumb, 1983)
Mary, a nine-year-old girl with a severe to profound mental handicap, lived in a residential special school. The teacher and her two aides carried out the intervention and recorded the results. Problem behaviours to decrease were defined as follows.

> "*Aggressive act* – any time Mary slaps (strikes with open hand), punches (strikes with closed fist), kicks (strikes with feet), or pulls hair (grabs hair with hands) of an adult or child.

Spitting – any time Mary orients towards an adult or child and projects saliva from the mouth in the direction of that person (the saliva does not have to make contact with the person).

Aggressive tantrum – any time Mary exhibits for a minimum of 10 seconds any combination of screaming, crying, and/or self-directed face-and-head-slapping while simultaneously displaying aggressive acts towards an adult or child."

During the baseline period staff used a pre-existing approach, in which they ignored the problem behaviour as far as possible but immobilised Mary until violence subsided where this was necessary to protect others. Recording aimed to count the total number of incidents of each of the three categories of behaviour each day.

After a baseline of 20 days an intervention procedure was implemented without any reported advance investigation of existing antecedents and consequences. Baseline procedures continued, but there was also a new technique involving provision of a reinforcing consequence for a defined period of time during which the problem behaviour did not occur (differential reinforcement of other behaviour or DRO). A timer was set for seven minutes. Any instance of problem behaviour resulted in its being reset for a further seven minutes (after a period of calming down in the case of an aggressive tantrum requiring immobilisation). When the timer rang, a staff member praised Mary lavishly, gave her something nice to eat, and then reset the timer. Under this procedure, the frequency of problem behaviours fell to a low level. For instance, aggressive acts averaged 10 per day during the baseline, but only four per day during the programme. A reinstatement of baseline conditions returned it to 10.5 per day, but reintroduction of the programme led to an average of only one instance per day.

Subsequently, staff gradually increased the length of the timed period and, at follow-up 34 weeks later, the frequency of problem behaviours had fallen still further. Spitting had stopped completely, aggressive acts averaged 0.8 per day, and aggressive tantrums 0.2 per day.

The crucial feature of this intervention was the use of a reinforcing consequence for abstaining from problem behaviours, an example of differential reinforcement of other behaviour (DRO).

Example 3 (Fleming and Tosh, 1984)

Jane was a 20-year-old young woman attending an adult training centre, who regularly "blew-up" for no apparent reason. She would start by making unreasonable demands or failing to comply with appropriate requests, which led to sulking, anger, and verbally and physically aggressive behaviour. The intervention apparently occurred in the adult training centre, but it is not clear exactly who carried out the procedures. There is no description of the precise behaviours involved, nor are any systematic records offered.

There was some prior thinking about antecedents and consequences. It was felt that in the past there had been models for some of her problem behaviours which she might have copied, but that there were no clear antecedents for them in her present situation. However, since the behaviours occurred in a "chain", one behaviour in the chain could be thought of as an antecedent for the next, and this had implications for intervention. It was possible that staff attention was a reinforcing consequence.

The description of the intervention programme is, for the most part, brief and vague.

Jane was encouraged to think of the physical feelings she experienced as she proceeded through the sequence of problem behaviours described. With help and practice she defined a series of five points which she could reliably describe and recognise, for example, "butterflies in my tummy" and "hot face". A card was prepared on which were recorded numbers given to each of the five points. Jane had to recognise each point by the feeling she experienced and try to stop the sequence of behaviour at one of them (the report does not state which, or in what sequence). When she accomplished this successfully, she put a mark on the appropriate part of her card and then engaged in a pre-arranged alternative "behaviour", such as thinking of a pleasant event. She was praised for doing this. Over a period of four weeks Jane's behaviour rapidly improved and she became able to control herself early in the behavioural sequence. The "blow-ups" disappeared and this improvement survived gradual fading out of the intervention procedure.

Despite the inadequacies in the published description, this study is of interest for its development of a "self-control" technique. The card procedure and accompanying instructions might be thought of as antecedents for making problem behaviour less likely and appropriate behaviour more likely. The praise is best thought of as a reinforcing consequence for the alternative behaviours (including the "stopping" and recording procedures) which were being developed (in other words, as an example of differential reinforcement of incompatible behaviour or DRI).

Example 4 (Luiselli, 1984)

Danny was a 15-year-old boy in a residential special shcool. He had a profound hearing loss, vision in one eye only, and bordered on mental handicap. Problem behaviours included aloofness, withdrawal, and aggressive and destructive acts which caused injury to staff. It required two or three staff to subdue him when these acts occurred. Implementation was carried out in the classroom and the living unit by the staff there, and in sessions alone with the researcher. Recording was also a joint enterprise.

The behaviours tackled are not specifically defined, but were clearly recognised by staff. Aggressive behaviour (for example, assaulting someone) and destructive behaviours (such as destroying an object) were separately recorded. Each incident was reported by staff to the researcher, who converted the observations to the number of times each type of problem behaviour occurred during each week. During baseline measures staff physically restrained Danny when necessary and admonished him when he had calmed down. He also had to pick up the pieces after destroying something and was again lectured. Non-directive counselling by a school psychologist was provided once a week.

During the six-week baseline period it was noted that Danny frequently showed physical signs of anxiety before outbursts: flushing of the face, trembling of the hands, and a tense, rigid appearance of the upper body. These could be viewed as antecedents of the aggressive and destructive behaviour.

After the baseline period an intervention programme was begun which involved several different procedures. Firstly, a token system was set up. The day was divided into about 15 different "activities". Danny could receive one point at the end of each activity. The report does not state what he had to do for this, but it apparently included abstaining from aggressive and destructive behaviours. Three times daily there were sessions in which he could exchange his points for toys and games, or he could save his points to "purchase" a weekend activity or a major outing further ahead. Secondly, there was a response cost procedure in which, after Danny had been restrained (where necessary) and 1 to 2 minutes after he had calmed down, five points were crossed off his points sheet for each aggressive act and three points for each destructive one. Thirdly, Danny was taught to identify his bodily states that indicated anxiety and to use a relaxation procedure to help him "feel better". He was taught to sit in a comfortable position in a chair, close his eyes, and breathe deeply in a slow, regulated pattern. He could go to special "relaxation areas" for this. Staff suggested relaxation if they observed the telltale signs, and they praised Danny when he went to the relaxation area on his own initiative or on request.

These procedures were supplemented by making up books and stories about various coping skills, including one in which Danny felt tense and upset, asked if he could relax, did so, returned to class, and received praise. Danny drew each event in the story books. This was a method of mentally rehearsing the behaviour which drew on Danny's skill at drawing. It required little communication through language, which he found difficult. Over six weeks Danny's aggressive responses averaged 0.83 per week during this programme, as opposed to 1.6 per week during the baseline. For destructive behaviour, the programme was continued for 21 weeks, but the average number of incidents decreased only to 0.33, compared with 0.5 during the baseline.

A modified programme was next introduced, first for aggressive and later for destructive behaviour. It is assumed that all the original treatment procedures continued but that, additionally, Danny had to go through an entire week without engaging in the problem behaviour to earn his weekend activity. Aggressive outbursts then averaged only 0.3 per week over 23 weeks, and destructive behaviour did not occur at all over eight weeks.

Intervention procedures were then gradually withdrawn. Firstly, points were discontinued, and Danny had to abstain from the problem behaviours all day to gain access to toys and games, abstain all week to earn the weekend activity, and abstain for two consecutive weeks for more major outings. At first he was given a card for each behaviour, to carry about instead of the points sheet, and the date and time of each occurrence was noted on it, but this was soon discontinued. Later, the skill-training sessions, and eventually all other features of the programme, were discontinued. Follow-ups over two years found no aggressive or destructive behaviour occurring.

This intervention used a set of antecedents for making appropriate behaviour more likely and problem behaviour less likely; points were used as reinforcing consequences for abstaining from violent behaviour (differential reinforcement of other behaviour or DRO); and removal of tokens was a reducing consequence for problem behaviours (response cost).

Example 5 (Touchette, MacDonald, and Langer, 1985)

Joan was a 14-year-old girl in a residential school for autistic adolescents. She had a severe mental handicap, did not speak at all, and had a long history of assaults on staff and peers which had sometimes caused them injury as well as severely disrupting educational activities. The intervention was carried out by school staff, with measuring both by them and by the researchers.

For measuring purposes, assaults were defined as two hits, kicks, or head butts towards staff or peers within 10 seconds, or a single hit to the face, or a single object thrown at someone. All of Joan's waking hours were divided into half-hour intervals. For each interval, staff recorded whether there were no assaults, one assault, or more than one assault. The total number of assaults was also recorded and the number per week calculated.

The pattern of occurrence of assaults was used to try to reach conclusions about antecedents and consequences promoting this problem behaviour. It was found that the behaviour occurred most often during the time Joan attended group pre-vocational and community living classes. Other group activities did not provoke the same reactions, nor did other kinds of learning activities. It seemed likely that the activities in the pre-vocational classes included antecedents which made assaults more likely. At weekends and during evenings, on the other hand, assaults were at their lowest, so the activities then presumably did not include the offending antecedents.

In the intervention, which began after a baseline period of three weeks, activities during the pre-vocational class time were changed to resemble the weekend and evening activities. Assistants engaged Joan in such activities as listening to stories and trying on cosmetics, and the activities were changed every 15 minutes. The assistant moved away for a time if Joan indicated she had had enough for a while. In the first week of this new approach, there were less than 10 assaults, whereas during the baseline the number had varied from 53 to 82 per week. The number of half-hour intervals in which assaults occurred also decreased dramatically.

During the next week a gradual return to the original programme was begun. At first Joan returned to the pre-vocational classes for 15 minutes of each hour they operated. Over the next 12 months, her time in these classes was increased very gradually until she was there for most of the time. Assaults occurred hardly at all.

This intervention is interesting in that antecedents making problem behaviours more likely to occur were removed, despite lack of precise knowledge of what they were, and this decreased the problem behaviour.

Example 6 (Belcher et al., 1982)
This study was carried out with Tommy, a 19-year-old young man with a severe mental handicap who was also blind. Tommy had tantrums which were dangerous to others. The intervention and its recording was carried out in a classroom setting by a teacher and aides.

The behaviours measured are not described precisely, but every episode and its duration was noted, and the number of episodes per day and the time occupied by them per day was calculated. This was done first during a baseline period, in which Tommy's tantrums were handled by spoken reprimands, withholding of praise, and provision of snacks and other reinforcers for appropriate behaviour.

Prior investigation suggested that there was a sequence of behaviour in Tommy's tantrums. They started with calling names repeatedly, throwing work, and pushing his chair back from the table. This led on to a range of other behaviours, including throwing his chair, stripping nude, and scratching anyone who came near. The earlier behaviours could be regarded as antecedents for those that followed. It was hoped that, if the three early behaviours in the sequence could be stopped quickly,the others would not occur. It was thought that this might be achieved by using an interruption procedure which, by turning Tommy round through 360 degrees, would confuse him for a moment (since he was blind) and thus allow, as it were, a new start on the appropriate behaviour required.

After a four-week baseline an intervention programme was devised in which, every time one of the three early behaviours occurred, a teacher told Tommy to stop, pulled his chair away from the table, told him to stand, and then guided him through one 360 degree turn. He was then made to sit down again to continue working. If any clothing was removed or work thrown, the teacher replaced it and generally tidied up. Throughout these procedures, which each lasted for up to about five minutes, the teacher demanded in an authoritarian voice that Tommy should stop and get on with his work properly. He was also occasionally praised and rewarded for working, but behavioural interruption was the only new procedure used. The frequency of tantrums had averaged 2.8 per day during baseline. This went down to 1.5 during the first week of the programme, and to one or less for the remaining 11 weeks. The duration of tantrums also decreased, averaging 28.4 minutes per day during baseline, and remaining below two minutes per day during weeks 7 to 12 of the intervention. Four weeks of measuring at follow-up nine months later found no tantrum episodes at all.

In this intervention, interrupting the problem behaviour was used as a reducing consequence for it.

Example 7 (Williamson *et al.*, 1983)

This description concerns a nine-year-old boy with a profound mental handicap and cerebral palsy, who was active physically but had no spoken language. Advice had been sought about his disruptive classroom behaviour, which included dangerous throwing of toys, along with opening and closing of doors and turning of door knobs. The intervention was conducted in the classroom at a day care developmental training centre. Procedures were carried out by the teachers, but measuring was by independent observers.

The problem behaviour was labelled "inappropriate behaviour", and was defined as "touching a door knob", "opening doors", "being within four feet of a door", and "throwing objects". "Appropriate behaviours" were defined as "manipulating toys in a manner that was not a danger to the subject or other persons", "quietly playing or sitting", and "walking or jumping in the classroom". Records were kept of the number of times appropriate and inappropriate behaviours occurred during each recording period of 30 minutes each day. For measuring, the number of times appropriate and inappropriate behaviours occurred during each period were added to give an overall total. The occurrence of each of these two kinds of behaviour was then calculated as a percentage of the total.

Systematic observation of antecedents and consequences indicated that the problem behaviours were often followed by teacher attention. It was also thought possible that the sensory consequences of the behaviour, such as seeing a thrown object in flight or hearing it crash-land, might be reinforcing the behaviour. These observations were taken into account in intervention programme design.

After an initial baseline period of eight days, when no intervention was in action, there was a sensory extinction phase. Door knobs were altered so that normal turning did not open the doors, and any toy played with was attached to the child's wrist by a 12-inch string, so that it could not be seen flying across the room or be heard crashing to the floor when thrown. Thus, some of the natural consequences of these actions were eliminated.

This intervention lasted for eight days and the average percentage of inappropriate behaviour dropped from the baseline level of 54.8 per cent to 16.4 per cent, while appropriate behaviours increased from 56.6 per cent to 75.2 per cent.

In a later phase, appropriate behaviours were systematically attended to and inappropriate behaviours systematically ignored, while the procedures for eliminating sensory consequences continued. This combination led to further improvements.

The technique of most interest here was sensory extinction, in which the reducing consequence was preventing naturally occurring sensory consequences from reinforcing problem behaviour.

Example 8 (Clark *et al.*, 1973)

An eight-year-old girl with a mental handicap called Bertha, who attended a special class, showed three groups of behaviour which caused particular concern: chokes and arm wraps, other attacks towards people, and attacks towards materials. The intervention was carried out by the two teachers in the classroom and recording was by independent observers.

Each of the three groups of problem behaviour was described more specifically: for instance, a choke was the placement of one or both hands around the neck of another child in a "stranglehold" fashion; whereas an arm wrap involved a "bear hug" round a child's neck, shoulder, or body. For recording purposes, the observation period was divided into 10-second intervals, and an observer noted whether each category of behaviour did or did not occur in each interval. The number of intervals per hour in which a problem behaviour occurred was then calculated, at first during baseline conditions in which the teachers ignored disruptive behaviours as far as possible and attended to Bertha when they were absent.

After a baseline of nine days an intervention procedure was implemented, without any reported study in advance of existing antecedents and consequences. Whenever Bertha engaged in a choke or an arm wrap she was placed in a small, empty booth for three minutes (which deprived her of attention and other kinds of stimulation). She was released as soon as there had been no crying, yelling, or banging for 15 seconds. The frequency of these behaviours decreased rapidly and dramatically, from an average of 13 occurrence intervals per hour during the baseline to an average of less than one per hour. Later, the same was done for the other problem behaviours with similar results.

In this study, exclusion time-out was used as a reducing consequence for problem behaviours.

Example 9 (Barton and Lagrow, 1983)

The young woman in this study was 21 years old. She had a profound mental handicap and was deaf/blind. She lived in a residential establishment with workshop and school programmes. She had a long history of destructive, aggressive, and self-injurious behaviours which made her a danger to herself and to others and limited her ability to join in the school's educational and vocational programmes. The intervention was carried out in Mary's everyday environment by the researchers and staff members, but recording was carried out by the researchers alone.

Observation was made throughout Mary's working day of the number of incidents per day of "aggressive behaviour", which included biting, hitting, head-butting, scratching, overturning furniture, and tearing her own or others' clothing. Self-injurious behaviour was measured similarly.

After 42 days of baseline, an intervention programme was begun without any reported advance investigation of antecedents and consequences. Whenever Mary exhibited one of these behaviours she was told "No", taken to another part of the building, and subjected to an overcorrection procedure. This consisted of holding her arms first at right angles to her body, then above her head, and then down at her sides, each for 30 seconds. This was repeated for 10 minutes on some days, and 20 minutes on others. Mary's aggressive behaviour decreased rapidly to a very low level; from an average of 98 aggressive acts per day during the baseline to an average of only four per day for a 25-day intervention period. There followed a 12-day period in which there was a similar intervention for self-injurious behaviour as well. Aggressive behaviour then fell to an average of one episode every three days. During follow-up over 14 weeks, the improvement was maintained.

In this study, making someone engage in an unwelcome activity as a reducing consequence for aggressive behaviour effectively decreased its frequency. This is usually called overcorrection.

Example 10 (Gross, Berler, and Drabman, 1982)

George was a four-year-old boy with a mental handicap in a special class. He did not speak or walk, but could crawl. He bit or gouged other children, often causing bleeding. This behaviour interfered seriously with the instructional programme, as well as being dangerous. The intervention and its recording were carried out in the classroom by the teacher and an aide.

Two classes of aggressive behaviour were tackled: biting and gouging. Biting was carefully defined as George fixing his teeth on to any bodily part of another person. Gouging was defined as clenching his hand with another person's flesh between his fingers and palms. During the baseline, whenever George exhibited aggressive behaviour, an adult grabbed his hand, said "No", and slapped the back of his hand. This procedure had already been in operation, and had made the aggressive behaviour somewhat less frequent. The number of incidents per day was recorded during baseline and intervention.

Advance investigation had established that George displayed aggressive behaviours towards his teachers when they worked with him. A variety of consequences had proved ineffective and it was felt that hand-slapping, which the teachers reported to have had *some* effect, should be replaced by something less aversive. This last consideration dictated the design of the intervention.

After 11 days of baseline, the intervention programme began. It made use of a plastic household sprayer, consisting of a six-inch high bottle with a nozzle that squirted water when a trigger was squeezed. It was adjusted to emit a jet of water rather than a mist. Whenever George performed an aggressive behaviour, an adult said "No" and squirted water on his face. This was effective within five days, decreasing George's aggressive behaviour from an average of 6.7 incidents per day during the baseline to 2.5 per day over 11 days of intervention. Return to baseline for nine days was followed by 22 further days of intervention, when the average number of incidents was only 0.8 per day and George was sometimes not aggressive for four or more consecutive days. Follow-up six months later found no aggressive behaviour in four recording periods, even though the sprayer had been removed from the classroom five months earlier.

In this study, subjecting George to an unwelcome experience was used as a reducing consequence for his violent behaviours.

Example 11 (Rotatori *et al.*, 1980)

This example concerns an 18-year-old young woman with a severe mental handicap in a special class. She had no speech. She engaged in various disruptive behaviours, including hitting other students, tearing materials, and throwing objects. The procedures were carried out by the school psychologist, the two teachers, and the aide. From the published description, it is not clear who did the recording.

The percentage of time engaged in "disruptive behaviours" was measured during a baseline period and during intervention in three different situations: the art/music classroom, the self-help classroom, and the room used for lunch.

After baselines of different lengths in the three different situations, an intervention was begun in each without any reported investigation in advance of antecedents and consequences. All disruptive behaviours were ignored, while all "on-task" behaviours were reinforced by praise. For instance, in the room used for lunch, the young woman was praised for finding her place at the table, opening her milk, drinking her milk, eating each item of food present, wiping her face and hands with a napkin to indicate she had finished, and returning her tray to the counter. In each setting, there was a decrease in the percentage of time spent in aggressive behaviours until they were completely eliminated. For instance, in art, the young woman engaged in disruptive behaviour an average of 28 per cent of the time during the eight-session baseline, but not at all during the last six days of the 32-session intervention. "On-task" behaviours increased in frequency.

In this study, reinforcing appropriate behaviour incompatible with the problem behaviour (differential reinforcement of incompatible behaviour or DRI) was accompanied by ignoring, used as a reducing consequence for aggressive and other disruptive behaviours (an example of extinction).

Example 12 (Luiselli, Myles, and Littman-Quinn, 1983)

This study concerned a 15-year-old boy called Keith with a severe to profound hearing loss and partial vision. He could communicate through sign language, but at a limited level. He was in a residential establishment for people with visual and auditory impairments. Keith engaged in aggressive and destructive behaviours which were causing extensive damage to property and people. It sometimes took two or three adults to restrain him. The intervention was carried out in the classroom and the living unit by the respective staff, who also did the recording.

Two classes of problem behaviour were identified. One was aggression, defined as Keith striking an adult or child with his closed fist, open hand, or head, or dragging his fingernails against their skins. The other was destruction, defined as his breaking an inanimate object by banging it against surfaces or tearing it with his hands. In each case behaviours were observed for six hours a day, five days a week, the number of instances per day of aggression and destruction being counted separately. This was done first during a baseline when no special measures were taken, and then during the intervention.

Prior investigation suggested that Keith's aggression was directed exclusively at adults and was reinforced by adult attention.

After a 10-day baseline a procedure was introduced into the classroom for reinforcing appropriate behaviours. Each time Keith responded correctly (not further defined) he was given a poker chip. When five such tokens had been accumulated, he could exchange them for a soft drink, a piece of chocolate, candy, or 2 to 3 minutes looking at picture books. After three days (not really long enough to judge effects) this procedure was supplemented by a "time-out" procedure for aggression only. Each time an incident occurred, Keith was placed in a small room with the door closed for three minutes. He was released as soon as he had been in there for one minute with no screaming, banging of walls, or thrashing about. The frequency of his aggression decreased from the baseline average of 64.5 instances per day to an average of 1.0 per day during approximately 75 days of intervention. Time-out was then introduced for destruction as well, and this behaviour soon also decreased to a very low level.

During this last stage a baseline measuring period was implemented in the residential unit, after which rewards (soft drinks, candy, picture books) followed 15-minute periods in which no aggression or destruction occurred. When either behaviour occurred, the timer used was reset for a new 15-minute period. This procedure did not consistently decrease the frequency of the problem behaviours. After 17 days it was supplemented by a time-out procedure similar to that used in the classroom, and this decreased both types of behaviour to negligible frequency.

In both settings the reward procedures were gradually faded out. After a four month vacation, five days of recording produced no incidents of either aggression or destruction in either setting.

In this study, reinforcing consequences of appropriate behaviour were accompanied by an unwelcome experience as a reducing consequence for aggressive and destructive behaviours. In the classroom, reinforcement was of behaviour incompatible with problem behaviours (differential reinforcement of incompatible behaviour or DRI), whereas in the living unit it was for abstaining from problem behaviour (differential reinforcement of other behaviour or DRO). The unwelcome experience used in both settings involved removal from adult attention and other sources of stimulation which might have been reinforcing the problem behaviour — an example of time-out.

PART C

Specific problems

SECTION 4. SELF-INJURIOUS BEHAVIOUR

Definition, causes, and incidence

Definition

The types of behaviour included in this section are those which result in rapid damage to a person's own body by mechanical means. They include: hitting or banging some parts of the body with other parts or against objects; biting; pinching; tearing; gouging with fingernails; tooth-grinding (known as *bruxism*); and hair-pulling (sometimes called *trichotillomania*).

Various other problem behaviours are commonly referred to in the literature as "self-injurious behaviour" and this section will sometimes be the best to follow in devising intervention programmes for them, but not always. The main kinds of behaviour involved here are:

behaviours which are not immediately self-injurious but which may cause damage over a period. One of these is thumb-sucking, which has been claimed to lead sometimes to dermatitis and associated infections, and sometimes to dental deformities. Where such problems are so acute that the behaviour needs to be decreased in frequency more or less immediately, the suggestions in this section will be relevant. If not, other sections may prove more helpful. Section 5, on stereotyped behaviour, for instance, is likely to be more helpful for thumb-sucking. Vomiting and food refusal may both cause physical harm over a period but, because of their specific association with feeding these are dealt with in Section 6 of this book which is devoted to feeding problems.

behaviours which are not necessarily self-injurious, but may be, such as eye-poking. If they *are* injurious, the suggestions in this section apply. If not, other sections are likely to offer better guidance; see Section 5 for eye-poking for instance.

Causes

There are several theories about the causation of self-injurious behaviour, some of which suggest basically medical reasons. For instance, the behaviour is especially characteristic of two medically described syndromes in which mental handicap and other problems are thought to be associated with biochemical abnormalities. These are the Lesch-Nyhan syndrome and the Cornelia de Lange syndrome (similar claims for Klinefelter's syndrome are less agreed). One theory is that people with these syndromes have a lowered sensitivity to pain, and there is a little recent support for this in a demonstration of decreased self-injurious behaviour in two people by use of the drug naloxone (*Narcan*), which is thought to increase pain sensitivity. Another suggestion is that self-injurious behaviour is sometimes a reaction to pain from other sources, and in some ways brings relief from that. Support for this view comes from the finding that head-banging sometimes develops or increases when children have infection of the middle ear (the infamous otitis media). Perhaps associated with that is the proposal that self-injurious behaviour leads to production in the body of chemical substances related to opium which promote pleasant states of mind and body. Such states may well make pain less noticeable and so may reinforce the self-injurious behaviour.

There is, however, no convincing evidence that self-injurious behaviour is usually caused medically, nor that it is always an inevitable consequence of any of the medical conditions referred to above (though most individuals with Lesch-Nyhan syndrome engage in it at some time in their lives). Moreover, there is evidence that self-injurious behaviour can be learned and is subject to the usual influences which have been shown to affect human learning. There is evidence, for instance, that it increases if reinforced by attention, and that children sometimes learn to use it for escape from unwelcome experiences, such as a difficult task, or even parental physical abuse. Rhesus monkeys have been trained to hit themselves in response to a particular sound, by regularly following it with a mild electric shock which provokes such self-abuse. It is also possible that self-injurious behaviour is sometimes a means of obtaining stimulation in an otherwise barren life. It is often found in bare institutional environments and in monkeys reared in isolation, and it has been shown to decrease in people with severe mental handicaps when stimulation, such as by toys or vibration, has been provided. On the basis of this theory, self-injurious behaviour can be thought of as being reinforced by its own stimulating effects.

It is possible that self-injurious behaviour can sometimes (perhaps often) begin for medical reasons; but whether or not it persists depends on the antecedents and consequences in a person's environment. If, for instance, Darren bangs his head because his ear hurts and this brings a great deal of attention from the people around him, the resulting reinforcement of head-banging may cause it to continue after the ear affliction has been remedied. A lowered sensitivity to pain, of course, would mean that the usual reducing consequences would be less available to counteract such effects.

Another view of interest is that self-injurious behaviour can sometimes be an intensification of behaviour which is considered to be normal at certain stages of development. It has been observed, in mild forms, in a significant proportion of pre-school children who do not have mental handicaps (the range in various studies being from seven to seventeen per cent), beginning around 7 to 8 months of age and disappearing before the age of five years. Children who remain for a long time at an early stage of development may form well-established self-injurious habits, and various antecedents and consequences may act in ways that intensify these.

Incidence

Self-injurious behaviour occurs in a significant number of people with mental handicaps in institutions 4–37 per cent in various studies, though the number in whom the behaviour results in significant damage or causes undue anxiety for people with responsibility is little more than one per cent. In community settings, a West German study reported an incidence of one per cent and, while a British study of children found a 12 per cent incidence, a study in schools in the USA found only 2.6 per cent. The behaviour can stop or diminish of its own accord (in 20 per cent of self-injurers in one study), but it is more common for it to continue unabated, or to increase, in the absence of intervention. Head-banging is by far the most common of the more serious manifestations, and this is frequently accompanied by biting and scratching (the two next most common), and by gouging and hair-pulling, as well as by aggressive and stereotyped behaviour. Recent evidence indicates that tooth-grinding is also extremely common, occurring in 20 per cent or more of long-term residents of mental handicap hospitals. Most people with mental handicaps who injure themselves do so in more than one way. One study of people living in residential establishments found that 30 per cent of those who self-injured engaged in three or more types of self-injurious behaviour.

Self-injurious behaviour is generally more common among people with the most profound handicaps; in one institutional study, 88 per cent of self-injurers being this handicapped.

Why are they a problem?

Self-injurious behaviours are regarded as a severe problem for a variety of reasons. Firstly, they are painful and upsetting to at least some of the people who engage in them. Secondly, the damage that results can be a threat to health, or even to life. For instance, infection can easily set in, severe bleeding and severe laceration or loss of flesh can occur (sometimes fingertips have been bitten off), injury to the eyes can cause blindness, bones can be broken, concussion is possible, and there is even a report of a limb having to be amputated. Though there is a threat to life, however, I have not yet found any record of a self-injurious behaviour actually causing death. Thirdly, preoccupation with the problem behaviour interferes with the learning of more appropriate behaviours, including those involved in interacting socially with others. Constructive interaction between people who self-injure and those who try to help them can also be very difficult to organise, particularly since self-injurious behaviours are sometimes a response to attempts to get people to acquire more appropriate behaviours. Fourthly, the behaviours can produce anxiety, distress, and a feeling of hopelessness in parents or responsible staff, which can affect the quality of their work and caring generally.

The dangerous effects of self-injurious behaviour, and the resulting anxieties it generates, make it necessary for steps to be taken to prevent or decrease it immediately rather than in a planned, gradual way, and this can produce secondary problems. The attention from attempts to distract or restrain people who self-injure can reinforce their self-injurious behaviours and thus make them occur more frequently or with greater intensity. In desperation, people with responsibility may resort to the use of physical restraints or may request medication.

Methods of physical restraint include splints to restrain the arms, helmets to prevent damage by head-banging, and even more comprehensive restrictions, like tight garments which keep most of the body motionless or straps that fasten a person to a bed or a chair. These measures decrease opportunities for the person to learn to engage in appropriate behaviours. With some people, who apparently like the experience, such restraint can reinforce the self-injurious behaviours so that they increase. If the restraint is very prolonged it can lead to deterioration of muscles and shortening of tendons. One recent study in institutions in the USA found that mechanical restraint, despite all these disadvantages, was used with 27 per cent of the self-injuring inhabitants. A British total population study found similar restraint was used in 13 per cent of all people with severe mental handicaps in one health region.

Attempts have also been made to control self-injurious behaviour with a wide variety of drugs, the major tranquillisers predominating. Such attempts have, on the whole, met with little success unless the dosage has been so high as to render the person virtually inactive. It has also been found that some individuals who show self-injurious behaviour react to normal doses of medication, that would send most people to sleep, by remaining wakeful and becoming resistive, combative, uncooperative, or abusive; or by increasing their self-injurious behaviour. Despite this, the recent American study of institutions quoted above found that 32 per cent of the self-injuring inhabitants were given medication and the British total population study found a figure of 44 per cent.

Intervention techniques

Defining the problem

When defining self-injurious behaviour it is important to describe precisely, not only the specific behaviours to be decreased, but also the specific appropriate behaviours which are to replace them. Ideally, the appropriate behaviours selected should be incompatible with the self-injurious behaviours. For instance, Ken cannot manipulate a toy and hit himself simultaneously, so increasing the frequency of toy play may make Ken's self-hitting less likely. Choosing a behaviour with the same purpose as the problem behaviour could also be helpful. If Zoe bangs her head to avoid a task, she could be encouraged to shake it instead (provided avoiding the task can be allowed).

Examples of behaviour descriptions are:

Tony hits his face violently with his fist at any time, or any place, and with any person, whenever arm restraints are not fitted.

Tony holds and manipulates a cuddly toy continuously for five minutes, anywhere and at any time when it does not interfere with other important activities.

Measuring the problem

Self-injury tends to be a frequently occurring problem behaviour, so that short periods of measurement are usually sufficient, say, half-an-hour. Where it is less frequent, longer measuring periods will be necessary.

Counting instances will probably give a valuable measure, since a single act can usually be defined with reasonable clarity. If the action occurs a large number of times without an intervening break, however, it may be better to record the *proportion* of the observation period in which the behaviour occurs. Some self-injurious behaviours are so severe that a means of prevention will be needed rapidly. If successful, this leaves nothing to measure. If the prevention methods are used only briefly when the behaviour is observed, however, measurement can be made of the number of times the behaviour *starts*.

Identifying existing antecedents and consequences

It ought to be particularly important to investigate existing antecedents and consequences of self-injurious behaviours since, for someone who seeks to do something which is regarded by most people as a very unwelcome experience, changes in antecedents and consequences cannot be planned on the basis of normal reactions. It is, therefore, surprising that, in published studies, such investigations are very rarely reported. In one interesting study, a teenager with a severe mental handicap was removed from an institution to a treatment centre and his head-hitting was investigated under four different conditions. In one of these he had to carry out difficult tasks from his educational programme; in another he was given materials to play with and warned that he was hurting himself each time he engaged in head-hitting; in a third he was left alone in a room with nothing interesting to do; and in the fourth he was able to play as he wished with available toy materials. Self-injury occurred much more frequently during the alone condition than during the other three conditions. It seemed likely, therefore, that the self-injury was being reinforced by the stimulation it provided, and that supplying interesting activities or materials was an antecedent making the problem behaviour less likely to occur. Unfortunately, the reasoning and intervention that followed did not relate very logically to these findings and the study is not, therefore, included in the examples that follow.

Various antecedents thought to have precipitated self-injurious behaviours in people with mental handicaps can be considered. The environmental setting may have little stimulation and few interesting activities; or may be unduly noisy; or may have too many people about, or too few. Antecedents from people's internal state can include discomfort; because of the way they are positioned, or from clothing, or from pain resulting from a medical condition. Specific event antecedents can include: restriction of movement, having to wait for a routine or event to commence; interruption of an activity (such as a stereotyped behaviour, or even a self-injurious behaviour different from the one being studied); proximity or absence of particular people; being required to do something unwelcome or difficult; a change of position or location, or being somewhere unfamiliar; specific noises; having something wanted taken away; being denied their own way; and being teased or assaulted by others. Antecedents involving demands on people or denying them something are particularly common precipitants of self-injury.

Consequences which have been thought to reinforce self-injurious behaviours can include: attention (even if scolding or punitive); being taken for a walk, or given food or toys; being left alone to engage in stereotyped behaviour or other welcome activity; physical restraint; and escape from demands by others.

Changing antecedents and consequences for intervention programmes

Research studies have focused more on decreasing self-injurious behaviours than on increasing appropriate alternative behaviours. This is largely because working on appropriate behaviours allows self-injury to occur during the period before the objective is achieved, and this is typically quite long. Concentrating on the self-injurious behaviours themselves is likely to decrease them more rapidly. Often, however, this is achieved by using consequences which are quite unpleasant. There is much to be said for considering trying to increase appropriate behaviours, preferably as the priority; but if that is impracticable, at least to use them as an accompaniment to devices for decreasing the problem behaviours.

Use of antecedents for making appropriate behaviours more likely has been quite rare in interventions for self-injurious behaviour. It can, however, sometimes be effective. In Example 1, for instance, continuous provision of toys increased grasping and mouthing of them in a young woman with a profound mental handicap and her finger-biting decreased concurrently. In one published study a 10-year-old boy with a profound handicap and autistic features was taught, by methods including physical guidance, to slap the therapist's hand instead of his own head. The hand-slapping spontaneously transferred to other adults and, since it was light and playful, became an acceptable play behaviour to substitute for the head-hitting. Other antecedent devices may derive from the attempts of some people with mental handicaps to restrain themselves from self-injury. One young man, for instance, was helped by wearing a jacket with large pockets, since he then tended to thrust his hands into them, apparently to restrain himself from hitting his head. Relaxation techniques have been used in one study.

Use of reinforcing consequences to increase appropriate behaviours has quite often been reported, though usually in combination with devices for decreasing the self-injurious behaviours. It can, however, sometimes work on its own, though experimental demonstrations have tended to be in rather artificial circumstances. Example 2, for instance, describes how reinforcing abstaining from head-banging (differential reinforcement of other behaviour or DRO) in a 14-year-old boy with a severe mental handicap decreased that behaviour, but this was in an experimental room and there was no experimental demonstration of improvement in everyday situations. Prior study of reinforcing consequences for the problem behaviour may suggest possibilities for reinforcing *appropriate* behaviour. For instance, if it looks as though self-injurious behaviour is reinforced by attention, then attention might be used as a reinforcing consequence for alternative behaviours that are more acceptable.

It is best to choose *specific* appropriate behaviours to reinforce, since DRO can result in increases in other self-injurious behaviours which are not the subject of intervention. Example 3 describes how head-hitting was decreased in a 13-year-old boy with multiple handicaps by reinforcing him for operating a walking frame. Since this kept his hands occupied, it was incompatible with head-hitting. This procedure was, therefore, an example of differential reinforcement of incompatible behaviour (DRI). If it is hard to think of a specific desirable behaviour to reinforce, perhaps any other *non*-injurious behaviour could be reinforced. Examples 1 and 4 illustrate combinations of DRO and DRI. Example 1 includes reinforcement of toy play as an alternative to finger biting which is, arguably, an example of differential reinforcement of equivalent behaviour (DRE).

Use of antecedents to make self-injurious behaviours less likely has been almost totally neglected in the literature. However, in Example 5, a 19-year-old young man with a mental handicap had his head-hitting much decreased by daily jogging sessions and these may well have acted as an antecedent. In Example 6, 22-year-old Harry held two plastic glasses to restrain himself from self-hitting and self-biting. Prior provision of vibratory stimulation (for example, from a vibrator attached to a chair) has sometimes been found to be effective. Other means of providing stimulation as an alternative to that which can be gained from self-injurious behaviour have also been successful. For instance, in one study, provision of brightly coloured toys decreased eye-poking, an activity which is known to produce visual effects. There is also evidence that positive behaviours from others, such as praising, patting, and hugging, can help stave off self-injurious behaviour.

Research into antecedents of self-injurious behaviour (see page 159) also suggests changes that might be made in antecedent conditions. If the behaviour is provoked by interference by other people with mental handicaps, this can be prevented; if by uncomfortable clothing, it can be adjusted; and if by demands to undertake difficult or welcome tasks, easier or more welcome ones can be substituted.

Reducing consequences are the intervention techniques best supported by research evidence. The most effective of these has been electric shock, followed by forced inhalation of ammonia, though electric shock has been found to have a high relapse rate and there have been instances where it has *increased* the frequency of self-injurious behaviour. Since such methods are highly unlikely to be used in practice in this country, it is necessary to rely on approaches where demonstrations of success have been less numerous and less dramatic.

Prevention of reinforcement can work in some instances. There have been instances of doing this by preventing sensory consequences; for example, by putting gloves and a helmet on 14-year-old James to prevent pain from eye-gouging (Example 7), and by various time-out procedures. For exclusion time-out, periods of something like 15 minutes have been needed for effectiveness, and as self-injurious behaviours could continue throughout this time, this may be unacceptable. This can also apply where social reinforcement is prevented by long-term isolation, as was done with nine-year-old Elaina (Example 8). The report does not indicate how much she damaged herself in the process, though the procedure *did* work. Less intrusive forms of time-out have involved removing reinforcers or other welcome experiences when a self-injurious behaviour occurred. For instance, 14-year-old James (Example 7) had toys removed for 30 seconds, 22-year-old Harry (Example 6) lost access to his restraints for five minutes, and Jane (Example 4) had a vibratory back massager turned off for 15 seconds or so. Behavioural interruption was reported in one study, in which a six-year-old boy had his toys removed and his hands held motionless for 10 seconds every time he engaged in eye-gouging. In using approaches of this kind, it is best to undertake *in advance* investigation of the kinds of experience likely to act as reinforcers for the person who is self-injuring. This is, however, rarely reported in the literature.

Planned ignoring is hardly ever used for self-injurious behaviour because of the associated risks. However, it has been shown to be effective if used for a long time. Use of protective applicances (see later) would make it more feasible, though there would then need to be methods for gradually discontinuing their use.

If more severe reducing consequences are needed, making a person do something unwelcome might be considered. For instance, eight-year-old Robert's head and chin-banging (Example 9) were virtually eliminated by a consequence in which his head and arms were put through a set series of movements repeatedly. Like other consequences of this kind, the procedure with Robert was called overcorrection, though there was no sense in which anything was being corrected. The movements were not appropriate behaviours and their only useful purpose was to deter the self-injurious behaviour. Use of arm exercises, however, is the method employed in most published studies of overcorrection for self-injurious behaviours. In some instances of self-biting, self-hitting, and eye-poking, the movement has consisted of repeatedly moving the hand to the abused part of the body and then away again without making contact, and in some cases of arm-biting and face-picking the person has been made to cleanse the wounded area lengthily with an antiseptic. Even so, the effectiveness of these measures could have been due to the unwelcome nature of the activity, and there is no evidence that making them genuinely corrective increases their effectiveness.

If unwelcome activities are difficult to organise or are thought unlikely to be effective, doing something unwelcome to a person can, as a last resort, be considered. Squirting water into the face (as with seven-year-old Jerome in Example 10), or lemon juice or citric acid into the mouth, has been shown to work; but perhaps more acceptable is putting a light cloth or some other light screening device over the person's eyes or the whole face for a short period. This has been found surprisingly helpful. For instance, it virtually eliminated hair-pulling in a nine-year-old girl with a profound handicap (Example 11). Another possibility is physical restraint, which eliminated self-hitting in seven-year-old John (Example 12). Restraining protective devices have also been used for very brief periods for this purpose.

Combinations of the foregoing methods are very common in interventions to decrease self-injurious behaviour. Most of these have involved DRO, usually in combination with consequences to reduce the problem behaviours. Example 6 describes how DRO was combined with a "time-out" procedure to decrease self-hitting and self-biting in a young man with a severe mental handicap, and it has also been combined with other methods of eliminating reinforcement for self-injurious behaviours, making the person do something unwelcome and doing unwelcome things to him. Many other combinations of methods are possible. Example 1, for instance, describes a combination of an antecedent for increasing an appropriate behaviour with DRO and DRI procedures. The daunted reader may like to be reassured, however, that there is no evidence for any general conclusion that methods are better used in combination than used singly. The key question to answer is: "What method or combination of methods is most likely to be effective for this particular problem in this particular person?".

Additional measures

Intervention sometimes includes *medical procedures*. If someone has otitis media this needs to be cured. If a person has a diminished pain sensitivity, some doctors may wish to raise it with medication, but this measure has barely proceeded beyond the research stage at the moment. Nor is any other kind of medication widely held to be helpful at present.

What undoubtedly needs to be added to the recommended intervention procedures for many people is some form of *protection to prevent serious injury*. This can never be regarded as a total intervention process, unless the person who self-injures finds it unwelcome (as in the case of physical restraint) and it is consistently used for short periods of less than half-an-hour as a consequence of the self-injurious behaviour.

However, used in thoughtful ways at other times, such protection can keep the person safe and allay anxieties in those who are trying to help which might otherwise interfere with programme planning.

Protective devices include: protective environments, such as padded rooms, chairs, or cots; protective clothing, such as helmets to minimise pain and injury from head-banging, and gloves and padded slippers with similar functions for a number of other kinds of self-injurious behaviour; protective applications like Vaseline to reduce the efficiency of pinching; protective attachments, such as a flat disc attached to the wrist by a wrist-band to prevent wrist-biting, and a plate attached to the teeth to prevent biting of the lower lip; and physical restraints.

Physical restraints can be of many kinds. A splint which restricts movement at the elbow prevents a person's hands from reaching the head. A "cape" of firm material, put over the shoulders, restricts arm movement. A flat disc fastened to the palm prevents fingers from bending sufficiently to grasp and pull out hair. Sometimes, tight-fitting clothes can be put on to restrict arm movement. In extreme instances, a person can be strapped to a chair or bed and the offending limbs fastened securely.

Physical restraints should be designed to allow as much movement as possible compatible with preventing injury. Arm splints have been made, for example, which restrict movement of the elbow in a way that prevents a person from hitting the head but which still allows manipulation of objects if seated at a table. With hinges and ingenuity, it is even possible for such splints to allow just enough movement for feeding but not quite enough for striking the head forcefully. By making the hinges lockable, self-injurious movements can be prevented while a person is unsupervised, but freedom of movement allowed without removal of the splint when it is required to engage in some more appropriate behaviour which can be watched and guided. Where a cape of firm material is used to restrict arm movements, this can be shaped so as to restrict movements down as far as the elbows, while allowing the forearms and hands to be almost completely unrestricted. Various plastic materials are available which can be heated and then moulded to whatever shape is required for a particular restraining device.

Articles by Spain, Hart, and Corbett (1984) and Patterson (1982) (both also in Murphy and Wilson, 1985) provide fuller information on protective appliances for the interested reader (including information on sources), but for practical purposes help will usually be required from an occupational therapist if such devices are needed. A dentist may be able to help in providing protective devices for the lips and mouth.

The precise ways in which protective devices are used must be related to the total intervention programme. It is important, firstly, to determine whether a particular device is a welcome, unwelcome, or even a neutral experience to a particular person. If it is a welcome experience it might be used as a major element of the programme – being used systematically as a reinforcing consequence for a period in which self-injurious behaviours do not occur. If it is unwelcome, it could, similarly, be a regular reducing consequence for self-injurious behaviour. If it is not used in these specific ways it can *interfere* with a programme. For example, if a device is welcome and is applied when self-injurious behaviours are occurring or have just occurred, it may then reinforce the unwanted behaviours. If it is unwelcome, and it is applied when appropriate behaviours are occurring or have just occurred, it may reduce those wanted behaviours, leaving the way open for return of behaviours that are self-injurious. It is sometimes possible to change the experience of a particular protective device from a welcome to an unwelcome or neutral one by giving less attention when it is applied. This is easier if devices are designed to be easy to put on and take off.

Secondly, if protective devices are to be helpful as constituents of a total intervention programme, their use needs to be minimised. So long as protection is sufficient, the less restrictive they are the better, and they should be worn only for short periods.

Thirdly, as part of the total programme, protective devices must be taken into account when evaluating the measured effects of the intervention and must be faded out in a sufficiently gradual manner when the objectives of the programme have been reached.

Subsequent action

Example 1 illustrates the modification of a programme to improve results. A 17-year-old young woman with a profound mental handicap bit her fingers less when provided with toys which were fixed in position so that she could not throw them away. However, the problem behaviour was still at an unacceptable level, so the toys were supplemented by reinforcing toy use and reinforcing abstaining from biting. Biting then decreased quite rapidly.

Transfer of an intervention from one situation to another is described for eight-year-old Robert in Example 9. His head and chin-banging was almost eliminated in the research centre he attended daily, but remained a problem at home until an essentially similar programme was implemented there.

Example 6 illustrates the planned fading out of an intervention programme. Harry, aged 22, abused himself in various ways, but the frequency of this behaviour decreased markedly when he had to abstain for progressively longer periods of time to earn periods of wearing restraining metal splints. Later, he was provided with two plastic glasses to hold as an alternative form of restraint and these were made progressively smaller each day until he abandoned them for other devices. Eventually, he wore spectacles as the only token "restraint" device and then showed virtually no self-injurious behaviour.

Illustrative studies

Example 1 (Lockwood and Bourland, 1982)

The person in this study was a 17-year-old young woman with a profound mental handicap, who lived in an institution. She could not walk and had a history of finger-biting. Intervention and recording were carried out by the experimenters and/or assistants in the daily living environment.

Finger-biting was defined as any contact of the woman's hand with lips or mouth. Also studied was an appropriate behaviour, toy use, defined as grasping or mouthing a toy. Instead of beginning with a baseline period, two intervention methods were alternated during daily sessions of one hour in the living unit. Each session was divided into four 15-minute periods. Usually, the two procedures were each used for two 15-minute periods, the particular sequence being changed daily. Occasionally, however, the whole hour was devoted to one procedure only. For each session, measures were taken of the percentage of time spent biting and the percentage of time spent in toy use.

Existing antecedents and consequences for the self-injurious behaviour were investigated, but nothing consistent was identified. Both intervention procedures at this stage, which lasted eight days, involved provision of toys, such as the kind of colourful rubber and soft plastic toys which infants enjoy chewing. One procedure was to put them, loose, in the woman's lap at the beginning of a 15-minute period and not replace them if they were thrown away. The other was to suspend them at eye level about 8 inches from her face, so that they could not be thrown away. Both procedures provided an opportunity for the young woman to grasp or mouth the toys, more appropriate behaviours which might give her similar satisfaction to that obtained from biting her fingers. During the periods when toys were attached the woman spent less time on biting and more time in toy use than she did during the times when the toys were loose. Plainly, the toys were antecedents which made appropriate behaviours more likely and problem behaviour less likely to occur, and the attached toys constituted more effective antecedents for both purposes than the loose ones. This was presumably because they provided more continuous opportunities to engage in the appropriate behaviours involved in toy play.

In a further phase of the study the toys were attached throughout the one-hour sessions, and there were somewhat complex procedures for reinforcing appropriate behaviours with praise and affectionate stroking of the face and rubbing of the arms. Firstly, there was reinforcement for *not* biting fingers for defined periods, an instance of differential reinforcement of other behaviour (DRO). The length of time required before reinforcement was given was selected according to what the most recent measurement had shown to be relatively easy for the young woman to achieve. It therefore varied from day to day, being 15 seconds early in the intervention and approximately 15 minutes after about 20 sessions. If finger-biting occurred during the interval selected, timing of that interval was stopped and then recommenced from the beginning as soon as biting ceased. Secondly, the woman was reinforced for toy use, which the authors claimed was incompatible with finger-biting. This would make it an example of differential reinforcement of incompatible behaviour (DRI). It could also be claimed that it served the same purpose (play) and was therefore differential reinforcement of equivalent behaviour (DRE). The period of continuous toy use required for reinforcement was related to recent records of that behaviour so as to make it easy for the woman. Finger-biting suspended the timing in the same way as in the DRO procedure. When these procedures were introduced, measuring continued as in the first phase. Biting almost disappeared after four sessions (having been as frequent as 60 per cent during one session in the first phase), while toy use reached a very high level after seven sessions (always over 60 per cent, whereas it had been below 20 per cent for some sessions for both interventions during the first phase). Both these improvements were maintained over the remainder of the 24-session second phase.

In this later phase, provision of toys as an antecedent to increase appropriate behaviours was accompanied by reinforcement of appropriate behaviours on both a DRO and a DRI basis.

Example 2 (Weiher and Harman, 1975)
This study describes work with a 14-year-old boy with Down's syndrome, who was described as "severely retarded and psychotic", and was resident in an institution. He could not walk or talk, had limited vision, and was not toilet trained. If allowed, he would bang his head against the floor, walls, or other hard surfaces, causing himself physical damage which left scars. For most of the time he was kept in a restraining chair which

prevented self-injury. The intervention and measurement were carried out by the experimenter in a special room.

The special room in which the study was conducted was furnished and arranged to resemble the boy's everyday environment. He was released from his restraining chair and, during a baseline period of seven days, was placed on the floor for four minutes daily, wearing a heavily padded cap worn over a lighter helmet liner and secured by a chin-strap. Each head-bang was recorded.

Intervention sessions began at the same daily times as the baseline observations, with no reported study of existing antecedents and consequences carried out in advance. Whenever there was no head-banging for three seconds, the boy was given half a teaspoonful of spiced apple sauce. If head-banging occurred before three seconds was up, the timer was reset for another three seconds. Each training session continued until 4oz of apple sauce had been given – about three-and-a-half minutes initially. Whenever the boy banged his head less than 10 times in each of two successive sessions, the length of time required for abstaining from the behaviour to earn reinforcement was lengthened; first to six seconds, then to varying intervals of increasing average length, eventually varying from 30 to 120 seconds for intervention sessions 45-49. This made the training sessions gradually longer. From session 23 onwards, the boy was told "Good" just before he received apple sauce. From session 33 onwards the heavily padded cap was removed, and from session 46 the lighter helmet liner was also discarded. All head-banging was recorded throughout and, after variable rates of occurrence in early sessions, it ceased from session 32 onwards (it had averaged 14.34 per minute during the baseline). At the same time, smiling, laughing, and other vocal noises increased markedly and the boy often clung to the experimenter's hand or leg and frequently climbed into his lap. It looked as though appropriate behaviours in relation to the experimenter might be replacing the head-banging, since removing reinforcement for a session had no harmful effect on two occasions when the experimenter was still in view, but led to some resumption of head-banging on an occasion when the experimenter could not be seen. There were reports of some decrease in head-banging outside the experimental situation, and it was hoped that further training of the boy in these wider settings could be undertaken.

The technique of reinforcing absence of self-injurious behaviour used so successfully in this study is an example of DRO, since any behaviour other than the problem one was effectively being reinforced. It will have been noticed that various changes were made to the initial intervention as time went on. These were designed to bring handling back towards something more normal, without losing improvements. Thus reinforcement was made less frequent and less predictable, the social reinforcer "Good" was introduced, and protective devices were removed.

Example 3 (Crisp and Coll, 1980)
Paul, a 13-year-old boy in an institution, was multiply-handicapped, being spastic in all four limbs, having a profound mental handicap, and requiring almost total nursing care. He hit his head with both fists unless restrained, sometimes more than 100 times per minute, and had many scars. It was not clear whether ward staff or experimenters carried out the initial intervention procedures, but measuring was carried out by a separate observer.

A one-day baseline involved observations during 45 minutes while Paul was sitting in a chair in the day-room. The number of head-hits was counted during 10 randomly distributed one-minute periods.

The intervention was begun without any reported study of antecedents and consequences being carried out beforehand. It consisted of reinforcing a specific behaviour incompatible with the self-injurious behaviour (DRI). Paul was strapped into a mobile walking frame and taught how to propel it. To do this, he had to grasp a horizontal bar on the walking frame with both hands (incompatible with head-hitting) and push his left foot against the floor. Prompting and reinforcement were used to achieve this, but the precise form of these techniques is not described. This was done in one session on each of three consecutive days and the head-hitting was counted during 10 randomly selected, one-minute periods in each session. The incidence was found to range from 0 to 6 per minute, whereas during the baseline it had been between 75 and 105.

There were further phases in this study. Firstly, there was a return to the baseline conditions for a day, when head-hitting ranged from 90 to 105 hits per minute; and then the intervention was reintroduced for three days, when it occurred hardly at all. Over the next 30 days, the DRI procedure was used more extensively, while non-systematic observations indicated a continued near-absence of head-hitting. Follow-up 18 months later found that mobility teaching had been continued by the ward staff, who had also taught Paul to use a wheelchair, and that self-injurious behaviours had been completely eliminated.

Example 4 (Nunes, Murphy, and Ruprecht, 1977)

Jane was a 12-year-old girl living in an institution. She had a severe mental handicap, could walk and follow simple commands, but could not talk. Her self-injurious behaviour consisted mainly of slapping her face with her hands, beating her ears with her closed fists, and slamming her arms against tables when seated. The intervention and measuring were carried out by a teacher.

During the baseline of 10 days, Jane was seated at a table in a partitioned corner of the classroom, a disassembled puzzle was put in front of her, and she was told to put it together. The frequency of self-injurious behaviours was recorded during a 15-minute session in the morning and a similar one in the afternoon each day, though no precise description of the behaviour or measuring procedure is given.

No investigation of existing antecedents and consequences was reported as having been carried out before the intervention, which was in the same setting as baseline measuring. The intervention used a vibratory back massager, placed between Jane's back and the back of the chair. This was kept on at any time when Jane was manipulating the puzzle, unless there was any instance of a self-injurious behaviour, in which case the teacher said, "Hands down", and turned off the massager. It stayed off until no self-injurious behaviour had occurred for at least 15 seconds, then it was turned on and the teacher said, "That's good". During this intervention, which lasted for nine days, the average number of self-injurious behaviours per session was 6.2, compared with 115.00 during baseline.

There followed another baseline, with the massager in position but turned off, which lasted six days, and then a modification of the first intervention for six days. This time, Jane received 15 seconds of vibration whenever she had not engaged in any self-injurious behaviours and had been touching the puzzle continuously for a defined period. The period was one minute during the first three days and subsequently three minutes. The rate then averaged 3.2, compared with 95.0 in the second baseline.

Several different techniques were used in this study. In the first intervention the withdrawal of the vibration was a reducing consequence for self-injurious behaviour. In the second intervention the vibration was used as a reinforcing consequence, in a procedure that was a mixture of DRO (reinforcement for not self-injuring) and DRI (reinforcement of the incompatible behaviour of manipulating the puzzle).

Example 5 (Baumeister and MacLean, 1984)
One of the people in this study was a 19-year-old young man in an institution, who had a severe mental handicap, who could walk and could follow simple instructions, but who did not talk. He hit himself on the head, face, chest, and shoulders, causing bruising and swelling. It is not clear exactly who carried out the intervention, which was in the daily living environment, though ward staff were involved. Measuring was by specially recruited observers.

There were two measuring periods, from 9.00 to 10.00 am and from 3.00 to 4.00 pm daily. Each period was divided into 30-second intervals and a note was made of whether each of several categories of behaviour, including head-hitting, did or did not occur during each interval. For each behaviour, the final measure for each session was the percentage of 30-second intervals during which it occurred.

While no systematic investigation of existing antecedents and consequences is reported, it is stated that the young man spent much time in ritualistic pacing in the day room. This might have suggested that various kinds of exercise could be welcome to him which might be usable in some way in the intervention programme.

After a baseline period of 14 sessions an intervention procedure was introduced which consisted of a one-hour jog from 1.00 to 2.00 pm, covering one mile for the first two weeks, two miles for the next two weeks, and three miles for the two weeks after that. The jogging took place outdoors or indoors, according to the weather, and the young man was accompanied by a staff member who set the pace. During this intervention, the incidence of head-hitting progressively decreased, more so in the afternoon than in the morning. During baseline, for instance, the afternoon incidence had varied from 29 to 40 per cent, whereas during the three mile phase, it ranged from 0 to 19 per cent.

This is a mysterious form of intervention, and it is possible only to speculate about how it works. Perhaps the most likely answer is that the whole process of getting the young man to jog was an antecedent which made the problem behaviour of head-hitting less likely to occur, though why it should have that effect is not clear.

Example 6 (Foxx and Dufrense, 1984)
Harry, a young man of 22 years, lived in an institution and was described as severely retarded and psychotic. He had a useful command and understanding of spoken language. Self-injurious behaviours included striking his nose, head, and thighs with his fists, and biting his arms. His nose was permanently disfigured and his arms were covered with scars. He wore hinged, metal arm splints for most of the time but these still allowed some self-injury which occurred whenever demands were made on him that he did not want. The intervention and measuring were carried out within the institution by the experimenters and institution staff members together.

The behaviours to decrease were head-blows, defined as any part of either hand coming into contact with any part of the head, exclusive of pats or strokes, or the fist or knee coming into contact with the nose; thigh-hitting, defined as either fist coming into contact with the thigh(s); and biting, defined as any part of Harry's body coming into contact with his teeth. Baseline recording was carried out for six five-minute sessions during the first hour of one day. Harry's restraints were removed and he was placed in a locked room, where he engaged in various activities, such as educational tasks and eating a meal. Two adults were present for half the sessions, and he was alone, though observed, for the others. Recording sessions were divided into 10-second intervals and the presence or absence of self-injurious behaviours noted for each. The percentage of intervals with self-injurious behaviours was calculated.

Careful observation of Harry's behaviour had suggested that restraints could play a major part in an intervention programme. Harry became agitated and self-injurious when they were removed, asked for them back, helped put them on, and seemed relaxed when wearing them. When the restraints had been removed he would attempt to restrain *himself*, by putting his hands inside his clothing or holding on to a staff member. Wearing restraints was plainly a welcome experience. It was, therefore, decided to use restraints as reinforcement for periods of non-injury, and to remove them as a reducing consequence (time-out) when a self-injurious behaviour occurred.

The first phase of intervention took place soon after and on the same day as the baseline. It occupied 18 sessions, one following immediately after another, in the same room as the baseline. It was administered by two adults. At the beginning of each session, Harry's restraints were removed and he was told that he could earn them back if he did not self-injure; but that if he hit himself the adults would leave the room with his restraints and he would remain there without them for five minutes. He was then encouraged to participate in various educational and play activities, and reinforced for doing so with praise and occasional food or drink. If no self-injurious behaviour occurred during a session, he was allowed to wear the restraints for five minutes. The duration of no self-injury required was five minutes at first, but was later increased. During the time-out periods, Harry's self-injurious behaviour, screaming, and door-banging were ignored. Measuring showed that he self-injured in 92.5 per cent of the intervals during baseline and 14.5 per cent during the intervention. On another day, a new baseline and similar intervention procedures produced results of 90 per cent and 5.7 per cent respectively.

Further phases of intervention took place in the living unit and were conducted by the staff there. At this point Harry began to restrain himself, by holding on to objects which he refused to relinquish and which made other kinds of restraint less necessary. At his request, he was given two large plastic glasses to hold, one in each hand. He was then given progressively smaller glasses each day, and when a very small size was reached, they were cut in half each day until he was holding only the rims. He was then persuaded to abandon them, to wear a wristwatch to "restrain" himself, and to interlock his fingers. After a few days he asked for spectacles as a "restraint" device and these were provided (with non-prescription lenses). He continued to wear these for the next four-and-a-half years, with virtually no self-injurious behaviour in the last four years of this period. He was taught to participate in various other meaningful activities, which no doubt helped.

In this study the restraints were being used as a reinforcing consequence in a DRO procedure (since they were applied following periods when Harry behaved in any way that was not self-injurious); and their removal acted as a reducing consequence for self-injurious behaviour in a time-out procedure. The glasses, watch, and spectacles appeared to function as antecedents for making problem behaviour less likely.

Example 7 (Dorsey *et al.*, 1982)

James was 14 years old, lived in an institution, and was mobile. He had a severe mental handicap, severe loss of vision, and some hearing impairment. The problem tackled was his frequent eye-gouging, which consisted of inserting his index finger into the eye socket between the eyeball and eyelid to the depth of the second joint. This resulted in swelling, of both the eyeball and its surrounding tissue. He had once fractured a cataract in the process. The initial intervention was carried out in the everyday environment by the experimenter and specially recruited assistants, as was measuring throughout; though the intervention procedures were eventually transferred to institution staff.

For intervention purposes the problem behaviour was described as contact of the fingers with the skin within the orbit of the eye, or insertion of the fingers into the eye-socket. During a baseline of 10 days this behaviour was measured, in the day area of the institution, during two 20-minute sessions (one morning and one afternoon) each day. The presence or absence of the behaviour was noted during a series of 10-second intervals (five consecutive, then a 10-second rest, then another five, and so on). The percentage of intervals per session in which the behaviour occurred was then calculated, and morning and afternoon measures were kept separately.

The intervention began without any reported advance study of existing antecedents and consequences. At first it was in the afternoons only. James was provided with visually stimulating toys (such as a flashlight and mirrors) but these were removed if eye-gouging occurred and then returned after 30 seconds without eye-gouging. This reduced eye-gouging from the average of 92 per cent during baseline to an average of 73 per cent. In a further phase of intervention, lasting nine days, James wore continuously during the sessions a pair of foam-padded gloves and an American football helmet lined with additional foam padding. While these devices did not prevent his bringing his hand to his eye, they *did* prevent injury. For measuring purposes, during this phase the problem behaviour was redefined as contact of a glove with the face mask. The average occurrence was then four per cent, a dramatic decrease. Finally, for the afternoons, there were 17 sessions in which the stimulating toys were provided and no protective equipment was worn initially. Every time eye-gouging occurred, the protective equipment was put on for two minutes and the toys were removed. The equipment remained on until no attempts at eye-gouging had occurred for 30 seconds. The average occurrence was then 1.2 per cent. After five of the 17 sessions this last procedure was also introduced for the morning, where the baseline procedures had been operating until this point. The average occurrence for mornings was then 0.7 per cent. For the last five days of this phase there was no eye-gouging at all, either in the morning or the afternoon.

This study illustrates a number of techniques. The continuous application of protective equipment could be regarded as an antecedent which made the problem behaviour less likely to occur, but it could also be considered as a reducing consequence since it prevented the reinforcement which was thought to be provided by the sensory effects of eye-gouging. Removal of toys and the application of protective equipment were both used as reducing consequences and could be regarded as examples of time-out, since they removed opportunities for reinforcement for a period whenever the problem behaviour occurred.

A second, slightly later experiment with James is also of interest, since the responsibility for intervention was eventually transferred to direct care staff operating under normal, everyday circumstances and for longer periods. A baseline period similar to that in the first experiment was operated for six days. Protective equipment was applied and toys removed as consequences of eye-gouging by special workers for 11 days, and then by direct care staff for about two months. In both cases, implementation was for five days a week for the five hours between finishing school and bedtime. The results were similar to those obtained by the original experimenters.

Example 8 (Jones, Simmons, and Frankel, 1974)
Elaina was a nine-year-old girl who had been hospitalised because of her self-injurious behaviours. She had a severe mental handicap and such autistic behaviours as resistance to change, stereotyped behaviour, and echolalic speech. Her self-injurious behaviours consisted of hitting her arms, hands, and knees against her teeth, and pinching and jabbing various parts of her body. These behaviours all produced open wounds on the skin and she was almost continuously restrained with a neck collar and arm tubes. Intervention procedures and measuring were carried out in the hospital by ward staff.

An intervention programme was implemented without any baseline measuring or study of existing antecedents and consequences being carried out in advance. For a two-hour session each morning and each afternoon. Elaina's restraints were removed and she was put in a room on her own, but with a supply of toys. Immediately after each session she was taken back to the ward and placed in a different room on her own for five minutes. She was then taken to her bedroom, where her arms and neck were washed, bandaged, and placed in tube restraints. She was then allowed to return to the ward. This complex procedure was carried out to avoid the bandaging and placing in restraints acting as consequences of what happened in the main isolation room. While in the room, she was not given any attention, so that reinforcement of self-injurious behaviour by attention was not possible. She was, however, observed through a one-way mirror, and the instances of self-destructive behaviour were counted. These were identified as: hitting, rather oddly defined as any discrete gouging of the body by the teeth; and jabbing, defined as any forceful contact between the fingers and any other part of the body. Over a period of 17 weeks, the number of instances per week fell from about 34,000 to zero, and remainted at zero for the next seven weeks. Separate measures for hitting and jabbing found that hitting began at a high rate and decreased steadily; whereas jabbing began at a relatively low rate, increased as hitting decreased, and then decreased. During week seven Elaina began to resist having restraints applied on the ward and was allowed to be free of them. There was then some self-injurious behaviour on the ward. This was measured from week 15 onwards when there were 20 hits or jabs per hour, but these decreased to zero by week 21 and remained there until week 24.

From week 25 onwards the time spent in the isolation room was gradually decreased and replaced with structured activities, such as school, outings, and recreation. By week 59, isolation was abolished. Hitting or jabbing did not reappear as a result, but there was a recurrence in week 72 for no apparent reason. Elaina was again given sessions in the isolation room and six weeks later it had greatly decreased. At this point, a separate drug programme confused further attempts at evaluating the approach.

In this study, the problem behaviour appeared to be decreased by a reducing consequence which consisted of withholding reinforcement. However, it would also be possible to interpret placing Elaina in the isolation room as an antecedent which made the problem behaviour less likely to occur.

Example 9 (Harris and Romanczyk, 1976)

Robert was eight years old, profoundly deaf, and severely visually handicapped. He had a moderate to severe mental handicap and no speech. Among a variety of unusual behaviours he banged his head and chin frequently. He attended a child behavioural research centre daily from his foster home. Intervention procedures were carried out by centre staff, but it is not clear who did the measuring.

The behaviour to be worked on was defined as contact of head or jaw with any object, including his own body or another person's body. Baseline measures took place in the context of educational activities with an individual tutor, and all occurrences for each day were counted over a period of 14 days.

Despite prior analysis of existing antecedents and consequences these do not appear to have contributed to the design of the intervention, which involved guiding Robert's head and arms through a specified series of movements every time a head- or chin-bang occurred. Robert's head was moved up, then down, then to the left, and then to the right; the whole process being repeated for five minutes. Then his arms were guided to his side, then in front of his body, then over his head, then out to the side at shoulder level, and then back to his side. This sequence was also repeated for five minutes. Any occurrence of self-injurious behaviour during these procedures led to starting the relevant five-minute period of administration again. After completion of these movements Robert was returned to the task that had been interrupted. From an average baseline frequency of 32 instances per day, self-injurious behaviour decreased to an average of five per day, during the first week of the intervention and two during the second week. Incidence then remained at, or very near, zero for the period of nearly nine months to the time of the written account.

Robert continued to engage in self-injurious behaviour at home until a similar programme there produced similar results. Again, the improvement was maintained over some months.

In this intervention, head- and chin-banging were decreased in frequency by making Robert engage in unwelcome activities as a reducing consequence for those behaviours. The procedure was called overcorrection.

Example 10 (Bailey, Pokrzywinsky, and Bryant, 1983)

Jerome was a seven-year-old boy with a severe mental handicap, autistic features, and epilepsy. He had little in the way of self-care skills, and very delayed language. He frequently bit his hand, causing injury and scarring. The study took place in the special class of an ordinary school which Jerome attended. Intervention procedures and measuring were carried out variously by an experimenter, experimenter's assistant, teacher, and classroom aide.

Jerome also put his hand and fingers in his mouth frequently to play with his teeth, tongue, and lips. Since this was difficult to distinguish clearly from biting, the behaviour selected for intervention was defined as "any contact of hand(s) or finger(s)to the lips, tongue, teeth, or oral cavity, except if such contact occurred in an appropriate eating context". Baseline data were, whenever class routine allowed, collected during four 15-minute sessions per day, scheduled to coincide with different regular activities. The number of occurrences per session was measured by using a wrist counter. There was a total of six sessions.

The intervention was begun with no reported advance investigation of existing antecedents and consequences. Every time a self-injurious behaviour occurred a fine mist of water, at room temperature, was sprayed on Jerome's face from a plastic bottle. At the same time the adult said, "No", in a firm voice. Sessions were selected in the same way as for the baseline, but the intervention procedures were used for some of these sessions only. Measuring was the same as in the baseline but was kept separate for the intervention and no-intervention sessions.

During baseline, the average number of mouthing behaviours was 43.5 per session. Over the 41 intervention sessions, the average was 5.1, while for the 27 no-intervention sessions it was 20.5. There was then a return to baseline management, with an average of 29.8 over 17 sessions. A reintroduction of the intervention produced an average of 2.9 for 14 intervention sessions and only 3.1 for 29 interspersed, no-intervention sessions. Thus, not only did the procedure decrease the frequency of the problem behaviour to a very low level, but the change generalised to times when the intervention was not in progress.

It should be mentioned that this procedure, of subjecting Jerome to an unwelcome experience as a reducing consequence for self-injurious behaviours, appeared to surprise and irritate rather than distress him, which might be reassuring to those who have doubts about the acceptability of the technique.

Example 11 (Barmann and Vitali, 1982)
A nine-year-old girl with a profound mental handicap living at home frequently pulled her hair during play and meal times. This resulted in inflammation of the scalp and large bald spots. After early demonstration, intervention procedures were carried out at home by the parents but measuring was by independent observers.

The problem behaviour was defined as any occurrence in which the girl's fingers came into direct contact with the scalp hair for three seconds or longer, resulting in a deliberate and forceful pulling action. During the baseline of 10 days, she wore a large bib made of opaque terry cloth. When hair-pulling occurred she was told "No (name), hands down", but no other action was programmed. Recording was for 90 minutes per day five days per week. After each recorded occurrence, other occurrences were not recorded until five seconds had passed, so the frequency measures obtained were of an unusual kind.

During the intervention the same sessions were used as in baseline recording. The researcher (for the first three days) or the parents (subsequently) responded to each instance of hair-pulling by saying, "No (name), hands down", and then pulling the bib loosely over the child's face and holding it for five seconds in a position which allowed comfortable and normal breathing. Over 23 sessions, the average daily frequency of hair-pulling was 17.8, compared with 51.3 during baseline. For the last 10 intervention sessions, hair-pulling did not occur. Monthly follow-ups for seven months involved measuring during a single 90-minute session, and showed that treatment gains were maintained even though the facial screening procedure was no longer used as a reducing consequence for the problem behaviour.

In this study "facial screening" was used as a reducing consequence for hair-pulling.

Example 12 (Rapoff, Altman, and Christophersen, 1980)

John was a seven-year-old boy in a special school who was blind and had a severe mental handicap. He did not speak. He hit, bit, and scratched his arms, hands, and head, producing bruises, open sores, and scars. Intervention and measuring were carried out by the teacher in the classroom.

The problem behaviour selected for intervention was self-hitting, defined as striking the head, forehead, or facial area with either or both hands. The teacher recorded the frequency of this behaviour in the classroom each day, using a wrist counter. The results were converted to a rate per minute for each day. However, during the one day of the baseline, the teacher ignored self-hitting or, if she was working with John, continued to attempt to get him to engage in the task at hand. This produced an unacceptable amount of self-injurious behaviour. The baseline procedure (and consequently the measurement) was, therefore, in operation for 20 minutes only.

The intervention procedure used restraint as a reducing consequence for self-hitting. When John hit himself the teacher said, "No hitting", made him sit in a different chair, held both his hands behind his back for approximately 30 seconds, and then required him to sit unrestrained for a further 10 to 20 seconds. If he did this without self-hitting he was then allowed to return to ordinary activities. This continued for 10 days during which the average rate of self-hitting was 0.3 instances per minute, compared to 6.3 per minute during the baseline. A one-day return to baseline conditions produced an average of 0.47 per minute and a return to the intervention procedures reduced the rate to zero within three days, where it remained at two-week, one-month, and two-month follow-ups. One year later, the teacher reported that self-hitting was rare and never injurious.

PART C

Specific problems

SECTION 5. STEREOTYPED BEHAVIOURS

Definition, causes, and incidence

Definition

Stereotyped behaviours, sometimes called *stereotypic behaviours* or *stereotypies,* are behaviours which are frequently, and usually continuously, repeated in the same form and which, from a common sense point of view, appear to have no cause or purpose. People who engage in stereotyped behaviours may, for instance, clap their hands repeatedly and very rapidly in front of their faces for several minutes at a time, or may sit in their chairs rocking backwards and forwards for much longer periods. Other examples include: rolling, nodding, or shaking of the head; side-to-side swaying or spinning round of the body; tapping with fingers or objects; pressing fingers on to the eye or into the eye socket; gazing at a light; rapid blinking; waving fingers between the eye and a bright light; rapid forced breathing; sniffing; repeatedly putting objects to the mouth to suck; moving objects in various ways; twirling hair or string; patting, slapping or rubbing self; waving or swinging arms; picking or scratching self; screaming or making other irritating noises; grimacing; nonsensical talking or speech sounds; repeating leg and foot movements; hand wringing or grasping; pill-rolling; dancing or jerking; hugging self; laughing to self; grooming self; chewing things; putting hands over eyes; eye crossing; pacing up and down, running, or hopping; walking on toes; putting out tongue; pulling and smearing saliva; blowing or puffing; and so on. Often, these behaviours are repeated in what seems to be a rhythmic fashion.

Some behaviours which fit this description cause physical damage to the people engaging in them, but they are normally separated off under the label self-injurious behaviour rather than stereotyped behaviour and are not dealt with in this Section. Section 4 has already been devoted to them. Two very similar behaviours could be divided between the two categories because one was more vigorous, and therefore more harmful, than the other.

The boundaries of the stereotyped behaviour category can also be unclear in other ways. It is not always certain whether behaviours that have been described as "compulsive" or "obsessive" should be included. A person who insists on daily attachment of pieces of string to items of furniture, for example, is performing quite complex and often varied actions which seem very different from something like repeated drumming on the table. Other behaviours may have a clearly understood purpose which, again, might exclude them from the category. People who repeatedly remove their clothes, for instance, might do so for the purpose of achieving nudity, which they prefer. Masturbating is another repetitive behaviour which can have a clearly understood purpose, and it can be argued that thumb-sucking has too. Instances have been quoted in the literature of repeated rubbing of the face caused by an allergy and rubbing at the crotch because of pain from a cyst in the testicles. Some of the suggestions that follow might nevertheless apply to intervention for some of these problems.

Causes

Stereotyped behaviour is often also referred to as *self-stimulatory behaviour,* and there is much evidence to suggest that its purpose is often to provide stimulation in an otherwise uninteresting existence. Such behaviour frequently occurs in children who are brought up in unstimulating institutions, and this is paralleled by its high prevalence among monkeys and apes reared in isolation. It is also particularly associated with handicaps which reduce a person's ability to receive or to register sensory stimuli. The more severe the mental handicap, the more frequent the stereotyped behaviour. The evidence from blind children is particularly impressive, in that they very commonly engage in stereotyped pressing of the eyes and eye sockets which is known to produce sensations of light. In one investigation, such behaviour was found to be common among children with defects of the eye itself, but it did not occur in children with damage to the optic nerve, which presumably prevents the effects of eye-pressing from reaching the brain and thus prevents this behaviour from being effective as stimulation. More direct evidence comes from experimental demonstrations, commonly with people with mental handicaps, which indicate: that there is more stereotyped behaviour in confined spaces where there are no objects to manipulate or attend to; that stereotyped behaviour becomes less frequent when measures are taken to increase playing with toys or other activity; that eliminating the sensory consequences of a stereotyped behaviour (by, for instance, carpeting the top of a table to eliminate the sound that can be made by spinning a plate) virtually eliminates that behaviour; that stereotyped behaviours can be decreased by talking to the people engaging in them; and that stereotyped behaviours increase after free movement has been restricted for a while.

However, some of the evidence for the self-stimulation explanation can be interpreted in other ways, and there is also evidence which suggests that this is far from being the whole story. Stereotyped behaviours have also been shown to increase under *high* stimulation, particularly when there is a great deal of noise, and also in unfamiliar environments which are potentially very stimulating. Indeed, these observations have led to suggestions that the behaviours are designed to achieve a certain *level* of stimulation, not too high and not too low. There is also evidence, however, that stereotyped behaviours are increased by tiredness, by frustrating situations, and by hunger, suggesting again that the explanations can be more varied or complicated than a self-stimulation view alone suggests.

Some repetitive movements seem to be neurological in origin, such as some forms of head-nodding and the hand-wringing which occurs in Rett syndrome. There is occasional speculation about medical causes of stereotyped behaviours generally, but no explanations of this kind have achieved much prominence. There is, on the other hand, much evidence that stereotyped behaviours can be learned, since they can be increased by various forms of reinforcement and decreased by removal of reinforcing consequences or by provision of reducing consequences.

There is good evidence for another point of view: that stereotyped behaviours can be associated with normal development. They are certainly normal in infancy. The most notable study of the phenomenon in non-handicapped children of 12 months of age or less, found that it was closely related to physical development. Rocking on hands and knees was most frequent just before crawling developed, stereotyped kicking just before walking, and rhythmic hand and arm movements just before complex manual skills. Stereotyped behaviours, therefore, may consist of simple, coordinated actions which need to be practised before their development or before their incorporation into more mature and skilled behaviours. In people with mental handicaps, such behaviours might sometimes simply indicate the stage of development reached. Further studies of non-handicapped infants found that early stereotyped behaviours could also acquire other functions. They could lead adults to attend to the infants; by picking them up or feeding them, for instance. Since the behaviours were less common in infants who were rocked, jiggled, bounced, and were carried more, a self-stimulation function was also thought likely.

These various findings led to the suggestion that stereotyped behaviour can be a general response to a variety of situations. When infants need to communicate, exert control over people, find stimulation, or take exercise, such behaviour may be their only means of doing so. If a stereotyped behaviour is reinforced by the resulting sensory stimulation, or by consequences in the environment, it can continue beyond its normal developmental stage. If there is a long time delay between stages, as occurs in people with severe mental handicaps, fixed stereotyped habits can develop.

Incidence

Stereotyped behaviours are very common in people with mental handicaps. An incidence of something like 40 per cent has been quoted for children and 18 per cent for adults. The incidence is higher in institutions than in the community (two thirds of the residents in one study). In institutions it has been found to occupy more of people's time, compared with the time spent by people living in the community, almost half the time in a few instances. The more severe the mental handicap the more likely stereotyped behaviour becomes, and additional sensory handicaps increase its likelihood even further. The most common form of the behaviour by far is body-rocking, with putting things in the mouth and complex hand and finger movements the next most frequent.

Why are they a problem?

Bearing in mind the self-stimulatory nature of much stereotyped behaviour, its normal occurrence in children, and its common occurrence among adults without mental handicaps (who are much given to such behaviours as leg-swinging and finger-tapping), it should not be assumed that it is always necessarily a problem. Indeed, such behaviour may be an *aid* to development. Even so, there is no doubt that it *can* be a problem. Some forms, while not actually causing immediate injury, can lead to skin afflictions or dental deformities − thumb-sucking for instance. Others, particularly when they involve noise or a great deal of vigorous activity, can be irritating or disturbing to others. Most stereotyped behaviours look odd and, if performed publicly, reduce social acceptability and therefore affect social adjustment. George, aged 10 (Example 12), was very unattractive to other children, for example, because his constant sucking of objects and associated dribbling left his hands and clothing constantly wet. The behaviours can also interfere with learning as it is difficult to engage in a stereotyped behaviour and learn things at the same time. Some people have been found to manage it, and others readily switch off their stereotyped behaviour at learning times. Some children, however, have been found not to learn successfully while such behaviours are occurring and to make progress only when measures are taken to suppress them.

It is suggested, therefore, that the effects of each particular stereotyped behaviour on various important aspects of an individual's life should be considered carefully before deciding whether it is a problem and needs an intervention programme.

Intervention techniques

Defining the problem

A clear description of a stereotyped behaviour is usually easily achieved, simply *because* it is stereotyped. An example, indicating the precision ideally required is:

> "When sitting in a chair with no obstruction in front, Karl rocks his body backwards and forwards between the back of the chair and his thighs, at any time, in any situation, or with any person".

As pointed out earlier, behaviour should not necessarily be regarded as a problem just because it is stereotyped. If it is performed only when no other activity is required, does no harm, can be tolerated by others, and can be restricted to situations where social acceptability is not much affected, perhaps it should be treated as a form of play, and allowed. The emphasis should then be on building up appropriate behaviours as alternatives.

Even when a stereotyped behaviour *is* thought to be a problem and to need attention, increasing alternative behaviours should be the method of choice whenever possible. It may be that the behaviour is problematic only because it interferes with the performance of appropriate behaviour. If the appropriate behaviour can be made sufficiently frequent by influencing it directly, it may not matter if the stereotyped behaviour still occurs. In Example 12, for instance, 10-year-old George's teacher tackled his sucking of fingers or hair by using a disapproving tone to tell him to stop, and reinforcing by sweets and praise his constructive play with objects as alternative appropriate behaviours. Although the decrease in George's stereotyped behaviours was not dramatic, constructive handling of objects improved and the teacher felt this to be an important step forward.

An example of a suitable description of an appropriate behaviour which might be developed as an alternative to rocking is:

"When sitting in a chair with no obstruction in front, Karl sits in an upright, comfortable position, and follows with his eyes the activities of other people continuously for five minutes".

Note that this behaviour is incompatible with rocking. However, incompatibility is important only where the stereotyped behaviour is a real problem. If it is just vaguely worrying, but has no clearly harmful effects, then the appropriate behaviours chosen as alternatives should be those which are most important for the person to engage in for other reasons.

Measuring the problem

Since stereotyped behaviour occurs frequently, periods of measurement can usually be short, sometimes only a few minutes. Since its frequency is sometimes very great, however, counting individual instances may require intense concentration. For a continuous stereotyped behaviour, like finger-sucking, it is difficult to know what to count as a single instance. In this kind of situation it is preferable to record the *proportion* of the observation period occupied by the behaviour. Alternatively, the person can be observed for a short time at regular intervals, a note made of whether the behaviour is occurring or not on each occasion, and the proportion of observation periods in which it is occurring can be calculated.

Identifying existing antecedents and consequences

A number of different kinds of antecedents have been identified, most of which are to do with the setting. It is well worth looking for: absence of stimulation, of things to attend to, of interesting activities, and of people with whom to interact; restriction of movement; demands to carry out difficult tasks; and too much stimulation, such as loud noise or an unfamiliar situation. In one study there was more stereotyped behaviour with the television on than when it was quiet or when music was played. Internal states, like tiredness, frustrating situations, and hunger are other possible antecedents.

Consequences for stereotyped behaviours have not been much investigated, since they rarely appear to need any. The mere performance of a behaviour, and the sensations it produces, is usually sufficient to increase its frequency. It can be thought of almost as reinforcing itself. However, it is possible that it can sometimes be reinforced (or additionally reinforced) by various forms of attention, or by freedom from or escape from attention.

Changing antecedents and consequences for intervention programmes

As mentioned earlier, increasing appropriate behaviours should be the first choice in designing intervention procedures. Identification of antecedents which are making stereotyped behaviours more likely to occur can help in selection of antecedents to make appropriate behaviours more likely. Absence of stimulation or of other people can be replaced by their presence; rapid increases in stimulation can be replaced by gradual ones; frustrating situations can be made less frustrating. Provision of interesting objects is the most obvious antecedent for appropriate behaviours, and can sometimes be effective. Example 1, with a 24-year-old woman with a profound mental handicap and autistic features, shows how giving her acceptable scented objects led to her smelling them instead of digging her fingers into her rectum and smelling them. The evidence suggests that interesting objects should often be accompanied by such other antecedents as guidance in appropriate play or manipulation, or play interaction with other people. In one study of a girl with a severe mental handicap a decrease in problem behaviours of a largely stereotyped kind occurred when she was shown how to play with toys and, when necessary, was physically guided in doing so. Some objects can be more effective than others: in one study with young boys with autistic and other problems, for instance, hard toys were found to be more effective than soft. A wide range of toys and other objects can be tried to see which ones are most effective. Example 2 describes how favourite toys were used with an 18-month-old boy with a severe mental handicap as antecedents for appropriate behaviour, with a following decrease in hand-gazing. This study is interesting in that another antecedent, provision of glasses, was found to have a similar effect and the two antecedents combined were far more effective than either one alone.

Whether reinforcing appropriate behaviour alone will effectively decrease stereotyped behaviours depends on the effectiveness of the reinforcing consequences. For 12-year-old Graham (Example 3), attention, praise, stars, and sweets were effective reinforcers for abstaining from nose-picking — a differential reinforcement of other behaviour (DRO) procedure. Where a stereotyped behaviour is thought to serve as stimulation, reinforcement of some play or other leisure behaviour may be particularly helpful as it has the same function. This would be differential reinforcement of equivalent behaviour (DRE). If there is difficulty in finding effective reinforcers there is much to be said for using the stereotyped behaviour itself for this purpose. A period of abstaining from a stereotyped behaviour, or performance of an alternative appropriate behaviour, can be reinforced by a period during which the stereotyped behaviour is allowed. The use of such reinforcement specifically to decrease stereotyped behaviours has not yet been put to test in an experimental study. It has, however, been demonstrated experimentally that it can increase appropriate behaviours. There have also been instances where reinforcement by allowing people freedom to do as they like for a while, in circumstances where what they like will probably include stereotyped behaviour, has had this effect (Examples 3 and 5 in Section 2).

An audible timer can be a help in these differential reinforcement of other behaviour techniques. To help nine-year-old Shirley, in one of my workshops, to overcome her constant chewing of clothes, equipment, toys, and other things, a timer was set repeatedly for one minute. She was told that if she did not put anything in her mouth until "the clock goes buzz" she would get a kiss, which she did (accompanied by praise). That the success of the intervention was related to this device was indicated by one incident in which Shirley held something near her mouth, said "Buzz", and put it down again.

Reinforcing appropriate behaviour is useful in itself, but it cannot be assumed that it will necessarily decrease stereotyped behaviours. In research studies, sometimes it has and sometimes it has not. There have even been instances where the stereotyped behaviours have *increased*. Where a stereotyped behaviour is regarded as a serious problem, therefore, measures will be needed for decreasing it directly, though these should always be accompanied by techniques to increase appropriate alternative behaviours.

The literature contains only a few instances of antecedents to make stereotyped behaviours less likely to occur. Identification of antecedents making stereotyped behaviour *more* likely were helpful in a study where television appeared to have this effect. Replacing it by quietness or music decreased the problem behaviour. Example 4 describes how daily jogging made subsequent stereotyped behaviour less likely in a boy with autistic features, perhaps because of some effect on his general state. Telling a person in advance *not* to engage in the behaviour is another device which has been described. Example 6 in Section 2 describes how a man with a profound handicap was trained to refrain from stereotyped hand-flicking when he was told, "Do not shake your wrist".

Unfortunately, reducing consequences for stereotyped behaviours are the successful devices most commonly mentioned in the literature. They include devices which are usually regarded as unacceptable in this country, such as slapping and pinching, electric shock, and whiffs of smelling salts. Regrettably, the less unpleasant the consequence is the fewer successful applications are reported in the literature, sometimes because no-one appears to have investigated. Thus, interrupting the behaviour and directing someone to do something else may be effective, but I have not found a report of an investigation using this technique on its own.

One class of mild consequence, prevention of reinforcement, has been found to be effective in reducing stereotyped behaviours. It depends on the preliminary identification of consequences which are reinforcing the problem behaviours. In Example 5, for instance, it was thought that a 10-year-old boy with severe mental and visual handicaps was obtaining reinforcement for spinning objects on a table by the sounds that resulted. Deadening of the sound by carpeting the surface virtually eliminated the behaviour. Other examples in the literature are: reducing snorting, bursts of musical sounding notes, and sloshing or slurring sounds by putting on earphones with a continuous noise which masked the sounds made; attaching a vibrator to the hand to mask stimulation from stereotyped hand and arm movements; blindfolding or turning off lights to prevent visual reinforcement from finger and hand manipulation; and stopping light switches from functioning or fitting soft material to deaden the sound made by repeatedly switching them on and off. In some instances, more than one kind of sensory stimulation had to be prevented. It should be noted that all these investigations were in experimental rooms rather than everyday settings, and some ingenuity may be required to carry out similar procedures in the latter.

Ways of preventing reinforcement for problem behaviour, known as "time-out", have been used successfully in a number of studies. In Example 6, for instance, a 28-year-old man with a profound mental handicap lost access to food and praise, social interaction, and interesting activity for two minutes every time he banged his hand on a desk or chair. It is worth noting, however, that *exclusion* time-out has been found to *increase* the rate of stereotyped behaviours in some studies.

If a stereotyped behaviour is a really serious problem, and more severe reducing consequences are needed, making a person do something unwelcome is a device that has repeatedly been shown to be effective. One possibility is to make the person practise the problem behaviour repeatedly to try to make it an unwelcome experience. This is reported for clothes-ripping in a young man with a severe mental handicap, as part of a package of several intervention techniques in Example 10. More commonly investigated is the technique called overcorrection, in which predetermined, unwelcome actions have to be carried out repeatedly by the person every time a problem behaviour occurs. In Example 7, for instance, which features a nine-year-old girl with a severe mental handicap and autistic features: stereotyped hand movements had to be followed by repeatedly moving her hands up, then down, then out, then in front of her, and holding each position for 15 seconds; genital touching had to be followed first by washing hands and using disinfectant, and then by the hand movements; while rocking had to be followed by repeatedly standing up, then sitting down, then leaning forward, and then leaning backward, maintaining each position for 15 seconds. Use of hand or arm exercises is the most common form of overcorrection reported in the literature. Periods of one minute or less have been found effective in some studies.

If unwelcome activities are difficult to organise or are thought unlikely to be effective, doing something unwelcome to a person may be considered if the situation is desperate. Physical restraint can, in certain forms, be an acceptable device. Example 8 shows how stereotyped behaviours in a 26-year-old woman with a profound handicap were decreased by making her keep her hands still for two minutes each time a stereotyped behaviour occurred. Another method is to put a light cloth or some other light-screening device over the person's eyes or face for a short period. In Example 9 this is described for a four-year-old boy with a mental handicap, whose eyes were covered by a therapist's hand every time he engaged in a stereotyped ritual involving looking at shoes, laughing, and saying, "shoes". Plunging someone into darkness is somewhat more extreme and less acceptable, while squirting water into a person's face or lemon juice into someone's mouth is probably beyond the acceptable limits for intervention for this class of behaviour.

In the literature combinations of the above methods are extremely common. Where a stereotyped behaviour presents a really severe problem, a combination of devices to decrease it with devices to increase alternative appropriate behaviours is likely to be the best choice. Most successful combination studies include reinforcement of any appropriate behaviour (that is, abstaining from problem behaviour) combined with some kind of reducing consequence for the stereotyped behaviour.

In Example 10, which describes elimination of clothes-ripping in a young man with a severe mental handicap, reinforcing appropriate behaviour is combined with *two* kinds of reducing consequences. First, the young man had to rip repeatedly for 15 minutes, a procedure designed to make the behaviour unwelcome to him. Then he had to dress and redress repeatedly, which was probably an unwelcome activity. In Example 11, light-gazing was decreased in a child with multiple handicaps by combining reinforcement for abstaining from the stereotyped behaviour with a brief period of head restraint for engaging in it. In Example 12, the reducing consequence was even more mild. Here, 10-year-old George was told to stop in a disapproving tone every time he sucked his finger or his hair, and he was reinforced by sweets and praise for constructive play with objects.

Additional measures
There is very little else to suggest. It is doubtful whether fitting restraining devices can ever be justified for stereotyped behaviours. Major tranquillisers have been shown to decrease their frequency when used in low doses, but such improvements can be accompanied by drowsiness and there have been instances where such medication has made people more resistive, combative, restless, uncooperative, or abusive after treatment. There is often, therefore, some reluctance to prescribe such medication. Provision of spectacles decreased hand-gazing in a pre-school boy with a severe mental

handicap and visual impairment in Example 2, but this could be interpreted as an antecedent to make appropriate behaviour more likely.

Subsequent action

Example 9 describes an intervention which was begun in the residential unit of a hospital, and then extended to the child's home at weekends. It concerned four-year-old Keith, who engaged in ritualistic behaviours related to shoes, and had his eyes covered so that he could not see every time he engaged in one of these behaviours. The rituals decreased rapidly when this procedure was introduced in the hospital, but no improvement occurred at home until the same procedure was also implemented there later on.

The gradual fading out of an intervention is described in Example 8, in which a 26-year-old woman who engaged in stereotyped head movements, mouthing of objects, and tapping of bricks was reinforced for engaging in simple tasks. Any occurrence of stereotyped behaviour was interrupted and the woman's hands were made to remain in her lap for two minutes. This two-minute period of restraint was halved (approximately) for every 30 minute period without stereotyped behaviour, but returned to two minutes' duration whenever two instances of the behaviour occurred within 30 minutes. In this way, the restraint was gradually diminished till it was momentary. It also became rare because of the marked decrease in the problem behaviour.

Illustrative studies

Example 1 (Smith, 1986)

The person in this study was a 24-year-old woman who had a profound mental handicap and was autistic, did not speak, behaved aggressively, injured herself, was hyperactive, and showed stereotyped behaviours which included digging in her rectum with her fingers and then sniffing them. She lived in a community-based group home and attended a vocational training programme. Intervention and measuring were carried out by a counsellor in both these settings, and a more senior member of staff checked the accuracy of the measuring.

The behaviour measured was rectal digging followed by finger sniffing, but this is not defined more precisely. All incidents were recorded during a continuous seven-hour period five days a week, and the number of incidents per day was calculated. During this time, the problem behaviour was not attended to, but the young woman was praised and rewarded for cooperating with work and home routines without being aggressive. This baseline period lasted for a month.

Observation showed that rectal digging occurred very briefly but the sniffing that followed lasted longer. It seemed likely, therefore, that the smell of faeces reinforced the problem behaviour. It was decided, therefore, to give the woman a range of other scented materials to smell, including scented hand lotion, perfume, scented lipstick, and sachets. Since the baseline observations showed that the problem behaviour occurred approximately every 10-15 minutes, these scents were presented approximately every 15 minutes. The woman was handed the scent, or the scented material was placed on her hands and her wrists, and she was allowed approximately 30 seconds to smell it. She was then directed back to everyday activities. Rectal digging was ignored, apart from continuing efforts to engage the woman in appropriate activites. Measuring continued as in the baseline, when the average daily incidence was 35. This showed a rapid initial decrease in the problem behaviour to less than 10 a day and, after about eight months of intervention, to less than one a day. Fading out of the programme was not considered necessary because it was easy to provide scents and the woman enjoyed them.

In this intervention provision of scented material was an antecedent which brought about the appropriate behaviour of smelling it, with the result that the problem behaviour of rectal digging and finger-sniffing decreased.

Example 2 (Gallagher and Berkson, 1986)

One of the children in this study was an 18-month-old boy with a severe mental handicap and difficulties with vision. He was not able to sit and did not interact with other children, but he could manipulate simple play objects. The report does not specify where the intervention occurred or who carried it out, but it was probably in an institution. Measuring was by independent observers.

The problem behaviour was hand-gazing, defined as any eye-to-hand fixation. The child was placed on the floor on his back and toys were placed where he could easily reach them. During four five-minute observation periods in each of 12 measuring sessions over a three-month period, the child was observed momentarily every 15 seconds and a note was made of whether hand-gazing was or was not occurring. The average percentage of occasions on which it occurred was calculated.

Observation of the child led to suspicions that he might have vision difficulties. He was referred to an optometrist and found to be short-sighted. It was thought possible that his poor sight decreased stimulation from his environment and that hand-gazing compensated for this. Spectacles were, therefore, provided but these were not worn all the time. Instead, during two observation periods per week over 22 weeks, the child was sometimes observed with his favourite toys nearby and spectacles on, sometimes with spectacles but no toys, and sometimes with toys but no spectacles. The report does not state what happened at other times. The average percentage of occurrences of hand-gazing (the baseline) was: 48 per cent with no glasses-no toys; 30 per cent with toys-no glasses; 26 per cent with glasses-no toys; and four per cent with glasses and toys. Thus, both the toys and the glasses decreased hand-gazing and the two combined almost eliminated it.

In this intervention provision of toys and provision of glasses could both be interpreted as antecedents which made the problem behaviour of hand-gazing less likely to occur. Probably, both measures achieved this by making appropriate behaviours, such as toy play and looking at the environment, generally more likely. It was noticed, for instance, that when the glasses were on, the child held his head more upright and looked around, but when they were taken off his head dropped and his attention focused on his hands.

Example 3

The teacher of 12-year-old Graham was involved in one of my workshops. Graham had a severe mental handicap, but he could talk in simple sentences and was just beginning to draw and to learn the shapes of letters and numbers. The intervention and its measuring were carried out by the teacher in the classroom.

Graham's teacher identified his main problems as grinning insolently, staring vacantly into space, and nose-picking. She decided to work first on nose-picking – the most offensive behaviour. The number of incidents of nose-picking was measured for two 15-minute periods each week.

After a 10-day baseline period, an intervention was begun. It was based on observations which indicated that Graham liked demonstrations of affection and praise, which he would seek in a variety of ways including putting his arms around an adult and saying, "I like you". He was told that if he kept his fingers away from his nose he would be given a sweet; and that, at the end of the day, he would be given a gold star if he tried very hard not to do it. His teacher then observed him briefly at hourly intervals. If, at the time of observation, Graham was not picking his nose he was given one sweet from a *Dolly Mixture* and his teacher put her arm round his shoulder and praised him. At the end of the day he was given a gold star if he had not picked his nose at all, and a silver star if he had not done it as much as usual. He was also praised publicly in assembly several times for his improvement. Over the nine days of measuring during the intervention, the average number of incidents per measuring period was 1.2, whereas during the baseline it had been 9.1. Nose-picking was eliminated within three days, but the average was raised to 1.2 by an attempt during two days to reward two-hourly instead of hourly.

That the improvement was directly related to the programme was shown by Graham's occasionally asking for a sweet and saying, "Me no pick nose". The improvement was maintained over several months, except that it had to be reestablished each time Graham returned to school from a holiday.

In this intervention Graham was effectively reinforced for any behaviour other than nose-picking, the procedure known as differential reinforcement of other behaviour (DRO).

Example 4 (Watters and Watters, 1980)

D, who was 10 years old, was one of five boys with autistic features in an investigation conducted in a classroom. His problem behaviour was described as "rocking back and forth". The intervention was carried out by the teacher, but measuring was by outside observers.

Measuring was carried out during language training sessions, *D* being observed for five-second periods on a randomised basis, and a record made of whether he was rocking or not on each occasion. The percentage of observation periods in which he rocked was calculated.

There was no baseline as such, and no advance study of antecedents and consequences; nor was this an "intervention", but more of an experimental comparison. The main comparison was between the effects of jogging with the teacher in the playground for 8 to 10 minutes immediately before the language session, and a variety of academic tasks similarly timed. Another prior activity was watching television. These three "preconditions" were arranged a number of times, in random order, over a period involving 27 language training sessions. The average percentage of rocking was 48.3 following academic tasks, but only 20.7 following jogging. No results are given for watching television, but it is claimed this was no better than the academic task.

That jogging as an antecedent acted by making a stereotyped behaviour less likely, rather than by making an alternative appropriate behaviour more likely to occur, was tested further by measuring the percentage of correct answers in the language training session after the different "preconditions". No difference of significance was found, so the effect seems to have been directly on the stereotyped behaviour. Why it should have this effect is not known.

Example 5 (Rincover *et al.*, 1979)

One of the children in this study was Reggie, aged nine years, who had severe mental and visual handicaps, responded only to very simple language, and had hardly any meaningful speech. He showed a high rate of stereotyped behaviour and little appropriate play. The investigation was carried out by the researchers in an experimental room containing nothing but the experimental materials.

The problem behaviour was identified as spinning objects on hard surfaces and, in the experimental room, a plate was provided for the purpose. For both baseline and intervention there was a daily 15-minute session, usually for four days per week. In each session there were 60 five-second observation intervals with Reggie sitting at a table. The observers recorded whether plate-spinning did or did not occur during each interval. The percentage of intervals during which it occurred was then calculated.

After a baseline of 11 sessions there followed three sessions in which the table-top was completely covered by a quarter-inch thick carpet, which deadened the sound made by the plate but did not prevent it from spinning. This was done because advance observation in the everyday classroom and discussion with the teacher had shown that, when Reggie spun an object he leaned towards it as though listening, and it was therefore possible that the behaviour was reinforced by the sound it made. Whereas, most of the time during baseline, Reggie had shown a high rate of plate-spinning (up to 100 per cent), it did not occur at all during this intervention. When the carpet was subsequently removed for four sessions, plate-spinning recurred at a similarly high rate, and then reduced to a very low rate again when the carpet was restored.

It seemed, in this intervention, that the plate-spinning became less frequent because it was prevented from being reinforced by the sound it made (sensory extinction). It should be added that, in further sessions, Reggie was taught to play with a music box, so that he could receive auditory reinforcement for more appropriate play.

Example 6 (McKeegan, Estill, and Campbell, 1984)

A 28-year-old man with a profound handicap and autistic features, living in a group home, could move around freely and understand basic requests but had no speech. His former aggressive and self-injurious behaviour had been eliminated, and the time had come to work on his stereotyped behaviour. The intervention took place in a large day room, and was conducted by home staff, though measuring was by separate observers.

The problem behaviour was defined as a highly repetitive, open handed, forceful slap on a table top or chair near where he was sitting. Measuring was for the whole of each six-hour day session. The total number of hand-banging incidents per day was recorded, and the rate per hour calculated for each day.

During the baseline of three days, the pre-existing programme was in operation. The man wore a large ribbon on his shirt. While he wore this and did not engage in any aggressive, self-abusive, or disruptive behaviours, he was given praise and something to eat intermittently. The ribbon (and with it the reinforcement) had previously been removed for a short period each time he engaged in one of these problem behaviours, but this was no longer necessary; it now acted as a reminder only.

The intervention was based on advance study of antecedents and consequences. Since the hand-banging occurred in a number of settings, and regardless of the presence or absence of others, no obvious antecedents were identifiable. It was, known however, that the ribbon had been an antecedent for appropriate behaviour and its removal a consequence for problem behaviour in the earlier programme, so it was decided to use the same procedure to reduce the frequency of hand-banging. Every time the behaviour occurred, the ribbon was removed for two minutes, all materials being used were removed, staff did not interact with the man, and no food or praise was given. If hand-banging continued, this time-out period was extended until 30 seconds of appropriate behaviour had occurred. After each time-out period the ribbon was restored, together with all the other benefits above. During the baseline period the frequency of hand-banging varied from 46.7 to 70 instances per hour, whereas during the first 10 days of the intervention it was never more than two. Improvement was maintained during the next 25 days and the problem behaviour did not occur at all during a five day follow-up six months later.

In this intervention the problem behaviour was reduced by removing access to all likely reinforcing consequences for a period (time-out).

Example 7 (Czyzewski, Barrera, and Sulzer-Azaroff, 1982)
This study involved a nine-year-old girl in a residential home who had a severe mental handicap and was autistic. She could walk but not talk, and engaged with high frequency in a wide range of self-stimulatory and self-injurious behaviours such as rocking, hand movements, masturbation, and self-biting. The intervention was conducted in her classroom and the school playground and was carried out by the experimenter, recording being by a staff member.

The problem behaviours were defined as: repeatedly touching fingers to or into the mouth; repeatedly touching the palm or back of the hand to the mouth or chin area; bringing any part of the hand to the ear and holding it there for a minimum of two seconds; rhythmic waving of hand or fingers 8 to 10 inches in front of the face; holding the hand still 6 to 10 inches in front of the eyes and looking at it; touching the genital area with the hands, with or without overtly masturbatory movements; and rhythmically shifting the body torso from side to side. There were two daily 15-minute recording periods during the baseline. Throughout this period the observer noted, for 15-second intervals, whether or not each of the behaviours identified occurred, with a five-second gap after each interval to record this. During these times, the girl was engaged in her regular classroom activities.

The intervention, not preceded by any reported study of antecedents and consequences, consisted of making the girl engage repeatedly in a specific set of actions each time a particular problem behaviour occurred. For stereotyped hand movements she had to put her hands up, then down, then out, and then in front of her, holding each position for 15 seconds and continuing for approximately two-and-a-half minutes. For touching the genitals she had to wash her hands and apply disinfectant (the account does not say where) for one minute, then follow the procedure for stereotyped hand movements for two-and-a-half minutes. For rocking she had to stand up, then sit down, then lean forwards, then lean backwards, holding each position for 15 seconds and continuing for two-and-a-half minutes. Physical guidance was used to bring this about if necessary. These procedures were implemented daily for three-and-a-half hours during regular classroom activities, and recording was the same as that used during the baseline although, because it was interrupted by the intervention procedures, it was spread out over longer periods. The average number of intervals per day during which stereotyped hand movements occurred was 30.17 during the six-day baseline, but only 4.3 during the intervention of seven days. When treatment was suspended for three days, it rose again to 34.0, but when intervention was reintroduced it was almost eliminated (average 1.0). The initial frequencies for rocking and genital touching were much lower, but the changes were in the same direction.

In this intervention, making the girl engage repeatedly in specified movements (according to one of the procedures that have been called overcorrection) seems to have acted as a reducing consequence for stereotyped behaviours.

Example 8 (Azrin and Wesolowski, 1980)

One of the seven people in this study was a 26-year-old, institutionalised woman with a profound handicap, who had no speech and interacted with others hardly at all. She spent a large amount of her time in stereotyped head movements, mouthing objects, and tapping bricks on tables. The intervention took place in a daily classroom lesson devoted to intensive instruction in motor skills with a single instructor. An additional trainer was required for the intervention and recording was by independent observers.

The woman was observed for 10 minutes at a time, either once or twice per day. Every 10 seconds, the observer recorded whether or not she was engaged in stereotyped behaviour. The percentage of occasions on which it was occurring was calculated for each day.

After five days of baseline recording an intervention was begun, without any recorded prior study of antecedents and consequences. The woman was given 90 minutes' daily individual training specifically designed to eliminate the stereotyped behaviour. She sat at a table and the instructor guided, instructed, and reinforced her in very simple tasks. Each correct movement was reinforced by praise and stroking, and there were also snack rewards. The second trainer stood behind her, "shadowed" the part of the body involved, and physically prevented any move towards stereotyped behaviour. After 30 minutes this training was replaced by a procedure in which, for every instance of stereotyped behaviour, the trainer pulled the woman's chair back from the table, told her not to do it, guided her hands gently to her lap or the edge of the table, and ensured they remained there for two minutes. If attempts at stereotyped behaviour occurred in the last 10 seconds of this period, it was extended until there had been no attempts for 10 seconds. This phase continued until no stereotyped behaviour had occurred for 30 consecutive minutes.

The woman was then included in the class situation, given praise, stroking, and snacks for correct responses in tasks, and the verbal reprimand, response interruption, and restraint for stereotyped behaviour. The duration of restraint was reduced by about half for every 30-minute period without stereotyped behaviour, but returned to two minutes whenever two instances occurred within 30 minutes. In this way, the restraint was gradually reduced to a momentary event. During the baseline period stereotyped behaviour occurred in over 40 per cent of the recording time, but after the individual training it hardly occurred at all. By the fourth day back in the classroom situation the incidence was below one per cent.

In this intervention interruption and restraint appeared to act as a reducing consequence for stereotyped behaviour.

Example 9 (Barrett, Staub, and Sisson, 1983)

Keith was a four-year-old boy with a mental handicap and a range of severe behaviour problems in a psychiatric hospital short-term residential unit for such children. Shortly after admission he became so preoccupied by shoes that they began to dominate his daily routine. The particular part of the intervention described here was carried out initially in the hospital residential unit, and then extended to the boy's home at weekends, probably by hospital staff and parents respectively, though this is not altogether clear. Measuring was by independent observers in the hospital and by the parents at home.

Among the shoe-related behaviours tackled was a ritual in which, every time he was required to greet someone or go from one place to another within the hospital residential setting, Keith stared at somebody's shoes for 2 to 3 seconds, laughed with his eyes closed for 2 to 3 seconds, and finally said "shoes" very loudly. The number of times this ritual occurred in the hospital residential unit during seven hours each day was recorded.

After a baseline period of seven days an intervention procedure began, without any reported advance investigation of antecedents and consequences. Each time the ritual occurred Keith would be told that he was engaging in the behaviour concerned. A hand would then be placed over his eyes so that he could see nothing, while the back of his head was held with the other hand. This continued until Keith had accepted it without fuss for 30 seconds. Over 12 days of this intervention the average daily frequency of the ritual was only 8.1, whereas it had been 43.6 during the baseline. For the last five days of the intervention the ritual did not occur at all. There then followed a phase in which the warning statement alone was used for the first instance each day, provided the behaviour ceased immediately. Incidence of the ritual remained very low for eight days, after which Keith was discharged home. By then the intervention had already been extended successfully to the home at weekends. Follow-ups over the next 12 months, after all intervention procedures had ceased, found the improvement had been maintained.

In this intervention visual screening acted as a reducing consequence for a stereotyped ritual. Essentially the same procedure was also effective, in both classroom and hospital residential unit, for kissing, licking, and touching of other people's shoes and for repeatedly saying or singing the word "shoes".

Example 10 (Carroll et al., 1978)

Ronnie was a young man with a severe mental handicap living in an institution who repeatedly tore off items of his clothing. The intervention took place in the everyday setting but was carried out by the experimenters. Its effects were measured by independent observers.

The problem behaviour was defined as partially or completely removing any article of clothing in which the material was torn. Records were kept of the number of times this occurred, though the length and time of the daily recording periods is not stated.

After a seven day baseline an intervention was begun without any reported study of antecedents and consequences in advance. After each ripping incident, Ronnie was taken to a separate room and made to rip the damaged garment repeatedly for 15 minutes. He then had to dress and undress repeatedly for the next 15 minutes. His movements were "shadowed", and physical guidance was used where necessary. If ripping was attempted during this second phase, the whole procedure was restarted. In addition to these reducing consequences, all non-disruptive behaviours were regularly reinforced with sweets, praise, and patting Ronnie or shaking his hand. At first this was done for every 10 minutes of the appropriate behaviour, but over a two-day period this was reduced in stages to varying times averaging one hour, where it remained. With this intervention package, Ronnie's clothes-ripping, which had varied from seven to 30 incidents per recording period during the baseline, reduced to a zero rate within five days.

In this intervention, negative practice and overcorrection were used as reducing consequences for stereotyped behaviour. Their use was combined with one kind of reinforcing consequence for appropriate behaviour (differential reinforcement of incompatible behaviour or DRI).

Example 11 (Barton, Repp, and Brulle, 1985)

The person being helped in this study was one of four children with multiple handicaps in a summer school. The intervention was carried out in the classroom by the teacher and teacher's aide, who also did the recording.

The problem behaviour was light-gazing, and was recorded as such any time the child spontaneously turned his head towards a light, window, or other light source and remained in that position. Records were kept throughout most of the day on note cards attached to the clothes of staff members and the number of occurrences per minute was calculated for each day.

After an 11-day baseline an intervention programme began. It consisted of a procedure for reinforcing any behaviour other than light-gazing and a procedure for reducing the light-gazing. For the reinforcement process the time was divided into periods, and the child was reinforced at the end of each period if light-gazing had not occurred. A tape recorder was used to produce an audible reminder at the end of each period. The length of the period (in minutes) was related to the baseline at first (1/mean rate), and then to performance during the intervention (1/previous day's rate), so that it started at about two minutes and twenty seconds and then gradually increased. Reinforcing consequences were individually determined but no further information about them is provided. The reduction procedure consisted of holding the child's head in the facing-front position for three seconds every time light-gazing occurred. These reinforcing and reducing procedures operated throughout the school day. Light-gazing had occurred at rates varying between 0.29 and 0.77 per minute during the baseline, but during the intervention declined progressively over a period of 37 days, until it was at 0.1 or less during the last five of these days.

In this intervention differential reinforcement of other behaviour (DRO) was accompanied by an overcorrection procedure as a reducing consequence for the stereotyped behaviour.

Example 12

George was a nine-year-old boy with a severe mental handicap, no speech, and a spastic condition affecting all four limbs. His teacher, Mrs. P., took part in one of my workshops. She reported that George: put everything in his mouth; sucked his rather long hair and his fingers; ate *Plasticine*, paper tissues, and elastic bands; and sucked and dribbled on hard apparatus, such as bricks. These behaviours made him unattractive to other children because of his constantly wet hands and clothing. He needed instead to learn to handle objects purposefully and constructively.

Mrs. P. decided to work on sucking fingers and hair, and measured the number of incidents during a half-hour session each day.

After eight days of baseline recording Mrs. P. began her intervention without any reported advance investigation of existing antecedents and consequences. She had decided to base her programme on disapproval for sucking fingers or hair (previously this had been tackled by distracting George's attention with something else) and approval for more constructive use of his hands. For 30 minutes each morning George was provided with some simple tasks involving manipulation of objects and was praised for each constructive action with them ("Good boy"). Additionally, there was more praise and a sweet at the end of the half-hour session which did not depend precisely on how he had behaved. If he put his fingers or his hair in his mouth he was told, "Take your fingers/hair out of your mouth" in a quiet and disapproving manner. The activities used were taking cylinders of graded sizes out of holes and putting them back in the right ones, putting one object inside another, moving objects from one container to another, assembling and taking apart nesting cubes, and taking objects off wires.

Measuring continued during the 30-minute programme periods. During the first eight sessions of baseline recording the average number of incidents per session was 8.5, varying from six to 12. For the following four sessions George was sucking his fingers continuously, and this was thought to be related to a heavy cold. For the eight sessions of recording during the intervention, the average incidence was 5.6, varying from three to eight. This improvement was moderate only. However, there was a significant increase in constructive handling of objects. This was not measured during the baseline, when George would not do it anyway, but it was measured during the intervention, and the number of constructive handling actions averaged 9.6 per recording period, varying from four to 15. Mrs P. reported that George now seemed to like such activities, and he persisted at one of the tasks for the full half-hour during the last recording session.

In this intervention disapproval used as a reducing consequence for the stereotyped behaviour was combined with reinforcement of alternative appropriate behaviour incompatible with the stereotyped behaviour; an example of differential reinforcement of incompatible behaviour (or DRI).

PART C

Specific problems

SECTION 6. FEEDING PROBLEMS

Definition, causes, and incidence

Definition

Almost any kind of problem behaviour can occur in association with feeding: non-compliance, aggressive behaviour, self-injurious behaviour, and stereotyped behaviour are all possible at the meal table. Approaches to these problems are covered in other sections. In this section the emphasis is on problem behaviours specifically associated with eating.

A problem obviously related to eating is stealing of food. This has been reported most commonly at mealtimes, where it frequently takes the form of grabbing handfuls of food that is really for a neighbour, though any other food within reach is also fair game. People can also go foraging for food, particularly when their food intake is being restricted to prevent them from becoming overweight, and they may, in these circumstances, attempt to escape detection.

A related problem is *scavenging* or *pica*. This is commonly defined as eating non-nutritive substances such as string, sweet wrappers, needles, items from refuse containers, pills, paper, soil, cigarette ends, stones, and a whole host of others. Some people with mental handicaps even consume their faeces, a behaviour termed *coprophagy*. Some authors include in the definition of pica the eating of food obtained from the wrong places – by picking it up from the floor, for instance.

Vomiting and rumination are problems that occur *after* eating. The distinction between these terms is not consistent in the literature. However, if the term *vomiting* is used it usually implies that the regurgitated matter is immediately ejected from the mouth. *Rumination*, on the other hand, usually implies that it is retained in the mouth for a while, perhaps chewed, and then either reswallowed, allowed to run out of the mouth, or ejected.

Another behaviour related to food is refusal to eat. A person may put up a hand to fend off the food, turn the head away, and struggle, cry, or scream. If someone trying to feed Roy, for example, manages to put some food in his mouth, Roy may neither chew it nor swallow it, thus preventing any more food being put in. Alternatively, the food may be ejected. Sometimes, vomiting occurs before the meal is finished. Food refusal may be general, or restricted to certain foods or to food presented in certain forms.

Other problems related to food include: eating too fast; eating without utensils; spilling food; eating directly off the plate; throwing food; and over-eating. These are rarely serious problems, usually just indicating a need for training in appropriate eating habits. Over-eating has been studied hardly at all in people with severe mental handicaps. Throwing food is probably best thought of as an example of either non-compliant or aggressive behaviour, which are dealt with in Sections 2 and 3 respectively.

Causes

The prevalence of feeding problems in the condition known as the Prader-Willi syndrome has led to suggestions that such difficulties sometimes have medical causes. People with this syndrome, which is associated with chromosomal abnormality, have a mental handicap (though usually it is not severe), eat to excess, and are usually overweight. They commonly go foraging for food, steal food, and are prepared to eat things of no nutritive value, including refuse and pills.

It has been claimed that pica can sometimes be the result of iron deficiency, on the grounds that one group of 12 children with the problem were all found to be iron deficient and were cured of pica by adding iron to their diets. This behaviour is also said to be more common in countries where iron deficiency is widespread. Interpretation is complicated, however, because pica can *cause* iron deficiency.

The absence of suggested medical causes for rumination has been more or less predetermined by those who have defined it, since they nearly always describe it as regurgitation *not* having any medical cause. Plainly, however, there *can* be medical causes of regurgitation. One is gastroesophageal reflux, in which stomach contents are ejected into the oesophagus because of abnormalities of the muscles where they join. This occurs mostly in people with cerebral palsy and can lead to problems similar to those described as rumination. Stomach or intestinal infections can have similar effects.

Problems of food refusal and overselectivity can be caused by various abnormalities of muscular function, again arising mainly from cerebral palsy. In one study it was estimated that, of 52 cases of delay in taking solid food, nearly 80 per cent were the result of neuromuscular disorders. It seems inappropriate to regard these difficulties as behaviour problems, but they can lead to situations in which people may refuse to take food which they are capable of learning to tolerate and may throw tantrums when pressed. Regurgitation can also occur as a result.

Medication, given for other reasons, can also have an adverse effect. For instance, phenytoin, used to control epilepsy, can reduce sensations of taste, and cause gastric upset and gum disorders, all of which can influence food intake.

There is much evidence that the problem behaviours described can be learned and that antecedents and consequences affect such learning in the usual ways. This applies to people with Prader-Willi syndrome just as much as to those who have similar problems without any medical origin. Food is itself a powerful reinforcing consequence, so that food-stealing brings it own reinforcement. Even pica is likely to result in occasional finds of food, which will intermittently reinforce scavenging. People with very severe handicaps, because of their limited scope for gaining access to other reinforcers, may rely heavily on food and eat almost as much as they can get. Regurgitating what they have eaten so that it can be eaten again may well be a way of obtaining reinforcement, particularly since it has been shown that feeding to capacity decreases the behaviour. Moreover, the regurgitation is elicited by straining movements of the body, sucking movements of the tongue, and probing of the mouth and throat with the fingers, which suggests some motivation to bring it about. There is also evidence which suggests that sensations from having food in the mouth for some time and chewing it are welcome. Children in institutions, at least in the past, have often been deprived of these sensations by speedy and mechanical approaches to feeding; and when, in various investigations, the process has been made more prolonged and more stimulating for them, it has lessened the rumination.

Where people with mental handicaps live in unstimulating conditions some problem behaviours may also be reinforced by attention that would not otherwise be forthcoming, such as the thorough cleansing process needed to clear up the mess after eating faeces. It has been suggested that food refusal problems may also owe much to antecedents and consequences in the environment.

There may, of course, sometimes be an interaction between medical and learning factors. If a person with a mental handicap living in unstimulating conditions vomits for some physical reason, and the results are welcome (attention, for instance), the behaviour may subsequently be repeated voluntarily.

Other problem behaviours related to feeding can occur as part of normal development. Pica, for instance, is very similar to behaviour that occurs in non-handicapped children between one and two years of age and, not uncommonly, beyond that age. If its consequences are reinforcing and other satisfactions are hard to come by for a child who has a mental handicap, the behaviour may well persist and become an established habit.

Incidence

Pica occurs quite commonly in people with mental handicaps living in long stay institutions. In two studies, it was found to occur in eight and 26 per cent respectively of residents. Rumination has been found to occur in 5.3 to 9.6 per cent of such populations, and vomiting in its wider variety of forms in up to 25 per cent. I have not located any information about incidence outside institutions.

Over-eating, leading to obesity, has been found to be a problem among people with mental handicaps in general, but it seems to be less prevalent among those with severe mental handicaps than in those whose handicaps are milder. The scanty data that exist, however, suggest that this problem is less common among people with mental handicaps as a whole than it is in the general population.

Why are they a problem?

Some feeding problems are so severe that they threaten life. Rumination, for instance, can lead to dehydration and malnutrition, and these in turn to lower resistance to disease. Mortality rates for people with this condition have been quoted from 12.5 to 50 per cent, but no doubt other factors are also involved. Refusal to eat is also potentially threatening to life, though as a last resort tube feeding directly into the stomach can keep a person alive. Deaths as a result of pica have not been located in the literature either, though there is always the risk of someone eating something dangerously poisonous (such as household paint containing lead) or extremely damaging.

Most of the problems mentioned have detrimental effects of some kind on health. Rumination, food refusal, and refusal to eat solid food can lead to loss of weight and retarded development. The vomited material in rumination is acid and can damage teeth. Pica can lead to swallowing of poisonous or dangerous substances. Lead poisoning has been reported and this can damage the brain. Some objects may cause intestinal blockages. Intestinal parasites, such as whipworms, may be taken in, particularly when faeces are eaten. The infestation is then sometimes chronic and can lead to diarrhoea or constipation, malnutrition and, consequently, anaemia. According to some authorities, however, over-eating leading to obesity is probably not a serious problem from a health point of view, unless the individual is overweight to an extraordinary degree, that is, something like double the recommended weight.

There are other harmful effects which make intervention in this group of problems a priority. People whose faces and hands are covered in faeces, or whose clothes are covered with vomit, and who smell very unpleasant, are hard to accept socially. It is tempting for those responsible for their daily care to keep away from them; and their companions, unless they are totally undiscriminating, will avoid them. In addition to this, people's preoccupation with these undesirable habits is likely to interfere with their learning of more appropriate behaviours.

Intervention techniques
Defining the problem
For some problems associated with feeding, eliminating the problem behaviour itself is a high priority and the behaviour needs to be clearly defined without delay. Examples of the kind of specific descriptions required are:

> Within five minutes of completing any meal, whoever supervises the process, Bob regurgitates some of it and retains some in the mouth and chews it.

> Whenever Philip is not being observed by hospital staff, he searches for loose objects of almost any kind and consumes them.

In some instances the main feature of the intervention should be to increase alternative appropriate behaviours. Even where directly decreasing the problem behaviour has to be given precedence, appropriate behaviours should also be encouraged. Examples of suitable descriptions of appropriate behaviour are:

> When occupation is not arranged for her by an adult, Diane finds a toy and plays with it with her hands for at least five minutes.

> At meal times, Harry holds his spoon in one hand and holds on to his plate with the other for at least three minutes.

Measuring
Most behaviours specifically related to feeding can be counted without too much difficulty. Either they occur as distinct acts, like eating an unsuitable object or grabbing

one handful of food from a neighbour's plate, or they occur at particular times, such as at breakfast or lunchtime. The latter makes it possible to record whether at each mealtime, a particular kind of rumination did or did not occur. They are not necessarily frequent, however, so long periods of measuring may be needed to achieve records of sufficient size to be interpreted meaningfully. For rumination, larger and more useful measures can sometimes be obtained by recording the number of *separate* times it occurs after every meal, or the proportion of, say, the first hour after each meal which is occupied by it. Much depends on the precise pattern of occurrence.

Identifying existing antecedents and consequences

Some of the most obvious antecedents of problem behaviours related to eating are not very helpful in planning an intervention. Food-stealing may be prompted by the sight of food, but this can hardly be changed at mealtimes. Pica might be prompted by the sight of an object, but it is hard to remove all objects. If people go foraging for objects to eat, this seems to require no external antecedents. The main antecedents of rumination are those emanating from eating itself, which should certainly not be removed. However, there is evidence that very rapid and unstimulating feeding methods can function as antecedents, and these can be changed. Such methods of feeding can also make food refusal more likely. The influence of setting antecedents has been shown by evidence that disruptive mealtime behaviours are less if eating takes place in family, rather than cafeteria, style.

Some consequences of eating-related behaviours also seem inevitable – reinforcement by the food itself, for instance, or by the stimulation of eating movements. It is, however, possible that various forms of attention can be reinforcing for a behaviour such as pica or food refusal. These can be modified.

Changing antecedents and consequences for intervention programmes

As already suggested, some antecedents and consequences associated with the problem behaviour can often be removed, modified, or used in different ways. Where this is not so, new antecedents and consequences will have to be employed. Even though the emphasis in planning interventions must sometimes be on directly eliminating the problem behaviour, measures to increase appropriate behaviour should always be sought. Where the problem behaviour is not immediately dangerous, appropriate behaviours should be the main focus.

Anything that prompts appropriate eating behaviour is potentially useful as an antecedent for encouraging other behaviours as alternatives to the problem behaviours. Demonstration, explanation, and physical prompting can be used, for instance, to teach proper use of a spoon or to encourage people to eat more slowly as part of a programme to reduce weight. It cannot be assumed that this will lead to a decrease in the problem behaviour, but it does help sometimes.

One study illustrating these procedures featured six children with severe mental handicaps, very limited eating skills, and a range of such inappropriate behaviours as screaming, spitting, throwing food, getting out of the chair, playing with food, licking the table or floor, and allowing food to fall out of the mouth. The intervention procedure was complex. The antecedent elements were: firstly, to divide each of the three daily meals into two "mini-meals" each of 15 minutes' duration, which provided more opportunities for learning; and, secondly, to provide manual guidance in spoon feeding. Two trainers were involved. One of them sat by the child's non-preferred arm and physically prevented it from being used for eating or disruptive behaviour. The other held the child's preferred hand and guided it to spoon food from the plate and transfer it to the mouth. The trainer's hand was gradually shifted to the wrist, then to the forearm, upper arm, and shoulder in succession, so that appropriate eating was brought about with progressively less guidance.

More complex guidance techniques have been described in weight reduction pro-grammes in which people with severe mental handicaps have been taught about healthy eating and the need for exercise, and have been given instruction in weight reduction techniques.

Methods of guidance too specialised to deal with here have been recommended for eating problems associated with cerebral palsy. Useful sources are Coupe *et al.* (1987), Palmer and Horn (1978), Utley, Holvoet, and Barnes (1977), Morris (1977), Warner (1981b), and a particularly comprehensive account by Anderson (1983). People with difficulty in controlling their movements can be helped by provision of devices for anchoring food and drink containers, such as non-slip mats and non-tip meal trays.

An antecedent device which has been used specifically for refusing to eat certain kinds of food is to camouflage those foods with something more appealing.

Reinforcing consequences for appropriate behaviours can be used in two main ways: to reinforce abstaining (that is, engaging in any behaviour *other* than the one that is a problem); and to reinforce specific behaviours incompatible with, or with the same purpose as, the problem behaviour. Example 1 shows how differential reinforcement of other behaviour (DRO) was used to decrease the incidence of food-stealing in a woman with a severe mental handicap by giving her tokens (exchangeable for various items of more concrete value) for periods of abstaining. Example 2 describes an application of the same procedure for rumination in a young man with a profound mental handicap, who was reinforced with food for periods of not ruminating. Two examples from my own workshops illustrate differential reinforcement of incompatible behaviour (DRI). In Example 3 five-year-old Sally, whose problem consisted of a range of behaviours to resist eating the first course of her school dinner, was reinforced for taking each spoonful of first course by being given a spoonful of the sweet, accompanied by praise. She could not do this and resist taking it at the same time, so an increase in the appropriate behaviour made a decrease in the problem behaviour highly likely. In Example 4, food-stealing at dinner in 12-year-old David was greatly decreased by giving him an extra spoonful of food (together with praise) for keeping his hand under the table while he and the teacher counted up to a certain number, this being repeated several times after completion of each course. In weight reduction programmes people with severe mental handicaps have been reinforced both for adhering to their specified programmes and for weight loss.

There are several examples in the literature of modifications of the feeding process used to generate antecedents to make problem behaviours less likely. An antecedent affecting internal state which has been used in a number of studies is *satiation*, in which people are, at each meal, fed until they can take no more. Since they are then no longer hungry, they should no longer engage in behaviours which are reinforced by food. Example 5 describes how this technique was used to decrease rumination in an adult with a profound mental handicap. This course of action should be used only on a short-term basis, so that the people involved do not become seriously overweight. Unfortunately, there is evidence to show that satiation is effective more because of the calories the food contains than because it fills people up, though bulky low-calorie meals have brought some success. For rumination, satiation does not usually present a weight problem at first because the person being fed is usually underweight.

An interesting recent study found that giving a solution of one part of granulated alum in 10 parts of water decreased rumination when given in advance of its occurrence. Alum produces an uncomfortable dry sensation in the mouth, and it was suggested that this stimulation was an acceptable substitute for the stimulation of vomit and therefore made rumination unnecessary. Alum is a normal food ingredient and unlikely to be harmful, but it is an unusual treatment, so that consultation with a doctor is advised before considering it.

An antecedent-based approach for rumination based more on specific environmental changes assumes that rumination is a means of obtaining stimulation which is denied by institutional methods of feeding. If the needed stimulation is supplied during the feeding process, it is assumed that the person will no longer need to engage in the behaviour. Example 6 describes how regurgitation was eliminated in a boy with a profound mental handicap by a feeding method which involved increased stimulation and active participation by the boy in the feeding process. The boy was encouraged to grasp the teat of the feeding bottle rather than have milk squirted into his mouth, and to bite food off a spoon rather than having the attendant scrape it off against his teeth. A method, similar in principle, has been used in the special care unit of an English school with a boy with multiple handicaps. The approach was to offer the boy food only when he gave some indication that he was ready – by reaching for the spoon or dish, or by looking at the dish and making some kind of noise. Rumination was decreased further by prolonging the eating procedure, a teacher placing the boy's hand carefully round the spoon and "spinning out" the time taken in helping him to hold it and scoop up the food. Even holding a child with a mental handicap during and after a meal has been found to decrease rumination.

In another study, rumination was decreased in a man with a profound handicap by giving him the same total amount of food at each meal, but spacing it out into five portions each eaten 15 minutes apart. This was accompanied by interruption of the ruminating, and graduated guidance which helped the man to fill his spoon to a normal level and to do this only after swallowing the previous spoonful.

Another antecedent device is to alter the nature of the food. Increasing the solid content is one approach that has been used, and Example 10 describes how milk-based foods were eliminated as part of an intervention for rumination in a five-year-old girl with a mental handicap. Conversely, the food can be made more liquid for people who find it difficult to cope with solid food.

Reducing consequences have been the most widely used techniques for tackling problems related to feeding. Dramatic results have been obtained with such techniques as electric shock, but these would not be tolerated in this country. Putting irritating liquids into the mouth have also been used in a number of studies, and this might be justified as a last resort where problems are otherwise totally intractable. Example 10 describes putting a lotion for discouraging nail-biting into the mouth as part of an intervention package for rumination when other devices had been found to have only a short-term effect.

The mildest types of reducing consequences are those that prevent reinforcement of problem behaviour. Extinction, the prevention of natural reinforcing consequences, has been used in a number of studies. Example 7 describes how altering the timing of the shower of a seven-year-old boy with a profound mental handicap prevented it from reinforcing eating and smearing faeces. In Example 10 regurgitation was thought to be reinforced by parental attention in a five-year-old girl with a mental handicap, and this was reduced as part of an intervention package by cleaning up the mess from behind, with minimal eye contact, conversation, or other attention. Extinction of refusing to eat solid foods has sometimes been achieved by offering nothing but solid food, in other words, never allowing the behaviour to be reinforced by obtaining the preferred liquid food. Satiation and use of alum have already been described as antecedents because they are introduced in advance. They may also act by preventing reinforcement of the problem behaviour, at least until the individual learns to predict that no reinforcement will occur when these procedures have been implemented.

Time-out techniques have been used a little. In Example 8, for instance, a young man with a profound handicap was provided with music unless he ruminated, when it was switched off for a short period. Removal to a time-out room has also been used. In Example 1, with a 28-year-old woman, whenever food-stealing incidents were discovered the trainer removed tokens that had been won for not stealing food. This is an example of response cost.

If more severe reducing consequences are required, making someone do something unwelcome can be reasonably acceptable. Where this technique has been used for feeding-related behaviours it has usually involved activities which might be thought of as correcting the problem behaviours. In the study of six children with severe mental handicaps referred to earlier, for instance, the reducing consequence for inappropriate behaviour at mealtimes was to be guided in cleaning up any spilled food, followed by practising loading food and taking it to the mouth three times before being allowed to eat. In Example 9, a young man with a profound handicap who ate cigarette ends was made to clean out his mouth and scrub his hands to excess, and then empty and wipe ashtrays. Making a person brush his teeth and wipe his lips with an oral antiseptic was, in one study, found to be very effective for reducing rumination. Unwelcome activities not related to the problem behaviour have also been used. For instance, functional movement training (moving the arms to a series of different positions repeatedly, for example, up, down, out, to the front) was found to be effective in decreasing such behaviours as refusing to open the mouth, spitting food out, turning the head away, and grabbing the plate or throwing the spoon in a 10-year-old child with a profound mental handicap. These are all techniques which have been called overcorrection.

There are also some unwelcome things that might be done to a person that are more acceptable than others, such as blindfolding, physical restraint, and water mist which have all been used to reduce food-related problems. In Example 8, saying "No" sharply was part of the intervention procedure for decreasing rumination in a man with a profound handicap and was finally effective on its own.

Combinations of various approaches have been reported in the literature. Example 10 describes how regurgitation in a five-year-old girl with a mental handicap was tackled by a combination of cutting down on milk-based foods as an antecedent, withholding parental attention when she regurgitated (extinction), providing attention as often as possible when she did not (DRO), and finally adding an unpleasant-tasting liquid as a reducing consequence for the problem behaviour. In Example 1, differential reinorcement of other behaviour (DRO) by awarding tokens for abstaining from food-stealing was accompanied by removing tokens as a reducing consequence for the problem behaviour. In Example 8 two reducing consequences for rumination in a man with a profound mental handicap were combined: turning music off in a "time-out" procedure, and saying "No" sharply.

Additional measures

Medical procedures have sometimes been used for food-related problems that do not have known medical causes. Food refusal, for instance, has been treated by forced feeding, intravenous feeding, and tubes inserted directly into the stomach or intestine. However, these methods do not promote effective eating habits, and the insertion of tubes is said to bring health risks of its own. Clearly, medical advice is needed on whether there are physical causes which can be treated.

The nature of the food given to a person may be relevant to treatment for physiological as well as psychological reasons. In Example 10, for instance, where the decreasing of milk-based foods was part of an intervention package for rumination in five-year-old Sarah, success could have been due to either reason, if indeed these measures were relevant to the outcome at all.

Medication has sometimes been used to control vomiting, but there is no clear evidence that is is helpful for people in whom no medical cause of vomiting has been found.

Subsequent action

Example 10 provides an illustration of how one intervention programme was replaced by a more effective one. Rumination in five-year-old Sarah, as already described, was tackled by restricting milk-based foods and drinks, and by minimising attention following regurgitation and providing much attention when she abstained from the behaviour. After a period of improvement, regurgitation mysteriously increased again. Sarah's parents then put an unpleasant-tasting liquid in her mouth each time she regurgitated and the regurgitation then decreased again and was finally eliminated.

In Example 1, an intervention programme for food-stealing in a young woman was transferred from one environment to another. Tokens for abstaining were first given in a training room in the hospital and the procedure was then transferred to a recreation room. Modified programmes were also introduced at various times into the wider hospital environment, into her group home after discharge from hospital, and finally into an apartment style living arrangement.

Gradual fading out of an intervention programme is illustrated by Example 3. A five-year-old girl was at first reinforced for taking each spoonful of the first course of her lunch by a spoonful of the sweet. She was gradually made to take more spoonfuls of the first course before the sweet reinforcement was given.

Illustrative studies

Example 1 (Page *et al.*, 1983a)

The person in this study was a 28-year-old woman, who had a severe mental handicap, was extremely overweight, and lived in a small group home. For the intervention she was admitted to a hospital. The procedures were carried out first in a training room, where she was left on her own with furniture, books, and magazines, and then in a recreation room, where there was a wider variety of activities available and staff and other patients were present. Implementation was by a special trainer and recording was carried out by independent observers.

The problem to decrease was food-stealing. Since, during the intervention sessions, no eating was supposed to take place, the behaviour was defined as any instance of food coming into contact with the young woman's lips. She was prompted to engage in some activity, told that the food was not to be eaten, and then left on her own. The number of occurrences of stealing was observed through a one-way mirror in 15- and 30-minute observation sessions, and the rate per minute was calculated. After a baseline of 16 sessions the intervention was begun without reported investigation of antecedents and consequences in advance. The procedure was the same as during the baseline, except that tokens (exchangeable at the end of a session for low-calorie snacks, or saveable for more costly items such as magazines and cosmetics) were given for periods without stealing. She was also praised. The periods were 30 seconds long at first, but were gradually increased to two hours. During the baseline in the training room, the rate of stealing averaged 1.0 per minute, whereas during the intervention it occurred hardly at all. A similarly high baseline rate in the recreation room was reduced to zero when the intervention procedures were introduced.

This intervention illustrates the use of reinforcement through a token system of any behaviour other than the problem one (differential reinforcement of other behaviour or DRO). Full interpretation, however, is complicated by early extension of essentially the same approach to the whole hospital environment throughout the day, combined with taking tokens away if regular inspection of the woman's room revealed possession of illicit food or food containers or wrappers (response cost). A marked loss in weight indicated that the overall effect was beneficial. Later, a modified version of the intervention was implemented in the group home by the staff there after the woman was discharged from hospital. Later still, it was transferred to an apartment-style living arrangement. The woman's weight continued to decline throughout these changes.

Example 2 (Conrin *et al.*, 1982)

John was a 23-year-old young man with a profound handicap, who had no spoken language, was blind, and had a deformity of the spine. He ruminated regularly after meals, beginning immediately the meal was finished and continuing for about two hours. The intervention was carried out in the everyday situation, probably by institution staff, with recording by independent observers.

For half an hour after each meal John was seated in a chair and a stopwatch was used to measure the number of seconds spent in ruminating during each recording period. The timing began each time a swelling of the cheeks indicated regurgitation, and was suspended when a movement of the Adam's apple and subsidence of the cheek swelling showed that the material had been re-swallowed.

After a baseline of five sessions an intervention programme was introduced without recorded advance study of antecedents and consequences. For every 15 seconds without rumination, John was given small pieces of biscuits or small amounts of peanut butter. This continued for half-an-hour. During the baseline John ruminated almost throughout the observation sessions; whereas for the eight sessions with reinforcement for every 15 seconds free of rumination, this behaviour averaged only 30.4 seconds per half-hour session. Subsequently the period of abstaining required before reinforcement was lengthened, until eventually it was every 10 minutes. Soon ruminating fell to an average of less than 20 seconds per half-hour session, where it remained for a period containing over 70 meals. Though the problem behaviour was not completely eliminated, John's weight increased from 79 lbs during baseline to 111 lbs by the end of the programme.

In this intervention John was effectively reinforced for engaging in any behaviour other than ruminating, that is, an instance of differential reinforcement of other behaviour (or DRO).

Example 3
Sally, aged five years, was a pupil of Mrs. X., a teacher in one of my workshops. She had a severe mental handicap, could sit but not walk, had virtually no speech, and was not at all toilet trained. Although she could hold a biscuit and suck it she made no attempt to chew and, although she would put all sorts of other objects into her mouth, she made no attempt to put her lunch in. She would reach for her plate, but then only tip it or knock it over. Her thumb or fist was continually in her mouth, making it difficult to feed her; and she was resistant to being fed the first course, often ending up having a tantrum in which she screamed, threw herself back in her chair, went rigid, went limp, and slid or fell forward in her chair, or bit her own fist. Both the intervention and its measurement were carried out by the teacher in school.

The problem behaviour was not precisely defined, Mrs. X. preferring to work on an appropriate behaviour incompatible with the one that was a problem. This was defined as willingly taking a spoonful of first course during the school mid-day lunch. During the baseline no attempt was made to influence this. Sally was fed the first course until she was unwilling to continue, but was given no sweet. The number of spoonfuls willingly accepted was recorded for each meal.

After a baseline of eight days an intervention programme was introduced. Existing antecedents and consequences were not studied, but the programme was based on the observation that Sally usually willingly accepted her sweet and appeared to enjoy it. She was also thought to like being told she was "a good girl". Each lunch time, therefore, she was offered a spoonful of first course and, if it was taken willingly, was reinforced by a spoonful of sweet and by "Good girl". If this was also taken she was praised again and offered another spoonful of first course, which was again followed by praise and a spoonful of sweet if it was taken willingly. This continued, each lunchtime, until the food was either definitely refused or not swallowed. Sometimes an initial refusal was followed by a re-offering, accompanied by the words "Good girl", until the food was either accepted or definitely refused. Over 14 days, the number of spoonfuls of first course accepted averaged 5.3, whereas during the baseline it had been 2.5. Perhaps more telling is the observation that, in the eight baseline measurements, Sally took more than three mouthfuls only once, while during the programme she exceeded this in eight of the 14 measurements. Mrs. X. herself thought there had been some improvement and was pleased that there were now no temper tantrums during the mealtime. She felt also that she herself now had a more relaxed attitude to the problems, which helped. Follow-up the next term found Mrs. X. still using the approach described and Sally's improvement maintained. She was now prepared to take a number of spoonfuls of first course before being reinforced by a spoonful of sweet. Within weeks Sally was eating the *whole* of the first course for just a few spoonfuls of sweet.

In this intervention the problem behaviours involved in refusing food were more or less eliminated by a procedure in which the girl was reinforced for a behaviour incompatible with them: willingly taking spoonfuls of first course. This procedure is known as differential reinforcement of incompatible behaviour (or DRI).

Example 4

Mrs. K., who attended one of my workshops, chose to work with David. He was 13 years old, had a severe mental handicap, was blind, and was very overweight. He showed a wide range of behaviour problems which included snatching and scooping up other children's food from their plates at lunchtimes, finger-sucking, rocking, repeated flushing of the toilet, crying and screaming when crossed, throwing furniture, and pushing other children off chairs. Both the intervention and its measurement were carried out by the teacher in school.

Mrs. K. decided to begin by tackling the problem of scooping up food from other children's plates at lunchtimes. The number of incidents was recorded at lunchtime each day.

After 10 days of baseline recording the intervention began, without study of existing antecedents and consequences. Mrs. K. identified an appropriate behaviour incompatible with food-stealing: David keeping his hands under the table when he was not supposed to be eating. Mrs. K. explained to David that, after each course was completed they were going to count to 10 together, while David kept his hands under the table and that, if he did this, he would have an extra spoonful of food. This was done several times after each of the two courses, and each extra spoonful was accompanied by praise and a pat on the shoulder. After four days, the counting was extended to 20, and after another four days it was dropped.

For the 10 days of recording during intervention the average number of food-stealing incidents was only 1.9, compared with 16.1 during the baseline. At the end of the workshop Mrs. K. intended to lengthen gradually the period for which David had to keep his hands under the table before being reinforced, and then eventually to discontinue the reinforcement.

In this intervention frequency of the problem behaviour of food-stealing was decreased by reinforcing an appropriate behaviour incompatible with it − keeping hands under the table; a procedure known as differential reinforcement of incompatible behaviour (or DRI).

Example 5 (Jackson *et al.*, 1975)

The intervention described here was with a 29-year-old man with a profound mental handicap living in an institution, whose vomiting and rumination had resulted in very severe weight losses which had put his life in danger. The intervention was carried out in the everyday institution environment. Recording was by independent observers, but it is not clear whether the programme was carried out by the experimenters or by institution staff.

Each session in both the baseline and the intervention was an hour long, and a session followed immediately upon each of the three meals of the day. Immediately after the meal the young man was returned to his home room and measuring began. A vomiting response was defined as any occasion when vomitus left the mouth. The number of such responses per session was recorded using a mechanical hand counter. During the baseline, this measuring followed normal institution meals.

After 15 baseline sessions an intervention commenced, without reported study in advance of the effects of antecedents and consequences. The young man was fed double the usual size of the meal, and then additional food until he refused food twice with a one-minute interval between the refusals. Immediately after the session, he was offered about half a litre of milkshake to maintain satiation throughout the day. During the baseline the number of vomiting responses per session varied from about 80 to about 320, whereas during the intervention it was always below 40. The rate increased with a return to baseline and decreased again when the programme was reinstated. From then onwards, the young man received double portions of the standard meals, and follow-up after 10 days of this modifed procedure found an average of 17.2 responses per session over six meals. About six weeks after the start of the first intervention period, the young man's weight had increased from 35.83 kg to 49.44 kg.

In this study it appears that satiation with food prevented reinforcement of the young man's vomiting behaviour, which therefore decreased. Alternatively, since the food was eaten in advance it could have been acting as an antecedent, or may have come to do so as the young man learned to predict its effects.

Example 6 (Ball, Hendricksen, and Clayton, 1974)
The person in this investigation was an 11-year-old boy in an institution who had a profound mental handicap, visual handicap, motor difficulties due to cerebral palsy, and no speech. He was on a diet of puréed food and milk given by a feeding bottle, and vomiting typically occurred during the meal. The intervention was carried out in the ordinary hospital setting by one of the hospital staff, though recording was by independent observers.

The investigation was organised in sessions immediately before the boy had his main meals. He was fed 60cc of apple sauce by spoon, then 60cc of milk from a bottle and another 60cc of apple sauce, the feeding being spaced so that the length of sessions remained around the same average level. Regurgitation was defined as any flow of previously ingested food. The number of clear-cut, separate regurgitations per session was measured.

During the baseline measuring, the standard institutional feeding method was used. Puréed foods were given by spoon, which was quickly withdrawn with a scraping movement against the boy's upper teeth, excess food then being scraped off the chin. Milk was squirted into his mouth with no contact with the teat.

After a baseline of seven feeding sessions the intervention began, with no reported advance investigation of the effects of antecedents and consequences. A feeding technique was used which emphasised the boy's active part in the feeding process. The bottle remained in his mouth, he seized it between his teeth while it was moved back and forth or up and down in a "tug of war", and the teat was occasionally moved from one corner of the mouth to the other for more varied stimulation. For the puréed foods, the spoon was held in his mouth and the food removed by his teeth movements. When biting slowed down, the spoon was tapped against the front teeth to start it again. During the baseline, regurgitations occurred at an average rate of 1.7 per session, whereas during the first six intervention sessions it averaged 0.3. There was then a return to baseline conditions, which increased the rate to 1.7 again. Reinstatement of the special feeding methods decreased regurgitation to zero.

In this intervention the special feeding method acted as a set of antecedents which made the problem behaviour less likely to occur.

Example 7 (Friedin and Johnson, 1979)

John was a seven-year-old boy with a profound mental handicap resident in a development centre. Although he could walk and understand a few very simple instructions, he could not talk, had very few self-help skills, and had only just been toilet trained. The intervention was carried out and records kept by centre staff, with monitoring by a psychologist.

Two behaviours were identified, though treated as one for both intervention and measurement purposes. Faeces-eating was defined as the presence of faeces in or around the mouth and on the hands. Faeces-smearing was defined as the presence of faeces on the hands and any part of the body and/or furniture or walls. Delegated staff recorded incidents on a chart, posted near the staff office, together with details of the precise times and places. Records were kept from 4.30 pm to 7.00 pm each day, since this was the period of most frequent occurrence.

Intervention began after a three-week baseline, and was planned in the light of particular prior observations. The high, and increasing, incidence of the problem behaviour in the early evening, and John's apparent enjoyment of being showered, dried with a towel, and dressed in fresh clothing led to the hypothesis that these cleaning up procedures reinforced the problem behaviours. An evening shower was usual around 7.00 pm and the faecal problems resulted in John having his earlier than he would otherwise have done. Shower time was therefore changed to 4.30 pm for John alone, and he was often allowed to play in the shower for a few additional minutes before being dressed in pyjamas. For any incidents of eating or smearing of faeces at any time of the day, he was simply washed; and if these occurred in the afternoon before 4.30 pm, he was not showered. Over the course of 30 weeks, the shower time was gradually changed to the hour between 6.00 pm and 7.00 pm. At first, John was showered before the rest of the group, but eventually he was mixed into the order. There were five incidents of eating and/or smearing faeces during the three-week baseline, and only six during the first 20 weeks of intervention. There were no instances during the last 10 weeks of this, nor at follow-up eight weeks later. There was also a decrease during the times outside 4.30 to 7.30 pm.

In this investigation the problem behaviour appeared to decrease as a result of eliminating reinforcing consequences which had formerly maintained it. This is the procedure normally referred to as extinction.

Example 8 (Davis, Wieseler, and Hanzel, 1983)

This investigation was carried out with a 26-year-old young man in an institution, who had a profound mental handicap and a long history of rumination. The intervention was implemented and recorded first by the experimenters in specially arranged settings, and later in the man's classroom in the institution, when the teacher was involved.

Rumination was defined and counted as the constriction of the man's throat muscles to regurgitate food. The number of incidents per session was at first recorded in each of three daily 12-minute sessions, half-an-hour after each meal. The sessions took place in an experimental room where the man was given a pegboard and bluegrass music was played for him.

After 15 days of baseline recording, an intervention programme was begun for the after-breakfast session only. It was based on the prior observation that the man found putting pegs in a pegboard a welcome activity, and that he often smiled and laughed when bluegrass music was played and had tantrums when it was turned off. During the intervention, therefore, as in the baseline the man was seated with a pegboard and a cassette recording of the music was played. Each time he ruminated the music was turned off for 10 seconds. If he ruminated again during this time, the music stayed off for 10 seconds after that. During the session the same procedure also operated for out-of-seat behaviour and other problems. The average number of ruminations per session decreased from 25 during the baseline to seven over 15 days of intervention. In later phases the frequency was decreased further by turning the music off for 30 seconds instead of 10. It was then decreased to zero by saying, "No", sharply at the same time as turning off the music.

After the above achievements, and various other procedures which operated at other times of the day, the 30 seconds of music deprivation and saying "No" procedures were transferred to the classroom, after a baseline period there. The after-lunch session procedures were implemented by the class teacher. They rapidly eliminated rumination in the classroom, and this continued when the music was gradually decreased in volume and finally discontinued.

In this investigation music was provided when there was no rumination, a form of differential reinforcement of other behaviour (DRO), and the music was switched off for a specified period whenever rumination occurred (time-out from reinforcement of appropriate behaviour). The procedure was made more effective by adding a sharp verbal, "No". Two reducing consequences for the problem behaviour were, therefore, eventually combined.

Example 9 (Foxx and Martin, 1975)

One of the people in this investigation was Bobby, a 33-year-old man living in an institution, who had a profound mental handicap and who scavenged for cigarette ends, picking them out of unflushed toilets, off the floor, or from ashtrays, and consumed them. The intervention was carried out on the ward by a "trainer" (it is not clear if this was a regular staff member or not) and recorded by independent observers.

The behaviour was defined as the gathering and eating of cigarette ends. During the baseline a cigarette end was placed in an easily seen ashtray every 15 minutes, during an eight-hour period each day, and a record was made if Bobby took it during that interval. Whenever he was found with a cigarette end he was admonished, and was made to spit it out and wash his hands and mouth.

After four days of baseline recording an intervention was begun, without reported advance study of antecedents and consequences. The ashtray was checked after 15-minute waits and, if Bobby had taken the cigarette end, he was subjected to an overcorrection procedure. For 10 minutes he had to brush his mouth, teeth, and gums gently with a soft toothbrush soaked in an antiseptic mouthwash. For the following 10 minutes he had to wash his hands and scrub his fingernails in warm soapy water with a soft fingernail brush. Finally, 10 minutes was spent in emptying and wiping out ashtrays. He was physically guided when necessary. At the end of this process another cigarette end was placed in the ashtray for the next 15-minute period. During the baseline, Bobby took the cigarette end every time, but this decreased to 50 per cent on the first day of intervention, and was near zero within four days. He remained at this level throughout the eight week period in which the intervention continued.

In this study, making a young man engage in unwelcome activities in an overcorrection procedure was a reducing consequence for the problem behaviour.

Example 10 (Hewitt and Burden, 1984)

Sarah was five years old. She had cerebral palsy and a severe mental handicap. She lived at home with her parents, who carried out the intervention at home under the guidance of a clinical psychologist.

The problem behaviour was regurgitating food, which Sarah then appeared to enjoy eating. The parents kept a record of the number of occurrences by methods which are not described.

After a week an intervention programme was initiated. It was based on a variety of trial observations. Firstly, it was thought that Sarah regurgitated more frequently after milk or milk-based foods. Secondly, the behaviour did not occur at school. Thus, the nature of the food and the home environment could be regarded as antecedents for the problem behaviour. Thirdly, informal observation showed that the parents reacted to regurgitation by talking to Sarah and providing eye contact while she was cleaned up and her clothes were changed. These reactions could have been reinforcing the problem behaviour.

The intervention programme attempted to minimise these influences. Milk-based food and drink was restricted and, when regurgitation occurred, Sarah's parents did not respond for five minutes or more. If it was necessary to deal with the mess they then did so from behind, avoiding eye contact and conversation, and being as impersonal as possible. In addition they provided, as often as they could, direct eye-contact, conversation, physical contact, and play when Sarah had not regurgitated. Over the next five weeks there was a steady improvement. In that period regurgitation occurred only 18 times, whereas it had been 44 during the baseline week. Mysteriously, it then increased steadily again over the next seven weeks, almost to its former level. It was decided to try doing something unwelcome to Sarah as a consequence of regurgitation. Lemon juice in the mouth appeared to be enjoyed, but she grimaced and turned her face away when a liquid to deter nail-biting was put into her mouth. This was therefore done each time she regurgitated, from behind with no eye contact or conversation. The problem behaviour then declined sharply, and over a six-month period was eliminated completely.

In this study the problem behaviour was decreased: first by minimising antecedents and consequences thought to have been promoting it and by reinforcing abstaining (that is, reinforcing any other behaviour); and later by adding to this a reducing consequence for the problem behaviour itself.

PART C

Specific problems

SECTION 7. DROOLING

Definition, causes, and incidence

Definition

Drooling is the escape of saliva from the mouth. Usually it dribbles out of an open mouth, but there is a report of one young man who held his mouth closed until it was over-full, the saliva then coming out in a mouthful.

Causes and incidence

Drooling can occur in people with mental handicaps who are not known to have a clearly relevant medical condition, but study of the problem has centred on those with cerebral palsy, where the incidence is fairly high. In a Scottish Spastics Centre, for instance, 21 out of the 232 children there drooled to various degrees, though only 10 did so constantly and profusely. In these instances the cause is nearly always thought to be a difficulty in using mouth and tongue muscles effectively. Firstly, saliva may easily escape through the mouth because of difficulty in keeping the lips closed. Secondly, the normal movements of the tongue and the muscles around the mouth, which propel the saliva to the back of the throat, may be disordered. Indeed, the tongue sometimes operates to move it in the *opposite* direction. Thirdly, there may be some difficulty in swallowing, though usually this is not a problem if the saliva can get right to the back of the throat. So far as is known, the amount of saliva produced is normal.

Drooling can occur also as a side-effect of medication, such as when haloperidol is used to control violent behaviour.

Why is it a problem?

Constant drooling makes a person very unattractive and therefore affects social adjustment. It is notable that, in Example 3, a young man with a severe mental handicap who lived in a hospital was able to move from a hospital ward to a pre-discharge villa just because of increased control over his drooling.

Intervention techniques

Defining the problem
Definition is fairly standard, and varies little from:

> Alex allows saliva to exude from mouth sufficiently to make his chin wet constantly.

Most intervention approaches have concentrated on increasing alternative appropriate behaviours, such as closing the lips or swallowing saliva. An example of a suitable description of such behaviours might be:

> Whenever saliva accumulates in the mouth sufficiently for there to be a risk of drooling, Alex swallows it.

Measuring the problem
Three main methods of measuring have been described. One is to weigh a bib worn by the person before and after a fixed period of time, and thus calculate the weight of saliva which has come out. Another is to observe at regular intervals, note whether the person is wet or dry, and calculate the percentage of intervals the person is found to be wet. A third is similar, but the criterion is whether there is a movement of saliva on lips or chin at the moment of observation. It is also possible to measure alternative appropriate behaviours, such as keeping the mouth closed or swallowing.

Identifying existing antecedents and consequences
This has been studied hardly at all.

Changing antecedents and consequences for intervention programmes
Research studies, which have been few, have focused almost entirely on increasing alternative appropriate behaviours, these usually being to keep the lips closed or to swallow. Before scientific study began, treatment was usually by speech or occupational therapists, and some of their methods have been incorporated into recently validated procedures. These methods tend to emphasise making muscle tone more normal, and appropriate movement patterns easier. A suitable posture is considered important, and the head is supported if necessary. Keeping the jaw closed, by finger pressure on the lips, chin, and under the chin, is thought to inhibit unwanted movements of the jaw and tongue which are likely to occur in people with cerebral palsy and so interfere with normal functioning. Pressure from the finger under the chin is also used to influence tongue movements which aid swallowing. Stroking the throat gently down both sides of the Adam's apple with the thumb and index finger is thought to promote swallowing, while finger pressure between the upper lip and nose is said to lead to closure of the lips and swallowing. Games of sucking (particularly with a straw) and blowing can be used to strengthen lip and tongue movements, and the person can be shown these movements in a mirror as they occur in order to increase awareness of them.

These various approaches can be viewed as specific event antecedents which make appropriate behaviours more likely to occur. Example 1 illustrates their use to promote mouth closing and swallowing with an 11-year-old boy with a mental handicap and cerebral palsy. Before attempting any measures of this kind it is wise to ask for a demonstration by a speech therapist or an occupational therapist, who may also recommend other procedures, such as running ice along the lips to aid closure.

Simply teaching someone to swallow may be insufficient. The person may also need guiding techniques to encourage swallowing to occur at the right times. In published studies such techniques have included teaching swallowing on command and using an auditory reminder. Both of these were used in Example 2, in which a seven-year-old girl with a severe mental handicap was taught first to swallow to command, and then to do so every time she heard a "bleep" from a simple electronic device which she wore. It is also possible to use a "reminding" device for keeping the lips closed. The person holds an electronic device, called the *Exeter Lip Sensor,* between closed lips for short periods. Whenever the lips are opened the sensor makes a noise, reminding the person to close them again. This continues until the person keeps the lips closed even when the device is not being worn.

Reinforcing consequences for appropriate behaviour have also been used. In Example 2 much praise was given for having a "dry chin" when the behaviour was being generalised from speech therapy sessions to the classroom. Example 4 describes similar reinforcement (combined with a reducing consequence for drooling) used with a 15-year-old girl with a profound handicap and cerebral palsy. This procedure effectively reinforced abstaining from drooling or any behaviour other than drooling (an example of differential reinforcement of other behaviour or DRO). A modification of the *Exeter Lip Sensor* (the *TS Model)* can be used for reinforcing mouth closure. This device is connected to a tape recorder which plays a tune or a story while the mouth is closed, but stops if it opens.

Drooling is more a failure to produce appropriate behaviour than engagement in problem behaviour. Therefore, use of antecedents and consequences to decrease it might not be expected. Nevertheless, Example 4 includes a technique which is plainly designed as a reducing consequence for drooling. Every time the girl's chin was found to be wet, she had to wipe her lips and chin 10 times with each of five tissues. In another similar study, an 11-year-old girl had to clean up the saliva with a paper towel and press a tissue lightly under her lips for 30 seconds every time she drooled.

It is clear that combinations of techniques have been the norm in the small number of studies published. Intervention techniques have also been used to promote wiping of the mouth but this, though useful, is not really a method of decreasing the problem behaviour.

Additional measures

One device which has been used to keep the mouth closed is a *chin cup,* a firm structure worn round the chin and attached to a headstrap with elastic. It was designed to produce a degree of light, upward pressure on the chin, sufficient to maintain mouth closure when needed without interfering too much with eating and drinking. It was also intended to give people an idea of closing their mouths, and can therefore be thought of as an antecedent to make this behaviour more likely to occur.

Surgical procedures have sometimes been used to counter drooling. These have included removal of salivary glands, cutting the nerve supply to these glands so that they do not function fully, cutting the ducts which carry saliva from the glands to the mouth, and re-routeing some of these ducts so that the saliva emerges nearer to the back of the throat. Often, these techniques are only partially successful, and some can have adverse side-effects. All four major salivary glands must be removed to halt the flow of saliva effectively, and this is difficult and dangerous. Cutting the nerves is difficult to achieve completely, and can also destroy the sense of taste. Cutting salivary ducts can lead to infection and other complications. While one recent study reported considerable success with children with cerebral palsy, it seems unlikely that anyone would wish to use such measures unless the drooling were severely incapacitating and a range of other methods had been tried and had failed.

Atropine (*Atropinol*) and propantheline (*Pro-Banthine)* can help to "dry up" drooling in severe cases, but such medication is rarely used because it also dries up other secretions thereby increasing the risk of infection in the eyes and chest, and tooth decay is increased. These drugs can also lead to constipation.

Subsequent action

Example 3 illustrates transfer of an intervention programme to a new environment. A young man in a mental handicap hospital was taught to swallow to reduce his drooling. This was first carried out in a training room, then transferred to the hospital workshop.

Example 2 includes some degree of fading out of an intervention programme. A seven-year-old girl was taught to swallow in response to an audible reminder every 30 seconds, and was then encouraged to control her dribbling without it for short periods.

Illustrative studies

Example 1 (Ray, Bundy, and Nelson, 1983)

The person in this study was an 11-year-old boy with a mental handicap, whose cerebral palsy affected all four limbs, living in a residential centre for children with mental handicaps. He could not walk or sit unsupported, and his head control was short-lived. He had no speech, but could respond to simple instructions. His mouth was usually open, though he could close it on command. He could swallow, but his tongue made forward-thrusting movements as he did so. His shirt was frequently wet from drooling and he required frequent bib changes to keep him dry. The intervention and its recording was carried out by the experimenter in an individual room.

The boy was seated in a wheelchair with head and trunk supported for daily, half-hour sessions. During the course of each session, he was given six ounces of a fruit drink and presented with a variety of games. He was then taken to a day activity room where other children were present, and the amount of saliva falling on an absorbent bib for the next hour was measured by weighing it before and after.

After a 10-session baseline an intervention programme was begun. Some consideration of antecedents plainly preceded this, but this is not specifically described. The experimenter placed the middle finger of his left hand under the boy's chin, and his thumb on the side of the boy's face. Intermittent tapping and jiggling were used to decrease unwanted jaw movements and facilitate mouth closure. While this was happening the boy drank six ounces of a fruit drink to stimulate saliva production, since a pool of saliva was thought to stimulate swallowing. The skin above his upper lip was stroked regularly, another device thought to promote swallowing. The average weight of saliva on the bib during this programme was substantially less than during the baseline, though there was an increase for one day only when the programme was introduced.

In this study, various antecedents were used to decrease drooling by increasing the alternative appropriate behaviours of mouth closing and swallowing.

Example 2 (Kellow, 1982)

The intervention here was carried out with a seven-year-old girl with a severe mental handicap, who could swallow but had poor ability to move and close her lips and move her tongue. The intervention was carried out in school by the teacher and a visiting speech therapist, partly in speech therapy sessions and partly in the classroom.

No precise description of behaviours, measuring, or advance investigation of antecedents and consequences is reported. The intervention proceeded in several stages. Over a period of about nine months the teacher and the speech therapist worked at lip and tongue movements. The girl learned to put her tongue in and out in response to demonstration and command, while simultaneously looking in a mirror. By similar methods she learned to close her lips, helped also by manual guidance. Licking sugar off her lips was used to exercise the tongue and stimulate the lip muscles. Pictures were used to show the mouth shapes for making the vowel sounds *oo, ee,* and *ah.*

The next stage was to teach the girl to swallow to command, and to the sound of a xylophone. When she had mastered this she was introduced to the *Dribble Control Box,* a simple but ingenious device developed by a team from Meldreth Manor School, a residential Spastics Society school for pupils with severe mental handicaps and cerebral palsy. It is a cigarette-pack-sized box which is pinned to the child's clothes and which emits a 2-3 second "bleep", the volume and frequency of which can be adjusted to suit the individual. The girl was asked to listen to the bleep from this device while the trainer said, "Listen, swallow". The bleep was repeated at 30-second intervals during sessions of 15 minutes. Soon the trainer just looked at the girl when the bleep sounded, and she swallowed. She was given lots of praise, squeezes, and hugs to reinforce this behaviour. Her response to this training was positive and quite rapid, though, when the school summer holiday started a week or two after beginning the programme, she still sometimes needed a demonstration and a touch under the chin to cue swallowing. The speech therapist visited the child's home and explained the programme to her mother, who continued it during the holiday.

The following term the child's teacher started to generalise the training to the classroom. She taught her to swallow to the bleep while engaged in another activity, such as doing a puzzle. The welfare assistant then watched her and reminded her when necessary. Lots of praise was given to her for having a "dry chin". Progress was good in the classroom, apart from a temporary setback when she had a cold and dribbling increased. By the end of the term she was wearing the box for most of her classroom time, with short spells when she was encouraged to control her dribbling without it. Her mother reported that she could manage without it for a while at home. The plan during the following term, however, was for her to wear it more or less continuously until she could use it without verbal reminders and without regression during colds. It could then be faded out.

By the end of the next term the girl was wearing the box all day in school and was able to maintain swallowing without a verbal cue. Over the following year the situation remained much the same, the device being successful in keeping her swallowing while she had a throat infection.

In this study drooling was decreased by a combination of specific event antecedents and reinforcing consequences to increase alternative appropriate behaviours.

Example 3 (Barton, Leigh, and Myrvang, 1978)

Melvin was 24 years old, lived in a long-stay mental handicap hospital, had a severe mental handicap and cerebral palsy which affected the whole of his left side, and had difficulty in articulating speech. He could swallow on request, but drooled profusely and was constantly wet. The intervention and its recording was carried out by the experimenters, at first in a special training room, but later in hospital workshops.

Drooling was defined by its effects − wetness on the chin or dripping off the lips. The alternative behaviour of swallowing was defined as a definite upward movement of the Adam's apple, accompanied by characteristic mouth movements. Baseline and intervention took place in a varying number of 15-minute sessions each day, with Melvin seated at a table and the observers outside the room looking through a one-way mirror. The time was divided into 10-second periods and records were kept of whether, during each of these periods, there was any drooling, swallowing, or wiping of the lips. Similar measures were carried out in everyday situations, such as the sheltered workshops, the ward, and during speech therapy sessions.

After a baseline of a few sessions an intervention was begun, without reported study in advance of antecedents and consequences. Melvin was taught to swallow when reminded. He was then seated at the table with a buzzer, a token dispenser, and a mirror in which he was asked to check his appearance. The item for which he was saving tokens was in view on a shelf. Swallowing was reinforced every time with tokens, and drooling was indicated by a buzz on the buzzer. As soon as these procedures were implemented there was a dramatic decrease in drooling, and this was maintained during training room sessions. When training was transferred to the workshops there was a slight increase, but the rate was still very low. Swallowing had been rare during the baseline, but improved to an acceptable level during the training room sessions and dropped only slightly on transfer to the workshops. The improvements were maintained over a one-year follow-up period, during which Melvin's increased control over his drooling enabled him to be moved to a pre-discharge villa.

Teaching Melvin to swallow when reminded is not described in any detail, but would have involved the use of antecedents and consequences. The main intervention described consisted essentially of using tokens to reinforce appropriate behaviour inconsistent with drooling − an example of differential reinforcement of incompatible behaviour (or DRI). The purpose of the buzzer is not altogether clear.

Example 4 (Drabman et al., 1979)

Katie was 15 and she attended a non-residential centre for people with mental handicaps. She had cerebral palsy affecting the whole left-hand side of her body. The intervention was carried out in the classroom and the playground by the teacher and an aide.

The problem behaviour was not defined directly, but its effects were. Katie's finger was wiped over her chin and lower lip; a record was kept of whether it was wet, very wet, or dry; and her mouth and chin were then wiped completely dry for the next recording period. "Wet" was defined as any moisture on the fingers, and "very wet" by saliva dripping from the chin. An observation was made every 30 minutes, presumably throughout the day. The average percentage of observations for which Katie was wet, very wet, and dry was calculated for each week.

After a three-week baseline an intervention procedure was implemented without reported advance investigation of antecedents and consequences. At each 30-minute drooling check the teacher praised dryness, but if the fingers were wet, told Katie this, said it was bad, and then made her wipe her lips and chin 10 times with each of five tissues. Physical guidance was given when necessary. During the wiping, Katie was constantly told that she was wet and that was bad, and that she should stay dry. During the baseline the proportion of dry checks was negligible, but over the first three intervention weeks it was between 20 and 40 per cent. During the next four weeks, checking was every 15 minutes, and dry checks increased steadily to 60 per cent in the last week. During a further eight weeks checks were every seven-and-a half minutes (with help from the observers), and there was a further slight improvement. Continued improvement was found at a follow-up six months after the intervention ended.

In this intervention praise as a reinforcing consequence for appropriate behaviour was combined with making Katie wipe her mouth repeatedly as a reducing consequence for the problem behaviour (overcorrection).

PART C

Specific problems

SECTION 8. AVOIDANCE BEHAVIOURS

Definition, causes, and incidence

Definition

Included in this section are those problem behaviours in which people avoid objects or activities that are necessary to their daily lives. Such problems are more commonly defined in terms of feelings of fear. The American Psychiatric Association, for instance, refers to a *phobia* as "a persistent, irrational fear of, and compelling desire to avoid, an object or a situation". To describe such feelings in behavioural terms, it is necessary to look for those behaviours which can be interpreted as fear: running away, trembling, crying, going white, and clinging to or hiding behind a familiar adult. Attempts to make people with phobias face up to the feared object or situation, may result in struggling or tantrums. People with mental handicaps have been reported as being afraid of such things as being physically examined, heights, baths and bathrooms, dogs, toilets, riding on buses and escalators, strangers, mannequins, and public places. Some of these fears are commonly labelled by technical terms. *Agoraphobia*, for example, is fear of going out of the home, *acrophobia* is fear of heights, and *claustrophobia* is fear of enclosed spaces. There is even a name – *anthophobia* – for fear of flowers.

Some difficulty can arise in distinguishing problems of this kind from non-compliance. If people are disinclined to carry out a task, and run away, cry, or have a tantrum to avoid it, is this best regarded as fear-induced, or simply a refusal to do as they are asked? A judgement has to be made for each individual problem in each individual person. If the first judgement does not result in effective action, it is necessary to think again.

Causes

No sound evidence about the causes of these avoidance behaviours has been located, though there have been speculations about how various antecedents and consequences may have promoted them, and about how irrational beliefs on which they might be based could have arisen. It has been suggested, for instance, that escape from the feared object reinforces the avoidance behaviour, or that such behaviour can be reinforced by attention. A wide range of fears, such as fear of strangers, animals, heights, unfamiliar objects or places, darkness, storms, doctors, and separation from their parents, is quite normal in non-handicapped young children. Their presence in older people with mental handicaps could be a reflection of delayed development.

Incidence

There does not seem to be any systematic knowledge available about the prevalence of avoidance behaviours in people with mental handicaps.

Why are they a problem?

Avoidance behaviours can cause problems if they interfere significantly with a person's life. Fear of going to the toilet, or fear of bathrooms, clearly interferes with the development of certain self-help skills, as well as having implications for social acceptance. Other fears may be only minimally restricting, such as fear of dogs or heights. A few fears that have been described in the literature may even be advantageous, such as fear of touching rats. Some degree of fear of strangers can also have advantages.

Intervention techniques

Defining the problem

An example of the kind of description needed for an avoidance behaviour is:

> On appearance of a stranger in any situation, Sophie backs away, cries, and hides.

A major part of the intervention usually consists of increasing the frequency of alternative, more appropriate behaviours, for instance:

> On appearance of a stranger, but in the presence of familiar people, Sophie approaches and says, "Hello".

> On appearance of a stranger, but in the presence of familiar people, Sophie continues current activities.

It is often appropriate to divide the tasks needed to overcome the behaviour into a series of steps to be mastered in sequence.

Measuring the problem

Evidence is insufficient to make specific suggestions, except that it may often be more appropriate to measure the alternative appropriate behaviours rather than the behaviour which is a problem.

Identifying existing antecedents and consequences

The object or situation that is being avoided is itself an antecedent and it is important to establish, as far as possible, *exactly* what it is. Is it, for instance, *all* strangers, or only those wearing white coats? There is very little guidance in the literature on the kinds of antecedents and consequences which maintain avoidance behaviours.

Changing antecedents and consequences for intervention programmes

The main emphasis in published studies has been on increasing approach behaviours to whatever was formerly avoided; in other words, increasing behaviours that are incompatible with avoidance.

Antecedents for increasing these appropriate behaviours have included various forms of guidance, and also devices for altering people's general state or their reaction to frightening situations. Example 1 illustrates guiding antecedents. Here, three children with mental handicaps were helped to overcome fear of strangers by the mother's demonstration of and guidance in the behaviours of walking up to and greeting a stranger. In three other studies, similar techniques were used to help adults with mental handicaps in institutions overcome fear of dogs. In two of these studies appropriate interaction of adults and dogs was recorded on videotape and played back to the adults to demonstrate appropriate behaviour.

Examples 2, 3, 4, and 5 illustrate antecedent devices for altering people's states or reactions. These approaches stem from a range of intervention techniques called *systematic desensitisation,* used mainly so far with adults of normal intelligence, but with some applications to children and to people with mental handicaps. In the classical version of such approaches, stimuli or actions which frighten someone are arranged in order, according to the amount of fear provoked, starting with the least alarming. The person is then induced to relax by an elaborate procedure in which a comfortable position is assumed, and one group of body muscles after another is relaxed until the whole body is relaxed. In this state the person is asked to imagine approaching or taking part in the least feared item in the "anxiety hierarchy". When the person can do this without experiencing any anxiety, the next item in the hierarchy is considered, and so on. At appropriate points, the imagined actions are tried out in the real world. It is believed that the relaxation induces a state that is incompatible with anxiety, which thus enables the person to overcome fears. Example 2 illustrates this technique. A 21-year-old man with a severe mental handicap, who was afraid of standing on or jumping off raised surfaces, overcame this fear by a procedure in which he was induced to relax many of his muscles and then imagine himself standing on or jumping off surfaces of gradually increasing height. Only when he could do this for each task without showing fear was he asked to actually perform the task. There was, of course, guidance as well.

In other versions of sytematic desensitisation, different methods can be used to bring about a state that is incompatible with anxiety. For example, the imagined part of the procedure can be dispensed with and the person made to face the sequence of feared situations directly in the real world. This last variation is usually referred to as *in vivo desensitisation.* Examples 3, 4, and 5 embody both these changes, which are likely to be more feasible and more effective with people with mental handicaps, although there is little firm evidence on the point. In Example 3, the required state was brought about in a 21-year-old man with a mental handicap by playing draughts with him. This enabled him to accept and touch the mannequins which he had formerly avoided, without any intervening imagination stage. Example 4 describes how a four-and-a-half-year-old boy with autistic features was able to overcome his fear of toilets flushing by being tickled to make him laugh continuously during visits to the toilet. Example 5 used the presence of a favourite nurse to overcome a seven-year-old's fear of physical examination by male doctors. The device was based on prior observation that a male doctor was an antecedent for avoidance behaviours. The design of the hierarchy also appeared to be related to advance study, since the boy had also been found to be particularly afraid of instruments, and these antecedents were, therefore, excluded from the earliest steps. In one study (Example 6), the method used was labelled desensitisation, even though there were no measures specifically to decrease anxiety. Adults with severe mental handicaps who were afraid of using escalators, were guided through the sequence of steps involved, from the least to the most feared. This was called *contact desensitisation*. The interventions for overcoming fear of dogs which were mentioned earlier also used a hierarchy, without measures being taken specifically to decrease anxiety.

No attempt will be made in this book to describe systematic desensitisation procedures in full. Readers may like to study the suggestions of Morris and Kratochwill (1983), which are really for use with non-handicapped children. As they stand, however, they seem too complex for use with many people with severe mental handicaps, and the simpler approaches described in Part B, Section 6 are likely to be more relevant.

In all the foregoing examples there was also reinforcement for engaging in the behaviour which the person had been trying to avoid. Use of this differential rein-forcement of incompatible behaviour (DRI), more or less on its own, is illustrated by Example 7. Here a seven-year-old girl, apparently fearful of a number of activities, was asked to engage in them once a day, and praised and given marks for their successful accomplishment. Such methods have also been used to help overcome fear of dogs and of riding on buses and in cars. Differential reinforcement of equivalent behaviour (DRE) may be relevant in some instances – for example, where avoidance behaviours are attention-seeking, attention can be given instead for attempts to approach.

In the examples so far, the emphasis has been entirely on increasing appropriate behaviour. Antecedents and consequences for directly decreasing the problem behaviour have, therefore, not been relevant. However, in Example 8, part of the intervention consisted of a time-out procedure used as a reducing consequence for wetting slacks in a 15-year-old boy, this problem behaviour being part of his pattern of avoiding using the toilet.

Example 8 also illustrates the use of a combination of methods, since spoken suggestions were used as antecedents for the appropriate behaviour of urinating in the toilet, which was also reinforced by gold stars, exchangeable for privileges (an example of differential reinforcement of incompatible behaviour or DRI). Example 9 is also best thought of in this way. It featured a 10-year-old boy who initially screamed and mutilated himself when attempts were made to make him drink from a cup. Circumstances were arranged to allow drinking from a cup to be reinforced by the drink itself. It was done by allowing the drink to be taken initially by a spoon, which the boy would do quite happily. A series of containers progressively more like a cup were then substituted for the spoon, until eventually he would drink from the cup itself. In this example antecedent changes allowed reinforcement of appropriate behaviour.

Subsequent action

Example 7 illustrates a change of programme to improve results. Sonia, aged seven years, was praised and given marks for performing 10 activities in which she was initially reluctant to engage. After 14 days she was performing all but two of these activities, namely, having a drink and playing with other children. A more elaborate programme was then introduced specifically for these activities, in which Sonia won tokens that were exchangeable for a prize for engaging in them. Progress then occurred in these tasks.

Examples 2 and 3 illustrate the transfer of an intervention through a series of behaviours. In Example 2, for instance, 21-year-old David was induced to relax and imagine himself engaging in the appropriate behaviour before being asked to put one foot on a two-inch high block. The procedure was then repeated for a range of increasingly worrying tasks, culminating in jumping off a 20-inch high chair.

Example 4 involved applications of the intervention in a number of different environments. A four-and-a-half year-old boy with autistic features overcame his fear of toilets flushing by being tickled when he used them, and this was done in a number of different settings. Example 5 involved transfer of a seven-year-old's decreased fear of physical examination from one doctor to another, though no special procedures were required to achieve this.

Example 8 includes procedures for fading out an intervention programme. Marty, aged 15, was reinforced with stars (exchangeable for outings) for urinating in the toilet, previously a feared activity. When some success had been achieved, the frequency of reinforcement was decreased by making it dependent on longish periods of staying dry. Finally, tokens were eliminated and improvements continued under a régime of praise and time-out for wetting, which had also been in operation during the intervention.

Illustrative studies

Example 1 (Matson, 1981a)

This study featured three relatively able children with mental handicaps, aged from eight to ten years, who had few friends and frequently complained of being fearful of strangers and acquaintances. The refusal to approach or speak to grown-ups meant that they could not stay with baby sitters or go on outings. The intervention was carried out by their mother in a clinic and at home, but measuring was by experimenters and, at home, partially by the father.

Fear of adult strangers was defined as the children refusing to approach or to speak to grown-ups other than immediate family members and their teacher. For both baseline and intervention, there were twice-weekly clinic sessions. During the baseline sessions, the mother took each child into the therapy room, having first told him to approach and greet a stranger who would be in there. Through a one-way screen the number of words exchanged with this adult were then measured, and a record was also made of how closely the child approached the stranger (distance in feet). The mother then took the child to a lounge and asked him to identify the level of fear he had experienced by pointing to one of seven levels on a kind of graph, describing them to him as "none", "a little", "some", and so on. This whole procedure was then repeated with three more adult strangers. There were similar measuring sessions in the children's own home.

After eight baseline sessions an intervention was begun without reported investigation in advance of antecedents and consequences. In the first clinic session each week the mother taught each child, in the absence of a stranger, the appropriate behaviour required. She accompanied the child to the spot where the stranger would be, told him what to say, and then asked him to repeat it. She rewarded him if he did it correctly. This was repeated until the child did it correctly on three successive occasions. There was more practice at home before the second weekly session, when there was one more practice trial. Then a stranger (different from during the baseline) was present again and the modelling and prompting procedure was repeated with each of four adults in turn. Measuring was carried out as in the baseline. As each session progressed, the mother's guidance was gradually faded out. Again, there was periodic measurement at home. These techniques were successful with all three children, all three measures changing in the direction desired. Follow-up six months later found the improvements had been maintained.

In this intervention demonstrations and instructions were used as antecedents for the appropriate behaviour required. Since it was also reinforced, the technique known as differential reinforcement of incompatible behaviour (DRI) was also being used.

Example 2 (Guralnick, 1973)

David was a 21-year-old young man with a severe mental handicap, living in an insitution, who was afraid of raised surfaces. This affected his participation in other treatment programmes. The intervention was carried out by the experimenter in his office. No measurement procedures are described. A behaviour defined for the first intervention was standing for three minutes on a 16-inch high ledge attached to the gym wall, and jumping to the floor without difficulty. However, this was not specifically measured.

An intervention began without reported advance investigation of antecedents and consequences. A series of large blocks and a strong chair with a seat 20 inches above the floor enabled a series of tasks to be devised in the office, in which David had to stand on and jump off surfaces of gradually increasing height. Each of these tasks could be further graded into "holding on to the wall" and "unsupported". It was planned to progress through these in the hope that achievements would transfer to the ledge in the gym.

In the first five half-hour sessions, however, David was engaged in pleasant conversation, fed, praised, and taught to relax the major muscle groups in his arms, legs, abdomen, and neck. In the sixth session he was made to relax and then asked to imagine himself walking over to a two-inch high block, which was on view, and briefly placing one foot on it. The experimenter asked questions like: "Are you standing in front of the block now?"; "Is your foot on it?". As soon as this had been done three successive times with no sign of fear, David was asked to perform the task. When, occasionally, he was unable to do this, further relaxation enabled him to do so.

In these ways, David progressed from the two-inch block through various stages to the chair seat. At each stage, sweets and other things to eat were given for spending progressively more time on the object. Eventually, David was easily able to stand on the 20-inch high chair seat without any support, move his head and eyes to observe all aspects of the room, turn completely around, engage in conversation, and jump to the floor, all with no apparent signs of fear. In fact, he had become eager to show off his new skills, apparently with extreme pleasure.

Soon after reaching the final target in the intervention sessions, David was reported to be standing on the ledge during gym lessons. Before long he was also jumping off it. Later he was able to climb a wooden ladder attached to a wall almost to the ceiling, and then turn to look out at the gym with little sign of fear. Later still, his improvements were found to be maintained in the gym.

In this study a relaxation procedure was used as an antecedent to help increase approach behaviours, and this behaviour was also reinforced (an example of differential reinforcement of incompatible behaviour or DRI). Since David was asked to imagine progressively more frightening situations when in the relaxed state, the approach is an example of the technique called systematic desensitisation.

Example 3 (Waranch *et al.*, 1981)

HA was a 21-year-old young man with a moderate mental handicap who lived at home with his parents. He avoided all places where he might come across mannequins, and therefore refused to join his parents for shopping and other outings. The intervention was carried out first at a clinic and then in the everyday environment. In the clinic it was implemented by therapists, who also measured behaviour helped by an independent observer. In the everyday environment the parents were also involved and reported back on progress.

Three kinds of behaviour were recorded. In the clinic three mannequins were each displayed to HA five times each in random order. One was a 46 cm clothed plastic doll, one an unclothed 64 cm plastic doll, and one a 135 cm adolescent store mannequin wearing shirt and trousers. At each presentation, a therapist first asked HA to come and touch the mannequin. If there was no response within 15 seconds, the therapist slowly took the mannequin to within HA's reach and again asked him to touch it. If he complied with the first request it was recorded as an "active approach", if with the second as a "passive approach". The recording sequence was carried out once before the intervention and again after each phase of intervention. In addition, HA's parents asked him to go to an indoor shopping complex with them two or three times a week for ice-cream, and reported back regularly on whether or not he did so.

The design of the intervention was related to initial observations that HA refused to touch the 46 cm doll, would not even look at the 64 cm doll, and enjoyed playing draughts. In sessions of approximately 50 minutes, a therapist played draughts with him. During the first session, the 46 cm doll was moved gradually closer to him. During the next two sessions, it was next to the table and HA was encouraged to touch it briefly between moves. Then it was seated between HA and the therapist, and HA was asked to pick it up and hold it each time he moved a draught. No such procedure was found necessary for the 64 cm doll, so the store mannequin was next introduced, initially lying in a chair covered by a sheet. The sheet was removed after four sessions, and the mannequin was moved to stand between HA and the therapist after another six sessions. HA was then asked to touch it before he moved a draught. At this point, HA was still refusing to go shopping with his parents. However, he agreed to go once with the therapist, who made him touch four different mannequins in various stores in order to receive ice-cream. His parents coninued to ask him at least once a week.

During the five baseline presentations of the 46 cm doll, HA touched it passively twice and asked for it to be taken away the other three times. He asked for the removal of the other doll and the mannequin on all five occasions. After training with the 46 cm doll, he actively approached both that one and the 64 cm one on all five occasions but still avoided the store mannequin. After training with the latter, he actively approached all three items five times. His parents reported that, after the shopping trip with the therapist, HA rarely refused to accompany them, and he made approximately 40 trips during the six-month period following completion of the intervention.

In this intervention playing draughts was used as an antecedent to make HA's avoidance responses to mannequins less likely and increase his approach behaviour to them. Being allowed to move a draught was also used as a reinforcing consequence for approach behaviours (an example of differential reinforcement of incompatible behaviour or DRI). The procedure is an example of systematic desensitisation, since playing draughts was used to produce an emotional state incompatible with avoidance reactions and, while in this state, HA was required to show approach behaviour towards objects that were increasingly frightening to him.

Example 4 (Jackson and King, 1982)

The person in this study was a four-and-a-half-year-old boy with autistic features, who was fully mobile and could understand simple instructions but had only a few spoken words. He reacted in a frightened way to the flushing sound of toilets, widening the pupils of his eyes, trembling, increasing the rigidity of his muscles, screaming, crying, breathing very fast, having tantrums, and running away. This interfered with school routines and was tiresome for his mother. The intervention and its recording was carried out by the mother at home and the teacher at school.

Definition of the boy's behaviour and the measuring techniques are not precisely described, but their nature is reasonably clear from the account of the intervention. There was careful investigation of antecedents. It was established that there was no fear reaction to sound other than the flushing of toilets, and that even the flushing sound had this effect only in the toilet. There was no effect when a recording of the flushing sound was played in another situation, or when it was accompanied by a photograph of a toilet. It occurred, however, in *any* toilet.

The intervention used the mother's observations that the boy loved being tickled to the point of laughter and that things to eat would be potent reinforcing consequences. After his trousers and underpants had been pulled down in the toilet, he was tickled on top of the chest and under the arms. As soon as he started laughing he was told to sit on the toilet. He usually laughed throughout this, and the toilet was then flushed many times during the next two or three minutes. If necessary, there was further tickling to keep him laughing. If he showed no fear reactions, he was given a cheese flavoured crisp and praised. This was done repeatedly in toilets in a number of different settings, though the report does not state the sequence. It was certainly to some extent "one after the other" because it is stated that, after three settings, the food reinforcement was faded out. The fear reactions were eliminated in all of these settings, the number of trials needed varying from five to eight. Follow-ups after three and six months found toilets being used without fuss everywhere.

In this intervention tickling was used as an antecedent to bring about the behaviour of laughing, since this was incompatible with fearful behaviour. Since reinforcement followed, the intervention could be regarded as an instance of differential reinforcement of incompatible behaviour (DRI). The authors describe it as systematic desensitisation, on the assumption that laughter produced an emotional state incompatible with fear reactions, and that this was carried out systematically in a planned sequence of situations.

Example 5 (Freeman, Roy, and Hemmick, 1976)

A seven-year-old boy with a mental handicap showed a variety of problem behaviours. Among these was fearful avoidance of physical examination by male doctors. On the approach of such a doctor he would run, screaming, in the opposite direction, and in the examination room he would refuse to undress, run round the room, and have temper tantrums. There was associated trembling, and rapid pulse and breathing. The intervention was carried out in hospital by a male doctor and a female nurse. No measuring procedures are described, nor any rigorous description of behaviours to change.

Prior study established that the boy had a particular fear of procedures involving instruments, and that he had a particularly good relationship with one nurse on the ward.

The intervention procedure began without any preceding baseline phase. A hierarchy of requirements for the physical examination was constructed, presumably based on beliefs about the relative strengths of his various fears. It consisted of 11 steps, ordered as follows: enter examination room; undress to shorts; allow blood pressure to be taken, and examination with stethoscope; permit touching of body parts; listen to chest and heart with stethoscope; allow examination of stomach; allow examination of genital area; allow examination of reflexes with reflex hammer; allow examination of throat with tongue blade; allow examination of ears with otoscope; and allow examination of eyes with ophthalmoscope. For each of seven daily sessions (length not specified), the boy's favourite nurse took him to the examining room and took him through the steps in the hierarchy, which occurred without undue problems. There followed a phase in which the doctor came in, performed the first few steps, and then remained in the room while the nurse carried out the rest; the procedure being terminated for the day after the first step in which any signs of anxiety occurred. Gradually, the doctor carried out more of the procedure, and eventually all of it without the nurse in the room. Finally, an unfamiliar doctor did it. The familiar doctor was able to go through the whole procedure with the boy's full cooperation within four sessions. When the unfamiliar doctor took over, no problem behaviour occurred, and the same applied when the boy was subsequently examined by a plastic surgeon.

In this study the presence and guidance of a favourite nurse were antecedents which made appropriate behaviour more likely and the problem avoidance behaviour less likely to occur. It is an example of systematic desensitisation, since the nurse's presence was used to decrease anxiety while the boy was required to face up to progressively more of a hierarchy of feared experiences.

Example 6 (Runyan, Stevens, and Reeves, 1985)

One of the people in this study was a 33-year-old woman in an institution, who had a severe mental handicap, a moderate hearing loss, and no speech. The intervention was carried out in a public shopping centre at a time when the shops were closed. It is not clear whether the intervention and its recording was carried out by the experimenters or by the regular residential centre staff.

The problem was fear of using escalators. A hierarchy of increasingly frightening behaviours was drawn up. The first seven items involved approaching the staircase between the up and down escalators, using it with prompting from the trainer, and using it independently. The other items were:

" 8. Approaches to within 1.5 m of working up-escalator.
  9. Stands at bottom of working up-escalator for 10 seconds.
  10. Rides up-escalator with trainer's arm around subject entire way.
  11. Rides up-escalator hand-in-hand with trainer entire way.
  12. Rides up-escalator with trainer one step behind.
  13. Rides up-escalator with trainer 10 steps behind.
  14. Rides up-escalator with trainer climbing alongside on stairs.
  15. Rides up-escalator alone.
  16. Approaches to within 1.5 m of working down-escalator.
  17. Stands at top of working down-escalator for 10 seconds.
  18. Rides down-escalator with trainer's arm around subject.
  19. Rides down-escalator hand-in-hand with trainer.
  20. Rides down-escalator with trainer one step ahead.
  21. Rides down-escalator with trainer 10 steps behind.
  22. Rides down-escalator with trainer descending stairs alongside subject.
  23. Rides down-escalator alone.
  24. Rides up-escalator and down-escalator alone.
  25. Rides up and down another escalator alone."

During the baseline period, the trainer instructed the woman (with accompanying gestures) to engage in the appropriate behaviour from the hierarchy, repeated this if necessary after 10 seconds, and gave her another 10 seconds to comply. If she succeeded, the next behaviour in the hierarchy was tried. As soon as an item was not attempted the test was terminated, and the "score" was the number of the highest item completed.

After a baseline of twelve 35-minute sessions the intervention programme was begun without any reported advance study of antecedents and consequences. For each item needing to be mastered (presumably the lowest one not completed), the trainer demonstrated it, then told the woman to do it, and then physically prompted or guided her if necessary. If she said "No", or moved away, the attempt was discontinued for a while. When an item was successfully completed, the woman was praised. Items requiring physical prompting or guidance were repeated until they were completed in response to verbal instructions alone. During the baseline the woman's "score" varied between eight and ten. As soon as the programme was introduced she completed all items up to and including 18, and within four sessions the whole hierarchy was completed.

In this study a hierarchy of behaviours leading to full escalator use was defined, verbal instructions and physical prompting and guidance were used as antecedents to make each behaviour occur, and praise was used as a reinforcing consequence. The authors label the approach contact desensitisation.

Example 7

Sonia aged seven years, had a severe mental handicap, was mobile, was able to speak in sentences, and was reasonably competent in self-help skills. She was, however, timid over contacts with adults, or with messy substances. She would draw away and say "No", stiffen, or seem generally afraid. Her teacher, Mrs. M., took part in one of my workshops and carried out the intervention and measured its effects in the classroom.

For intervention purposes, Mrs. M. chose 10 activities in which Sonia was reluctant to engage and asked her to do each of them once a day. There was no baseline measurement, but a record was kept of whether or not Sonia performed each activity each day. For the intervention, which began without reported study in advance of antecedents and consequences, Sonia was praised each time she performed one of the 10 activities. She was also given marks (part of a pre-existing class system) for "doing well", though the precise way in which this was done was not specified. The tasks, and the number of days out of 14 that they were performed, were: climbing in and out of boxes (14); eating her lunch (13); drinking milk or orange (3); sand play or gardening (14); desk work without adult (7); desk work with adult (13); play activities with other children outside the classroom without adult encouragement (1); putting on and taking off coat (8); painting or sticking (14); and play involving being lifted off the floor (5).

At the end of the 14 days, the only serious refusal problems concerned drinking milk or orange and playing with other children. While continuing the above scheme, therefore, Mrs. M. worked out a more specific programme for those two behaviours. Every time Sonia accepted a drink or accepted an invitation which the teacher had asked other children to make for Sonia to join them in their play outside the classroom environment, Sonia was allowed to choose a coloured piece of paper to put in an envelope, and a symbol was put on a chart. She was told that these were each worth a penny and that she could choose a prize to buy with them at the end of term. She was organised to count them daily to see how many she had won. These "tokens" were given immediately for drinking, and on return to the classroom for playing with another child. In addition, other adults were told of her success and they regularly added their praise to Mrs. M's. The procedures were used for five days, during which Sonia drank her milk or squash every day. She accepted an outside invitation to play on only three of the five days, but this was slightly better than before. The programme was continued, in the hope of further progress.

In this intervention, Sonia was reinforced for the behaviours she would otherwise avoid – an example of differential reinforcement of incompatible behaviour (DRI).

Example 8 (Luiselli, 1977)
This intervention was with Marty, a 15-year-old young man in an institution, who had a severe mental handicap, could speak only in three-word phrases, could carry out simple commands, and could perform simple self-care and work skills. Though originally toilet trained, he had recently taken to avoiding the toilet, breathing rapidly and deeply and putting his fingers in his ears when it was mentioned, and urinating in his slacks. Both the intervention and its measurement was carried out by the institution staff in their everyday environment. Two behaviours were identified. Wetting, identified by any clearly visible signs of moistness in the slacks, was to be decreased. Urinating in the toilet, identified by its sound heard through the toilet door, was to be increased. The number of wettings of slacks per week was measured.

The intervention programme was begun after a baseline of three weeks, and was related to the observation that Marty's favourite activity was going on trips into the community with an attendant. Every time he urinated in the toilet, he was given a gold star which was put on a chart in the toilet and he was also praised. At specific times during the day it was suggested to him that he might go, and he was reminded of the stars. In the first week he had to win three consecutive stars to go on the outing; in the second week six consecutive stars; in the third week, all the stars possible for one day; and in the fourth week, all the stars possible on two consecutive days. Whenever Marty did wet his slacks he was made to sit by himself for 40 minutes, still wearing them wet. During the baseline, Marty wet his slacks an average of 15.6 times per week, whereas the average during the four weeks of intervention was 5.5.

Following this initial intervention tokens were discontinued and Marty was praised for having dry slacks and allowed his outing if he was dry to a specified extent. Wettings then continued to decrease, to an average of 3.1 per week over 14 weeks. Tokens (exchangeable for slightly different privileges) were later reintroduced for staying dry for specified periods, and the wettings averaged 3.0 per week for 10 weeks. After this Marty was simply praised for being dry and made to sit on his own if he wet his slacks. At follow-up six months and 12 months later, wetting was absent.

In this intervention suggestions for visiting the toilet were used as antecedents to make appropriate behaviour occur, stars were used to reinforce this behaviour (differential reinforcement of incompatible behaviour or DRI) and isolation time-out was used as a reducing consequence for inappropriate behaviour.

Example 9 (Wickings *et al.*, 1974)

This study concerned a 10-year-old boy with a profound mental handicap, who showed "psychotic symptoms" and had no speech, but who could walk, use the toilet, dress himself to some extent, and feed himself slowly with a spoon. The intervention was carried out by the staff of the special hospital unit he attended during the week, and by his mother at home at weekends.

The problem was described as an acute fear of drinking from a cup. If there was a filled cup or glass in the same room he screamed continuously and tried to knock it off the table. At mealtimes he accepted the presence of a cup, but used a spoon to transfer the drink to his mouth. Attempts to make him drink from the cup were met by difficult behaviour, which included injuring his face by tearing at it. No measuring of these behaviours is described, and investigation of antecedents and consequences is limited to noting the contrast between his reaction to a cup and his reaction to a spoon.

The intervention began by using a plastic splinting material to mould a spoon the same size as his usual teaspoon and using it instead. After a week of this, another spoon was made, with a slightly larger and deeper bowl and a shorter handle. In subsequent versions, the spoon handle was shortened further and the bowl was made larger and given a flattened base. It now stood on a table like a cup and had a little liquid poured in to it. The boy tolerated these gradual changes and accepted enough liquid in the "spoons" to require him to take, first two sips, and then three. By various other minor engineering feats, a series of containers progressively more like a cup were used, until eventually the boy would use an ordinary cup or mug. Each of these changes was introduced by the nursing staff and then sent home for use there. The results generalised to the home without difficulty and were maintained when he returned to school. The full programme took eight months, but this was mainly due to experimentation with materials and it was felt that it could have been achieved within a few weeks without that.

The best interpretation of this study is probably that the boy was reinforced (by the drink) for reacting appropriately to antecedents progressively closer to one which initially triggered off problem behaviour. However, manipulation of antecedents was the crucial factor in allowing this to happen.

PART C

Specific problems

SECTION 9. TOILETING PROBLEMS

Definition, causes, and incidence

Definition

Problems associated with toileting include incontinence of urine (*enuresis*), incontinence of faeces (*encopresis*), and the often associated undue retention of faeces, as well as unduly frequent visits to the toilet and smearing of faeces on walls and furniture. Eating of faeces (*coprophagy*) is another problem but this has already been dealt with in Section 6 on Feeding Problems. Toileting problems have not been extensively studied with people with mental handicaps. They have commonly been thought of as aspects of developmental delay, and therefore matters for routine training rather than identification as problem behaviours. As a result it is difficult to find any clear definitions on which to base investigation of causes, incidence, and intervention.

Enuresis has been defined as the involuntary passing of urine, at least twice a month for children between the ages of five and six years and once a month for older children. However, 70 per cent of people with mental handicaps in institutions have been found to be enuretic in some sense, 79 per cent of four-year-old children with Down's syndrome to wet the bed at least once a week (as compared with 27 per cent of non-handicapped children of the same age), and 41.5 per cent of institutionalised adults to be nocturnally enuretic. At the moment, therefore, deciding what to regard as a problem for people with severe mental handicaps is difficult. Plainly, however, people who wet only at night have less of a problem than those who are incontinent during the day as well.

Encopresis has been even more neglected. There is no agreement over what should or should not be thought of as a soiling problem, and soiling is not commonly identified as a specific problem among people with mental handicaps. It is useful, however, to distinguish between straightforward failure to acquire bowel control, and instances where it is more a matter of bowel control being too effective. A person may have stopped bowel movement and become seriously constipated, the faeces then leaking out slowly as a fluid or being expelled involuntarily as small hard lumps.

Too frequent visits to the toilet can be thought of as a milder version of incontinence. Smearing is probably only a toileting problem by chance, in that the person might do the same with mud instead if it were available.

Causes

Little can be said for certain about the causes of toileting problems in people with mental handicaps. However, there could well be medical causes, or at least medical origins, in some instances. Urinary disorders and infections, for instances, can lead to difficulties in passing or controlling the passing of urine. Diabetes can cause excessive production of urine. Various disorders and infections can also cause diarrhoea, and hence soiling. Alternatively pain, from fissures in the anus or from passing of hard faeces, can inhibit bowel movement and lead to constipation. Eventually either the control will give way allowing motions to be passed in the wrong places or retention will continue until the rectum becomes packed with a hard mass of faeces and bowel movements cease altogether. Small bits may then be forced out occasionally, or a stage may be reached in which liquid faeces leaks round the hard faecal mass and stains the clothing. It has been found that in this situation the muscles of the anus constantly exert more pressure to close the opening than is normal and there is often decreased sensation in the area so that the person is not aware of the need to pass a motion.

For most people, however, toileting problems are best thought of as a failure to learn appropriate habits, since systematic training frequently ameliorates them. There are also claims that undue pressure for toilet training can lead to avoidance of normal toileting behaviours, either through fear or as an act of rebellious non-compliance. This might set in motion the sequence of events described above for soiling. However, there is little sound evidence and it remains an opinion.

Smearing might well be a stimulating activity which brings its own reinforcement as well as attracting attention from others. These consequences can also reinforce the soiling which precedes smearing.

Incidence

Surveys in British institutions for people with mental handicaps have reported "incontinence" rates varying from 6.4 to 16 per cent of adults, with higher rates than this for people with more severe handicaps and for children. This is hardly surprising in the absence of clear definitions. Clearly, enuresis in some form is more common than this; but the incidence of toileting problems cannot be said to have been clearly established.

Why are they a problem?

People who present problem behaviours related to toileting become unacceptable to others and this can adversely affect their social relationships. Such problems can also lead to discomfort from wet or dirty clothing. Dealing with this places an extra burden on carers who will then have less time for offering other helpful attention to the people concerned. Difficulties with toileting also interfere with educational and recreational activities in which people might otherwise engage. There is also a danger of infection spreading.

Intervention techniques

Defining the problem

Defining a toileting problem can be relatively simple. For example, a problem behaviour might be described as follows:

> Whenever he feels an urge to pass urine, Clive does so immediately, regardless of the situation and clothes worn.

At the same time it is usually advisable to define also alternative incompatible behaviours, such as:

> Whenever he feels an urge to pass urine, Clive controls it, goes to the toilet, and passes it there.

If soiling is associated with chronic constipation, however, there is no problem behaviour as such − the body simply takes over and faeces are expelled involuntarily. The emphasis then must be entirely on appropriate behaviour to increase.

It is important to realise that using the toilet appropriately requires a complex set of skills. Appropriate urination, for instance, involves starting to urinate when the bladder pressure reaches a certain level, detecting this pressure level, holding back urine, urinating when the bladder is not full, manipulating clothing, going to the toilet or asking to be taken, adopting body positions necessary for the urine to be passed into the toilet bowl, and planning ahead to use toilet facilities when they are available. A whole series of alternative appropriate behaviours may, therefore, need to be taught in a planned sequence.

Measuring the problem

The simplest way of doing this is to record the number of incidents of the problem behaviour, or of alternative appropriate behaviours. With some methods of intervention for wetting, however, the incidence may be artificially increased by giving the person a great deal to drink, and this makes counting instances less meaningful. A suitable alternative then is to measure the proportion of urine emissions which take place appropriately in the toilet. Another possibility might be to measure the time for which a person stays clean and/or dry.

Identifying existing antecedents and consequences

For a person who is simply untrained, no external antecedent is needed to explain the occurrence of urination or defaecation. This is an automatic part of the body's functioning. The urge to perform could be regarded as an antecedent, but there is little point in this since it is not something that needs to be changed. It has been suggested that another internal antecedent, pain, can lead to retention of faeces, and this is worth identifying if something can be done to alleviate it. Certain external antecedents can also influence when and where the behaviours occur. In Example 1, for instance, it was suggested that seven-year-old Dora defaecated when wearing her nappy and she did not soil herself at all when she was dressed in pants instead. It looked as though the nappy was an antecedent which made defaecation more likely to occur.

It seems likely that defaecation and urination are pleasurable in themselves, and therefore need no external reinforcing consequences for their occurrence. External consequences, however, can influence when and where the behaviours occur. For instance, one boy with a mental handicap used to soil himself and then smear the faeces with his hand. Simply doing this may have been reinforcing in itself but the attention he received afterwards was probably more so, and this is likely to have reinforced both the soiling and the smearing. It consisted of bathing him, talking to him, dressing him in clean clothes and, sometimes, giving him a cup of tea.

Changing antecedents and consequences for intervention programmes

Intervention programmes for toileting problems have tended to be complex, but use of antecedents and consequences both for decreasing problem behaviour and increasing alternative appropriate behaviours occur as elements in them.

One antecedent which has been used to increase the frequency of urination is giving a great deal to drink. It does not influence whether the urination occurs as appropriate behaviour or not, but it increases the opportunities to learn to make it appropriate. Thus, in Example 2, 14-year-old Alan was given additional drinks during an intervention programme in which reinforcement and time-out were used to increase appropriate use of classroom commodes and decrease soiling and wetting. There is a parallel in using increased fibre in the diet to enhance the sensitivity of the bowel so that people receive clearer internal signals when they need to defaecate, and in using suppositories (gelatinous bodies which are inserted in the anus to promote passing a motion by their stimulating and lubricating effects). Both of these measures were used to bring about defaecation in a chronically constipated, five-year-old boy with a mental handicap in Example 3, so that he could be reinforced by popsicles, music, and praise for opening his bowels in the toilet. Laxatives can have a similar function.

Example 3 also provides an illustration of using an antecedent specifically for bringing about appropriate behaviour. The boy had balance problems, and this was thought to contribute to his crying and refusing to sit on the toilet. When provided with a footstool, which helped him to sit with more stability, he remained seated there.

For people with physical handicaps, special seating arrangements may be needed. This is too complex a field to be covered here. Readers are referred to Finnie (1974) for general guidance, and to Greenfield and Milne (1985) for descriptions of commodes, potty chairs, over toilet aids, toilet trainer seats, and lists of suppliers. These aids can all be used as antecedents to bring about relaxed internal states which will help promote necessary behaviour changes.

Taking people to the toilet, telling them what to do there, and providing them with physical guidance are specific event antecedents which have been used. For instance, in Example 6 a 26-year-old man with a profound mental handicap was, if necessary, led to the toilet, physically seated upon it, and his legs were moved into position as part of a programme for overcoming daytime wetting.

Reinforcing consequences for appropriate behaviours have been a major feature of some intervention programmes, though always in association with other measures. One common approach is to take someone to the toilet, say, every half-hour, sit the person on it for, say, a quarter-of-an-hour each time, and then provide some reinforcing consequence for eliminating there. In Example 1, for instance, seven-year-old Dora was taken to the toilet at regular times and reinforced by *Smarties*, praise, and games of pat-a-cake, at first for remaining on the toilet and later for defaecating there. In Example 2

14-year-old Alan was seated on a commode every half-hour, and given cuddles or various things to eat and drink for urinating or defaecating there. In Example 3 a five-year-old child was provided with a suppository at intervals and seated on the toilet for up to 15 minutes. Music, and things to eat and drink, reinforced remaining there and bowel movements were reinforced by popsicles and praise. In all these studies reinforcement of appropriate behaviour was accompanied by other devices.

Antecedents to make problem toilet behaviours less likely are rarely mentioned in the literature. I have located one (Example 1) which consisted of changing an antecedent thought to be making such behaviour more likely. Seven-year-old Dora was thought more likely to defaecate when wearing her nappy than at other times. She was, as a result, dressed in pants instead of a nappy, and soiling then ceased. In another case, a boy with a mental handicap who smeared faeces was dressed in a cat-suit, which reduced his opportunities to engage in the behaviour.

A range of consequences have been used to reduce problem behaviours. An early consideration is the removal of consequences which advance investigation suggests may be reinforcing them (extinction). In Example 1, seven-year-old Dora was laid on a changing table and cleaned, powdered, and changed every time she soiled, a procedure she appeared to enjoy immensely. When she was changed standing up instead, soiling decreased greatly.

Interrupting the problem behaviour is a common reducing device. It virtually always utilises an alarm system, in which the moisture in urine or faeces completes an electric circuit which triggers off an alarming noise. During the day an alarm system is incorporated into the person's pants, the "buzzer" being incorporated into a box worn on a belt around the waist. In addition to its effect on the person with the toileting problem, it also alerts people with responsibility so that they can tell the person to stop the problem behaviour and take the person to the toilet to carry it out there instead. At night, the alarm is more usually incorporated into a pad on which the person sleeps and the buzzer box is usually beside the bed. Hopefully, the alarm awakens the person when urinating or defaecating starts and the person can then go or be taken to the toilet to complete the behaviour.

It is usual for a set sequence of recommended activities to follow the sounding of an enuresis alarm, so that interruption is never the only consequence. For instance, for bed wetting, it has been suggested that a person who has urinated should, with guidance if necessary, switch off the buzzer, visit the toilet or use a pot to empty the bladder, help the carer to remake the bed with dry sheets and dry alarm pads, switch the alarm back on, and then return to bed. Thus, not only is the problem behaviour interrupted, but there is a loud alarming noise, sleep is disturbed, and the person has to leave his bed and perform what is probably an unwelcome task in changing the sheets. These are all potential reducing consequences. A procedure for daytime wetting is decribed in Example 8, in which the parents of a seven-year-old boy with a profound mental handicap responded to a pants alarm by saying, "Potty", then immediately running with the boy to the bathroom, disconnecting the alarm, and telling him to sit on the toilet.

There can be many complications in the use of alarms, especially those used at night. Designs must meet safety specifications, remaining below specified current and voltage levels. They should also be designed to prevent "buzzer ulcers" occurring. Hunt, Long, and Long (undated) provide further guidance in this area. Different alarms have different sounds, and it is necessary to select one that will have an effective sound for a particular person. One variation is an alarm which makes a vibrating sound under the pillow. This sometimes wakes people who are not disturbed by other buzzers, including people who are deaf. Some alarms have a light, so that the person does not have to wake up in the dark. Slight procedural defects can upset the process. For instance, people with mental handicaps need to become accustomed to an alarm before it is used so that they do not fear or sabotage it. Nylon sheets, it is often claimed, should be avoided, since they do not allow urine through very easily. They also encourage perspiration and produce static electricity which can set off the alarm in the absence of urination. The person with the problem needs to be naked below the waist to give the best chance of urine getting on to the pads. After each instance of the alarm going off the pads must be replaced and any wet sheets must be washed, since a residue of dry urine can combine with sweat to produce a false alarm. Detailed guidance, explained very clearly, is provided by Morgan (1981). Hunt, Long, and Long (undated) include procedures on maintaining equipment in a fit state for use. However, professional guidance is *essential* for using these devices. It is also essential that the advising professionals are themselves trained well beyond routine use of the equipment itself.

Time-out has also been used as a reducing consequence, in combination with other devices. In Example 2, for instance, 14-year-old Alan took part in games and other activities and received attention while he remained clean and dry, but he was removed from this situation and ignored for half-an-hour if he had an accident.

Making a person do something unwelcome has also been incorporated as a reducing consequence in various intervention programmes. In Example 3, whenever the five-year-old boy passed faeces anywhere other than in the toilet, he was made to sit on the toilet for five minutes without any of the reinforcing consequences which were provided for sitting there at other times. In Example 4, the soiling of an eight-year-old boy with a mental handicap was tackled by a procedure which included *full cleanliness training*, a form of overcorrection. His parents inspected his pants every 15-20 minutes and, if he had soiled, he had to clean himself and to wash his soiled clothes for at least 15 minutes. In Example 5, a nine-year-old boy with a mental handicap had to undergo an over-correction procedure involving practice in going to, sitting on, and returning from the toilet several times, as well as engaging in cleaning up operations, every time he wet his pants.

Doing unwelcome things to a person has also been used to reduce problem behaviour in this area; but apart from the enuresis alarm procedures referred to earlier, only in forms such as spanking which cannot be recommended for use in Britain.

Virtually all intervention programmes described in the literature combine two or more techniques (though it has not been demonstrated that this is necessary for success). In one such "package", the soiling of the five-year-old boy in Example 3 was overcome by an intervention which combined: use of a stabilising stool as an antecedent to make problem behaviours less likely; dietary changes and suppositories as antecedents to promote appropriate behaviours; popsicles, music, and praise to reinforce sitting on the toilet and defaecating there; and sitting on the toilet as a reducing consequence for defaecating elsewhere.

The *forward-moving procedure* is another "package". This involves wearing an alarm system triggered electrically by the flow of urine. When it sounds, the person with responsibility moves very rapidly to the person who is urinating and says, "Stop", or the equivalent. This, together with the alarm, frequently makes the person stop urinating. The problem behaviour is therefore followed by reducing consequences. The person is then taken to the toilet, placed in the right position for urinating into it, and encouraged to do so, all of which are antecedents for appropriate behaviour. If the person obliges, reinforcement is provided. As progress is made, the person is taught to respond to the alarm by going to the toilet unprompted, and to remove and replace clothing as needed. Example 7 describes the rapidly successful use of this procedure with a nine-year-old boy with a profound mental handicap. In this example the alarm was of a kind which sounded precisely at the times while urine was flowing, but stopped when it was not. I know of no sources for such apparatus in this country. However, Example 8 describes a modified version of the procedure which could be used with easily obtainable pants alarms. This was a home-based intervention with a seven-year-old boy with a profound mental handicap. When the alarm sounded, his parents said "Potty", ran him to the toilet, turned the buzzer off, and seated him on the toilet. At first, he was reinforced for any elimination there, but later only for elimination in the toilet.

Associated with the forward-moving procedure is practice in turning the flow of urine on and off. However, little guidance is available on how this is brought about with people with mental handicaps, or how it is fitted into the training sequence.

Dry bed training is an intensive "package" designed specifically for nocturnal enuresis which might be considered if the "lighter" packages above fail to work. It has the following elements:

Intensive training. About half-an-hour before bedtime, the person is given two cups of a favourite drink in order to provide more opportunities for urination to occur. While in bed, the person is awakened every hour and told to visit the toilet. Prompting by physical guidance is used if necessary to achieve this; but to the minimum extent necessary, and faded out as soon as possible. The person then sits on the toilet for five minutes. If the person responds to these antecedents by urinating in the toilet (detected by an alarm system in the toilet bowl in which the urine completes an electric circuit to trigger off a sound) praise is given, with two cups of drink and a favourite food to eat. The person then returns to bed. If no urination occurs, the person is returned to bed, given two cups of drink there, and praised for getting up and going to the toilet. In either case, the person is also directed to touch the dry sheets and is praised for them being dry before returning to sleep.

Procedures if accidents occur. The person sleeps on the pad part of an enuresis alarm. When the alarm sounds, the carer turns it off and reprimands the person for being wet. The person then has to go to the toilet and undergo a form of overcorrection, called *cleanliness training*. In cleanliness training the person has to remove the wet sheet, wipe the mattress, take the wet sheet to the laundry room, bring a fresh sheet from another room, and remake the bed. This is followed by positive practice overcorrection in getting up and going to the toilet. This involves lying down in bed for three minutes, being woken up with the minimum prompting necessary, going to the toilet, sitting on it for up to 30 seconds, and then returning to bed, all without any reinforcement. This procedure is repeated for 45 minutes. The alarm is then reactivated and the person allowed to return to sleep.

Monitored post-training phase. Extra drinks, favourite things to eat, praise, and hourly awakening are discontinued as soon as there is no more than one accident per night and the person urinates in the toilet on at least half of the hourly visits. The procedures for accidents, however, continue as before.

Normal procedure (on the hospital wards where it originated). When no accidents have occurred for seven days, the remaining special intervention procedures are discontinued, but the bed is inspected in the morning and, if it is wet, the person with a mental handicap has to remake it. If there is wetting on two days in any week, the monitored phase is reinstated.

Rapid toilet training is a daytime version of dry bed training. It has the following elements:

Procedures when no accidents occur. The person is seated in the toilet area for eight hours a day at first, being required to sit on the toilet every half-hour and remain there for half-an-hour, or until elimination takes place if this occurs first. The urine completes an electric circuit in an alarm system in the toilet bowl which then makes a sound. When this happens, the person is given sweets, hugged and praised, and given as much to drink as possible. (If elimination does not occur the person is still given the drinks, since this increases the rate of urination and therefore speeds up training.) The toileting procedure is accompanied by such prompts as are necessary to get the person to undress appropriately before sitting on the toilet and dress again and flush the toilet afterwards. In addition, the person is given food and praise at five-minute intervals if dry. An alarm system in the pants is worn, which is set off by the passage of urine. It is, therefore, unnecessary to check physically whether or not the person's pants are dry.

Procedures when accidents occur. If the pants alarm sounds it is disconnected and a complex series of reducing consequences follows. The person's attention is gained by being shaken and being told not to wet. Cleanliness training is then given. This procedure begins by the person being undressed and given a tepid shower. The person must then change into dry clothes, carry the wet clothes to a sink, immerse them in water, wring them out, and hang them out to dry. The person then returns to the toilet and has to mop up the floor or chair, being manually guided to the minimum extent necessary to ensure that this is done. After the cleanliness procedure, the person's chair is removed and there is a one-hour time-out period when no food, drink, or attention is available and any meal due is delayed.

Maintenance procedures. The use of the alarm apparatus is discontinued, but pants are inspected at mealtimes, snack-times, and bedtime. On each occasion, the person is praised if dry. If wet, the person is reprimanded, goes through the cleanliness training procedure used in the intervention, and then has meals delayed or snacks omitted. After some weeks checks are made only at mealtimes and bedtime. Eventually these are discontinued, though cleanliness training for accidents remains in use.

There is no particular reason for supposing that rapid toilet training and dry bed training should be adhered to rigidly. More intensive and less intensive variations have been reportedly successful. A version of dry-bed training is described in Example 5. A nine-year-old boy with a profound mental handicap was given plenty to drink, guided to visit the toilet regularly, reinforced for urinating there, and made to clean up and practise visiting and sitting on the toilet a number of times whenever he wet his pants. In Example 6, the procedure with a 26-year-old man with a profound mental handicap differed from the original in that the time-out period was only half-an-hour, repeated practice at using the toilet was substituted for the cleanliness training, and no alarm was used in the toilet bowl.

Another package which might be helpful as an alternative that is less demanding and less threatening than rapid toilet training or dry bed training could consist of regular toileting, with reinforcement of elimination on the toilet, and taking of the person to the toilet when an enuresis alarm sounds. I have found no reference in the literature to use of such a procedure with people with mental handicaps, yet it could be the best reconciliation between effectiveness, economy of time for people with responsibility, and avoidance of unnecessarily unpleasant procedures.

Additional measures

Medication has sometimes been used for enuresis (usually imipramine – trade name *Tofranil*) in the absence of known medical causes, but I have found no reports of this with children with severe mental handicaps and it is apparently ineffective with adults. With children generally, improvements are frequently lost when medication stops. Furthermore, medication like imipramine and its relatives can adversely affect sleep or mood, or cause a dry mouth, its long-term effects on children are not known, and accidental overdoses are dangerous (can, indeed, be fatal), which leads to reluctance to prescribe it.

Medical involvement will certainly be required for some of the methods already mentioned, even though these can be interpreted in terms of the behavioural concepts on which the intervention approaches are based. This includes prescription of laxatives, suppositories, and enemas for soiling associated with constipation. Enuresis can be caused by infections of the urinary tract, by diabetes, and by epileptic seizures, all of which are susceptible to medical intervention. It is also advisable to check with the person's doctor that there is no medical reason why an increase in fluid intake should not be instigated.

Finally, it is worth mentioning that using *Mycil* powder (sold by chemists for athlete's foot) as a talcum powder can reduce the smell arising from urinary incontinence and thus improve a person's social acceptability in advance of solving wetting problems.

Subsequent action

Example 2 describes the modification of an existing intervention with a view to increasing its effectiveness. Alan, a 14-year-old boy with a profound mental handicap, was placed on a commode regularly and reinforced for passing urine or faeces while there. At other times he engaged in games and other activities, and received attention and drinks, but he was removed from these attractive experiences for half-an-hour every time he had an accident. This was followed by increased appropriate use of the toilet but no reduction in accidents. The distinction between the pleasant situation and "time-out" was therefore made more obvious by putting a plastic bib on him and placing the "rewards" in it, but taking it off during "time-out" periods. The number of accidents then decreased significantly.

Example 7 describes a more radical change of programme. A procedure in which a seven-year-old boy with a profound mental handicap was taken regularly to a toilet and offered guidance in and reinforcement for using it achieved no success. It was replaced by use of a pants alarm, taking the boy quickly to the toilet when it sounded, and reinforcing appropriate behaviour there. This procedure, and subsequent adjustments as he made progress, led to independent toileting and no accidents.

Systems using enuresis alarms can fail for reasons enumerated earlier, and it may be necessary to use a different kind of alarm or change the method of use in some other way to achieve success.

Fading out intervention programmes without loss of improvements has been well provided for in dry bed training and rapid toilet training, which have been developed specifically for people with severe mental handicaps. The procedures have been described earlier.

Illustrative individual studies are, however, rare, though Example 6 provides one. The variation on rapid toilet training used there was described earlier. As soon as it resulted in one independent visit to the toilet in the 26-year-old man, prompting was discontinued completely, he was moved gradually further away from the toilet until he was out of the toilet area altogether, and the length of time between pants checks was gradually increased. The accident rate remained low on this less intensive programme.

A measure now recommended when using the simpler procedure of guiding a person to go to and use the toilet every time an enuresis alarm sounds, is to follow improvement by a continuation of the programme with an increased drinking rate. If this too is successful, it makes it easier for the person to maintain the improved behaviour when returning to a normal drinking rate. With people with mental handicaps, however, it has been more common to build increased fluid intake into the original intervention programme, though this should have the same effect on maintenance.

Rapid toilet training also includes a procedure for generalising improved behaviour from the toilet area to other settings by gradually moving the person further from the toilet. Again, Example 6 illustrates this. Generalisation may often require implementation of the same programme within all of the situations a person encounters.

It should be noted that successful interventions for toileting problems are quite often followed by a relapse at some stage. However, re-implementation of the intervention usually restores the improvement and makes further relapse less likely.

Several of the examples describe fading out of some elements of an intervention programme. In Example 3, for instance, a somewhat complex programme was used to reduce soiling in a five-year-old. It included use of a suppository every two days (or when the child looked as if he wanted to defaecate) and regular visits to the toilet, with reinforcing consequences for remaining there and for motions. When some improvements had been gained, the suppository was reduced in size and used less frequently, while reinforcers for sitting on and using the toilet were made intermittent and then gradually eliminated.

Illustrative studies

Example 1 (McNamara, 1972)

Dora, aged seven years, attended a British junior training centre (prior to the transfer of children with severe mental handicaps to education). She spoke only a few words and concentrated very poorly on most activities. The intervention programme was carried out by the centre staff, and it seems likely that they also did the recording.

The problem behaviour was defined as soiling the nappies she wore. During a baseline period records were kept of all such occurrences and the times at which they took place.

Intervention proceeded in various stages. Advance study of antecedents discovered that Dora eliminated regularly between one-and-a-half and two-and-a-half hours after meals and the mid-morning break. At these times, therefore, she was seated on the toilet and reinforced for staying there with *Smarties* and praise at first and, later, by playing pat-a-cake with the teaching assistant. At first, she also had to be reinforced with *Smarties* at intervals for accompanying the assistant to the toilet. These procedures were successful.

It was also intended to reinforce her massively for defaecating in the toilet, but she did not oblige.

The next stage of intervention was based on informal and systematic observations. On one occasion Dora got off the toilet and made for her nappy, defaecating en route. It was thought possible that nappy-wearing was an antecedent for soiling. This was tested by dressing her in pants for a few days, when she did *not* soil, which supported the idea. It was also observed that, when a nappy was dirtied, Dora would tug at the teacher's overall and her own nappy and then either lead the teacher to the bag of clean nappies or bang on the changing table. On the changing table she would lie down and wait to be cleaned, powdered, and changed, a procedure which she seemed to enjoy enormously. It seems likely that these procedures were reinforcing soiling. She was therefore changed standing up, while the other intervention procedures continued (though it is not clear if she was still dressed in pants). Soiling then decreased from three times a day to an average of just under once daily. The report does not state whether she then defaecated in the toilet.

In this investigation action was taken at the regular times at which Dora defaecated, presumably in the hope that she would learn to recognise internal sensations which would then act as antecedents for the behaviour of passing faeces. In addition, a supposed antecedent for soiling was eliminated by removing her nappy, appropriate behaviours were reinforced, and certain reinforcing consequences for problem behaviours were eliminated.

Example 2 (Barton *et al.*, 1975)

Alan was a 14-year-old boy with a profound mental handicap in a hospital-based special school. Though able to follow very simple instructions, his attention was very difficult to attract and maintain, and he would not wash or dress himself. He was frequently wet and often soiled, and there was no sign that he was aware of any discomfort. Intervention and recording were carried out by the staff.

The behaviours to be changed are not specifically defined in the written account, but simply labelled as "accidents" and "appropriate use of toilet". The former was recorded as the number per week and the latter as "percentage success".

The intervention programme was used with the whole class and no advance study of the effects of antecedents and consequences is reported. Commodes were placed in the classroom, and the children were placed on them every half-hour, remaining there until they used them or for 15 minutes. Success was reinforced with sweets, drinks, peanuts, biscuits, and cuddles. When not on a commode the children were engaged in games and simple activities, during which they received attention and drinks as long as they remained clean and dry. Whenever a child had an accident, he or she was removed from the games and given no attention for half-an-hour. During a baseline week, Alan's records showed only one instance of appropriate toilet use, whereas in the first three weeks of the programme, there were 14, 24, and 43 instances respectively. There were three accidents during baseline week, and two, five, and four respectively during the first three weeks of the programme. It was thought possible that he did not understand that reinforcement was provided only while he was clean and dry. He therefore had a plastic bib put on, into which various reinforcing offerings were placed. The bib was taken off during the time-out period. After this the number of accidents was never more than one, and was sometimes nil, per week. The extra drinks were also decreased so that instances of appropriate use of the toilet also become less frequent, varying from five to 14 per week. These levels were maintained over a year, though the precise conditions under which maintenance occurred are not clear − it is simply stated that the amount of time spent in training was decreased. The procedure was also gradually generalised to the school toilets, and this was accomplished without difficulty with Alan.

In this study extra drinks were antecedents for passing urine (thus giving more opportunities for learning appropriate behaviour), appropriate behaviour was reinforced in various ways, and time-out was used as a reducing consequence for problem behaviours.

Example 3 (Groves, 1982)

The subject of this study was a five-year-old boy with a mental handicap, particular delay in language, and autistic features in his behaviour. Though he had achieved dryness, he had a history of chronic constipation since early infancy, cried and refused to sit on the toilet, and had never achieved bowel control. Bowel movements were brought about by enemas (injections into the bowel to stimulate and lubricate passage of faeces). The intervention and measurement procedures were carried out by the parents at home.

Recording procedures were somewhat complex and not very clearly described, but the essential behaviours defined for measuring during both the baseline and the programme were large bowel movements without enema administration, soiling (presence of faeces in the pants at two-hourly checks), and self-initiated sitting on the toilet with defaecation. The number of instances of each was noted for each day and converted to various measures for comparison purposes.

After a four-week baseline an intervention programme was introduced. A detailed study of the problem was carried out before designing the programme. It appeared that difficulty in keeping solid food down and preference for soft foods contributed to chronic constipation. When this was not relieved by use of enemas, faeces would leak out in liquid form, or occasionally be passed involuntarily in small hard lumps. The boy also had balance problems, and this was thought to contribute to his crying and refusal to sit on the toilet. It was also supposed that he had difficulties in recognising sensations from inside his body which should have signalled that the muscles preventing evacuation of the bowel needed relaxing. Dietary changes were, therefore, introduced in advance of the programme, consisting mainly of increases in fibre and natural foods. The child-sized enema was replaced by an adult-sized suppository to increase bowel distention and its associated sensations. A footstool was provided to improve balance and body stability on the toilet. Every two days, or when the child made straining movements or gave other indications of needing to pass a motion, a suppository was inserted and he was seated on the toilet for a maximum of 15 minutes. Subsequently, he was seated on the toilet again for a maximum of five minutes, at 30-minute intervals, until a motion was passed. He was not forced to stay on the toilet, but popsicles, drinks, and recorded music were used as reinforcing consequences for remaining seated there. Bowel movements while on the toilet were reinforced with "social and physical praise" and popsicles.

Whenever the child passed faeces anywhere other than in the toilet, he was seated on the toilet for five minutes without any reinforcement. The result of this full-scale programme, which ran for four weeks, was that 100 per cent of all large bowel movements occurred on the toilet. During baseline, none had occurred on the toilet. No other changes were noted from baseline performance.

From the fifth intervention week onwards, measures began to be introduced to fade out the programme. After three large bowel movements in the toilet, the amount of suppository used was reduced by half, and the frequency of use was also decreased. Reinforcement for sitting on the toilet and for passing motions there was made intermittent and was then gradually phased out. Measures were also introduced to generalise the behaviour to situations outside the home. Further improvements occurred during and after these changes. Soiling of the pants was eliminated in three months, self-initiated use of the toilet occurred for 100 per cent of large bowel movements within three months, and the child was entirely self-sufficient in toilet use both at home and in school after five months. Follow-up over two years found no relapses.

In this intervention a stabilising stool was used as an antecedent to make problem behaviour less likely, and dietary changes and suppositories as antecedents to promote appropriate behaviours. The appropriate behaviours of sitting on the toilet and defaecating there were reinforced by popsicles, music, and social interaction. Sitting the boy on the toilet for defaecating elsewhere might be regarded as a reducing consequence for problem behaviour.

Example 4 (Doleys and Arnold, 1975)

Brian was an eight-year-old boy with a severe mental handicap who repeatedly soiled his pants at home, though rarely in school. There was some associated constipation, but no specific information about this was offered. The part of the intervention described here was implemented and recorded by the parents at home.

The behaviours measured were soiling and bowel movements in the toilet (not further defined). The number of each of these per week was noted.

After a four-week baseline an intervention procedure was commenced without reported study of the effects of existing antecedents and consequences. One day was spent in a psychology clinic overcoming Brian's refusal to sit on the toilet, which was henceforward no problem. From then on the parents were told to check Brian's pants every 15 to 20 minutes. If he had dry and clean pants he was reinforced, though the method is not stated. The parents were also asked to sit him on the toilet once an hour for about 10 minutes. On the way they were to ask him if he felt a need to go (in the hope that this would encourage him to attend to internal signals of the need) and, while he was there, he was reinforced for any apparent attempt to defaecate. Additionally, Brian chose a toy which was placed in his sight in the toilet. If he defaecated, he was allowed to have the toy. As soon as this had happened once, a chart with 10 squares was put on the toilet wall and Brian coloured in one square after each bowel movement. Twenty squares had to be coloured to win the second toy.

When a pants check revealed that Brian had soiled, he underwent a full cleanliness training. This involved a parent expressing displeasure, then Brian scrubbing his soiled pants for at least 15 minutes, and then bathing and cleaning himself. If he cried or was "disruptive" at the end of 15 minutes the procedure was to continue until he stopped. During the baseline Brian soiled his pants an average of three times a week and did not defaecate in the toilet at all. During the 16 weeks of the intervention described, the corresponding figures were 1.3 and 3.2 respectively.

For the next few weeks bowel movements in the toilet were reinforced by praise and food alone, pants were checked only every hour, and Brian was then simply asked if he wanted to go to the toilet and was not taken if he did not. The improvement was maintained, as it was also at a follow-up some weeks later.

In this intervention appropriate use of the toilet was encouraged by the antecedent of asking Brian if he wanted to go and the consequence of rewarding bowel movements in the toilet. Soiling was followed by the full cleanliness training programme as a reducing consequence.

Example 5 (Luiselli *et al.*, 1979)

One of the people in this study was a nine-year-old boy with a profound mental handicap, no speech or imitative behaviour, no response to instructions, no appropriate toilet behaviour, and much body-rocking and hand-flapping. The intervention was carried out and recorded in a special class in an ordinary school by the teachers there.

The behaviours identified and measured were urinating in the pants and urinating in the toilet. During the baseline, a normal toileting schedule was followed, the boy being taken to the toilet four times a day and seated on it for five minutes each time, the condition of his pants being noted. If he urinated in his pants, he was changed into dry clothes without comment. All instances of the two behaviours were recorded, and the number per school day noted.

After a baseline of 26 days an intervention programme, called rapid toilet training, was begun without reported study in advance of existing antecedents and consequences. For three hours each morning the boy was given drinks, initially and every half-hour, then taken to the toilet after every half-hour, and seated on it for 20 minutes or until he urinated there. If he had remained dry between two toilet visits he was reinforced by praise, touch, and things to eat; and the same applied if he urinated in the toilet. If he urinated in his pants he was subjected to five minutes of "overcorrection and positive practice". There is no description of the latter, but it is clear that "overcorrection" involved making him carry out some actions to put the situation right, such as cleaning up urine on the floor and chair and/or going to get dry pants and/or cleaning his genital region and changing into dry pants and/or washing and hanging out the wet pants; while "positive practice" involved making him go to the toilet, lower his pants, sit on it for a few seconds, get up, raise his pants, and return to his chair, repeating the sequence a number of times. It was not feasible to continue this intensive programme for the rest of the school day, so a less intense version took over. During the baseline the boy urinated in his pants twice a day on average and in the toilet not at all, whereas during the 13 days of intervention the corresponding averages were below one and above three respectively. By the end of the 13 days he was urinating in the toilet during at least 70 per cent of his morning visits (presumably measured for one morning).

At this point fading out of the intervention programme began. The boy took part in regular classroom activities and was taken to the toilet just five times a day and seated on it for five minutes each time. Otherwise the programme was much the same. This lasted 20 days and wetting was virtually absent. After that, checking of pants was gradually eliminated, and visits to the toilet returned to baseline levels. Urination in the toilet was still reinforced and positive practice and overcorrection used for wetting. Finally, reinforcement for urinating in the toilet was faded out. Pants-wetting remained virtually absent over a follow-up of about a year.

In this study drinks were used as antecedents to increase urination and this provided more opportunities for learning. Taking the boy to the toilet was an antecedent to make it more likely that he would urinate there. This appropriate behaviour was reinforced by praise, touch, and food, and the unwelcome activities involved in overcorrection and positive practice were used as reducing consequences for wetting.

Example 6 (Dickson and Smith, 1976)

Andrew was a 26-year-old man with a profound mental handicap in an institution, who had frequent wetting accidents. Both the intervention and its recording was carried out on the ward in a mental handicap hospital by the nursing staff, with the psychologist advising and monitoring closely.

The behaviours to be changed are not specifically defined in the written account, but the aims of the programme are given as training Andrew to go to the toilet of his own accord and decreasing his wetting accidents. The number of wetting accidents per week was measured.

Andrew's intervention programme was carried out without reported advance study of antecedents and consequences. It is not specifically described, but can be more or less pieced together by reference back to several other articles to which reference is made, together with some use of imagination. (This is necessary because I have not been able to find a satisfactory description of the use of these particular methods with any individual person in any other publication). The programme had three elements, presumably carried out concurrently since it is not indicated otherwise. They were: a bladder training procedure; an accident training procedure; and self-initiation training.

Bladder training procedure. For approximately eight hours a day initially, Andrew was restricted to a part of the ward screened off as a training area. At regular intervals (perhaps half-hourly) he was given as much to drink as he would take, so that the frequency of urination was increased to allow more training opportunities and, therefore, speed up the programme. Every half-hour Andrew was prompted to go to and use the toilet. The prompts used were the minimum needed. If a gesture, or word, or a single touch was sufficient, nothing else was used. If necessary Andrew was led to the toilet, physically seated upon it, and his legs moved into the appropriate position. This physical guidance, however, was gradually faded to a touch and then a gesture, and verbal instruction was also replaced by a brief gesture as soon as possible. If, on any occasion, minimal prompting failed to work, it was stepped up to the minimum necessary to be effective. Whenever Andrew performed on the toilet this behaviour was reinforced by giving him a sweet, or something else he liked to eat. In addition, his pants were checked every five minutes. He was encouraged to feel them himself to discriminate a dry condition from a wet one, and he was rewarded if they were dry.

Accident training procedure. Andrew wore a pants alarm, consisting of a circuit and a device for producing a warning noise housed in a box worn on a belt around the waist and attached by leads to electrodes connected to the outside of his underpants, slightly below the tip of the penis. Whenever he began to urinate the urine completed the electric circuit and crossed the gap between the electrodes, and the alarm sounded. When this happened an adult would gain his attention and then reprimand him. The alarm was then disconnected, and Andrew had to practise going to the toilet several times. If he did not cooperate with this he was manually guided, the guidance being faded out as he began to cooperate. No reward was given unless *he* took the initiative in going to the toilet. Following the toilet practice, there was a half-hour time-out period during which no drinks, rewards, or attention was given.

Self-initiation training. This developed from the prompting and fading procedure for going to the toilet described under the bladder training procedure. As soon as Andrew went once to the toilet on his own initiative, arrived dry, and attempted to sit on the toilet and push his trousers down, prompting was discontinued completely. After each "success" of this kind, he was allowed to go a little further away from the toilet, until eventually he was back in the main part of the ward. The length of time between pants checks was gradually increased. Under this régime, the number of wetting accidents decreased from 37 accidents per week during an unspecified baseline period, to three during the seventh week of training. To maintain this improvement, checking of pants was gradually reduced to six times a day, with praise for being dry and the same consequences as during the programme when wet. Mealtimes were included in the six occasions, and Andrew had to be dry to obtain the meal. This maintained a rate of about three accidents per week.

In this intervention: various kinds of prompting were used as antecedents to bring about appropriate toileting behaviour; self-initiated attempts to use the toilet were reinforced with things Andrew liked to eat; and staying dry was similarly reinforced (differential reinforcement of behaviour incompatible with the problem behaviour or DRI). The problem wetting behaviour was followed by reducing consequences. These included interrupting the behaviour with the pants alarm, reprimanding him, making him engage in the perhaps unwelcome behaviour of repeatedly using the toilet (overcorrection), and a time-out period.

This particular combination of techniques is a variation of the treatment package known as rapid toilet training.

Example 7 (Van Wagenen *et al.*, 1969)
One of the people in this study was a nine-year-old boy in an institution. He had a profound handicap, but could walk and had some ability to handle his clothes. He had no speech. The intervention was carried out by the experimenters, in a small room equipped with play materials and some adjacent toilets, in an establishment to which children were referred for toilet training.

Only appropriate behaviours were specifically identified, and these were selected on the basis of a training sequence. During the baseline the boy was frequently offered as much water as he would drink and was praised for drinking. He was dressed in cotton briefs and upper garments only, placed in a room with two other children, and observed for 3 to 4 hours daily. All urination events were recorded and assigned to one of six levels representing intermediate steps between "urinates on the floor" (level 1) and "walks in, removes clothes and urinates in commode, all without prompting" (level 6).

The baseline period lasted "a minimum of 5 days", after which an intervention programme was commenced without reported advance investigation of antecedents and consequences. The boy was one of three children being trained together, and frequent offers of unlimited quantities of water continued with the aim of increasing opportunities for learning. Instead of briefs he wore a somewhat complex enuresis alarm, which allowed urine to pass through it to emerge on the floor or in the toilet. An alarm worn on a belt sounded as soon as urine began to pass through, continued to sound throughout urine flow, and stopped when urination did. Training proceeded in the following steps:

As soon as the alarm sounded the trainer moved rapidly to the boy calling "Stop" or "No". The combined startling effect of these events often led the child to stop passing urine.

The trainer grasped the boy by the hand, led him quickly towards the commode, and placed him in the position for urinating. He then kept quiet and gently stroked the boy's back to get him to start urinating again. The alarm was still operating and, whenever it sounded in this situation, the trainer clapped his hands and made other effusive gestures of approval to reinforce the urination.

When the boy reliably urinated into the commode, the trainer faded out the prompting procedures. Instead of physically leading the boy, he went close to him and called and beckoned to induce walking to the commode. These less intrusive prompts were themselves discontinued as they became unnecessary.

When independent travel to the commode was achieved, the alarm was replaced by cotton training briefs, and the boy was taught to remove and replace them by physical guidance and reinforcement.

At the beginning of this intervention the boy urinated on the floor, but usually had some left over for the commode. Within eight days all urinating on the floor had ceased and he was consistently walking to the toilet without prompting, removing his briefs, and urinating in the commode.

The "package" described here is labelled the forward-moving procedure by the authors. The alarm and the trainer's reaction can be seen as reducing consequences for urinating on the floor, since they interrupt it. Guidance in visiting the toilet provides antecedents for appropriate toilet behaviour, which is then reinforced by approval.

Example 8 (Litrownik, 1974)

Steven, who was seven years old, had a profound mental handicap, no speech or response to simple instructions, and was totally incontinent. The intervention was carried out and its effects measured by the parents at home.

The behaviour to change was not specifically defined, but the number of "accidents" per day between 3.30 and 9.00pm was measured, together with a record of the times at which they occurred.

After a one-week baseline a programme was begun, based partly on observations made during the baseline. It had been found that accidents occurred at predictable times, such as after snacks, after dinner, and before bed. Steven's parents were therefore advised to sit him on the toilet three times a day at times when he usually urinated. This had to be physically prompted at first but, after a week, Steven was taking off his own pants and sitting on the toilet for at least two minutes at a time. Various antecedents were used to try to get him to eliminate, such as placing his hand in water, running water from a tap, and making various grimaces and grunts preceded by instructions to "Do this". He was also given large amounts to drink beforehand. However, he eliminated only twice over a nine-week period. These eliminations were immediately reinforced by food and praise, but there was no repetition of elimination as a result.

Following this initial failure a different method was tried. Steven wore a device which gave an auditory signal every time he wet (by the completion of an electric circuit).

When it sounded the parents said "Potty", and immediately ran him to the bathroom, disconnected the alarm, and "reinforced" him with food and praise. The description does not state what behaviour was supposed to be reinforced, but the procedures were meant to inhibit urination until Steven reached the bathroom. After two days the parents reacted in the same way, except that, after disconnecting the alarm, they told Steven to sit on the toilet, and they reinforced him if he did. On the third day of this changed procedure, Steven began to urinate in the toilet. For the next 18 days he was reinforced only when he did so. Another change was instituted shortly after this because Steven had started to pull at the alarm apparatus or to "fuss" before eliminating. When he did this his parents now said "Potty" and took him to the bathroom. During the first 14 days of this phase there were only three accidents, whereas there had been between four and six per day during the baseline. Steven's parents then returned to taking him to the bathroom at times when he usually urinated and telling him "Potty". Within 14 days he was going to the bathroom on his own, and during the 14 days after that there were no accidents. After another seven days without accidents the alarm apparatus was removed. Steven remained continent over a five-month follow-up period. The improvement transferred to school and was maintained on a two-week visit to relatives.

In the successful phases of this intervention Steven's problem behaviour was initially followed by interrupting it with the alarm and running him to the toilet, which may have been reducing consequences. Later he was told to sit on the toilet as an antecedent to bring about this appropriate behaviour, which was then reinforced by food and prai Later these reinforcing consequences followed only when he urinated in the toilet. Later still, saying "Potty" and taking him to the toilet were used as antecedents to bring about appropriate behaviours. The procedure is an adaptation of the forward-moving procedure described in Example 7, but appears to have used an ordinary pants alarm.

PART D

Making it possible

SECTION 1. TRAINING

Introduction

Parts B and C of this guide have outlined the main techniques of intervention for behaviour problems in people with severe mental handicaps. A number of conditions are, however, needed if these techniques are to be used effectively in practice. One of these is adequate training of the people who are to carry out the techniques.

The issues surrounding training will now be discussed and some basic suggestions offered. For more detailed practical suggestions readers are referred to Topping (1986), Yule and Carr (1987), McBrien and Foxen (1981), Foxen and McBrien (1981), and McConkey (1985).

Why train?

Reading alone is rarely sufficent preparation for applying behavioural techniques. Hopefully this book has described such techniques clearly enough to allow the most straightforward applications to be carried out without further guidance, and this *is* possible. However, such applications are not often undertaken without practical guidance, despite good intentions.

There are a number of reasons why guidance in person is needed to supplement written accounts:

However clear, written material can be misunderstood.

People may lack confidence that a technique will work for them. Are they to do all that planning for nothing? It is also possible for them to become discouraged during early attempts at application. Personal guidance can provide support and reassurance.

No-one is accustomed to pre-planning behaviour in the detail required for behavioural programmes. This requires considerable self-discipline, which is more likely to be maintained in the knowledge that someone is observing what is happening or that there is a need to report back to someone.

Actions required of people implementing behavioural programmes may sometimes conflict with their habitual ways of behaving. For instance, it is easier to complain of other people's problem behaviours than to praise or reward them when they behave more acceptably. The changes needed may be difficult to bring about without supervision.

It is helpful for people to have feedback on their performance from someone who is more knowledgeable, so that they know when they are operating effectively and when they are not.

Although the above arguments suggest that reading alone is rarely sufficient preparation for carrying out specific programmes, behavioural approaches also suggest *general* changes in ways of behaving towards people with mental handicaps. Various characteristics of behaving – such as having clear goals, looking for features of the environment that might be causing or maintaining problem behaviours and changing them, looking for things to praise rather than things to criticise, and acting consistently – are worth adopting generally. To be reminded of them in relation to problem behaviours can sometimes lead to a change of approach and consequent improvements, even though specific programmes are not planned. As in any field, there is a danger of becoming dogmatic about the need for specialised training, and this attitude can deter people from quite simple, helpful changes in approach which can be achieved without it.

Who should do the training?

The primary experts in behavioural approaches are applied psychologists. In the field of severe mental handicap, these are usually educational or clinical psychologists. Other professionals, however, can also acquire the expertise needed to train. Doctors, teachers, and nurses, for instance, have all been involved in training situations. The trainers may be employed by an organisation that has responsibility for people with mental handicaps, by training or educational establishments, or by private agencies.

It is also possible for people who have received a basic training to pass on some helpful techniques to colleagues by word of mouth and practical example. However, this should not be regarded as a complete form of training. One very promising training scheme, however, is *pyramid training,* in which trainers train others not only as practitioners, but also as trainers. One example of this is the *EDY (Education of the Developmentally Young)* training developed at the Hester Adrian Research Centre at Manchester University, in which educational psychologists have been trained as trainers and have then gone back to their employing authorities and taught other educational psychologists and also teachers. Similarly, the nursing profession has set up an advanced training in behavioural approaches, which is attended by experienced nurses who then return to their work settings to participate in training other nursing staff there. Teachers trained to use behavioural approaches sometimes pass on their skills effectively to other teachers or to parents. Parents have been used to train other parents. The more links there are in the chain of communication, however, the greater the danger that the message received will be different from the original.

What training experiences are necessary?

It is important to have a clear knowledge of the techniques required. The same could be said of an understanding of the underlying theory, but it is by no means clear that this always aids effective implementation. A reading or lecture input can provide for either need. There must also be provision for asking questions, and it is helpful to have a subsequent test of knowledge, with correction of errors and misunderstandings.

Supervised practice of techniques is extremely helpful, though success can sometimes be achieved without it. Examples are devising clear descriptions of behaviours, measuring behaviours, and drawing up programmes for hypothetical cases. Videotapes, of people showing problem behaviour for instance, can be very helpful in providing suitable material that can be used for such practice. Written exercises, and assignments carried out in groups, can promote sharing of ideas and discussion. Role-play can be invaluable, allowing trainers to demonstrate techniques and trainees to practise them. It is helpful to record role-play sessions on a videotape so that people's performance can be studied in detail afterwards.

Implementation of the first programmes carried out by trainees with people with mental handicaps should be seen as part of their training. Trainees can be watched by more knowledgeable supervisors, or asked to report back to them in detail. Recording forms like those in the Action Record in this book are helpful for such reporting back.

Follow-up is also highly desirable to ensure that effective practice is maintained and to allow trainees to raise problems which have cropped up and develop expertise with techniques not covered by the initial training. It is best if the follow-up can be ongoing, so that problems can be sorted out at any time.

How should training be organised?

The precise organisation of training will vary according to the needs of trainees, the availability of trainers, and the nature of the daily situations involved. In particular, there is a need to consider:

whether the training will be ongoing or provided in specific sessions;

whether it will be given individually or in groups;

and,

what level of expertise will be expected of trainees.

Each of these considerations will now be explored further.

Ongoing training or specific sessions?

An ideal situation is one where a resident expert can be available whenever needed. Training can then be organised at times which match the progress of the trainees and can be continued for as long as support is needed. Such situations are rare.

Usually training has to be organised on a sessional basis. It is then important to plan the timing of the sessions carefully. Each should be of a length sufficient for all needs to be covered without rushing. There should be sufficient time between sessions to allow the necessary application of what has been learned, but not so much that trainees are insufficiently supported or feel they are getting "nowhere". The right balance is hard to find and will vary enormously from person to person.

Individual or group training?

Individual training allows the maximum interchange between trainer and trainee. It has been developed to a high degree in the *EDY* training mentioned earlier. Full details are provided in McBrien and Foxen (1981) and Foxen and McBrien (1981). Briefly, the training has been used for teachers and non-teaching assistants working with children with severe mental handicaps in special schools, and for nurses and nursing assistants working with adults in hospitals. It attempts to teach basic behavioural principles and to help trainees design and carry out training programmes that will aid learning and development of people with severe mental handicaps and help to overcome behaviour problems. There are three phases.

> *Phase 1* consists of 10 practical sessions covering, respectively: basic behavioural principles; selecting reinforcers; using reinforcers to change behaviour; prompting; task analysis; shaping; imitation training; time-out; overcorrection; and generalisation and discrimination.
>
> These are taught by a combination of: short reading assignments; watching and rating of video demonstrations of techniques; role-play techniques; practising of techniques with people with severe mental handicaps with feedback from the trainer; ratings of performance; and a written test.

> *Phase 2* involves the trainer and trainee together applying what has been learned in setting up a behavioural programme for one person with a severe mental handicap in the everyday environment. The trainee runs the programme, reports back, and is provided with feedback and advice.

> *Phase 3* is similar, but the trainer gradually lessens the amount of support given, allowing the trainee to take more and more responsibility for the programme.

In principle, individual training allows the timing and length of training to be geared specifically to individual needs. In practice, however, this is limited by time constraints. The complete *EDY* training, for instance, consists of 34 sessions; and this is far longer than any other training scheme of which I am aware.

Most training has to be on a group basis, for reasons of economy. This arrangement does have advantages, however, in that trainees can share experiences and feelings with fellow trainees and feel supported by the group to which they belong. In the workshops I organised for teachers, this opportunity to share problems with each other was one of the most valued features.

What level of expertise is needed?
Given that the more involved and intrusive interventions will require expert guidance on an individual basis, most practitioners will not need to be trained in all the techniques described in Part B, though they should know about them. It is suggested that two levels of training can be identified which will apply to most people working in most environments.

There should be a *first-level training* in which people learn to: identify problem and appropriate behaviours, and measure them; identify existing influences maintaining problem behaviours; identify the necessary changes in antecedents and consequences; plan an intervention programme, with the main emphasis on ways of increasing appropriate behaviours; measure and evaluate the results; and plan future steps.

A *second level training* should cover the rest of the techniques in this guide. This is appropriate for people working in more specialised settings – for instance, in units where people with severe mental handicaps who have particularly serious behaviour problems are gathered together for help – and for people who will eventually train and supervise others.

Detailed proposals for these two levels of training follow. The need not to be dogmatic on the subject has already been referred to, however, and I would not wish anyone to think that this is the only helpful way of proceeding.

A suggested first-level training scheme

The following scheme is outlined as one possible way of providing intitial training in the use of behavioural techniques. It is intended for use with people who have had no experience of such techniques and for those who have used them to some extent but have had no systematic training in doing so.

The scheme consists of eight weekly workshop sessions, and a follow-up meeting about a month after Session 8. Each session is between two and two-and-a-half hours long, and contains whatever is needed of input, practice, discussion, and testing of knowledge and skills. Between sessions, trainees should each work with a selected person with a severe mental handicap and apply what has been learned in each session in that person's everyday environment. If possible, there should be regular visits to these environments by the trainer during and after the training period to observe, advise, and help the trainees. Ideally there should be no more than five trainees for each trainer, though where a number of trainers work jointly there may be some sessions (such as Session 1) when they are not all needed. The kinds of experience that are appropriate for each session are outlined below. The relevant sections of Part B of this book are noted for each. *Part C* should be regarded as a source of information about particular problem behaviours that crop up.

SESSION 1. Introduction and overview (Part B, Section 1 and Part D, Section 3).
The principles and concepts of behavioural approaches are introduced. These are illustrated by accounts of complete intervention programmes with people with severe mental handicaps. The trainees are then given an outline of the training and what it is intended to achieve. They then think about how the approaches might apply to the people with severe mental handicaps with whom they are involved, and each trainee is asked to select, before the next training unit, one of them with whom to work. Trainees

are each advised to choose a person whose problems are not too severe, since this will be their first attempt. Indeed, it is not vital for the person to present a problem of any seriousness at all. Everybody has some behaviour that would be better changed, and it is the process of behavioural change which is the subject of the training. In the following paragraphs, however, all behaviours chosen as needing to be decreased will be referred to as problem behaviours. Finally, legal and ethical questions are introduced and discussed.

SESSION 2. Defining the problem and selecting behaviours to work on (Part B, Sections 2 and 3).

The trainees each describe the person with severe mental handicap with whom they have chosen to work, and the problems the person presents. Form 1 of the Action Record is completed for this purpose. Input is provided on selecting and specifically describing problem and appropriate behaviours and analysing them further. Trainees practise writing behavioural descriptions. They are then each asked to prepare a description of all the problem behaviours of the person they have chosen (on Form 2 of the Action Record) and suggested appropriate behaviours to replace them (Form 3), and to have these ready for the next training session. If there are no problem behaviours of any seriousness, trainees are asked to identify *any* behaviours that would be better changed and their alternatives.

SESSION 3. Measuring behaviours (Part B, Section 4).

Trainees each present their descriptions of the problem and appropriate behaviours which they have prepared for the people with whom they will be working. The descriptions are checked and, if necessary, improved. Trainees then make a firm decision on which behaviours to work on, the emphasis being placed as far as possible on increasing appropriate behaviours. Input is now provided on measuring, with exercises carried out on various measuring techniques using role-play or videotapes. Trainees' knowledge is then tested. Ways of measuring the behaviours selected by the trainees are discussed. Trainees are asked to finalise the method of recording they will use, to carry in out in the daily situation, and to present the results (on Form 4) at the next session.

SESSION 4. Identifying existing influences (Part B, Section 5).

Records of measuring are examined and discussed, and alterations suggested where appropriate. Input is provided on how behaviours are influenced by antecedents and consequences and how these may be identified. Practice exercises are arranged for such identification, using role-play or videotapes. In readiness for the next session, trainees are asked to:

   continue measuring, improving on the process where necessary;

   investigate the antecedents and consequences of the problem behaviours selected for study and record the results on Forms 5 and 6.

SESSION 5. Deciding on changes to make in antecedents and consequences (Part B, Sections 6 and 7).

Records of investigation of existing antecedents and consequences are examined and their implications for practice discussed. Input is provided on changes which might be made in these to improve behaviours. The emphasis is on antecedents and consequences to increase appropriate behaviours, but there is also some discussion of changes to decrease problem behaviours. These are limited to the least intrusive. For consequences in particular, only very easily-used and low-key methods are included, such as planned ignoring and non-exclusionary time-out. Techniques are demonstrated, role-played, or videotaped and played back. Trainees' knowledge and understanding is tested. Before the next session, trainees are asked to:

continue measuring;

select changes in antecedents and consequences likely to be helpful for increasing appropriate behaviours, record them on Form 7, and underline those they propose to use;

select changes in antecedents and consequences likely to be helpful for decreasing problem behaviours, record them on Form 8, and underline any they propose to use.

SESSION 6. Planning and implementing the first attempt to overcome the problem (Part B, Sections 8 and 9).
Records of decision-making for changes in antecedents and consequences to increase appropriate behaviours and decrease problem behaviours chosen are examined, and modified if necessary. Input is provided on programme planning and implementation, examples of programmes are presented, and exercises on planning programmes are carried out. Trainees are each helped to plan a programme for use with the person with whom they will be working. By the next session, they are asked to:

think further about the programme, write a full description of it on Form 9, and begin to implement it;

continue measuring, but now using Form 10.

SESSION 7. Early evaluation and modification of intervention programme (Part B, Sections 8 and 9).
Trainees report back on their programmes and on how they are progressing. Doubts about whether the programme design is appropriate are examined and changes are considered – but made only if there are strong reasons for doing so. Problems arising during implementation are discussed and practice is provided in any techniques causing difficulty. Trainees are asked to:

continue the programme, with any modifications needed, but attempting to do so without any further changes to it;

record any changes on Form 11;

continue measuring.

SESSION 8. Further planning and implementation (Part B, Section 10).
Records of the behaviours are examined, trainees each report back on their experience, and progress is evaluated. There is discussion of whether the programme should continue in its present form, or whether it should be faded out or replaced by a modified or new programme. Plans are made for any changes necessary. Input is provided on means of

fading out the programme and maintaining and generalising changes. By the time of the follow-up session, trainees are asked to:

think more about how the programme has progressed and record on Form 11;

plan and implement any changes needed and record these on whichever forms are appropriate;

if appropriate, plan how to fade out the programme and maintain improvements, recording the plans on Form 12;

contact the trainer if advice or help is needed before follow-up.

SESSION 9. Follow-up (Part B, Section 10).
Records of the behaviours are examined, progress is evaluated, advice and help is provided as needed, and plans for future action are made. Form 12 is completed if this has not been done already – if improvements have not occurred, this should still be done as an exercise. Trainees discuss how they will be able to apply what they have learned in the future. They provide feedback to the trainer on what they have gained from the workshop and what further advice and help they need. Ideally, there should be continued contact with the trainer, unless guidance is readily available otherwise.

At the end of this training, trainees should have a basic knowledge of behavioural approaches and should be able to carry out interventions that do not require very intrusive methods. They should also be able to assist with more intrusive programmes, provided they are supervised by someone with adequate knowledge, skill, and experience of using such techniques.

It should be noted that useful results can be obtained with training that is even simpler and more abbreviated than that described above. My own workshops, from which a number of examples are described in Part C, were provided for teachers, most of whom had already attended a lecture at a larger course which outlined behavioural approaches. Each workshop consisted of: six sessions of about one-and-a-quarter hours each, on a once-a-week basis; at least one informal visit to each classroom during the workshop period; and some informal follow-up afterwards. Participants were guided to: identify behaviours to increase and decrease (Session 1); carry out baseline measurements (Session 2); identify reinforcers which might increase appropriate behaviour (Session 3); work out a programme for using these reinforcers systematically to change behaviours (Session 4); and measure and evaluate the results, and plan the next step (Sessions 5 and 6). This was sufficient to decrease most of the problem behaviours which concerned them.

A suggested second-level training scheme

It is more difficult to outline a suggested scheme for advanced training in behavioural techniques, since needs will vary considerably between different settings. The following proposals should, therefore, be regarded as only one of many possible schemes.

The scheme is again based on nine sessions of between two and two-and-a-half hours each, with a 1:5 trainer: trainee ratio. However, the sessions are further apart, allowing time for considerably more practice in the everyday environment between sessions. Each session, apart from the first: takes an advanced topic; provides the necessary input, demonstration, practice, discussion, and testing; and is followed up by application by the trainees, as appropriate, to several people with severe mental handicaps in their everyday environments. These exercises are reported on at the subsequent sessions. There is a considerable emphasis on sharing knowledge, skills, and training experiences with other people who already have some experience in this work. The content of the sessions is as follows. As for the first-level training, relevant Part B sections are noted and Part C is used for further information on particular problem behaviours as required.

SESSION 1. Introduction and overview.
This session starts with trainees describing their current work, and outlining difficulties encountered and gaps in their expertise. There is then some testing and revision to ensure that basic behavioural principles are not only mastered but remembered. The trainer then outlines the organisation of the training and negotiates with the trainees as to how it can be used to provide for their needs. For the next session the trainees are asked to identify a number of people with severe mental handicaps with whom they work, who present particular problems. This is intended to give some flexibility for practising what is learned in the everyday environment.

SESSION 2. Further analysis of behaviours to change (Part B, Section 3).
This session offers more detailed coverage of analysis of behaviours identified for change, and practice and testing takes place as necessary.

SESSION 3. Measuring (Part B, Section 4).
Trainees are reminded of the different techniques of measuring. They are asked to identify techniques they have not used and behaviours in the people whom they have selected which they think are difficult to measure. Input, practice, and testing is provided as necessary, and plans are made for exercises in the everyday environment after the session.

SESSION 4. Identifying antecedents and consequences (Part C, Section 5, 6, and 7).
This session concentrates on identifying existing antecedents for alternative appropriate behaviours (those for problem behaviours were covered in the first-level training) and on a wider range of possible changes in antecedents and consequences to modify behaviours, including more intrusive devices.

SESSION 5. Less intrusive interventions (Part B, Sections 8 and 9).
Trainees identify less intrusive techniques they have not used. These are discussed and plans for exercises are made.

SESSIONS 6 and 7. More intrusive interventions (Part B, Sections 8 and 9).
Such devices as isolation time-out, physical restraint, overcorrection, and facial screening are described and practised. If appropriate, they are carried out in the everyday environment, though this is under *direct* supervision if any risk is thought to be entailed.

SESSIONS 8 and 9. Programme modification, fading out programmes, maintaining change, generalisation (Part B, Section 10).
These are covered in more detail than in the first-level training. Trainees identify

relevant needs among the people with whom they are working and practise them in the everyday setting.

At the end of this training, trainees should be able to carry out a wider range of techniques with much less supervision. Further sessions can be organised to provide them with training skills and practice, and they can then possibly be recruited to help with first-level training. After sufficient experience of this, they will be able to organise first-level training themselves.

Where should training take place?

There are arguments for basing training in the everyday situation where the techniques are to be applied. This gives it a greater feeling of reality and does not present trainees with the additional task of transferring what they have learned in one situation to another. It also helps other people in the everyday situation to understand in advance what is going to be done. On the other hand, training provided elsewhere often allows greater concentration on learning techniques which can be difficult to acquire. It also makes training in groups more feasible, so that experiences and ideas can be shared.

Most training takes place away from the everyday situation. (Exceptions to this are the very promising home-visiting schemes for parents, particularly the *Portage Scheme* described by Bluma *et al.* (1976), which can include behaviour problems within their scope.) This removal of training from the everyday situation makes it particularly important that all staff who work in the everyday setting receive some kind of training, if only to provide them with a clear idea of what their colleagues are doing.

One situation where there is an additional argument for training outside the everyday setting is where people working in different settings need to cooperate very closely. Parent workshops, for instance, have been organised in schools by teachers, though not particularly for behaviour problems as yet, to help parents understand what the school is trying to do and to foster joint working. This clearly takes parents out of their everyday setting.

PART D

Making it possible

SECTION 2. PROVISION AND ORGANISATION OF RESOURCES

Topics covered

This section covers a group of related conditions which are important if behavioural techniques are to be implemented successfully. Firstly, there must be sufficient resources, both human and material, to allow the techniques to be carried out. Secondly, there must be appropriate organisation of both activities and resources. Thirdly, senior staff must provide the necessary supervision and support.

Resources

Effective implementation of the approaches described makes heavy demands on resources, mostly human resources. Much time is needed for individual observation, planning, and implementation. Though many techniques can be incorporated into everyday activities, there are others that need a person's full attention. Staffing levels should be sufficient to permit this and to provide help for parents and other relatives.

Actual staffing needs vary greatly from one situation to another. No attempt will be made to recommend staffing levels, except to say that, where several people with severe mental handicaps and very severe behaviour problems are gathered together for specialised help, the staffing ratio will sometimes need to be one staff member to two people with behaviour problems or better, if the problems are to be overcome rather than just contained. It is also important to remember that parents of people presenting problem behaviours should not have to devote the whole of their lives to coping with their young or grown-up children. They are entitled to some time of their own. In addition they should not be placed in a position where they have to neglect the rest of the family in order to cope with the person with behaviour problems. A great deal of regular help should, therefore, be available to any such parent who wants it and staffing levels should seek to make adequate provision for this.

Turning to material resources, it is important that the accommodation should allow and facilitate effective interventions. In the first place this means that it should provide for the basic needs of the people with severe mental handicaps concerned, regardless of whether they show behaviour problems or not. There should, for instance, be sufficient space to allow people to pursue their interests without getting too much in each other's way. However, the layout should be homely, with some relatively secluded corners and comfortable seating. Sleeping areas should allow a degree of privacy, and suitable provision for keeping personal possessions. Toilets should be private, comfortable, and easy to keep clean. There should be raised areas to provide a view for people who cannot stand and to allow people with responsibility to handle them easily. Provision should be made for outdoor activities.

In addition, the accommodation should facilitate the techniques needed to overcome behaviour problems. Doors should be lockable if necessary, so that staff are not diverted from constructive activities by having to catch escaping people who have no road sense. At least some walls, lights, and flooring should be designed to minimise damage from violence, or injury to those who abuse themselves physically. Safe sleeping areas are particularly important. One-way mirrors are valuable for observing behaviour un-obtrusively. A conveniently situated time-out room or area is important, designed to be uninteresting without being frightening. It should have soft walls, to minimise harm from attempts at self-injury, which are easily cleaned to reduce the effects of frequent vomiting or defaecating, and the design should allow people with responsibility to see in and people with severe mental handicaps *not* to see out. A specially designed toilet training area is invaluable.

Certain kinds of equipment may be needed. Again, this should provide for basic needs as well as for behaviour problems. Plenty of carefully chosen leisure materials, for instance, help to make life more interesting and behaviour problems therefore less likely. Equipment specifically for use in coping with behaviour problems is rarely excessively expensive, but a low budget can make even very modestly priced items difficult to obtain. Devices for counting and timing behaviours, to aid toilet training, to help control drooling, and to provide vibration as a reward for appropriate behaviours are all examples of equipment mentioned in this guide. Provision for safe storage of equipment is essential.

Further suggestions on accommodation and equipment can be found in Jones (1983), though his account focuses on children.

Organising staff and activities

There are many difficulties in organising staff resources and activities for effective behaviour change programmes. The most acute are likely to be those which involve using a relatively small amount of staff time to carry out all the assessment, recording, planning, and implementing of programmes. These are additional to the many essential activities which take place routinely in the setting where the programmes are being used. In attempting to solve the problem, all available helping hands need to be mustered and then organised carefully to ensure that as many vital functions as possible are carried out to the maximum possible extent.

The first step is to determine who is available to help. In addition to regular staff, students, parents and other relatives, and volunteers might be able to help. Overall planning requires a fairly detailed knowledge of behavioural techniques, but many of the component activities are relatively simple and can be carried out by people without specialist knowledge if the requirements are made quite clear to them.

Once the force is mustered, the task requirements need to be determined and specific jobs allocated to particular people at particular times. This kind of procedure has only recently been studied experimentally, but it has already been found to be helpful in a number of settings, including a school special care unit, an adult training centre, a school-based residential unit for children with moderate to profound mental handicaps, and a residential home for adults with severe and profound mental handicaps.

One method of staff organisation is *room management*. At any one time, each staff member has a definite role. In one study, for instance, one person worked on individual programmes, one (the mover) looked after routine needs, and another (the room manager) kept a general eye open to see that all the other people with mental handicaps were occupied as appropriately as possible. If necessary the individual worker returned the person being worked with to the room manager, and helped the mover. However, other versions are possible, much depending on the number of staff available and the tasks to be carried out. So far, it has been felt most appropriate to rotate roles, to prevent staff boredom and involve all staff members at some time in all aspects of management.

Applying this approach to planning behaviour change programmes, it would be ideal, at any time when programmes were in operation, to have at least one person with responsibility carrying out individual programme activities with people with mental handicaps, at least one person ensuring that routine needs and interruptions were covered, and one more person to see that the group as a whole was usefully occupied. This last person has been called the room manager or play manager, and has a vital but often neglected role to play. While some individuals are being given attention during learning or activity programmes, whether to do with behaviour or otherwise, those who are unattended: may sit and do nothing; or may engage in stereotyped behaviour, apparently to relieve the boredom; or may seek attention or interest by producing behaviour which is disruptive. As pointed out throughout this book opportunities to engage in acceptable activities when left unattended are important antecedents for decreasing problem behaviours. The room or play manager needs, therefore: to ensure that appropriate activities are available in advance for all the people present; to prompt each person in turn to engage in one of the activities; to redirect people to any activity to which they have ceased to attend or to try them with another; and to provide for changes in activity from time to time. Only a short time should be spent with each person in turn, since frequent attention must be paid to every person to ensure that as many people as possible are encouraged to be constructively engaged for as long as possible.

Supervision and support

What any one person with responsibility can do alone is limited. For effective application of the techniques in this guide, it is important that the most senior staff should facilitate, coordinate, encourage, and monitor the effects of others. Different senior staff can help in different ways.

Senior administrative staff responsible for the systems in an establishment can try to ensure that such systems are helpful. Is it really necessary, for instance, on a hospital ward where systematic attempts are being made to decrease feeding problems, for food to be delivered and dirty crockery retrieved in less time than it takes to carry out the intervention techniques? Behavioural methods of intervention need to be carefully planned and precisely carried out, and overall routines should take this into account.

Senior administrative staff can also try to help ensure that the human and material resources needed are made available, and that their distribution and organisation within the establishment are satisfactory. Staff shortages are particularly likely to lead to breakdown of intervention programmes, especially in the early stages, and there may be ways of ensuring that their effect on such programmes is minimised.

Senior staff with a more direct, supervisory position have a wider variety of roles. They are the people who should have the commitment and determination to see that important intervention techniques are carried out effectively. They, too, should play their part in trying to secure the necessary resources, and they are the people responsible for organising those resources as suggested earlier in this section. Such organisation needs to be done in a way which makes the staff for whom they are responsible feel involved and committed. This is best achieved by working out the proposed organisation after full consultation with everybody involved, and then meeting with everyone regularly to discuss how well it is working afterwards. If staff feel the organisation is partly theirs, they are likely to play a more enthusiastic part in making it work.

These senior staff also have an important role in ensuring that each member of staff has clearly assigned duties and carries them out. Each person with a severe mental handicap, for instance, should have some clearly defined goals, and one or more members of staff should have a clear responsibility to help that person reach them. The senior member of staff should ensure that the duties are written down and that, wherever appropriate, written records are kept to show that they are being carried out. Charts on the wall to show the progress being made by the people staff are trying to help could be a useful aid. Senior members of staff should communicate clearly and regularly with all staff to let them know whether they think they are carrying out their roles well or unsatisfactorily; and they must be prepared to offer advice, help, and emotional support if things are not going well.

A recently published study provides an interesting example of a staff supervisory system. A daily, one-hour activity period was introduced into a hospital ward. The staff were trained in the techniques required for this and the nursing officer and senior nursing officer associated with the ward were trained to use a specific monitoring system. Written descriptions of what was required of the staff were drawn up in consultation with them. Each day the ward charge nurse calculated and made graphs of the level of involvement of residents in activities during the activity hour. The graphs and other relevant data were sent each Wednesday to the nursing officer, who passed copies on to the senior nursing officer. Once a fortnight, the nursing officer made an unannounced visit during an activity period. He filled in a monitoring checklist and told the staff how well he thought they were doing. Once a month, he combined his fortnightly records of observation and action with the charge nurse's weekly summaries into a report which he sent to the senior nursing officer. The senior nursing officer made an unannounced visit during an activity period once a month and went through the same procedures as the nursing officer carried out in his fortnightly visit. He then prepared a report which incorporated the nursing officer's monthly report and data and sent it to the Sector Health Care Team. This team met monthly and made comments to the senior nursing officer which were fed back to ward staff by the nursing officer. These procedures, as a whole, were found to maintain staff use of the techniques which they had been taught and engagement of residents in the activities.

The ways in which senior staff should carry out their supervisory role might best be described under six headings, adapted from those recently identified as part of a system called *positive monitoring*:

Defining the aims and goals. This is preferably done in consultation with staff. All staff members need to be clear about the aims of the service as a whole and the part of the service in which they work. All staff members should have their own goals. Thus, in a situation where the overall staff aim is to overcome certain behaviour problems in the people with severe mental handicaps whom they are helping, individual staff members might be allocated the broad goals described in the room management procedure described earlier. Within these goals there would be more specific goals; to do with the kinds of behaviour change required, the kinds of routine needed and interruptions to be covered, and the kinds of activities in which the group as a whole should be engaged. The aims and the goals should be written down. Senior members of staff should make their own personal goals clear to other staff, particularly since these should include helping them to achieve *their* goals.

Specifying staff procedures. Procedures should be clearly specified so that staff members know how they should work to achieve each service aim and each personal goal. The procedures should be agreed in consultation with staff, and written down in a clear way that can be referred to easily. They should be reviewed regularly. The intervention programmes devised for behaviour problems can provide procedures for some of the aims and goals. Again, the procedures by which the senior staff help other staff in this aspect of the system should be clearly specified.

Helping staff follow procedures. Senior staff should make sure that all the other staff understand what is expected of them and can carry out the procedures required. They should either provide or seek appropriate training for them. Then they should discuss the procedures with them individually, and watch them in action. It is helpful if they identify the key elements in the procedures required and write them down. This forms a checklist which they can use to guide their observation of staff and help identify where they are having difficulties. Staff should then be given feedback on how well they have done and should be guided in making any necessary improvements. Staff can also use such a checklist to help each other improve. In regard to behaviour problems the elements of an intervention programme may often translate easily into a checklist of what is required of staff. For a particular problem presented by Frank, for example, staff may need to praise him every time he behaves in an appropriate way and turn away from him as soon as he begins to engage in the problem behaviour. Both activities can be difficult to carry out regularly if they are not clearly identified and help in acting in an appropriate manner is not provided.

Watching staff work. Even after the procedures have been mastered, senior staff should continue to watch the staff in action regularly. Various checklists can be devised to help evaluate specific aspects of their work. This should be done on a sampling basis, using a schedule agreed with the staff. Records of observations should be meticulously kept.

Giving and receiving feedback. Senior staff should think very carefully about the feedback they give to staff. It is often useful for them to write it down first to help clarify their thinking. The priority is to identify what each member of staff is doing well and to convey this very specifically and in an encouraging manner. Improvements over previous performance should particularly be mentioned. Where criticism is required the emphasis should be, not on what was wrong, but on what to do instead. Where a better alternative is not clear, possible solutions should be discussed with staff to see if one can be discovered. Senior staff should also encourage staff to give *them* feedback on how they carry out their supervisory functions, and on ways in which organisation could be improved. They should receive these suggestions without becoming defensive and should either act on them or explain why they do not. All these processes are facilitated by careful recording by senior staff during sampling periods, and by the other staff when they are not being observed. Charts on the wall to show the progress made by the people staff are helping can also be a useful and encouraging aid.

Reviewing job performance. Senior staff should undertake regular job reviews with each member of staff they supervise. The reviews should be regular and fairly frequent, and should be carried out without interruption. Lists of matters to be discussed can be drawn up by the senior and other staff concerned, and the reviews themselves should similarly be a mutual enterprise, with both people involved trying to be honest and constructive in what they say to each other.

In supervising and supporting staff, it is advisable to keep in mind the importance of morale. Low morale can lead to staff: putting off things they are supposed to do; depending too much on supervisory staff, rather than taking responsibility themselves; failing to overcome problems that they would formerly have solved; resisting desirable changes in practice; losing their concern about the people whom they are responsible for helping; or running down other staff. The consequences can be serious, both for the effectiveness of their work and their own happiness and stability.

Low morale can result: from discouragement, through lack of success in work tasks; from feeling overwhelmed by the demands of the job; or from a general loss of interest, perhaps because a staff member feels "in a rut". These causes have implications for the measures needed to maintain good morale. The kinds of training, supervisory, and support activities already described should help staff to achieve success in their work and, therefore, avoid undue discouragement. Adequate resources and careful allocation of tasks should help staff avoid being overwhelmed by the work. As much variety as possible should be built into the job, so that if one task is particularly wearing staff can look forward to a rest from it. Involvement in planning activities provides a break from direct contact with the people being helped. Loss of interest in the job, or feeling in a rut, can be made less likely by supervisory staff taking a personal interest in those they supervise, treating them with respect, consulting them, attending sympathetically to their problems and anxieties, making clear the overall philosophy and plan of the work, and helping staff work out their individual plans for their own approach to the job and their future careers.

The kinds of supports needed are summarised in Figure 27.

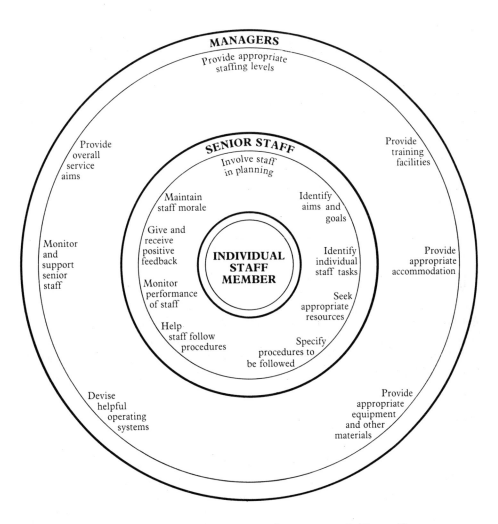

FIGURE 27. Summary of types of support needed by staff

PART D

Making it possible

SECTION 3. LEGAL AND ETHICAL CONCERNS

The needs

In addition to training, and provision and planning of resources, effective use of behavioural techniques in practice requires procedures for satisfying everyone concerned that the techniques, and their style of implementation, are legally and ethically acceptable. This should include people with mental handicaps (if they can understand), relatives, fellow professionals, other people with a legitimate interest, higher authority, and the public at large.

What does the law allow?

What law is relevant?

I cannot claim a detailed knowledge of the law. Added to this, there is no unified framework of law for people with mental handicaps. Such law as does exist is not always very specific. The task of presenting a helpful view of the matter is, therefore, difficult. In attempting to do so I have made much use of the *Mental Health Act, 1983* and the Mental Health Act Commission's *Draft Code of Practice (1985)* (not yet finalised or officially approved) which attempts to interpret and supplement parts of the *Act* to give a clearer overall picture. The *Act* itself is, however, concerned more with mental illness than with mental handicap and, to make the account more complete, other *statutory law* (that is, law established by Parliament) is also included, as well as *case law* (sometimes referred to as *common law*) which has been established through the decisions of judges given in the courts of law.

What kinds of offence are risked?

It has long been the legal position that, with certain exceptions, no treatment can be given to any person without that person's valid consent. A person can refuse to undergo it, and legal action can be taken if it is carried out without prior permission. Depending on the precise circumstances, action may or may not be taken under the *criminal law*, which administers punishments; but it is more helpful to discuss it further under *civil law*, which covers all relevant circumstances and which confines itself to awarding damages and imposing injunctions to prevent the offence from being repeated.

Under civil law, a person given treatment against his or her will might sue for damages on account of the following wrongful acts against individuals (known as *torts*):

Assault, which is a threat by one individual to inflict unlawful force on another. There need not be any serious danger – just threatening to touch someone against his or her will is an assault. What matters most is that the person *feels* threatened.

Battery (known as *physical assault against the person* in Scotland), which is the application of force to another person without that person's consent. There must be some direct contact with the other person's body, either in person or by some object. Again, just *touching* someone without that person's consent can be a battery, though it needs to be more than the everyday touching which occurs in crowded places, through shaking hands, or so on. Forcibly guiding a person to carry out an appropriate behaviour would qualify.

False imprisonment, which is the imposition of direct physical restraint upon another person without justification; that is, it does *not* refer simply to putting somebody in prison. The behavioural techniques of time-out, overcorrection, and physical restraint obviously fit the definition. However, almost any treatment given forcibly is likely to require such restraint.

Inflicting mental injury, though this is not so clearly defined. It could, for instance, be claimed that carrying out an intervention that is very upsetting to a person with a severe mental handicap is a tort in this category.

Negligence, of which there are two main forms that are relevant. The first is where a person with responsibility neglects to do something for someone with a mental handicap which it is that person's duty to do. One duty shared by everyone must be to help people with mental handicaps to overcome behaviour problems which will debar them from leading satisfying lives. Anyone who neglects to do this is legally at fault. The other form of negligence involves carrying out an action in an insufficiently careful way. If, for instance, someone placed in exclusion time-out is left there, locked in and unobserved, and injures him or herself by trying to break through a glass door to get out, the person responsible might well be judged as negligent in law. The amount of care required must depend on the age, abilities, and characteristics of each individual. Teachers, nurses, and others *in loco parentis* would, for instance, be expected to act in the same way as a reasonably careful parent.

The concept of consent is crucial in understanding the legal offences above. If the person consents to the intervention and it is carried out with proper care, legal action is unlikely to follow. However, consent that is valid in law requires that the person has been given sufficient information about what is proposed, that the person is competent to consent, and that consent is given voluntarily — that is, there must be no coercion, however subtle. It seems likely that many people with severe mental handicaps would *not* be considered competent to consent to the interventions described in this guide, because they would not have sufficient understanding of what was involved and of the possible consequences. Ultimately, this can be decided only by a court, and great care must therefore be taken in attempting to reach a decision about a person's competence on an everyday basis.

Law that allows intervention

Given that someone with a mental handicap is *not* competent to give valid consent, how can intervention procedures be carried out without offence to the law? One way is to make use of powers given by the *Mental Health Act, 1983* and similar legislation in Scotland and Northern Ireland. Given that certain carefully specified procedures are followed, a person can be detained compulsorily in hospital for treatment if it is necessary for that person's health or safety or for the protection of others. Under these circumstances, and again by following statutory procedures, any normal treatment can be given without consent, apart from surgery or sex hormone implantation. Reasonable force required to ensure administration of the necessary treatment then becomes lawful, and does not in these circumstances constitute assault or battery.

The powers of the Mental Health Act Commission are, however, a legal constraint of a kind. The Commission is a panel of part-time professionals and lay people whose functions include:

  reviewing the use of detention powers in hospitals;

  visiting and interviewing detained patients in hospital and investigating complaints;

  monitoring consent to treatment procedures; and

  issuing codes of practice for all professions.

In addition there are Mental Health Review Tribunals which investigate, and can overrule, decisions on admission, retention, and discharge of individual patients.

Compulsory admission to hospital is not, however, permissible simply as a convenient device for administering any kind of treatment needed. The *1983 Act* lays down certain restrictions, and these are interpreted in the Commission's *Draft Code of Practice.* The *Code* states: that the patient must have a mental disorder as defined (extremely vaguely) by the *Act;* that statements must be made about the patient's need for treatment, why it has to be given in hospital, and that it is likely to alleviate or prevent a deterioration of the patient's condition; and that the nearest relative must be consulted in advance. It makes clear that mental handicap alone is *not* sufficient grounds for such an admission, and the great majority of people handicapped in this way do not satisfy the criteria for it. How then, may treatment be provided *without* hospital admission?

The only circumstances in which treatment can legally be given without consent to an adult not detained under the *1983 Act* are those where there is a serious emergency, so that the treatment is needed: to save a life; prevent serious deterioration in the adult's condition; alleviate serious suffering; or prevent danger to the adult or to other people. It seems unlikely, therefore, that many of the kinds of intervention described in this guide would be allowed, since they are designed to be used in a planned way over a period rather than in an emergency. Some of the actions involved, such as physical restraints or medication, can be used in an emergency, but their use *purely* in emergencies is inadequate as intervention.

In the case of a person under 18 years of age, consent to an intervention can sometimes be given by the parent or guardian, by the local authority for a child in care, or by the High Court for a ward of court. This depends on the age and understanding of the child or young person concerned, and individual judgements have to be made in situations where parent and child disagree.

Parents have greater powers to *carry out* intervention procedures than many professionals, such as doctors and psychologists. The same applies to some extent to teachers or residential care workers who are *in loco parentis* and can reasonably expect to influence a child in the same way as a reasonable parent would do. Indeed, such workers have a duty to do so. Furthermore, the *Education Act, 1944* ruled that a child or young person must be provided with education according to age, ability, and aptitude, up to the age of 16 years (or 19 years if wished), and the *Education Act, 1981* makes it clear that all pupils with special educational needs who are still at school must have those needs provided for. The position is similar in Scotland *(Education (Scotland) Act, 1946; Education (Scotland) Act, 1981)* and Northern Ireland *(Education Act, 1947; Education Order, 1984; Draft Education Order (Northern Ireland), 1986)*. All children with severe mental handicaps have special educational needs, and those needs include learning to behave appropriately.

The powers of people *in loco parentis* are, however, diminishing. The *Education (No. 2) Act, 1986* removes the right of teachers to use corporal punishment, or to do anything else which would constitute a battery (or physical assault in Scotland), except where it is necessary to avert any immediate danger of personal injury to anybody, or immediate danger to someone's property. Teachers sued for battery can no longer claim that it was justified solely by their position as teachers. In March 1987 the Under Secretary of State for Health stated in the House of Commons that revised regulations for local authority community homes and voluntary children's homes would shortly prohibit the use of corporal punishment.

What intervention does the law allow and not allow?

The law specifically forbids certain kinds of behaviour which have sometimes been used for intervention, such as physical chastisement of adults, locking people in isolation, and depriving people of food or sleep. These are all measures that have imprecise boundaries, and some measures recommended may or may not be legal, regardless of how justified they are in other ways. Locking somebody in a room during a time-out procedure, while remaining outside the room and watching constantly, for instance, raises the question of whether the person is locked in isolation or not. Is withholding food for a short time until acceptable table behaviour occurs "depriving" somebody of food? Can facial screening or physical restraint be considered to be forms of physical chastisement?

For many interventions which are *not* specifically forbidden, valid consent is required before they can be used except, as explained earlier: in emergencies; or where a person can legally be detained in hospital for treatment; or where a parent or person *in loco parentis* carries out the intervention or has the power to give consent on behalf of a child.

However, it is doubtful if the consent restriction could be applied to all interventions. Such devices as physical prompting which is not resisted, reinforcing appropriate behaviour, reinforcing any behaviour other than a problem behaviour, and planned ignoring, often do not involve anything that would not take place in everyday action without any risk of legal sanction. The difference is that the actions involved are used more systematically than usual. Whether this makes any difference in law is not clear. It is, perhaps, fortunate that such approaches are unlikely to lead to legal action.

The problem that remains concerns practices which are less common and are, therefore, more likely to be questioned and taken to court. Adults with severe mental handicaps, who cannot understand what they are being asked to consent to and, therefore, cannot legally give consent, cannot in law be helped by such practices. This creates the strange position in which, legally, people are sometimes unable to receive the treatment they need. On the other hand, professional helpers who do *not* provide treatment that is needed can be found guilty of negligence if any harm results and there is any doubt on the consent question. The law has not yet specifically dealt with this anomalous situation. If it had to be resolved in a court, however, professional helpers should come out of it unscathed if they are seen to have acted reasonably, and to have followed the rules of conduct normal in their profession. The legal, therefore, merges into the ethical, which will be dealt with next.

Ethical questions

Ethical issues

The techniques described in this guide raise a number of ethical issues, the most important of which are outlined below.

> The techniques represent a variety of ways in which people in a relatively powerful position make and carry out deliberate plans to change the behaviour of those in less powerful positions. How can it be ensured that such actions are in the interests of people with severe mental handicaps? People with responsibility may be pursuing their own interests. If, for instance, nurses on a hospital ward can influence Roy, a potentially troublesome resident, to sit still in a corner all day in front of television programmes he cannot understand, life for them is much easier, but Roy's needs are neglected. People with severe mental handicaps should in any case have opportunities to exercise some choice about what they do. How far do approaches of the kind described in this guide deprive them of such opportunities?

> Problem behaviours can be people's reaction to living conditions which are unsatisfactory because, for instance: they deprive them of dignity; they provide them with no interesting experiences or activities; and they restrict their development as individuals. The problem behaviours can, as it were, be regarded as a protest. If people engaging in problem behaviours can be influenced to behave in more acceptable ways, is this simply covering up the unsatisfactory features in their lives? And if so does this mean that these features are less likely to be improved?

> Some of the techniques make use of experiences that are clearly unpleasant. Can this lead to people with severe mental handicaps being treated in a way that is cruel

or degrading? Some years ago four nurses were given suspended prison sentences for treatment which included giving mixtures of curry powder, washing-up liquid, and cinnamon, and rubbing patients' faces in urine. These measures were claimed to be elements in behavioural intervention programmes. While defenders of these particular measures would be hard to find, what should one think of devices like physical restraint, isolation time-out, overcorrection, or facial screening? Should they be used at all? And, if so, with whom?

Concern might also be expressed about intervention programmes in which people with severe mental handicaps are deprived of automatic access to items that are usually regarded as basic rights, which are then offered as reinforcers for appropriate behaviour. In certain token economies, for instance, hospital residents have had to "earn" their meals, comfortable beds, attractive clothing, pocket money, and even access to recreational activities. Is this ever justified? If so, how severe should a behaviour problem be before such measures are introduced?

Sources of ethical principles

I can claim no special knowledge as to what is, or is not, ethically acceptable. Everyone will have his or her own opinion. What is needed is a series of procedures for ensuring that these different opinions are taken into account when deciding upon intervention procedures.

To some extent, such procedures do exist. The safeguards of the *Mental Health Act, 1983* mentioned earlier, give some scope for preventing unethical activity. Further, some professions have codes of conduct which are influential in this way. For instance, the *Code* of the Association of Educational Psychologists decrees that educational psychologists must aim to protect the welfare of all people who seek their services or are the subject of their studies. They must not pursue, or allow others to use them to pursue, any purposes that are inconsistent with that principle. They must do nothing that might bring the profession into disrepute, or diminish the trust and confidence of the public. They must reach decisions independently of any concern for their own professional prospects or pecuniary interests. Furthermore, they must not collude with their employers in any activity detrimental to the wellbeing of children, young people, or their families. Educational psychologists belonging to the Association can be called to account if they breach any part of this *Code* and can, if necessary, be expelled. This does not necessarily prevent them from continuing to practise, however. It is doubtful, in any case, whether all workers involved with people with severe mental handicaps have such a code to follow.

There are other codes with different ranges of application. A government-sponsored working party has, for instance, offered ethical guidelines for behavioural approaches (Royal College of Psychiatrists, Royal College of Nursing, and British Psychological Society, 1980), but there is no legal obligation to follow this. The *Draft Code of Practice* drawn up by the Mental Health Act Commission (1985) makes many assertions which are basically ethical, though some also have legal status, and all might represent the attitude of a court of law. The *Code* says, or implies, that people with mental handicaps: should have as domestic a life style as possible and the opportunity to participate in ordinary life with appropriate supports; should have opportunities to make choices; and should enjoy age-appropriate personal possessions, entertainment, and outings. It further implies that all professionals, involved lay people and, where possible, people with mental handicaps themselves, should formulate and put into practice an individual progress plan; and that aversive, depriving, and restraining intervention techniques should be used only in exceptional circumstances, and only after carefully argued justification.

Finally there are the international codes, such as the *Universal Declaration of Human Rights (1948)* and the *European Convention on Human Rights (1950)* which lay down, for instance, that everyone has the right to liberty, security of person, and to treatment with dignity, and that no-one should be subjected to cruel, inhuman, or degrading treatment or punishment. The *United Nations Declaration on the Rights of Mentally Retarded Persons (1971)* states that people with mental handicaps should have the same rights as other people insofar as is feasible. These are essentially legal documents, but probably have their greatest influence ethically, since they are difficult to enforce.

From these ethical principles, and from the legal requirements described earlier, procedures need to be drawn up to ensure that people with severe mental handicaps and problem behaviour are helped in legally and ethically acceptable ways. The rest of this section offers suggestions as to how this may be done.

Procedures for less intrusive interventions

No reasonable person objects to parents, care staff, and school staff trying to teach children to behave in acceptable ways, or to establishments for adults having reasonable rules and expectations to which people with severe mental handicaps must conform and attempting to help them to behave in ways which will permit a more normal life. Plainly, there have to be ways in which these objectives can be reached. Provided these are not particularly unusual or frightening, most people are likely to approve. It would not be reasonable to establish elaborate safeguarding procedures which had to be implemented before any such methods could be used. Indeed, this would be a serious deterrent to doing anything constructive at all, or even to taking up employment in this field.

It is suggested, therefore, that for techniques which use only everyday antecedents, reinforcing consequences which do not make use of things which should be available as a matter of right, very mild reducing consequences like planned ignoring or non-exclusionary time-out, or combinations of these measures, no formal safeguarding procedures are needed. Indeed, the same might be said of some more intrusive techniques, such as isolation time-out or physical restraint, if they occupy only short periods of time, are adequately monitored, and can be carried out without active opposition from the person concerned. What is important, however, is to ensure that everyone who plays an important part in the life of a person with a severe mental handicap is consulted about, and has the opportunity to contribute to, all procedures to help that person realise the greatest possible potential and lead a satisfying and socially acceptable life. This applies to education, vocational training, and planning for leisure, as well as to decreasing problem behaviours.

In the early years, parents are the most important people of all in children's lives. They should play a major part in determining the aims, goals, and objectives for their children, both in and out of school and, except where they have formally renounced parental rights, in residential care situations. They should not need to "be consulted about" what other people are doing for their children; they should be helping to formulate plans for them from the beginning. In some pre-school situations, such as opportunity groups, parents are involved in running the provision and so are naturally closely involved. In home visiting schemes, such as the *Portage Scheme,* they are the people working with their children. Many special schools are in more or less daily contact with parents, meeting them regularly, sending written "home-school books" back and forth daily with news, comments, and suggestions, and sometimes organising workshops to make the school's work with the children clearer. As children grow older, they should be increasingly involved themselves, whenever possible, in determining their own aims and objectives, and their parents should continue their close involvement. This should continue into adulthood as long as people remain dependent upon their parents. Throughout this time all professionals involved should be interacting with parents in comparable ways.

It is important also for the various professionals involved to consult regularly with each other, not only to exchange information but to offer their plans for comment and, if necessary, criticism. They should be open to suggestions for modifying their aims and approaches, or coordinating them with those of other workers. The same applies to anyone helping in a voluntary capacity, and to any other people with severe mental handicaps who share the life of a person who has a behaviour problem if they are able to contribute.

If people with severe mental handicaps do not have parents to watch over their interests, or their parents do not have the skills to do so, it is important to look for alternatives. The local Social Services Authority will have a responsibility, but it is also advisable to arrange involvement of people outside statutory bodies. The United Nations *Declaration on the Rights of Mentally Retarded Persons (1971)* states that people with mental handicaps have a right to qualified guardians to protect their personal wellbeing and interest. In many states in the USA and Australia, there is a form of court-appointed guardian who can take decisions on treatment. In the USA, the *Developmentally Disabled Assistance and Bill of Rights Act, 1975* requires all states to establish independent agencies to pursue the rights of people with handicaps. The Canadian State of Alberta, and France, also have helpful legislation. While there are as yet no such systems in this country, the *Disabled Persons (Services, Consultation and Representation) Act, 1986* empowers the Secretary of State to make regulations governing the appointment of an "authorised representative" to act as an advocate for a person with a mental handicap. However, no date is set for even the implementation of this part of the *Act,* let alone the regulations, and it seems likely to founder for lack of resources. It is not clear how far it would lead to effective advocacy, even if implemented. The *Act* applies to England, Wales, and Scotland, and a similar *Act* is planned for Northern Ireland.

Relatives and volunteers can also be enlisted to help represent the interests of people with severe mental handicaps. Other sources are various kinds of advocacy groups, established on a legal basis in many states in the USA and in some other countries, and now springing up in the United Kingdom. Some operate with the help of "befriending non-professionals", who represent people with mental handicaps wherever it is allowed. Others act specifically to provide legal representation. Such groups could be involved routinely in decision processes.

If the above policies are pursued, there is likely to be little danger that professionals will use behavioural techniques to further their own ends rather than those of the people with severe mental handicaps for whom they have responsibility; or that they will use behavioural change as a cover for unsatisfactory provision for such individuals. Most professionals will, in any case, want to put the interests of their client first, and the procedures that have been outlined will enable them not only to do so but to be *seen* by everyone to do so.

Procedures for more intrusive interventions

Even if parents and others have been involved in planning and provision from the start, the use of the more depriving or aversive consequences for reducing problem behaviours may alarm them and will certainly, quite rightly, worry them. Use of such devices needs to be approached with caution, the more so the more aversive they become.

In Section B it was repeatedly suggested that reducing consequences should be used only when other techniques were insufficient, and that the most aversive reducing consequences should be avoided if at all possible. When all else has failed there comes a decision point, when the consequences of allowing the problem behaviour to continue have to be weighed against the consequences of using more depriving or aversive techniques.

For instance, should people be allowed to cause themselves severe and irreparable self-injury through thumping and tearing at their faces with their hands? Or should they be kept constantly in restraints? Or should they be subjected to an overcorrection procedure, or have a jet of water squirted into their face every time they move a hand violently towards their head? How aversive can reducing consequences be which aim to prevent constant regurgitation which is causing severe malnutrition in someone, or life-threatening violence towards other people?

No one person working with people with severe mental handicaps should have to, or be allowed to, make such decisions alone. It is suggested, therefore, that a definite sequence of procedures be set up to ensure that all important issues are considered by everyone concerned, and a specific and defensible line of action agreed. This should apply to *all* interventions where any risk of harm is involved, or where a reasonable person might feel uneasy for other reasons, *not* just to behavioural approaches.

The precise form of such a sequence will vary from setting to setting, but may well conform to the following general pattern.

Step 1. Discuss, with the person with a severe mental handicap if possible, with parents and other relatives, with other professionals, with employers, and with anyone else with a legitimate interest, the measures that have been taken so far and the implications of their lack of success. Are the behavioural changes that are being sought really in the interests of the person concerned or intolerable for others, or is a rethink necessary? If the former, are the environments in which the person exists really appropriate for that person's individual needs, or is there some unsatisfactory feature that accounts for continuation of the problem behaviour which could be altered? Have all possible less intrusive methods of intervention been tried, or are there still some which might be worth introducing?

Step 2. With the same group of people, describe clearly and discuss various possible new intervention procedures. Specify exactly: what the objectives of each alternative are; how they are expected to be reached; who will carry out each of the activities involved; what possible side-effects may occur; what additional risks are involved; what will be done to minimise side-effects and other risks; how progress is to be assessed; and how a decision will eventually be made that objectives have been reached. Always aim for the group to agree on the least aversive intervention which has a reasonable chance of success. It is important to ensure that everyone who has a part to play in this intervention is competent to carry out the allocated tasks, and that somebody who is highly trained and qualified in behavioural approaches is either involved directly in implementation of the procedures or is easily available for consultation.

Step 3. Seek to obtain appropriate consent to the proposed intervention, preferably from the person with a severe mental handicap personally. If the person is a minor, not competent to give consent, this should be sought from the parents, other relatives, or legal guardian. If there is any doubt at all as to whether an adult with a severe mental handicap is competent to give consent and there is no-one else who can be clearly held to be representing the interests of the person, then the matter might be submitted to an independent body designed for the purpose. One body of this kind is a "Human Rights Committee", a device not uncommon in the USA. This might perhaps consist of: various professionals with expertise of the kinds involved in the intervention; a legal expert; a parent, relative, legal guardian or other person in a protective capacity; another person with a mental handicap; and one or more disinterested lay people. Where the person is in the care of some statutory organisation, such as the National Health Service, or a local Social Services Authority, it is sometimes argued that such a committee should *always* be involved for more intrusive interventions. However, its use is very much a matter for debate. Whatever consent procedures are set up, they should allow for those with day-to-day responsibility to take appropriate action in an emergency and report to the consenting individual or body afterwards.

Step 4. Before proceeding try to ensure that the person, or the representative of the body, giving the permission signs a detailed consent form. This might include:

   a precise description of the behaviour to be modified;

   a precise description of the techniques proposed;

   a description of techniques already used and their outcomes;

   a description of possible alternative approaches to the one proposed;

   a justification of the proposals;

   a description of anticipated side-effects or risks;

   a description of recording procedures to be used and of the specific behaviours to be monitored;

   the anticipated outcomes and expected time required for the techniques to be effective;

the qualifications of the people implementing the programme;

the names of impartial persons not directly involved in the programme who are available to discuss it with relatives or, where possible, the person with the problem behaviour for whom the programme is designed.

In instances where people with severe mental handicaps consent and sign the form themselves, great care is needed to make certain that they understand everything on the form. It is wise also to get the consent form signed by an advocate or by an independent body representing the person.

Step 5. Make sure that, throughout implementation of the intervention, its progress is kept constantly under review by everyone involved, including whoever gave consent. The person or people who gave consent should have the right to withdraw it.

Record carefully everything relevant that happens during this period. Remember that it is important that everything is done in a professional manner, that all necessary safeguards are taken, and that all appropriate codes of practice are followed by everyone involved.

Final words

Powerful methods require careful safeguards to ensure that they are not used unethically. However, it is just as unethical to leave people with severe mental handicaps in states where they are a danger to themselves or to others, and/or are unacceptable to most people in the society in which they live, simply because of timidity about introducing techniques which could improve things. With care and cooperation, the body of knowledge described in this guide can be used to bring about a significant improvement in the lives of some of the most handicapped people in our society.

APPENDIX 1

Action record for problem behaviour

Introduction

The Action Record for Problem Behaviour is intended for use with the guide *Overcoming Difficult Behaviour,* which provides detail on the necessary assessment and intervention techniques. The Action Record consists of an initial brief guide to use, followed by 19 forms. These consist of Forms 1 to 12, which are likely to be needed for all interventions, and Forms 5A, 6A, 11A, 11B, 11C, 12A, and 12B, which will be helpful for some interventions but not others.

The forms are headed as follows.

Form 1. Contents of Action Record.
Form 2. Problem behaviours.
Form 3. Appropriate behaviours.
Form 4. Baseline measuring.
Form 5. Before and after a problem behaviour.
Form 5A. Before and after an appropriate behaviour.
Form 6. Existing patterns of antecedents and consequences.
Form 6A. Welcome and unwelcome experiences.
Form 7. Influences which may increase an appropriate behaviour.
Form 8. Influences which may decrease a problem behaviour.
Form 9. First intervention programme.
Form 10. Measuring for first intervention programme.
From 11. Evaluating and modifying a programme.
Form 11A. Modified or new intervention programme.
Form 11B. Measuring for a modified or new programme.
Form 11C. Evaluating and modifying a modified or new programme.
Form 12. Fading out a programme and/or maintaining the change.
Form 12A. Measuring while fading out a programme and/or maintaining the change.
Form 12B. Evaluating and modifying fading and/or maintenance procedures.

The forms cannot be used exactly in the order presented for all interventions. The set includes just one copy of every basic form likely to be needed in an intervention with one person. However, several copies of some forms may be needed within the same intervention. Permission is granted to reproduce, by any means, whatever duplicate copies are needed of these forms for that person's intervention. A new set will need to be purchased for subsequent interventions with that person, or for interventions commenced with other people.

Where more than one copy is needed of any particular form, it is recommended that users should add numbering of their own (i, ii, iii, for example) to the form number so that the forms can continue to be filed in numerical order and can easily be restored to order when disturbed.

Brief guide to using the forms

Form 1. Contents of Action Record

Write here any necessary details about the person whose behaviour is a problem. As the intervention proceeds, list each form as it is used on this initial form, so that you can quickly ascertain what the Action Record for a particular person contains.

Form 2. Problem behaviours

Write down all the problem behaviours you want to decrease in frequency. From the list, select the behaviour or behaviours you think best to work on first. Underline this/them. If necessary, analyse each behaviour selected into steps, and write these down on a separate Form 2, adding an extra code to the Form number (for example 2i). If this further analysis is carried out, decide which step or steps to tackle first and underline it/them.

Form 3. Appropriate behaviours

Write down all the appropriate behaviours you want to increase in frequency. This list cannot be exhaustive, so it is best to start with any behaviours whose absence is a problem in itself and behaviours that the person could engage in instead of the problem behaviour. Select the behaviour or behaviours you think best to work on first (which may often depend on your earlier selection of priority problem behaviours). Underline this/these. If necessary, analyse each behaviour into steps, component behaviours, or underlying behaviours if necessary, and write these down on a separate Form 3 (adding a new code for identification). If this further analysis is carried out, decide what behaviour(s) to tackle as a first step and underline it/them.

Form 4. Baseline measuring

Write down very specifically the behaviours you are going to measure to clarify the extent of the problem. Use a separate Form 4 (for example, i, ii, iii) for each behaviour. Determine a precise observation schedule for measuring each behaviour and write this down too. When recording, make clear in the first column the exact time and duration of the observation period if this is not described exactly by the observation schedule. The second column is for recording things as they happen (for example, a mark for each occurrence of a specific behaviour). The third column is for totalling such observations. Continue for at least 10 recording periods. If possible, complete Forms 5-8 over the same period of time that is used for this baseline measuring.

Form 5. Before and after a problem behaviour

Write down the specific problem behaviour selected. Then, each time it occurs, write what is happening immediately before it and immediately after it. If any regular pattern emerges, write it down on Form 6. If more than one problem behaviour is to be tackled, use a separate Form 5 (i, ii, iii, and so on) for each.

Form 5A. Before and after an appropriate behaviour

If a selected appropriate behaviour *does* occur occasionally it may be worth writing it down here and, on each occasion, writing what is happening immediately before it and immediately after it. If any regular pattern emerges, write it down on Form 6. If more than one appropriate behaviour is to be tackled, use a separate Form 5A for each. Remember to add you own code as before (for example, Form 5Ai).

Form 6. Existing patterns of antecedents and consequences

This form is for noting, in writing, regular patterns shown by use of Forms 5 and 5A, where used. Use a separate Form 6 (i, ii, iii, and so on) for each different behaviour. Anything that occurs frequently before a behaviour may be influencing the likelihood of occurrence of that behaviour and may therefore be an antecedent. Anything that occurs frequently after a behaviour may be influencing the likelihood of that behaviour occurring again and may therefore be a consequence.

Form 6A. Welcome and unwelcome experiences

Form 6A is intended for use where there is some uncertainty as to what experiences the person finds welcome and unwelcome. Even where these experiences are known in advance, the first column of the form can be used to write them down as a memory aid. If the form is to be fully used, look for experiences the person might find welcome or unwelcome and write them down. For each, note the person's reaction carefully and write that down. Finally, indicate whether the reaction shows the experience to be welcome, unwelcome, or neither. If necessary, present a range of experiences systematically and make similar written notes.

Form 7. Influences which may increase an appropriate behaviour

From the information gathered on Forms 5 and 6 (and 5A and 6A if used), try to identify antecedents likely to set off any appropriate behaviours selected. Write these down. Then try to identify consequences likely to reinforce any appropriate behaviours selected. Write these down.

Form 8. Influences which may decrease a problem behaviour

From the information gathered on Forms 5 and 6 (and 5A and 6A if used), try to identify antecedents likely to make a selected problem behaviour less likely to occur. Write these down. Then try to identify consequences likely to make a selected problem behaviour less likely to be repeated. Write these down.

Form 9. First intervention programme

Use the entries made so far to plan a first attempt to overcome the problem. Write an account of the planned intervention programme. Ensure that points 1–7 are all included in your description, except where irrelevant.

Form 10. Measuring for first intervention programme

This is essentially the same as Form 4, and is completed similarly. During implementation of the programme, use the same observation schedule and recording methods as on Form 4, unless there are good reasons for changing them. Continue observations for at least 10 recording periods.

Form 11. Evaluating and modifying a programme

Note in writing whether the behaviour changes wanted have occurred sufficiently, have occurred to some extent but not sufficiently, or have not occurred at all. Write down also any other details likely to be helpful in planning what to do next. In the light of this evaluation consider, and write down, whether the programme should continue unmodified, whether it should be gradually faded out in ways which maintain helpful changes, whether it should be modified in small ways to make it more effective, or whether it needs replacing by a different programme because it is so ineffective. Minor modifications should be written down. For major changes, on the other hand, use Form 11A.

If the objectives of the programme have been sufficiently achieved consider, and note, whether a programme is needed for other problem behaviours not included in the first programme. If so, go back to Form 2 and follow the same sequence as for the behaviours originally selected.

Form 11A. Modified or new intervention programme

If more than minor changes are to be made, write a description of the new or modified programme, following the same guidelines as on Form 9. If, on the other hand, gradual fading out of the programme, rather than modifying or replacing it, is needed, use Form 12 instead.

Form 11B. Measuring for a new or modified programme

Again, measure and record exactly as for Forms 4 and 10, continuing for at least 10 recording periods.

Form 11C. Evaluating and modifying a modified or new programme

The new or modified programme should be evaluated and further action planned, in much the same way as for Form 11.

Form 12. Fading out a programme and/or maintaining the change

Plan methods for gradually decreasing the contrived antecedents and consequences without losing behavioural gains. Write these down. Ensure that points 1–6 are all included in your description, except where they are irrelevant.

Form 12A. Measuring while fading out a programme and/or maintaining the change

Again, measure and record exactly as for Forms 4 and 10, continuing as long as necessary.

Form 12B. Evaluating and modifying fading and/or maintenance procedures

Write down how far the intervention programme has been successfully faded out and the behaviour changes maintained. In the light of this, plan and write down any necessary modifications or any other further action required.

Further action

Recording for any further action, such as a return to the original programme or planning an intervention for a different behaviour, should be catered for by obtaining a new set of forms.

Name: ....

Date of birth: ....

Group and/or establishment: ....

Completed by: ....

Action by: ....

Any special notes: ....

....

....

ACTION RECORD FORM 1

Contents of Action Record

List of Action Record Forms completed:

Form number	Date completed	Form number	Date completed

Name: .... **ACTION RECORD FORM 2**

Date of birth: .... **Problem behaviours**

Completed by: ....

What problem behaviours do you want to decrease in frequency?

Specific action involved	Circumstances of occurrence (places, times, events, people, etc.)

Name:	**ACTION RECORD FORM 3**
Date of birth:	**Appropriate behaviours**
Completed by:	

What appropriate behaviours do you want to increase in frequency?

Specific action involved with standards	Circumstances in which required (places, times, events, people, etc.)

Name:	**ACTION RECORD FORM 4**
Date of birth:	**Baseline measuring**
Completed by:	

Behaviour observed

Observation schedule
(state when, under what circumstances, for how long, what is observed, and what is to be recorded)

Records

Date and period of observation	Records of frequency or duration	Total for observation period

Name: ....   **ACTION RECORD FORM 5**

Date of birth: ....   **Before and after a problem**
                                                             behaviour
Completed by: ....

Behaviour

Occasion	What precedes	What follows

Name: ....   **ACTION RECORD FORM 5A**

Date of birth: ....   **Before and after an**
                                                                                  appropriate behaviour
Completed by: ....

Behaviour

Occasion	What precedes	What follows

Name: ....

Date of birth: ....

Completed by: ....

ACTION RECORD FORM 6

**Existing patterns of
antecedents and consequences**

Behaviour

Regular patterns of antecedents and consequences

Name:	**ACTION RECORD FORM 6A**
Date of birth:	**Welcome and unwelcome**
Completed by:	**experiences**

Experience	Reaction	Welcome or Unwelcome

Name: ....   **ACTION RECORD FORM 7**

Date of birth: ....   **Influences which may**
                                                                          increase an appropriate
Completed by: ....   **behaviour**

Behaviour

Antecedents

Consequences

Name: ....

Date of birth: ....

Completed by: ....

ACTION RECORD FORM 8

**Influences which may
decrease a problem behaviour**

Behaviour

Antecedents

Consequences

Name:	**ACTION RECORD FORM 9**
Date of birth:	**First intervention programme**
Completed by:	

Note the following information in the order given

1. Precise behaviours to increase and/or decrease, including standards and circumstances.
2. Antecedents and/or consequences planned.
3. Precise ways in which antecedents are to be used.
4. Precise ways in which consequences are to be made conditional on occurrence of behaviours.
5. Any other features of the programme.
6. Precise times and places for operating the programme.
7. How the programme is to be introduced and the person showing the behaviour involved.

Name:	**ACTION RECORD FORM 10**
Date of birth:	**Measuring for first**
Completed by:	**intervention programme**

Behaviour observed

Observation schedule
(state when, under what circumstances, for how long, what is observed, and what is to be recorded)

Records

Date and period of observation	Records of frequency or duration	Total for observation period

Name: ....   **ACTION RECORD FORM 11**

Date of birth: ....   **Evaluating and modifying
a programme**

Completed by: ....

How far has the first intervention programme achieved its objectives?

Should the programme continue in its present form, or should a modified or new programme be designed, or should the programme be gradually faded out? If the programme is to be modified, what changes are needed?

Name: ....   **ACTION RECORD FORM 11A**

Date of birth: ....   **Modified or new**

Completed by: ....   **intervention programme**

Note the following information in the order given

1. Precise behaviours to increase and/or decrease, including standards and circumstances.
2. Antecedents and/or consequences planned.
3. Precise ways in which antecedents are to be used.
4. Precise ways in which consequences are to be made conditional on occurrrence of behaviours.
5. Any other features of the programme.
6. Precise times and places for operating the programme.
7. How the programme is to be introduced and the person showing the behaviour involved.

Name:	**ACTION RECORD FORM 11B**
Date of birth:	**Measuring for a modified**
Completed by:	**or new programme**

Behaviour observed

Observation schedule
(state when, under what circumstances, for how long, what is observed, and what is to be recorded)

Records

Date and period of observation	Records of frequency or duration	Total for observation period

Name: ....   **ACTION RECORD FORM 11C**

Date of birth: ....   **Evaluating and modifying**
a modified or new programme

Completed by: ....

How far has the modified or new programme achieved its objectives?

Should the programme continue in its present form, or should a modified or new programme be designed, or should the programme be gradually faded out? If the programme is to be modified, what changes are needed?

Name: ....   **ACTION RECORD FORM 12**

Date of birth: ....   **Fading out a programme**
and/or maintaining the
Completed by: ....   **change**

Record the information relating to each of the following procedures in the order given.

1. How contrived antecedents are to be faded out.
2. How use of "natural" antecedents is to be increased.
3. How the amount, frequency and immediacy of contrived consequences is to be diminished.
4. How use of "natural" consequences is to be increased.
5. How variation in the procedures is to be increased.
6. Any other changes.
7. How the changes are to be introduced to the person and the person involved in decisions about the changes to be made.

Name: ....   **ACTION RECORD FORM 12A**

Date of birth: ....   **Measuring while fading out**
a programme and/or
Completed by: ....   **maintaining the change**

Behaviour observed

Observation schedule
(state when, under what circumstances, for how long, what is observed, and what is to be recorded)

Records

Date and period of observation	Records of frequency or duration	Total for observation period

Name: ....   **ACTION RECORD FORM 12B**

Date of birth: ....   **Evaluating and modifying**
fading and/or maintenance
Completed by: ....   **procedures**

How far have the procedures achieved their objectives?

What further action is needed?

APPENDIX 2

Sources of materials

Introduction

The following sources are not exhaustive – there are others. It is not possible, in a book like this, to vouch for the effectiveness of particular items for particular purposes with individual people. It is important to seek guidance locally from appropriate advisers on precisely which products to use for a particular intervention. Further, information of this kind rapidly becomes out-of-date. Readers may, therefore, like to obtain the more comprehensive lists, which are updated regularly, published by the Disabled Living Foundation. The address is: The Disabled Living Foundation, 380-384 Harrow Road, London, W9 2HU. 01–289 6111.

Measuring and reminding devices

Timers and hand tallies

Nottingham Rehab Limited, Ludlow Hill Road, West Bridgford, Nottingham, NG2 6HD. (0602) 234251.

Taskmaster Limited, Morris Road, Clarendon Park, Leicester, LE2 6BR. (0533) 704286.

Hestair Hope, St. Philips Drive, Royton, Oldham, OL2 6AG. 061–633 6611.

Timers

Nottingham Rehab Limited, Ludlow Hill Road, West Bridgford, Nottingham, NG2 6HD. (0602) 234251.

E.J. Arnold & Son Limited, Parkside Lane, Dewsbury Road, Leeds, LS11 5TD. (0532) 772112.

Philip and Tacey Limited, North Way, Andover, Hants, SP10 5BA. (0264) 332171.

Vibrators

Vibro-Medico, 20 Church Road, Hadleigh, Essex, SS7 2DQ. (0702) 557966.

Splint-making materials

Nottingham Rehab Limited (address above).

S.H. Camp Limited, Portfield Industrial Estate, Nevil Shute Road, Portsmouth, PO3 5RL. (0705) 697411.

Protective helmets

Radford Orthopaedic Company Limited, Rebecca House, Rebecca Street, Westgate, Bradford, West Yorkshire, BD1 2RX. (0274) 723729.

Remploy Limited. Medical Products, Russ Street, Broad Plain, Bristol BS2 0HJ. (0272) 277512.

Pryor and Howard Limited, 39 Willow Lane, Mitcham, Surrey, CR4 4US. 01 – 648 1177.

S.H. Camp Limited, (address above).

U. Williams and Co. Limited, 23/25 Wyche Grove, South Croydon, Surrey. 01 – 688 8308.

Specialised Orthotic Services, Trent Lane, Weston-on-Trent, Nr. Derby, DE7 2BR. (0332) 702232.

Hinged arm splint

John Florence Orthotics, Chailey Heritage, Chailey, Sussex. 082 – 572 2063.

S.H. Camp Limited, (address above).

U. Williams and Co. (address above).

Non-slip mats and non-slip meal trays

Nottingham Rehab Limited (address above).

S.H. Camp Limited (address above).

Aids to control drooling

Dribble control box

Ken Ketteridge, 10 Walpole Road, Cambridge, CB1 3TJ. It is made to order, and it is best to enquire informally by ringing him at Meldreth Manor School (0763 60771) during working hours or at home (0223 247326) at other times.

Exeter Lip Sensors

Bio-Instrumentation Limited, Holm Croft, School Road, Silverton, Exeter, EX5 4JH. (0392) 860475.

Enuresis alarms and associated equipment

Nottingham Rehab Limited (address above).

Headingley Scientific Services, 45 Westcombe Avenue, Leeds, LS8 2BS. (0532) 664222.

N.H. Eastwood & Son Limited, 118 East Barnet Road, Barnet, Herts, EN4 8RE. 01–441 9641.

Simcare, Peter Road, Lancing, West Sussex, BN15 8TJ. (0903) 761122.

Wessex Medical Equipment Company Limited, Unit 2, Budds Lane Industrial Estate, Romsey, Hants, SO51 OHA. (0794) 518246.

Astric Products Ltd., Astric House, Lewes Road, Brighton, BN2 3LG. (0273) 608319.

Connevans Limited, 54 Albert Road North, Reigate, Surrey, RH2 9YR. (0737) 247571.

Tech Toys, Telford Opportunities Centre, Halesfield 14, Telford, Shropshire, TF7 4QR. (0952) 223161.

Commodes

Nottingham Rehab Limited (address above).

Carters (J & A) Limited, Alfred Street, Westbury, Wilts. BA13 3DZ. (0373) 822203.

APPENDIX 3

Sources of information

Texts for selection of appropriate behaviours

Bailey (1983), Bluma *et al.* (1976), Browning *et al.* (1983), Cunningham and Sloper (1978), Gardner, Murphy, and Crawford (1983), Jeffree, McConkey, and Hewson (1977), Kiernan (1981), Kiernan, Jordan, and Saunders (1978), Longhorn (1988), Ouvry (1988), Perkins, Taylor, and Capie (1980a), Rectory Paddock School (1983), STEP (1985a), Whelan and Speake (1979), Whelan and Speake (1981).

Checklists for selecting appropriate behaviours

General purpose

Developmental Checklist (Perkins, Taylor, and Capie, 1980b), Progress Assessment Chart (Gunzburg, 1973), PIP Developmental Charts (Jeffree and McConkey, 1976), Portage Guide to Early Education (Bluma *et al.*, 1976), Assessment in Mental Handicap (Hogg and Raynes, 1987).

For people with profound and multiple handicaps

Anson House Preschool Project Checklists (Gunstone, 1985), Behaviour Assessment Battery (Kiernan and Jones, 1982), Steps to Independence (Best, 1987), A System for Assessment and Intervention for Preschool Profoundly Multiply Handicapped Children (Sebba, 1980), The Next Step on the Ladder (Simon, 1981).

For life and work-oriented tasks for more able people with severe mental handicaps

The Personal Record System (Whelan and Lancashire Social Services, 1980), Pathways to Independence (Jeffree and Cheseldine, 1982), The Scale for Assessing Coping Skills (Whelan and Speake, 1980), The Work Skills Rating Scale (Whelan and Schlesinger, 1980), The Bereweeke Skill-Teaching System (Felce *et al.*, 1983, 1986), The Hampshire Assessemnt for Living with Others (Shackleton-Bailey and Hampshire Social Services, 1980a), Hampshire New Curriculum (Shackleton-Bailey and Hampshire Social Services, 1980b), the Community Living Skills Assessment, Second Edition (STEP, 1985b), the Offerton Self-care Checklist (Burton *et al.*, 1981).

Specific areas

Pre-Verbal Communication Schedule (Kiernan and Reid, 1987), Paths to Mobility Checklist (Presland, 1989b), Checklist for Feeding Skills (Warner, 1981a), Affective Communication Assessment (Coupe *et al.*, 1985), Assessment of Early Feeding and Drinking Skills (Coupe *et al.*, 1987), Wessex Revised Portage Language Checklist (White and East, 1983).

Main texts for behavioural methods

Axelrod and Apshe (1983), Barrett (1986), Cheesman and Watts (1985), Cunningham and Sloper (1978), Evans and Meyer (1985), Favell and Greene (1981), Foxx (1982), Gardner (1983), Harrop (1983), Hersen, Van Hasselt, and Matson (1983), Jeffree, McConkey, and Hewson (1977), Kiernan (1981), Kiernan, Jordan, and Saunders (1978), Lavigna and Donnellan (1986), Lovitt (1978), Luce and Christian (1981), Matson and McCartney (1981), Perkins, Taylor, and Capie (1980a), Rincover (1981), Van Houten (1980), Westmacott and Cameron (1981), Wheldall and Merrett (1985), Whitman, Scibak, and Reid (1983), Yule and Carr (1987), Zarkowska and Clements (1988).

Other general references

Alberto, Troutman, and Briggs (1983), Aman (1985), Atkinson *et al.*, (1984), Axelrod, Brantner, and Meddock (1978), Barmann, Croyle-Barmann, and McLain (1980), Beail (1985), Bluma *et al.*, (1976), Browder and Shapiro (1985), Burgio, Page, and Capriotti (1985), Calamari, Geist, and Shahbazian (1987), Campbell and Small (1976), Corbett (1980), DHSS (1972), Danaher (1974), Donnellan *et al.* (1984), Drabman, Jarvie, and Archbold (1976), Ford and Veltri-Ford (1980), Foxx and Bechtel (1982), Foxx and Shapiro (1978), Friman, Cook, and Finney (1984), Gardner *et al.* (1983), Gast and Nelson (1977), Glynn (1982), Gourash (1986), Graziano and Kean (1968), Green (1977), Gutierrez-Griep (1984), Hall and Hall (1980a and 1980b), Harris (1985), Harris and Ersner-Hershfield (1978), Harvey (1979), Heaton-Ward (1977), Hogg *et al.* (1987), Huguenin and Mulick (1981), Hulse, Egeth, and Deese (1981), Jackson and Boag (1981), Jain and Arya (1987), Jones (1983), Krivacek and Powell (1978), Leitenberg (1965), Lindsay and Baty (1986), Luiselli

(1980), Luiselli, Myles, and Littman-Quinn (1983), Lutzker, McGimsey-McRae, and McGimsey (1983), Lutzker and Wesch (1983), Malott (1984), Mank and Horner (1987), Mansell *et al.* (1982), McBrien and Weightman (1980), McLaren and Bryson (1987), Meunier, Kissell, and Higgins, (1983), Michael (1975), Morgan and Striefel (1987/8), Mulick and Schroeder (1980), Murphy (1982), Murphy and Byrne (1983), Murray (1976), Nunes, Murphy, and Ruprecht (1977), O'Leary (1972), Oliver (1986), Pickering and Morgan (1985), Poling and Ryan (1982), Premack (1959, 1971), Presland (1981a, 1981b, 1989a, 1989b), Quine (1986), Ralph and Birnbrauer (1986), Repp, Barton, and Brulle (1983), Rincover (1979), Rolider and Van Houten (1985), Schoen (1983, 1986), Solnick, Rincover, and Peterson (1977), Sorce and Emde (1982), Spangler and Marshall (1983), Spreat *et al.* (1986), Sturmey, Crisp, and Dearden (1983), Touchette, MacDonald, and Langer (1985), Van Houten and Rolider (1988), Wacker *et al.* (1985), Yarnall and Dodgion-Ensor (1980).

Masturbation

Barmann and Murray (1981), Cook, Altman, and Haavik (1978), Czyzewski, Barrera, and Sulzer-Azaroff (1982), Foxx *et al.* (1986), Gunn and Rosser (1987), Krivacek and Powell (1978), Mitchell 1985), Murphy (1980), Whitman, Scibak and Reid (1983).

Stealing

Azrin and Wesolowski (1974), Ivimy and Card (1985), Van Houten and Rolider (1988), Whitman, Scibak, and Reid (1983).

Hyperactivity

Aman (1984), Aman *et al.* (1985a, 1985b), American Psychiatric Association (1980), Campbell, Anderson, and Green (1983), Fisher *et al.* (1985), Herbert (1980), Kavale (1982), Koller *et al.* (1983), O'Brien and Obrzut (1986), O'Leary (1980), Prior and Griffin (1985), Reid *et al.* (1984), Schworm (1982), Thurber and Walker (1983), Varley and Trupin (1982).

Air swallowing

Barrett *et al.* (1987).

Stripping

Carroll *et al.* (1978), Foxx (1976), Keogh and Whitman (1983), Mitchell (1985), Whitman, Scibak, and Reid (1983).

Self exposure

Lutzker (1974).

Aggressive sexual behaviour

Mitchell (1985).

Sleeping difficulties

Clements, Wing, and Dunn (1986), Hewitt (1985), Howlin (1984), Podboy and Mallory (1977), Tait, Brookes, and Firth (1976).

Behaviours characteristic of depression

Matson (1982).

Non-compliant behaviours

Alberto, Troutman, and Briggs (1983), Foxx (1977), Kiernan and Kiernan (1988), Koegel and Rincover (1974), Kuzynski et al. (1987), Mace et al. (1988), Martin (1971), McKeown (1978), Orton (1979), Russo, Cataldo, and Cushing (1981), Schoen (1983), Sininger and Yarnall (1981), Tomporowski (1983), Volkmar and Cohen (1982), Volkmar, Hoder, and Cohen (1985), Wehman and McLaughlin (1979), Weisberg, Passman, and Russell (1973), Williams and Forehand (1984).

Violent behaviours

Barton and LaGrow (1983), Belcher et al. (1982), Bethlem Royal Hospital and the Maudsley Hospital (1980), Campbell, Anderson, and Green (1983), Carney and Nolan (1979), Clark et al. (1973), DHSS (1976), Fleming and Tosh (1984), Gardner et al. (1986), Gross, Berler, and Drabman (1982), Harvey and Schepers (1977), Koller et al. (1983), Libby, Polloway, and Smith (1983), Luiselli (1984), Luiselli, Myles, and Littman-Quinn (1983), Luiselli and Slocumb (1983), Mulick and Schroeder (1980), Podboy and Mallory (1977), Reid et al. (1984), Rotatori et al. (1980), Touchette, MacDonald and Langer (1985), Wehman and McLaughlin (1979), Wiener and Crosby (1986), Williamson et al. (1983).

Self-injurious behaviours

Bailey, Pokrzywinsky, and Bryant (1983), Barmann and Vitali (1982), Barron and Sandman (1985), Baumeister and MacLean (1984), Blount et al. (1982), Campbell, Anderson, and Green (1983), Cataldo and Harris (1982), Crisp and Coll (1980), Demchak and Halle (1985), Dorsey et al. (1982), Edelson, Taubman, and Lovaas (1983), Favell and Greene (1981), Foxx and Dufrense (1984), Fulcher (1984), Greer et al. (1985), Griffin et al. (1986, 1987), Harris and Romanczyk (1976), Hollis and Meyers (1982), Horner and Barton (1980b), Jenner (1984), Jones, Simmons, and Frankel (1974), Lockwood and Bourland (1982), Lutzker and Wesch (1983), Murphy (1985), Murphy and Wilson (1985), Nunes, Murphy, and Ruprecht (1977), Oliver, Murphy, and Corbett (1987), Parrish et al. 1985), Patterson (1982), Rapoff, Altman, and Christophersen (1980), Richmond et al. (1984), Rojahn (1986), Schroeder (1985), Schroeder et al. (1980), Schroeder, Mulick, and Rojahn (1980), Silverman et al. (1984), Singh and Millichamp (1985), Spain, Hart, and Corbett (1984), Sturmey et al. (1988), Weiher and Harman (1975), Whitman, Scibak, and Reid (1983), Wieseler et al. (1985), Wurtele, King, and Drabman (1984), Wynn-Jones (1983).

Stereotyped behaviours

Aman (1984), Aman, White, and Field (1984), ARRI (1987), Azrin and Wesolowski (1980), Barrett, Staub, and Sisson (1983), Barron and Sandman (1985), Barton and LaGrow (1983), Barton, Repp, and Brulle (1985), Carroll et al. (1978), Czyzewski, Barrera, and Sulzer-Azaraff (1982), Dunlap, Dyer, and Koegel (1983), Gallagher and Berkson (1986), Hollis (1978), Hopper and Wambold (1978), Jan et al. (1983), LaGrow and Repp (1984), Lewis and Baumeister (1982), Lovaas, Newsom, and Hickman (1987), Maag et al. (1986), McKeegan, Estill, and Campbell (1984), Nellhaus (1983), Rincover et al. (1979), Smith (1986), Sturmey et al. (1988), Thelen (1981), Van Dijk (1982), Watkins and Konarski (1987), Watters and Watters (1980), Whitman, Scibak, and Reid (1983).

Feeding problems

Anderson (1983), Albin (1977a, 1977b), Azrin, Jamner, and Besalel (1986), Azrin and Armstrong (1973), Ball, Hendricksen, and Clayton (1974), Beukelman and Rodgers (1985), Conrin *et al.* (1982), Coupe *et al.* (1987), Crump (1987), Davis, Wieseler, and Hanzel (1983), Epstein and Wing (1987), Fox *et al.* (1982), Fox *et al.* (1985), Foxx and Martin (1975), Friedin and Johnson (1979), Hewitt and Burden (1984), Hinds and Oliver (1985), Jackson *et al.* (1975), Jones (1982), Lobato, Carlson, and Barrera (1986), Morris (1977), O'Neil *et al.* (1979), Page *et al.* (1983a, 1983b), Palmer, Thompson, and Linscheid (1975), Palmer and Horn (1978), Rast *et al.* (1981, 1985), Rotatori, Switzky, and Fox (1983), Singh and Bakker (1984), Singh and Winton (1985), Smith *et al.* (1983), Starin and Fuqua (1987), Tierney and Jackson (1984), Utley, Holvoet, and Barnes (1977), Warner (1981b), Whitman, Scibak, and Reid (1983), Wolf, Cohen, and Rosenfeld (1985).

Drooling

Anderson (1983), Barton, Leigh, and Myrvang (1978), Brown *et al.* (1985), Drabman *et al.* (1979), Finnie (1974), Harris and Dignam (1980), Kellow (1982), Koheil *et al.* (1987), Morris (1977), Mueller (1974), Palmer and Horn (1978), Rapp (1980), Ray, Bundy, and Nelson (1983), Trott and Maechtlen (1986), Warner (1981b).

Avoidance problems

American Psychiatric Association (1980), Bryon and Weston (1987), Burgio, Willis, and Burgio (1986), Chapman (1978), Dixon and Gunary (1986), Freeman, Roy, and Hemmick (1976), Guralnick (1973), Hatzenbuehler and Schroeder (1978), Jackson (1983), Jackson and King (1982), Lindsay *et al.* (1988), Luiselli (1977), Mansdorf (1976), Marks (1987), Matson (1981a), Morris and Kratochwill (1983), Peck (1977), Runyan, Stevens, and Reeves (1985), Waranch *et al.* (1981), Wickings *et al.* (1974).

Toileting problems

American Psychiatric Association (1980), Azrin and Foxx (1971), Azrin, Bugle, and O'Brien (1971), Barton *et al.* (1975), Bettison (1982), Bollard and Nettelbeck (1982), Campbell *et al.* (1983), Dixon and Smith (1976), Doleys and Arnold (1975), Dunlap, Koegel, and Koegel (1984), Finnie (1974), Greenfield and Milne (1985), Groves (1982), Hobbs and Peck (1985), Hunt, Long, and Long (undated), Litrownik (1974), Luiselli *et al.* (1979), McNamara (1972), Meadow (1980), Morgan (1981), Phibbs and Wells (1982), Smith (1981), Smith (1976, 1979), Smith *et al.* (1975), Smith and Smith (1987), Van Wagenen *et al.* (1969), Whitman, Scibak, and Reid (1983), Wilson (1980), Woodmansey (1967).

Staff training

Capie, Taylor, and Perkins (1980), Farrell (1985), Foxen and McBrien (1981), Hogg and Mittler (1987), McBrien (1985), McBrien and Foxen (1981), McCall and Thacker (1977), McConkey (1985), Moore, Nikolski, and Presland (1981), Presland (1981b), Presland and Farren (1984), Topping (1986), Toy and Hawthorne (1978), Wiener and Crosby (1986), Yule and Carr (1980).

Note. The article by Presland (1981b) provides a description of evaluative data for the workshops which were organised by the author and which have been a source for many of the recommendations within this guide.

Resources and organisation

Clements (1979), Firth and Myers (1985), Jones *et al.* (1987), Jones (1983), McBrien and Weightman (1980), Partridge, Chisholm, and Levy (1985), Porterfield (1987), Repp, Felce, and de Kock (1987), Spreat *et al.* (1985), Woods and Cullen (1983).

Legal and ethical matters

Advocacy Alliance (1984), Association of Educational Psychologists (1984), Bailey, Matthews, and Leckie (1986), Berry (1987), Brakman (1985), British Psychological Society (1978), Clarke (1986), Cook, Altman, and Haavik (1978), Donnellan *et al.* (1984), Dunbar-Brunton (1979), Frebertshauser (1987), Gast and Nelson (1977), Glaser and Morreau (1986), Gostin (1985), Griffith (1983), Gunn (1985, 1986), Harris (1983), Liell and Saunders (1986), Mental Health Act Commission (1985), Mittler (1979), Roos (1974), Royal College of Psychiatrists, Royal College of Nursing, and British Psychological Society (1980), Sandler *et al.* (1985), Singer and Irvin (1987).

Medical aspects

Aman (1985), Aman and Singh (1983), Barron and Sandman (1985), Burgio, Page, and Capriotti (1985), Campbell *et al.* (1978), Campbell, Anderson, and Green (1983), Campbell and Small (1976), Corbett (1980), Corbett and Pond (1985), Crammer, Barraclough, and Heine (1982), Fischbacher (1987), Gadow (1986), Gadow and Poling (1988), Glaser and Morreau (1986), Gourash (1986), Griffin *et al.* (1986), Hechtman (1985), Kavale (1982), Lipman (1986), O'Leary (1980), Oliver (1986), Oliver, Corbett, and Murphy (1987), Pulman, Pook, and Singh (1979), Reid (1985), Sacks (1980), Schalock *et al.* (1985), Schroeder (1985), Singh and Millichamp (1985), Singh and Winton (1984), Varley and Trupin (1982).

APPENDIX 4

Notes on controversial issues

Introduction

There are many controversies and other uncertainties in the field of behavioural approaches to human problems. Even the basic scheme of antecedents, behaviour, and consequences is not without its conceptual uncertainties; and it has no firm scientific foundation, being largely a commonsense-based framework within which to think about more certain knowledge. This basic scheme is not, however, particularly controversial – not yet, anyway – and will not be discussed here. Instead, issues will be discussed on which controversy is already in existence, and certain positions that have been taken up in this guide, which may be attacked by others working in similar fields, will be defended.

No attempt will be made to deal with criticisms of behavioural approaches generally. Discussion of relevant issues can be found elsewhere (Jones, 1983; MacMillan and Kolvin, 1977; O'Leary, 1972; Harrop 1983; Wheldall and Merrett, 1985).

Why use the term "reducing consequence"?

The term *reducing consequence* is used in this guide to mean "an event, object, or situation which, when it follows a behaviour, makes that behaviour less likely to occur again". It can also be defined as "an event, object, or situation which, if it regularly follows a behaviour, decreases the frequency of occurrence of that behaviour".

In the literature a number of other terms can be found which have been used with one or other of the above definitions. These are *negative reinforcer, punisher, attenuator, and decelerator.* These will now be discussed in turn, and the reasons for not adopting them in this book will be given.

Negative reinforcer. At one time this term was quite commonly attached to the definitions given for a reducing consequence, but it is now usually held to mean something quite different. A more common definition now is "an event, object, or situation which, if it is regularly in existence when a behaviour occurs and is regularly removed immediately following that behaviour, leads to that behaviour occurring more frequently". This definition is, of course, more or less opposite in meaning to the old one, but it is more logical since a reinforcer, by definition, *increases* the frequency of behaviour and it is, therefore, not sensible to have a variety of reinforcer which *decreases it.*

Punisher. This term is in common use today, but I have a number of objections to it.

Punishment is usually thought of as something actively unpleasant whereas the primary aim in behavioural approaches should, in my view, be to decrease problem behaviours by the least unpleasant method possible.

Punishment is commonly thought of as something which is imposed more because the person receiving it deserves it in a moral sense than because it is going to help that person. In this guide the main aim is to help, and the approaches selected should be based on that, rather than on what the person "deserves".

Another feature common in punishment is the deterrence of people other than the one punished. Again, in my view, this is not a consideration which should be involved in selection of consequences to decrease a behaviour.

There is often a revenge motive in punishment: the "eye for an eye" element which is meant to make the wronged person feel better. Again, this is not relevant to selection of consequences for the purposes set out in this guide.

The above elements of meaning in the term "punisher" make it difficult to apply the term to some consequences of a behaviour which decrease its likelihood or frequency, such as the prevention or removal of reinforcing consequences. As will be argued later, all sorts of conceptual confusion occurs when alternative terms, like "extinction" and "time-out", are used for such consequences to avoid referring to them as punishment.

Attenuator. This is derived from the verb to attenuate, which was defined by Lovitt (1978) as meaning "to weaken or decrease the frequency of a behaviour". Its non-technical meaning has more to do with decreasing the size, force, or value of something than with decreasing its likelihood or frequency. It could, therefore, be a misleading word to use.

Decelerator. This is derived from the verb to decelerate, which Lovitt (1978) defined to mean much the same as attenuate. Its non-technical meaning would cover the frequency aspects of something, but not the likelihood aspect.

The term reducing consequence has not, to my knowledge, appeared previously in behavioural literature, but the term *reduction* has. Lutzker, McGimsey-McRae, and McGimsey (1983) state that "behaviour reduction occurs when the frequency of a behaviour declines following contingent removal or addition of some event". Plainly, the term *reducer* is directly derivable from this. Its everyday use would enable people to speak meaningfully of reducing the likelihood and reducing the frequency of a behaviour. It has none of the confusing associations of the word "punisher". It is changed in this guide into reducing consequences because reducer sounds like a "thing", whereas the likelihood or frequency of a behaviour can be affected by any kind of change in the environment.

Why discard the concept of negative reinforcement?

Negative reinforcement is usually defined as increasing the frequency of occurrence of a behaviour by removing something from the environment whenever that behaviour occurs. The implication is that whatever is removed is unpleasant. The difficulties with the concept of negative reinforcement have been helpfully pointed out by Michael (1975) and by Green (1977). Two examples should suffice here:

> Suppose Luke, a person with a mental handicap, struggles with an adult to avoid being taken to the toilet and the adult gives up so that Luke does not have to go. The struggling could be said to have been negatively reinforced because the unpleasant experience of adult direction and control has been removed following it. However, it could also be said to have been *positively* reinforced because it is followed by the pleasant experience of Luke being allowed to do as he wishes.

> Suppose Luke is given an apple every time he goes willingly to the toilet. This would usually be described as *positive reinforcement* of going to the toilet. However, if Luke likes apples and knows the adult gives them at intervals, the experience of being without one could be thought of as unpleasant. Giving Luke an apple would remove this unpleasant experience and would therefore constitute negative reinforcement.

It seems that there is no clear distinction between "positive" and "negative" reinforcement. Any change that is pleasant is removing a situation that was less pleasant, and any removal from an unpleasant situation is a pleasant change. It is best, therefore, to think simply of a *reinforcing consequence,* which is anything that increases the likelihood or frequency of a behaviour that it follows. A distinction between positive and negative reinforcement offers no advantages and leads to confusion.

Iwata (1987) confuses the issues further by extending the definition of negative reinforcement to increasing the frequency of a behaviour by allowing a person to avoid a consequence that would occur if the behaviour did not take place. For instance, if Diane is woken by a buzzer every time she wets the bed, she can avoid this consequence by not doing so. According to Iwata, remaining dry is then being negatively reinforced. No clear reason is given for interpreting the events in this way, when it is simpler to regard them as punishment or reduction of the problem behaviour. This extended definition is, in any case, subject to the same objections as the more usual narrower one.

What is the purpose of identifying welcome and unwelcome experiences?

Welcome experiences are those which someone appears to welcome. *Unwelcome experiences* are those which someone appears to dislike or avoid. These are concepts which, to a large extent, depend on subjective judgement and therefore lack the scientific flavour which behavioural approaches are intended to have. Why then, should use of these concepts be recommended in this guide?

A major problem with concepts like antecedent, reinforcing consequence, and reducing consequence, is that they are defined by the events which follow them. There is, therefore, no obvious objective way of identifying them in advance. This has two main implications.

> It means that they are not genuinely scientific concepts themselves, since they allow explanation of events only *after* they have happened; whereas applied science is mostly about the prediction and control of events. Indeed, a feature of scientific explanation is that it involves predictions which can then be confirmed or falsified by the events concerned, thus testing out the validity of the predictions. Antecedents and consequences can be tested out in this way only if objective ways are found of making predictions, and the definitions provide no basis for this.

To make practical use of antecedents and consequences, they need to be identified *in advance,* and this is not possible from the definitions alone.

To overcome these two difficulties it would be necessary to add features to the definitions which would allow identification of the concepts in advance. Alternatively, an additional set of concepts could be sought which would enable prediction of what features or changes in the environment were going to function as antecedents and consequences for a particular behaviour in a particular person (Danaher, 1974). I know of only two strategies which have been used for such prediction which have any reasonable claim to be objective or scientific.

The first of these strategies is to subject someone systematically to a range of environmental features and changes as possible antecedents and/or consequences for one selected behaviour, and to record the effects of these on the occurrence of that behaviour. There are two alternative forms of this strategy.

One is to use, for the investigation, the actual behaviour for which an intervention programme is required. Among a number of studies of this approach are those by Iwata *et al.* (1982) and Sturmey (1988), who respectively observed self-injurious and stereotyped behaviour in people with mental handicaps under several different conditions. These varied according to the presence or absence of play material, requirement or non-requirement to carry out difficult tasks, and use or non-use of disapproval. This approach, however, though of considerable interest in extending current knowledge, is really a series of intervention programmes and not an *advance* strategy at all. It seems more relevant to build selection procedures into the intervention programme itself; for instance, by systematically using different potential reinforcers on different occasions (Yarnall and Dodgion-Ensor, 1980).

The other is to use some simple behaviour, different from the one that requires an intervention programme (Gutierrez-Griep, 1984; Murphy and Byrne, 1983; Murphy, 1982; Wacker *et al.*, 1985). The most common procedure is to allow someone to select preferred experiences by pressing a lever or some other very simple action. It is then assumed that experiences that reinforce lever-pressing are also likely to reinforce behaviours that need to be changed. Though the studies have demonstrated that preferences can be established in people with the most severe handicaps, I know of no evidence that the preferred experiences are necessarily the best to use subsequently in intervention programmes for different behaviours.

Both these forms present another problem: how to select the environmental features and changes which are to be investigated. None of the published studies mentions more than a small number, and it is certainly impossible to investigate every possibility.

The other strategy for predicting antecedents and consequences is to measure the naturally occurring frequency of occurrence of a wide range of desired and naturally occurring behaviours of the person concerned, and to list them in order of frequency with the most frequent at the top. It is then possible to make use of the *Premack Principle,* which states that any behaviour is reinforced by subsequent participation in any other behaviour which is of more frequent natural occurrence (Premack, 1959).

Using this principle it is necessary first to choose the behaviour whose occurrence is to be increased, and then to select any behaviour from further up the list to use as a reinforcing consequence. The principle could be extended to assert that any behaviour lower down the list could be enforced as a reducing consequence for a behaviour whose occurrence is to be decreased (Premack, 1971). However, the concept has been little researched with human beings (Danaher, 1974); and some of the research that has been carried out does not support it (Hulse, Egeth, and Deese, 1981). Virtually nothing is known about how it would apply to people with severe mental handicaps. There is a report of one demonstration in which making them engage in less frequent behaviours as a reducing consequence decreased the frequency of occurrence of more frequent behaviours (Krivacek and Powell, 1978); and there the judgement of frequency was a subjective one.

There are, moreover, the following difficulties in applying the principle to practice, which make it hard to recommend its use with much enthusiasm.

It applies directly only to reinforcers which constitute an activity in which someone participates. There are many reinforcers that are not like this.

Since the rate of occurrence of a behaviour depends on what antecedents and consequences are in operation at a particular time, how can the "natural" rate of the behaviour be determined? Indeed, is there any such rate?

The procedure is complex and time-consuming if carried out with any precision. Perhaps this is why, as far as I know, it never has been.

What usually happens in the selection of antecedents and consequences is that a person with responsibility first watches the behaviour of someone with a severe mental handicap. The person with responsibility then uses the information obtained, combined with other knowledge about the person observed and experience of people generally, to make intelligent guesses about what environmental features are most likely to function as antecedents and consequences for the behaviour to be worked on. The application of terms like *behavioural analysis* and *functional analysis* to the ABC process sometimes leads to the subjective nature of this kind of prediction being overlooked. The concept of welcome and unwelcome experiences openly acknowledges this subjective element, but tries to bring some system into it without requiring lengthy investigations of dubious validity.

Studies of the validity of such procedures have only recently begun. There is now some evidence that emotional reactions in young infants and children with mental handicaps can be reliably recognised by adults (Sorce and Emde, 1982). Furthermore, it is possible to introduce some objectivity into the procedure, in that actual selection of experiences by people with severe mental handicaps can often be used (Alberto, Troutman, and Briggs, 1983) and a wide range of experiences can be sampled. Alberto, Troutman, and Briggs list 22 experiences investigated with a blind and deaf boy with a mental handicap. Atkinson *et al.* (1984) asked staff working with children with autistic features to list potential reinforcers. They drew up a list of 263, which staff were then able to rank "don't know", "dislikes", "likes", and "likes very much", with reasonable reliability and reasonable agreement with the parents. Pace *et al.* (1985) and Green *et al.* (1988) recently found that children and young people with profound mental handicaps could demonstrate their preference for different experiences, and that the more preferred experiences were subsequently more effective at reinforcing compliance with simple instructions than were the least preferred. Green *et al.* (1988) also found that systematic observation of preferences produced different results from the ones obtained by asking staff to give their subjective opinions, and that it was only the experiences shown to be preferred by the systematic procedure that functioned as reinforcers.

Should extinction be regarded as a separate technique from other kinds of reducing consequence?

Traditionally, it has been the custom to separate *extinction* and *punishment* as two distinct techniques for decreasing problem behaviour. Extinction has been seen as preventing the behaviour from being reinforced (Drabman, Jarvie, and Archbold, 1976), whereas punishment has been seen as following it with an aversive experience (Harris, 1985). Both, however, are supposed to decrease problem behaviour and they therefore fit the definition in this guide of a reducing consequence.

Is there, therefore, any purpose in differentiating extinction and punishment as distinct types of reducing consequence? The arguments against doing so are as follows.

The original concept of extinction seems to have assumed that it consisted only of ensuring that reinforcing consequences which were formerly increasing a problem behaviour were no longer allowed to follow it. However, in the commonly used form of extinction known as *planned ignoring*, this is not the case. In this form the person with responsibility deliberately witholds attention following the behaviour, so that attention will not reinforce it. Rotatori *et al.* (1980), for instance, ignored hitting other students, tearing materials, and throwing objects as part of a classroom intervention programme for an 18-year-old young woman with a severe mental handicap. However, a person with responsibility who is not attending to the person showing the problem behaviour, must be doing something else instead. Often, this will be things like facing any direction other than that of the person with a mental handicap, or pointedly attending to other people in the room. Thus, something is *added* to the environment of the person with the problem behaviour at the same time as ensuring that reinforcing consequences are absent. These additions may be unwelcome and distinguishable from aversive consequences, such as squirting water into the face, only by their degree of unpleasantness.

People at an early stage of emotional development who have customarily been reinforced by, for instance, the sound of a plate spinning and then suddenly find they are not (Rincover *et al.*, 1979) could be upset by the experience. The removal of the sound could then be aversive to them and could therefore have much in common with consequences intended to be aversive in the first place.

Some consequences that are intended to be directly aversive also prevent problem behaviour being reinforced. *Overcorrection* procedures, now generally included in "punishment", require people to do something unwelcome for several minutes. During this time, it will be impossible for them to obtain such naturally occurring experiences as freedom to do as they wish, which may have been reinforcing the problem behaviour. Thus some forms of overcorrection could also be labelled extinction.

The reducing consequences commonly labelled *time-out* have been the centre of much controversy. The question is whether they are extinction or aversive consequences (Leitenberg, 1965). Plainly, they could be either.

It follows from these arguments that there is no reliable way of differentiating extinction from reducing consequences which are aversive. Any reducing consequence might have elements of both. It is much simpler, and probably just as helpful, to use the overall concept of a reducing consequence which can act by removal of welcome experiences, application of unwelcome experiences, or combinations of the two.

Why depart from the tradition of describing time-out as one distinct technique?

There are two serious objections to the term *time-out* or *time-out from positive reinforcement*: firstly, it has no agreed and clear definition; and, secondly, it is hard to distinguish from other supposed types of reducing consequence which have been described. The arguments for these objections are as follows.

There is no agreed and clear definition

Leitenberg (1965) pointed out, some 20 years ago, that "there is no single set of operations which adequately defines 'time-out (from positive reinforcement)' ". This is still the case today. Both Leitenberg and, more recently, Mulick and Schroeder (1980) and Harris (1985) have listed a variety of different procedures which have been given this label.

The definition of time-out (from reinforcement) usually includes the deprivation of one or more experiences for a predetermined period. Beyond this, the term is used in ways that differ from author to author and from study to study. The following uses can be identified.

Deprivation of something specific which is thought to have been reinforcing the problem behaviour. For example, Whitman, Scibak, and Reid (1983) report studies in which behaviours, like eating with the hands and stealing food, were thought to be reinforced by food consumption. They were tackled by procedures which included removing the meal for a short period every time such a problem behaviour occurred.

Removal from all influences which might have been reinforcing the problem behaviour. There are many examples of this in the literature. For instance, Luiselli, Myles, and Littman-Quinn (1983) had a 15-year-old boy with multiple handicaps removed from his classroom or cottage to a small bare room for three minutes (or such longer time as it required for him to behave appropriately in the minute before release) every time one of a number of defined aggressive behaviours occurred. The assumption is that anything in the classroom or cottage which may have been reinforcing the problem behaviour would then be unavailable.

Deprivation of access to experiences which have been reinforcing appropriate behaviours (that is, not the problem behaviour itself). In one study (Huguenin and Mulick, 1981), for instance, a young man with a severe mental handicap in a school situation was praised and given something to eat every 10 minutes if he worked without talking out loud or touching anybody. If he did engage in these behaviours, all school materials were removed and he was made to sit, inactive and ignored, for five minutes with no opportunity to gain reinforcement. Foxx and Shapiro (1978) and Solnick, Rincover, and Peterson (1977) describe similar procedures.

Deprivation of some welcome experience which is not known to have been reinforcing any behaviour at all. Thus Ford and Veltri-Ford (1980) and Barmann, Croyle-Barmann, and McLain (1980) provided music specially and then turned it off for a prescribed time when problem behaviour occurred. Nunes, Murphy, and Ruprecht (1977) did the same with vibration. In these instances, it could be claimed that the welcome experience was also reinforcing any behaviour other than the problem behaviour (DRO), which relates it to the technique described in the previous paragraph.

Time-out is hard to distinguish from other types of reducing consequence
If the definition adopted is deprivation for a period of something specific which is thought to have been reinforcing a problem behaviour, it is indistinguishable from *extinction*, as defined earlier. As Harris and Ersner-Hershfield (1978) state: "the words 'time-out' and 'extinction' are used interchangeably and inconsistently".

Experiences like being placed alone in an empty room could be very upsetting, in which case the procedures would be conceptually similar to more directly aversive techniques, such as unpleasant-tasting liquids or squirting water in the face. There is much discussion in the literature as to whether time-out defined in this way is primarily *withdrawal of reinforcers* or primarily a *directly aversive consequence*. The question remains unresolved, partly because there is no satisfactory definition of "aversive" which excludes withdrawal of reinforcers (Leitenberg, 1965).

The techniques referred to as *overcorrection* involve making people do something unwelcome for a period. This incidentally deprives them of access to reinforcers which would be available if they were left to their own devices. They could, therefore, qualify for the label "time-out". This argument also applies to *negative practice, physical restraint,* and other kinds of directly aversive experiences.

To cut a way through the confusion, I suggest that time-out should continue to be described separately from overcorrection, negative practice, and physical restraint, since these each have defining features which time-out lacks. Time-out itself can then be divided into *time-out from reinforcement of problem behaviour* and *time-out from reinforcement of appropriate behaviour.* The former is more closely related to extinction, and the latter more closely related to depriving techniques like response cost, than either of these two forms of time-out is related to the other.

What does "overcorrection" mean?

Foxx (1982), probably the leading authority on *overcorrection,* defines it as: "a Type I punishment procedure in which the misbehaving student is required to overcorrect the environmental effects of her misbehaviour and/or to practice appropriate forms of behaviour in those situations in which the misbehaviour commonly occurs". He defines Type I punishment as: "the application of an aversive event following a misbehaviour". However, one of his examples required a boy to lift his arms repeatedly above his head, then out from his sides, and then directly in front of him every time he punched his own head. Each position had to be held for 15 seconds and the whole sequence was repeated for 10 minutes. This is hardly appropriate behaviour it and does not correct anything. It does not, therefore, fit his own definition.

Both Foxx (1982) and Foxx and Bechtel (1982) add further defining characteristics, and the two lists do not entirely correspond. Foxx includes the use of short verbal instructions to carry out the overcorrection behaviour, but Foxx and Bechtel do not. Foxx and Bechtel say the overcorrection behaviour must be topographically similar to the problem behaviour (that is, it must involve the same body parts), whereas Foxx does not. Furthermore, Foxx and Bechtel also contradict themselves since they give, as one of their examples of overcorrection for soiling pants, a procedure involving mopping the floor and washing the soiled clothing, which involves quite different parts of the body from those involved in the act of soiling.

The fact of the matter is that many different procedures have been labelled overcorrection. Any attempt to draw lines between those that really are and those which really are not seems to result in arbitrarily chosen lists and general confusion. As Foxx and Bechtel themselves point out, overcorrection procedures are *combinations* of techniques. Thousands of combinations of techniques are possible. Surely the intention cannot be to attach a label to every one! If, on the other hand, a particular combination were found to be much more successful than most other combinations, then there would be a purpose in labelling it separately. There is much evidence that various packages that have been called overcorrection are more effective in certain circumstances than are some single measures. However, the distinctions made by Foxx and Bechtel do not distinguish effective from ineffective findings. For instance, they insist that the overcorrection act should be topographically similar to the problem behaviour, yet it has been found that *dissimilar* acts can be just as effective (Foxx and Bechtel, 1982).

The question to be resolved is whether more effective results can be obtained by:

defining a very exclusive package called overcorrection; or,

relying primarily on the concept of enforcing unwelcome activity as a reducing consequence and using the variety of procedures that have been labelled overcorrection as some of the most effective ways of doing this.

There seems to be no strong evidence that the first alternative will lead to better results, and I would contend that the second alternative is easier to understand and implement. Overcorrection then, in this guide, includes any unwelcome experience which a person is made to engage in repeatedly as a reducing consequence. The only exception is where repetition of the problem behaviour itself is the consequence. The procedure is then called *negative practice*.

How effective is medication?

Reference has been made at intervals in the text to the use of medication to decrease problem behaviour. I felt that I should give some indication of my sources, particularly since I am not a doctor and my credibility on medical matters is, therefore, low.

There has been a great deal of criticism in the research literature of the use of medication, particularly the major tranquillisers, for such purposes. It has been claimed that there is very little valid evidence that such medication decreases problem behaviours separately from its general sedative effect; and this effect decreases all behaviours, whether problem or appropriate, and at certain dosage levels sends people to sleep. There are accounts, too, of a variety of harmful side effects, of serious withdrawal symptoms when medication is stopped, and of detrimental effects on learning. Reviews of this research are provided by Gadow and Poling (1988), Singh and Millichamp (1985), Gadow (1986), Lipman (1986), and Aman and Singh (1983).

These alarming conclusions, however, are not universally accepted. Aman (1985) offers what seems a well-balanced, recent review. There is, he says, some reason to believe that some of the widely used major tranquillisers can decrease stereotyped behaviours, self-injurious behaviours, hyperactivity, and aggressive behaviours. The side-effects and adverse effects on learning are found in studies which used high doses. Perhaps the same applies to withdrawal symptoms.

Although the tone of Aman's review is favourable towards the use of medication, he says that evidence of effectiveness is limited. He also discusses the issue of dosage levels. One of the defences against the criticisms that have been levelled is that such criticisms apply only when medication has been misused. However, Aman describes methods of determining the best treatment as "hit and miss empirical", which might suggest that distinguishing between correct use and misuse in practice is by no means a straightforward matter. Gadow and Poling (1988), Glaser and Morreau (1986), and Schalock *et al.* (1985) also provide helpful discussion of current practices in monitoring the effects of medication on people with mental handicaps.

Most of the research seems to have been carried out in the USA, where medication is used extensively in residential establishments (Aman, 1985; Griffin *et al.*, 1986; Oliver, Corbett, and Murphy, 1987). Its significance in relation to practice in this country could be different, though one recent study in a mental handicap hospital found a high rate of use (Fischbacher, 1987). However, Corbett (1980), a British specialist, writes: "The results of treating behaviour disorders with drugs alone tends to be disappointing in the long-term, though there may be an initial response". He continues: "There are very few instances in which specific drugs seem to be effective in controlling individual symptoms; all psychotropic drugs which are in common usage have general effects". He does, however, note a few possible exceptions to this. He goes on to discuss the problems of determining appropriate dosage levels and describes it as "still an experimental technique". Corbett's recommendations are for "clinical trials in individual cases and careful monitoring" and for medication to be just part of an overall plan of management. Reid (1985) writes similarly, also from a British perspective.

Other relevant references consulted are: Crammer, Barraclough, and Heine (1982), who provide a detailed practical guide to use of relevant drugs; Barron and Sandman (1985), who demonstrated that major tranquillisers can actually aggravate some problem behaviours in people with severe mental handicaps; and Burgio, Page, and Capriotti (1985), Campbell *et al.* (1978), Schalock *et al.* (1985), Singh and Winton (1984), and O'Leary (1980), who compared medication, behavioural approaches, and combined approaches. Research on this last issue is sparse, but there are some encouraging findings.

Other medical issues

There is little evidence on dietary treatments, though Oliver (1986) has described some clinical cases. Reid (1985) briefly summarises our present state of ignorance.

Sources used for epilepsy and behaviour problems include Sacks (1980), Corbett and Pond (1985), and Gourash (1986).

Bibliography

Advocacy Alliance. *Guidelines for One-to-one Advocacy in Mental Handicap Hospitals.* London: Advocacy Alliance, 1984.

Alberto, P.A., Troutman, A.A., Briggs, T. The use of negative reinforcement to condition a response in a deaf-blind student. *Education of the Visually Handicapped,* 1983; **15**:2, 43–50.

Albin, J.B. The treatment of pica (scavenging) behavior in the retarded: critical analysis and implications for research. *Mental Retardation,* 1977a; **15**:4, 14–17.

Albin, J.B. Some variables influencing the maintenance of acquired self-feeding behavior in profoundly retarded children. *Mental Retardation,* 1977b; **15**:5, 49–52.

Aman, M.G. Hyperactivity: nature of the syndrome and its natural history. *Journal of Autism and Developmental Disorders,* 1984; **14**:1, 39–56.

Aman, M.G. Drugs in mental retardation: treatment or tragedy? *Australia and New Zealand Journal of Developmental Disabilities,* 1985; **10**:4, 215–226.

Aman, M.G., Singh, N.N. Pharmacological intervention. *In* Matson, J.L., Mulick, J.A. (Eds.). *Handbook of Mental Retardation.* New York: Pergamon, 1983, 317–337.

Aman, M.G., Singh, N.N., Stewart, A.W., Field, C.J. The Aberrant Behavior Checklist: a behavior rating scale for the assessment of treatment effects. *American Journal of Mental Deficiency,* 1985a; **89**:5, 485–491.

Aman, M.G., Singh, N.N., Stewart, A.W., Field, C.J. Psychometric characteristics of the Aberrant Behavior Checklist. *American Journal of Mental Deficiency,* 1985b; **89**:5, 492–502.

Aman, M.G., White, A.J., Field, C. Chlorpromazine effects on stereotypic and conditioned behaviour of severely retarded patients – a pilot study. *Journal of Mental Deficiency Research,* 1984; **28**:4, 253–260.

American Psychiatric Association. *Diagnostic and Statistical Manual of Mental Disorders (3rd Edn.).* Washington DC: American Psychiatric Association, 1980.

Anderson, C.A. *Feeding – A Guide to Assessment and Intervention with Handicapped Children.* Edinburgh: Jordanhill College of Education, 1983.

ARRI. Rett syndrome. *Autism Research Review International,* 1987; **1**:2, 6–7.

Association of Educational Psychologists. *Members' Handbook.* Durham: AEP, 1984.

Atkinson, R.P., Jenson, W.R., Rovner, L., Cameron, S., Van Wagenen, L., Petersen, B.B. Brief report: validation of the Autism Reinforcer Checklist for Children. *Journal of Autism and Developmental Disorders,* 1984; **14**:4, 429–433.

Axelrod, S., Apsche, J. *The Effects of Punishments on Human Behavior.* New York: Academic Press, 1983.

Axelrod, S., Brantner, J.P., Meddock, T.D. Overcorrection: a review and critical analysis. *Journal of Special Education,* 1978; **12**:4, 367–391.

Azrin, N.H., Armstrong, P.M. The "Mini-meal" – a method for teaching eating skills to the profoundly retarded. *Mental Retardation,* 1973; **11**:1, 9–13.

Azrin, N.H., Bugle, C., O'Brien, F. Behavioral engineering: two apparatuses for toilet training retarded children. *Journal of Applied Behavior Analysis,* 1971; **4**:3, 249–253.

Azrin, N.H., Foxx, R.M. A rapid method of toilet training the institutionalised retarded. *Journal of Applied Behavior Analysis,* 1971; **4**:2, 89–99.

Azrin, N.H., Jamner, J.P., Besalel, V.A. Vomiting reduction by slower food intake. *Applied Research in Mental Retardation,* 1986; **7**:4, 409–413.

Azrin, N.H., Wesolowski, M.D. Theft reversal: an overcorrection procedure for eliminating stealing by retarded persons. *Journal of Applied Behavior Analysis,* 1974; **7**:4, 577–581.

Azrin, N.H., Wesolowski, M.D. A reinforcement plus interruption method of eliminating behavioral stereotypy of profoundly retarded persons. *Behaviour Research and Therapy,* 1980; **18**:2, 113–119.

Bailey, I.J. *Structuring a Curriculum for Profoundly Mentally Handicapped Children.* Glasgow: Jordanhill College of Education, 1983.

Bailey, R., Matthews, F., Leckie, C. Feeling – the way ahead in mental handicap. *Mental Handicap,* 1986; **14**:2, 65–67.

Bailey, S.L., Pokrzywinsky, J., Bryant, L.E. Using water mist to reduce self-injurious and stereotypic behavior. *Applied Research in Mental Retardation,* 1983; **4**:3, 229–241.

Ball, T.S., Hendricksen, H., Clayton, J. A special feeding technique for chronic regurgitation. *American Journal of Mental Deficiency,* 1974; **78**:4, 486–493.

Barmann, B.C., Croyle-Barmann, C., McLain, B. The use of contingent-interrupted music in the treatment of disruptive bus-riding behavior. *Journal of Applied Behavior Analysis,* 1980; **13**:4, 693–698.

Barmann, B.C., Murray, W.J. Suppression of inappropriate sexual behavior by facial screening. *Behavior Therapy,* 1981; **12**, 730–735.

Barmann, B.C., Vitali, D.L. Facial screening to eliminate trichotillomania in developmentally disabled persons. *Behavior Therapy,* 1982; **13**:5, 735–742.

Barrett, R.P. (Ed.). *Severe Behavior Disorders in the Mentally Retarded: Nondrug Approaches to Treatment.* New York: Plenum Press, 1986.

Barrett, R.P., McGonigle, J.J., Ackles, P.K., Burkhart, J.E. Behavioral treatment of chronic aerophagia. *American Journal of Mental Deficiency,* 1987; **91**:6, 620–625.

Barrett, R.P., Staub, R.W., Sisson, L.A. Treatment of compulsive rituals with visual screening: a case study with long-term follow-up. *Journal of Behavior Therapy and Experimental Psychiatry,* 1983; **14**:1, 55–59.

Barron, J., Sandman, C.A. Paradoxical excitement to sedative-hypnotics in mentally retarded clients. *American Journal of Mental Deficiency,* 1985; **19**:2, 124–129.

Barton, E.J., Madsen, J.J. The use of awareness and omission training to control excessive drooling in a severely retarded youth. *Child Behavior Therapy,* 1980; **2**:1, 55–63.

Barton, E.S. Behaviour modification in the hospital school for the severely subnormal. *In* Kiernan, C., Woodford, F. (Eds.). *Behaviour Modification with the Severely Retarded.* Amsterdam: Associated Scientific Publishers, 1975, 213–232.

Barton, E.S., Leigh, E.B., Myrvang, G. The modification of drooling behaviour in the severely retarded spastic patient. *British Journal of Mental Subnormality,* 1978; **24**:2, 100–108.

Barton, E.S., Robertshaw, M.S., Barrett, H., Winn, B. The introduction and development of behaviour modification in an ESN(S) school. *Behaviour Modification (UK),* 1975; **8**, 20–38.

Barton, L.E., Barton, C.L. An effective and benign treatment of rumination. *Journal of Association of Persons with Severe Handicaps,* 1985; **10**:3, 168–171.

Barton, L.E., LaGrow, S.J. Reducing self-injurious and aggressive behavior in deaf-blind persons through overcorrection. *Journal of Visual Impairment and Blindness,* 1983; **77**:9, 421–424.

Barton, L.E., Repp, A.C., Brulle, A.R. Reduction of stereotypic behaviours using differential reinforcement procedures and momentary restraint. *Journal of Mental Deficiency Research*, 1985; **29**:1, 71–79.

Baumeister, A.A., MacLean, W.E., Jnr. Deceleration of self-injurious and stereotypic responding by exercise. *Applied Research in Mental Retardation*, 1984; **5**:3, 385–393.

Beail, N. The nature of interactions between nursing staff and profoundly multiply handicapped children. *Child: Care, Health and Development*, 1985; **11**:3, 113–129.

Belcher, T.L., Conetta, C., Cole, C., Iannotti, E., McGovern, M. Eliminating a severely retarded blind adolescent's tantrums using mild behavioral interruption: a case study. *Behavior Therapy and Experimental Psychiatry*, 1982; **13**:3, 257–260.

Bethlem Royal Hospital and the Maudsley Hospital. *Guidelines for the Nursing Management of Violence*. London: Bethlem Royal and Maudsley Hospitals, 1980.

Berry, D. Power to the plea. *The Guardian*, 1987; 4th March, 3.

Best, A.B. *Steps to Independence: Practical Guidance on Teaching People with Mental and Sensory Handicaps*. Kidderminster: BIMH Publications, 1987.

Bettison, S. *Toilet Training to Independence for the Handicapped: a manual for trainers*. Springfield, Ill: Charles C. Thomas, 1982.

Beukelman, F., Rogers, J.J. Noncontingent use of alum in the reduction of rumination. *Psychology in the Schools*, 1985; **21**:4, 500–503.

Blount, R.L., Drabman, R.S., Wilson, N., Stewart, D. Reducing severe diurnal bruxism in two profoundly retarded females. *Journal of Applied Behavior Analysis*, 1982; **15**:4, 565–571.

Bluma, S.M. Shearer, M.S., Frohman, A.H., Hilliard, S. *The Portage Guide to Early Education*. Wisconsin: CESA, 1976.

Bollard, J., Nettelbeck, P. A component analysis of dry-bed training for treatment of bedwetting. *Behaviour Research and Therapy*, 1982; **20**, 383–390.

Brakman, C. A human rights committee in a public school for severely and profoundly retarded students. *Education and Training of the Mentally Retarded*, 1985; **20**:2, 139–147.

British Psychological Society. *Report of the Working Party on Behaviour Modification*. Leicester: British Psychological Society, 1978.

Browder, D.M., Shapiro, E.S. Applications of self-management to individuals with severe handicaps: a review. *Journal of the Association for Persons with Severe Handicaps*, 1985; **10**:4, 200–208.

Brown, A.S., Silverman, J., Greenberg, S., Malamud, D.S., Album, M., Lloyd, R.W., Sarshik, M. A team approach to drool control in cerebral palsy. *Annals of Plastic Surgery*, 1985; **15**:5, 423–430.

Browning, M.M., Anderson, C.A., Bailey, I.J., Law, I.H., MacLeod, C., Suckling, M.H. *Identifying the Needs of Profoundly Mentally Handicapped Children*. Glasgow: Jordanhill College of Education, 1983.

Bryon, M., Weston, C.P., Treating dog phobia in residents of a large mental handicap hospital: a possible brief approach. *Mental Handicap*, 1987, **15**:3, 119–121.

Burgio, L.D., Page, T.J. Capriotti, R.M. Clinical behavioral pharmacology: methods for evaluating medication and contingency management. *Journal of Applied Behavior Analysis*, 1985; **18**:1, 45–49.

Burgio, L.D., Willis, K., Burgio, K.L. Operantly based treatment procedure for stair avoidance by a severely mentally retarded adult. *American Journal of Mental Deficiency*, 1986; **91**:3, 308–311.

Burton, M., Thomas, M., Cullen, C. *Offerton Self-care Checklist*. Manchester: Hester Adrian Research Centre, 1981.

Calamari, J.E., Geist, G.O., Shahbazian, M.J. Evaluation of multiple component relaxation training with developmentally disabled persons. *Research in Developmental Disabilities*, 1987; **8**:1, 55–70.

Campbell, M., Anderson, L.T., Green, W.H. Behavior-disordered and aggressive children: new advances in pharmacotherapy. *Developmental and Behavioral Pediatrics*, 1983; **4**:4, 265–271.

Campbell, M.D., Anderson, L.T., Meier, M., Cohen, I.L., Small, A.M., Samit, C., Sachar, E.J. A comparison of haloperidol and behavior therapy and their interaction in autistic children. *Journal of American Academy of Child Psychiatry*, 1978; **17**:4, 640–655.

Campbell, M., Small, A.M. The use of psychotherapeutic drugs in pediatrics. *In* Simpson, L.L. (Ed.). *Drug Treatment of Mental Disorders*. New York: Raven Press, 1976, 209–236.

Capie, A.C.M., Taylor, P.D., Perkins, E.A. Teaching Basic Behavioural Principles. Kidderminster: BIMH Publications, 1980.

Carey, R.G., Bucher, B. Positive practice overcorrection: the effects of duration of positive practice on acquisition and response reduction. *Journal of Applied Behavior Analysis*, 1983; **16**:1, 101–109.

Carney, M.W.P., Nolan, P.A. Management of the disturbed patient. *Nursing Times*, 1979; November 1st, 1896–1899.

Carroll, S.W., Sloop, E.W., Mutter, S., Prince, P.L. The elimination of chronic clothes ripping in retarded people through a combination of procedures. *Mental Retardation*, 1978; **16**:3, 246–249.

Cataldo, M.F., Harris, J.H. The biological basis for self-injury in the mentally retarded. *Analysis and Intervention in Developmental Disabilities*, 1982; **2**:1, 21–39.

Chapman, S. The use of relaxation techniques with very young children. *Association for Behaviour Modification with Children Newsletter*. 1978; **2**:2, 5–8.

Cheesman, P.L., Watts, P.E. *Positive Behavior Management: A Manual for Teachers*. London: Croom Helm, 1985.

Clark, H.B., Rowbury, T., Baer, A.M., Baer, D.M. Timeout as a punishing stimulus in continuous intermittent schedules. *Journal of Applied Behavior Analysis*, 1973; **6**:3, 443–455.

Clarke, D. *Mentally Handicapped People: Living and Learning, 2nd Edn*. Eastbourne: Baillière Tindall, 1986.

Clements, J.C. Goal planning in residential care of the severely mentally handicapped. *Behavioural Psychotherapy*, 1979; **7**:1, 1–6.

Clements, J., Wing, L., Dunn, G. Sleep problems in handicapped children: a preliminary study. *Journal of Child Psychology and Psychiatry*, 1986; **27**:3, 399–407.

Conrin, J., Pennypacker, H.S., Johnston, J., Rast, J. Differential reinforcement of other behaviors to treat chronic rumination of mental retardates. *Journal of Behavior Therapy and Experimental Psychiatry*, 1982; **13**:4, 325–329.

Cook, J.W., Altman, K., Haavik, S. Consent for aversive treatment: a model form. *Mental Retardation*, 1978; **16**:1, 47–51.

Corbett, J.A. Medical treatment of behaviour problems in people with mental handicap. *In* Simon, G.B. (Ed.). *The Modern Management of Mental Handicap*. Lancaster: MTP Press, 1980, 29–41.

Corbett, J., Pond, B. The management of epilepsy. *In* Craft, M., Bicknell, J., Hollins, S. (Eds.). *Mental Handicap: A Multidisciplinary Approach*. London: Baillière-Tindall, 1985, 373–381.

Coupe, J., Aherne, P., Crawford, N., Herring, J., Jolliffe, J., Levy, D., Malone, J., Murphy, D., Alder, J., Pott, P. *Assessment of Early Feeding and Drinking Skills*. Manchester: Manchester Education Committee (SERIS), 1987.

Coupe, J., Barton, L., Barber, M., Collins, L., Levy, D., Murphy, D. *Affective Education Assessment*. Manchester: Manchester Education Committee (SERIS), 1985.

Crammer, J., Barraclough, B., Heine, B. *The Use of Drugs in Psychiatry, 2nd Edn*. London: Gaskell, 1982.

Crisp, T., Coll, P. Modification of self-injurious behaviour in a profoundly retarded child by differentially reinforcing incompatible behaviour. *British Journal of Mental Subnormality*, 1980; **26**:2, 81–85.

Crump, I.M. (Ed.). *Nutrition and Feeding of the Handicapped Child*. Boston, Mass: College-Hill Press, 1987.

Cunningham, C., Sloper, P. *Helping Your Handicapped Baby.* London: Souvenir Press, 1978.

Czyzewski, M.J., Barrera, R.D., Sulzer-Azaroff, P. An abbreviated overcorrection program to reduce self-stimulatory behaviors. *Journal of Behavior Therapy and Experimental Psychiatry,* 1982; **13**:1, 55–62.

Danaher, B.G. Theoretical foundations and clinical applications of the Premack Principle: review and critique. *Behavior Therapy,* 1974; **5**, 307–324.

Davis, W.B., Wieseler, N.A., Hanzel, T.E. Reduction of rumination and out-of-seat behavior and generalization of treatment effects using a non-intrusive method. *Journal of Music Therapy,* 1983; **20**:3, 115–131.

Demchak, M.A., Halle, J.W. Motivational assessment: a potential means of enhancing treatment success of self-injurious individuals. *Education and Training of the Mentally Retarded,* 1985; **20**:1, 25–38.

Department of Health and Social Security. *Census of Mentally Handicapped Patients in Hospitals in England and Wales at the End of 1970.* London: HMSO, 1972.

Department of Health and Social Security. *The Management of Violent, or Potentially Violent, Hospital Patients.* Circular HC (76) 11. London: DHSS, 1976.

Dixon, J., Smith, P.S. The use of a pants alarm in day time toilet training. *British Journal of Mental Subnormality,* 1976; **22**:1, 20–25.

Dixon, M.S., Gunary, R.M. Fear of dogs: group treatment of people with mental handicaps. *Mental Handicap,* 1986; **14**:1, 6–10.

Doleys, D.M., Arnold, S. Treatment of childhood encopresis: full cleanliness training. *Mental Retardation,* 1975; **13**, 14–16.

Donnellan, A.M., Mirenda, P.L., Mesaros, R.A., Fassbender, L.L. Analysing the communicative functions of aberrant behavior. *Journal of the Association for Persons with Severe Handicaps,* 1984; **9**:3, 201–212.

Dorsey, M.F., Iwata, B.A., Reid, D.H., Davis, P.A. Protective equipment: continuous and contingent application in the treatment of self-injurious behavior. *Journal of Applied Behavior Analysis,* 1982; **15**:2, 217–230.

Drabman, R.S., Cruz, G.C.Y., Ross, J., Lynd, S. Suppression of chronic drooling in mentally retarded children and adolescents: effectiveness of a behavioral treatment package. *Behavior Therapy,* 1979; **10**:1, 46–56.

Drabman, R.S., Jarvie, G.J., Archbold, J. The use and misuse of extinction in classroom behavioral programs. *Psychology in the Schools,* 1976; **13**:4, 470–476.

Dunbar-Brunton, J. *The Law and the Individual (2nd Edn.).* London: MacMillan, 1979.

Dunlap, G., Dyer, K., Koegel, R.L. Autistic self-stimulation and intertrial interval duration. *American Journal of Mental Deficiency,* 1983; **88**:2, 194–202.

Dunlap, G., Koegel, R.L., Koegel, L.K. Continuity of treatment: toilet training in multiple community settings. *Journal of the Association for Persons with Severe Handicaps,* 1984; **9**:2, 134–141.

Edelson, S.M., Taubman, M.T., Lovaas, O.I. Some social contexts of self-destructive behavior. *Journal of Abnormal Child Psychology,* 1983; **11**:2, 299–312.

Epstein, L.H., Wing, R.R. Behavioral treatment of childhood obesity. *Psychological Bulletin,* 1987; **101**:3, 331–342.

Evans, I.M., Meyer, L.H. *An Educative Approach to Behavior Problems: a Practical Decision Model for Intervention with Severely Handicapped Learners.* Baltimore: Paul H. Brookes, 1985.

Farrell, P. *EDY: Its Impact on Staff Training in Mental Handicap.* Manchester: Manchester University Press, 1985.

Favell, J.E., Greene, J.W. *How to Treat Self-Injurious Behavior.* Lawrence, Kansas: H. & H. Enterprises, 1981.

Felce, D., Jenkins, J., de Kock, U., Mansell, J. *The Bereweeke Skill-Teaching System: Goal-setting Checklist for Adults.* Windsor: NFER-Nelson, 1986.

Felce, D., Jenkins, J., Dell, D., Flight, C., Mansell, J. *The Bereweeke Skill-Teaching System.* Windsor: NFER-Nelson, 1983.

Finnie, N.R. *Handling the Young Cerebral Palsied Child at Home. Second Edn.* London: Heinemann, 1974.

Firth, H., Myers, M. Supporting staff in community services. *Mental Handicap,* 1985; **13**:3, 100–103.

Fischbacher, E. Prescribing in a hospital for the mentally retarded. *Journal of Mental Deficiency Research,* 1987, **31**:1, 17–29.

Fisher, W., Burd, L., Kuna, D.P., Berg, D. Attention deficit disorders and the hyperactivities in multiply disabled children. *Rehabilitation Literature,* 1985; **46**:9–10, 250–254.

Fleming, I., Tosh, M. Self-control procedures: a useful means of helping people who are mentally handicapped to overcome problems of temper and aggression. *Mental Handicap,* 1984; **12**:3, 110–111.

Ford, J.E., Veltri-Ford, A. Effects of time-out from auditory reinforcement on two problem behaviors. *Mental Retardation,* 1980; **18**:6, 299–303.

Fox, R.A., Hartney, C.W., Rotatori, A.F., Kurpiers, E.M. Incidence of obesity among retarded children. *Education and Training of the Mentally Retarded,* 1985; **20**:3, 175–181.

Fox, R., Switzky, H., Rotatori, A.F., Vitkus, P. Successful weight loss techniques with mentally retarded children and youth. *Exceptional Children,* 1982; **49**:3, 238–244.

Foxen, T., McBrien, J. *Training Staff in Behavioural Methods: The EDY In-Service Training Course for Mental Handicap Practitioners: Trainee Workbook.* Manchester: Manchester University Press, 1981.

Foxx, R.M. *Decreasing Behaviors of Severely Retarded and Autistic Persons.* Champaign, Ill: Research Press, 1982.

Foxx, R.M., Bechtel, D.R. Overcorrection. *In* Hersen, M., Eisler, R.M., Miller, P.M. (Eds.). *Progress in Behavior Modification Vol. 13.* New York: Academic Press, 1982, 227–288.

Foxx, R.M. The use of overcorrection avoidance to increase the eye contact of autistic and retarded children. *Journal of Applied Behavior Analysis,* 1977; **10**, 489–499.

Foxx, R.M. The use of overcorrection to eliminate the public disrobing (stripping) of retarded women. *Behaviour Research and Therapy,* 1976; **14**, 53–61.

Foxx, R.M., Dufrense, D. "Harry": the use of physical restraint as a reinforcer, timeout from restraint, and fading restraint in treating a self-injurious man. *Analysis and Intervention in Developmental Disabilities,* 1984; **4**:1, 1–13.

Foxx, R.M., Martin, E.D. Treatment of scavenging behaviour (coprophagy and pica) by overcorrection. *Behaviour Research and Therapy,* 1975; **13**, 153–162.

Foxx, R.M., McMorrow, M.J., Fenlon, S., Bittle, R.G. The reductive effects of reinforcement procedures on the genital stimulation and stereotypy of a mentally retarded adolescent male. *Analysis and Intervention in Developmental Disabilities,* 1986; **6**:3, 239–248.

Foxx, R.M., Shapiro, S.T. The timeout ribbon: a nonexclusionary timeout procedure. *Journal of Applied Behavior Analysis,* 1978; **11**:1, 125–136.

Frebertshauser, L. Advocacy trusts play surrogate parent role. *TASH Newsletter,* March 1987, 4–5.

Freeman, B.J., Roy, R.R., Hemmick, S. Extinction of a phobia of physical examination in a seven-year-old mentally retarded boy: a case study. *Behavior Research and Therapy,* 1976; **4**, 63–64.

Friedin, B.D., Johnson, H.K. Treatment of a retarded child's faeces smearing and coprophagic behavior. *Journal of Mental Deficiency Research,* 1979; **23**:1, 55–61.

Friman, P.C., Cook, J.W., Finney, J.W. Effects of punishment procedures on the self-stimulatory behavior of an autistic child. *Analysis and Intervention in Developmental Disabilities,* 1984; **4**:1, 39–46.

Fulcher, G. A review of self-injurious behaviour (SIB). *Australia and New Zealand Journal of Developmental Disabilities*, 1984; **10**:2, 51–67.

Gadow, K.D. *Children on Medication, Volume 1: Hyperactivity, Learning Disabilities and Mental Retardation.* London: Taylor and Francis, 1986.

Gadow, K.D., Poling, A.G. *Pharmacotherapy and Mental Retardation.* London: Taylor and Francis, 1988.

Gallagher, R.J., Berkson, D. Effect of intervention techniques in reducing stereotyped hand-gazing in young severely disabled children. *American Journal of Mental Deficiency*, 1986; **91**:2, 170–177.

Gardner, J., Murphy, J., Crawford, N. *The Skills Analysis Model.* Kidderminster: BIMH, 1983.

Gardner, W.I., Cole, C.L., Berry, D.L., Nowinski, J.M. Reduction of disruptive behaviors in mentally retarded adults: a self-management approach. *Behavior Modification*, 1983; **7**:1, 76–96.

Gardner, W.I., Cole, C.L., Davidson, D.P., Karan, O.C. Reducing aggression in individuals with developmental disabilities: an expanded stimulus control, assessment and intervention model. *Education and Training of the Mentally Retarded*, 1986; **21**:1, 3–12.

Gast, D.L., Nelson, C.M. Legal and ethical considerations for the use of timeout in special education settings. *Journal of Special Education*, 1977; **11**:4, 457–467.

Glaser, B.A., Morreau, L.E. Effects of interdisciplinary team review on the use of antipsychotic agents with severely and profoundly mentally retarded persons. *American Journal of Mental Deficiency*, 1986; **90**:4, 371–379.

Glynn, T. Antecedent control of behaviour in educational contexts. *Educational Psychology*, 1982; **2**:3–4, 215–229.

Gostin, L.O. The law relating to mental handicap in England and Wales. *In* Craft, M., Bicknell, J., Hollins, S. (Eds.). *Mental Handicap: A Multidisciplinary Approach.* London: Baillière-Tindall, 1985, 58–72.

Gourash, L.F. Assessing and managing medical factors. *In* Barrett, R.P. (Ed.). *Severe Behavior Disorders in the Mentally Retarded: Nondrug Approaches to Treatment.* New York: Plenum Press, 1986.

Graziano, A.M., Kean, J.E. Programmed relaxation and reciprocal inhibition with psychotic children. *Behaviour Research and Therapy*, 1968; **6**, 433–437.

Green, C.W., Reid, D.H., White, L.K., Halford, R.C., Brittain, D.P., Gardner, S.M. Identifying reinforcers for persons with profound handicaps: staff opinion versus systematic assessment of preferences. *Journal of Applied Behavior Analysis*, 1988; **21**:1, 31–43.

Green, R.T. Negative reinforcement as an unrewarding concept – a plea for consistency. *Bulletin of the British Psychological Society*, 1977; **30**, 219–222.

Greenfield, E., Milne, J. *Summary Report of an Assessment of Toilet Aids for Handicapped Children.* 1985. DHSS Store, Health Publications Unit, No. 2 Site, Manchester Road, Lancs. OL10 2PZ.

Greer, R.D., Becker, B.J., Saxe, C.D., Mirabella, R.F. Conditioning histories and setting stimuli controlling engagement in stereotypy or toy play. *Analysis and Intervention in Developmental Disabilities*, 1985; **5**:3, 269–284.

Griffin, J.C., Ricketts, R.W., Williams, D.E., Locke, B.J., Altmeyer, B.K., Stark, M.T. A community survey of self-injurious behavior among developmentally disabled children and adolescents. *Hospital and Community Psychiatry*, 1987; **38**:9, 959-963.

Griffin, J.C., Williams, D.F., Starke, M.P., Altmeyer, B.K., Mason, M. Self-injurious behavior: a state-wide prevalence survey of the extent and circumstances. *Applied Research in Mental Retardation*, 1986; **7**:1, 105–116.

Griffith, R. The administrative issues: an ethical and legal perspective. *In* Axelrod, S., Apsche, J. (Eds.). *The Effects of Punishment upon Human Behavior.* New York: Academic Press, 1983, pp317–338.

Gross, A.M., Berler, E.S., Drabman, R.S. Reduction of aggressive behavior in a retarded boy using a water squirt. *Journal of Behavior Therapy and Experimental Psychiatry*, 1982; **13**:1, 95–98.

Groves, J.A. Inter-disciplinary treatment of encopresis in individuals with developmental disorders: need and efficacy. *In* Hollis, J.H., Meyers, C.E. (Eds.). *Life-Threatening Behavior : Analysis and Intervention.* Washington, DC:AAMD, 1982, 279–327.

Gunn, M. Human rights and people with mental handicaps. *Mental Handicap*, 1986; **14**:3, 116–120.

Gunn, M. The law and mental handicap: 6. Consent to treatment. *Mental Handicap*, 1985; **13**:2, 70–72.

Gunn, M., Rosser, J. *Sex and the Law: A Brief Guide for Staff Working in the Mental Handicap Field (England and Wales only).* London: Family Planning Association Education Unit, 1987.

Gunstone, C. *The Anson House Pre-school Project: Revised Checklist.* London: Barnardos, 1985.

Gunzburg, H.C. *Progress Assessment Chart of Social and Personal Development.* Stratford-Upon-Avon : SEFA, 1973.

Guralnick, M.J. Behavior therapy with an acrophobic mentally retarded young adult. *Journal of Behavior Therapy and Experimental Psychiatry*, 1973; **4**, 263–265.

Gutierrez-Griep, R. Student preference of sensory reinforcers. *Education and Training of the Mentally Retarded*, 1984; **19**:2, 108–113.

Hall, R,V., Hall, M.C. *How to Use Planned Ignoring (Extinction).* Lawrence, Kansas: H & H Enterprises, 1980a.

Hall, R.V., Hall, M.C. *How to Use Timeout.* Lawrence, Kansas: H & H Enterprises, 1980b.

Harris, J. Citizen advocacy. *Mental Handicap*, 1983; **11**:4, 145-146.

Harris, K.R. Definitional, parametric and procedural considerations in timeout interventions and research. *Exceptional Children*, 1983; **51**:4, 279-288.

Harris, M.H., Dignam, P.F. A non-surgical method of reducing drooling in cerebral-palsied children. *Developmental Medicine and Child Neurology*, 1980; **22**:3, 293-299.

Harris, S.L., Ersner-Hershfield, R. Behavioral suppression of seriously disuptive behavior in psychotic and retarded patients: a review of punishment and its alternatives. *Psychological Bulletin*, 1978; **85**:6, 1352-1375.

Harris, S.L., Romanczyk, R.G. Treating self-injurious behavior of a retarded child by overcorrection. *Behavior Therapy*, 1976; **7**, 235-239.

Harrop, A. *Behaviour Modificqtion in the Classroom.* London: Hodder and Stoughton, 1983.

Harvey, E.R., Schepers, J. Physical control techniques and defensive holds for use with aggressive retarded adults. *Mental Retardation*, 1977; **15**:5, 29–31.

Harvey, J.R. The potential of relaxation training for the mentally retarded. *Mental Retardation*, 1979; **17**:2, 71–76.

Hatzenbuehler, L.C., Schroeder, H.E. Desensitisation procedures in the treatment of childhood disorders. *Psychological Bulletin*, 1978; **85**:4, 831–844.

Heaton-Ward, W.A. The drug treatment of mentally handicapped patients. *In* Mittler, P. (Ed.). *Research to Practice in Mental Retardation: Volume III. Biomedical Aspects.* Baltimore: University Park Press, 1977, 213–220.

Hechtman, L. Adolescent outcome of hyperactive children treated with stimulants in childhood : a review. *Psychopharmacology Bulletin*, 1985; **21**:2, 178–191.

Herbert, M. Hyperactivity in the classroom. *Special Education : Forward Trends*, 1980; **7**:2, 8–11.

Hersen, M., Van Hasselt, V.B., Matson, J.C. (Eds.). *Behavior Therapy for the Developmentally and Physically Disabled.* New York: Academic Press, 1983.

Hewitt, K. Behavioural approaches to sleeplessness in children with severe learning difficulties. *Mental Handicap*, 1985; **13**:3, 112–114.

Hewitt, K., Burden, P. Behavioural management of food regurgitation: parents as therapists. *Mental Handicap*, 1984; **12**:4, 168–169.

Hinds, R., Oliver, C. Chronic vomiting in people who are mentally handicapped. *Mental Handicap*, 1985, **13**:4, 152–154.

Hobbs, T., Peck, C.A. Toilet training people with profound mental retardation: a cost effective procedure for large residential settings. *Behavioral Engineering*, 1985; **9**:2, 50–57.

Hogg, J., Lambe, L., Cowie, J., Coxon, J. *People with Profound Retardation and Multiple Handicaps Attending Schools or Social Education Centres*. Manchester: MENCAP Profound Retardation and Multiple Handicap Project, 1987.

Hogg, J., Mittler, P. *Staff Training in Mental Handicap*. London: Croom Helm, 1987.

Hogg, J., Raynes, N.V. *Assessment in Mental Handicap: A Guide to Assessment Practices and Checklists*. London: Croom Helm, 1987.

Hollis, J.H. Analysis of rocking behavior. *In* Meyers, C.E. (Ed.). *Quality of Life in Severely and Profoundly Mentally Retarded People: Research Foundations for Improvement*. Washington, DC: AAMD, 1978, 1–53.

Hollis, J.H., Meyers, C.E. *Life-Threatening Behavior: Analysis and Intervention*. Washington DC: AAMD, 1982.

Hopper, C., Wambold, C. Improving the independent play of severely mentally retarded children. *Education and Training of the Mentally Retarded*, 1978; **13**:1, 42–47.

Horner, R.D., Barton, E.S. Operant techniques in the analysis and modification of self-injurious behavior: a review. *Behavior Research of Severe Developmental Disabilities*, 1980; **1**:1, 61–91.

Howlin, P. A brief report on the elimination of long term sleeping problems in a 6-year-old autistic boy. *Behavioural Psychotherapy*, 1984; **12**, 257–260.

Huguenin, N.H., Mulick, J.A. Nonexclusionary timeout: maintenance of appropriate behavior across settings. *Applied Research in Mental Retardation*, 1981; **2**:1, 55–67.

Hulse, S.H., Egeth, H., Deese, J. *The Psychology of Learning. 5th Edn*. Tokyo: McGraw-Hill Kogakusha, 1981.

Hunt, G., Long, J., Long, J. *Nocturnal Enuresis Management, Systems and Equipment*. Oxford: Oxford Regional Health Authority, undated.

Ivimy, R., Card, H. "That's stealing". *Community Care*, 1985; 7th November, 19–21.

Iwata, B.A. Negative reinforcement in applied behavior analysis: an emerging technology. *Journal of Applied Behavior Analysis*, 1987; **20**:4, 361–378.

Iwata, B.A., Dorsey, M.S., Slifer, K.J., Bauman, K.E., Richman, G.S. Towards a functional analysis of self-injury. *Analysis and Intervention in Developmental Disabilities*, 1982; **2**, 3–20.

Jackson, G.M., Johnson, C.R., Ackron, G.S., Crowley, R. Food satiation as a procedure to decelerate vomiting. *American Journal of Mental Deficiency*, 1975; **80**:2, 223–227.

Jackson, H.J. Current trends in the treatment of phobias in autistic and mentally retarded persons. *Australia and New Zealand Journal of Developmental Disabilities*, 1983; **9**:4, 191–208.

Jackson, H.J., Boag, P.G. The efficacy of self-control procedures as motivational strategies with mentally retarded persons: a review of the literature and guidelines for future research. *Australian Journal of Developmental Disabilities*, 1981; **7**:2, 65–79.

Jackson, H.J., King, N.J. The therapeutic management of an autistic child's phobia using laughter as the anxiety inhibitor. *Behavioural Psychotherapy*, 1982; **10**:4, 364–369.

Jain, A.K., Arya, R.P. Pre-menstrual tension and behavioural problems in women with mental handicap. *Mental Handicap*, 1987; **15**:2, 64–67.

Jan, J.E., Freeman, R.D., McCormick, A.Q., Scott, E.B., Robertson, W.D., Newman, D.E. Eye-pressing by visually impaired children. *Developmental Medicine and Child Neurology*, 1983; **26**:6, 755–762.

Jeffree, D., Cheseldine, S. *Pathways to Independence*. London: Hodder & Stoughton, 1982.

Jeffree, D.M., McConkey, R. *PIP Developmental Charts*. London: Hodder & Stoughton, 1976.

Jeffree, D.M., McConkey, R., Hewson, S. *Teaching the Handicapped Child.* London: Souvenir Press, 1977.

Jenner, S. The effectiveness of abbreviated overcorrection-based treatments. *Behavioural Psychotherapy,* 1984; **12**:2, 175–187.

Jones, A.A., Blunden, R., Coles, E., Evans, G., Porterfield, J. Evaluating the impact of training, supervisor feedback, self-monitoring and collaborative goal setting on staff and client behaviours. *In* Hogg, J., Mittler, P. (Eds.). *Staff Training in Mental Handicap.* London: Croom Helm, 1987, 213–300.

Jones, M.C. *Behaviour Problems in Handicapped Children.* London : Souvenir Press, 1983.

Jones, S.H., Simmons, J.Q., Frankel, F. An extinction procedure for eliminating self-destructive behaviour in a 9-year-old autistic girl. *Journal of Autism and Childhood Schizophrenia,* 1974; **4**:3, 241–250.

Jones, T.W. Treatment of behavior-related eating problems in retarded students: a review of the literature. *In* Hollis, J.H., Meyers, C.E. (Eds.). *Life-Threatening Behavior: Analysis and Intervention.* Washington DC : AAMD, 1982, 3–26.

Karpowitz, D.H., Johnson, S.M. Stimulus control in child-family interaction. *Behavioral Assessment,* 1981; **3**, 161–171.

Kavale, K. The efficacy of stimulant drug treatment for hyperactivity: a meta-analysis. *Journal of Learning Disabilities,* 1982; **15**:5, 280–289.

Kellow, B. The Medeci Dribble Control Box. *Behavioural Approaches with Children,* 1982; **6**:4, 20–21.

Keogh, D., Whitman, T. Mental retardation in children. *In* Hersen, M., Van Hasselt, V.B., Matson, J.C. (Eds.). *Behavior Therapy for the Developmentally and Physically Disabled.* New York: Academic Press, 1983, 205–246.

Kiernan, C. *Analysis of Programmes for Teaching.* Basingstoke: Globe Education, 1981.

Kiernan, C., Jones, M. *The Behaviour Assessment Battery (Second Edn.).* Windsor: NFER-Nelson, 1982.

Kiernan, C., Jordan, R., Saunders, C. *Starting Off.* London: Souvenir Press, 1978.

Kiernan, C., Reid, B. *Pre-Verbal Communication Schedule.* Windsor: NFER-Nelson, 1987.

Kiernan, D., Kiernan, C. *Survey of Behaviour Problems in Special Schools: Feedback to Participating Schools.* Manchester: Hester Adrian Research Centre, University of Manchester and School of Education, Manchester Polytechnic, 1988.

Koegel, R.L., Rincover, A. Treatment of psychotic children in a classroom environment: 1. Learning in a large group. *Journal of Applied Behavior Analysis,* 1974; **7**:1, 45–59.

Koheil, R., Sochaniwskyj, A.E., Bablich, K., Kenny, D.J., Milner, M. Biofeedback techniques and behaviour modification in the conservative remediation of drooling by children with cerebral palsy. *Developmental Medicine and Child Neurology,* 1987; **29**:1, 19–26.

Koller, H., Richardson, S.A., Katz, M., McLaren, J. Behavior disturbance since childhood among a 5-year birth cohort of all mentally retarded young adults in a city. *American Journal of Mental Deficiency,* 1983; **87**:4, 386–395.

Krivacek, D., Powell, J. Negative preference management: behavioral suppression using Premack's punishment hypothesis. *Education and Treatment of Children,* 1978; **1**:4, 5–13.

Kuczynski, L., Kochanska, G., Radke-Yarrow, M., Girnius-Brown, O. A developmental interpretation of young children's noncompliance. *Developmental Psychology,* 1987; **23**:6, 799–806.

LaGrow, S.J., Repp, A.C. Stereotypic responding: a review of intervention research. *American Journal of Mental Deficiency,* 1984; **88**:6, 595–609.

LaVigna, G.W., Donnellan, A.M. *Alternatives to Punishment: Solving Behavior Problems with Non-aversive Strategies.* New York: Irvington, 1986.

Leitenberg, H. Is timeout from positive reinforcement an aversive event? A review of the experimental evidence. *Psychological Bulletin*, 1965; **64**:6, 428–441.

Lewis, M.H., Baumeister, A.A. Stereotyped mannerisms in mentally retarded persons: animal models and theoretical analyses. *In* Ellis, N.R. (Ed.). *International Review of Research in Mental Retardation, Volume 11*. New York: Academic Press, 1982, 123–161.

Libby, J.D., Polloway, E.A., Smith, J.D. Lesch-Nyhan syndrome: a review. *Education and Training of the Mentally Retarded*, 1983; **18**:3, 226–231.

Liell, P., Saunders, B. *The Law of Education (9th Edn.)*. London: Butterworths, 1986.

Lindsay, W.R., Baty, S. Behavioural relaxation training: explorations with adults who are mentally handicapped. *Mental Handicap*, 1986; **14**:4, 160–162.

Lindsay, W.R., Michie, A.M., Baty, F.J., McKenzie, K. Dog phobia in people with mental handicaps: anxiety management training and exposure treatments. *Mental Handicap Research*, 1988; **1**:1, 39–48.

Lipman, R.S. Overview of research in psychopharmacological treatment of the mentally ill/mentally retarded. *Psychopharmacology Bulletin*, 1986; **22**:4, 1046–1054.

Litrownik, A.J. A method for home training an incontinent child. *Journal of Behavior Therapy and Experimental Psychiatry*, 1974; **5**, 77–80.

Lobato, D., Carlson, E.I., Barrera, R.A. Modified satiation reducing ruminative behaviour without excessive weight gain. *Applied Research in Mental Retardation*, 1986; **7**:3, 337–347.

Lockwood, K., Bourland, G. Reduction of self-injurious behaviors by reinforcement and toy use. *Mental Retardation*, 1982; **20**:4, 169–173.

Longhorn, F. *A Sensory Curriculum for Very Special People: a practical approach to curriculum planning*. London: Souvenir Press, 1988.

Lovaas, I., Newsom, C., Hickman, C. Self-stimulatory behavior and perceptual reinforcement. *Journal of Applied Behavior Analysis*, 1987; **20**:1, 45–68.

Lovitt, T.C. *Managing Inappropriate Behaviors in the Classroom*. Reston, Virginia: Council for Exceptional Children, 1978.

Luce, S.C., Christian, W.P. *How to Reduce Autistic and Severely Maladaptive Behaviors*. Lawrence, Kansas: H & H Enterprises, 1981.

Luiselli, J.K. Case report: an attendant-administered contingency management programme for the treatment of a toileting phobia. *Journal of Mental Deficiency Research*, 1977; **21**, 283–286.

Luiselli, J.K. Treatment of an autistic child's fear of riding a school bus through exposure and reinforcement. *Journal of Behavior Therapy and Experimental Psychiatry*, 1978; **9**, 169–172.

Luiselli, J.K. Relaxation training with the developmentally disabled: a reappraisal. *Behavior Research of Severe Developmental Disabilities*, 1980; **1**, 191–213.

Luiselli, J.K. Treatment of an assaultive, sensory-impaired adolescent through a multicomponent behavioral program. *Journal of Behavior Therapy and Experimental Psychiatry*, 1984; **15**:1, 71–78.

Luiselli, J.K., Michaud, R.L. Behavioral treatment of aggression and self-injury in developmentally disabled, visually handicapped students. *Journal of Visual Impairment and Blindness*, 1977; **77**:8, 388–392.

Luiselli, J.K., Myles, E., Littmann-Quinn, J. Analysis of a reinforcement/time-out treatment package to control severe aggressive and disruptive behaviors in a multihandicapped rubella child. *Applied Research in Mental Retardation*, 1983; **4**:1, 65–78.

Luiselli, J.K., Reisman, J., Helfen, C.S., Pemberton, B.W. Toilet training in the classroom: an adaptation of Azrin and Foxx's rapid toilet training procedures. *Behavioral Engineering*, 1979; **5**:3, 89–93.

Luiselli, J.K., Slocumb, P.R. Management of multiple aggressive behaviors by differential reinforcement. *Journal of Behavior Therapy and Experimental Psychiatry*, 1983; **14**:4, 343–347.

Lutzker, J.R. Social reinforcement control of exhibitionism in a profoundly retarded adult. *Mental Retardation*, 1974; **12**, 46–47.

Lutzker, J.R., McGimsey-McRae, S., McGimsey, J.F. General description of behavioral approaches. *In* Hersen, M., Van Hasselt, V.B., Matson, J.C. (Eds.). *Behavior Therapy for the Developmentally and Physically Disabled.* New York: Academic Pres, 1983, 25–56.

Lutzker, J.R., Wesch, D. Facial screening: history and critical review. *Australia and New Zealand Journal of Developmental Disabilities,* 1983; **9**:4, 209–223.

Maag, J.W., Rutherford, R.B., Wolchik, S.A., Parks, B.T. Brief report: comparison of two short overcorrection procedures on the stereotypic behavior of autistic children. *Journal of Autism and Developmental Disorders,* 1986; **16**:1, 83–87.

Mace, F.C., Hock, M.L., Lalli, J.S., West, B.J., Belfiore, B., Pinter, E., Brown, D.K. Behavioral momentum in the treatment of noncompliance. *Journal of Applied Behavior Analysis,* 1988; **21**:2, 123–141.

Macmillan, A., Kolvin, I. Behaviour modification in teaching strategy: some emergent problems and suggested solutions. *Educational Research,* 1977; **20**, 10–21.

Mahoney, K., Van Wagenen, R.K., Meyerson, L. Toilet training of normal and retarded children. *Journal of Applied Behavior Analysis,* 1975; **4**:3, 173–181.

Malott, R.W. Rule-governed behaviour, self-management, and the developmentally disabled: a theoretical analysis. *Analysis and Intervention in Developmental Disabilities,* 1984; **4**:2, 199–209.

Mank, D.M., Horner, R.H. Self-recruited feedback: a cost-effective procedure for maintaining behavior. *Research in Developmental Disabilities,* 1987; **8**:1, 91–112.

Mansdorf, I.J. Eliminating fear in a mentally retarded adult by behavioral hierarchies and operant techniques. *Journal of Behavior Therapy and Experimental Psychiatry,* 1976; **7**, 189–190.

Mansell, J., Felce, D., de Kock, U., Jenkins, J. Increasing purposeful activity of severely and profoundly mentally handicapped adults. *Behaviour Research and Therapy,* 1982; **20**:6, 593–604.

Marks, I. The development of normal fear: a review. *Journal of Child Psychology and Psychiatry,* 1987; **28**:5, 667–697.

Martin, J.A. The control of imitative and nonimitative behaviors in severely retarded children through "generalised-instruction following". *Journal of Experimental Child Psychology,* 1971; **11**, 390–400.

Matson, J.L. Assessment and treatment of clinical fears in mentally retarded children. *Journal of Applied Behavior Analysis,* 1981a; **14**:3, 287–294.

Matson, J.L. A controlled outcome of phobias in mentally retarded adults. *Behaviour Research and Therapy,* 1981b; **19**, 101–107.

Matson, J.L. The treatment of behavioral characteristics of depression in the mentally retarded. *Behavior Therapy,* 1982; **13**:2, 209–218.

Matson, J.L., McCartney, J.R. (Eds.). *Handbook of Behavior Modification with the Mentally Retarded.* New York: Plenum Press, 1981.

McBrien, J.A. Behavioural training for nurses in mental handicap: an application of the EDY course. *Journal of Advanced Nursing,* 1985; **10**:4, 337–343.

McBrien, J., Foxen, T. *Training Staff in Behavioural Methods: The EDY In-Service Course for Mental Handicap Practitioners. Instructor's Handbook.* Manchester: Manchester University Press, 1981.

McBrien, J., Weightman, J. The effect of room management procedures on the engagement of profoundly retarded children. *British Journal of Mental Subnormality,* 1980; **26**:1, 38–46.

McCall, C., Thacker, J. A parent workshop in the school. *Special Education: Forward Trends,* 1977; **4**:4, 20–21.

McConkey, R. *Working with Parents: A Practical Guide for Teachers and Therapists.* London: Croom Helm, 1985.

McKeegan, G.F., Estill, K., Campbell, B.M. Use of nonexclusionary timeout for the elimination of a stereotyped behavior. *Journal of Behavior Therapy and Experimental Psychiatry*, 1984; **15**:3, 261–264.

McKeown, M. Educating Andrew: a case-study of behaviour modification with an autistic boy in the school setting. *Apex*, 1978; **6**:3, 23–24.

McLaren, J., Bryson, S.E. Review of recent epidemiological studies of mental retardation: prevalence, associated disorders and etiology. *American Journal of Mental Retardation*, 1987; **92**:3, 243–254.

McNamara, E. Dora: or how they met their Waterloo. *Special Education*, 1972; **61**:3, 9–11.

Meadow, R. *Help for Bed Wetting*. Edinburgh: Churchill Livingstone, 1980.

Mental Health Act Commission. *Mental Health Act 1983: Section 118: Draft Code of Practice*. London: DHSS, 1985.

Meunier, G.F., Kissell, R., Higgins, T. Scale of aversiveness of behavioral decelerators. *Perceptual and Motor Skills*, 1983; **56**:2, 611–614.

Michael, J. Positive and negative reinforcement, a distinction that is no longer necessary; or a better way to talk about bad things. *In* Ramp, E., Semb, G. (Eds.). *Behavior Analysis: Areas of Research and Application*. Englewood Cliffs, New Jersey: Prentice Hall, 1975, 31–44.

Mitchell, L.K. *Behavioral Intervention in the Sexual Problems of Mentally Handicapped Individuals*. Springfield, Ill: Charles C. Thomas, 1985.

Mittler, P. *People Not Patients: Problems and Policies in Mental Handicap*. London: Methuen, 1979.

Moore, S., Nikolski, I., Presland, J. A workshop for parents of young handicapped children. *AEP Journal*, 1981; **5**:5, 40–44.

Morgan, R. *Childhood incontinence*. London: Heinemann, 1981.

Morgan, R.L., Striefel, S. Restrictiveness of procedures to decrease behavior: views of school psychologists, administrators, teachers, and specialists. *Journal of Special Education*, 1987-88; **21**:4, 108–121.

Morris, R. J., Kratochwill, T. *Treating Children's Fears and Phobias: A Behavioral Approach*. New York: Pergamon, 1983.

Morris, S.E. *Program Guidelines for Feeding Problems*. Edison, NJ: Childcraft Education Corporation, 1977.

Mueller, H. Feeding. *In* Finnie, N.R. *Handling the Young Cerebral Palsied Child at Home, 2nd Edn.* London: Heinemann, 1974, 111–130.

Mulick, J.A., Schroeder, S.R. Research relating to management of antisocial behavior in mentally retarded persons. *Psychological Record*, 1980; **30**:3, 397–417.

Murphy, G. Decreasing undesirable behaviours. *In* Yule, W., Carr, J. (Eds.). *Behaviour Modification for the Mentally Handicapped*. London: Croom Helm, 1980, 90–115.

Murphy, G. Sensory reinforcement in the mentally handicapped and autistic child: a review. *Journal of Autism and Developmental Disorders*, 1982; **12**:3, 265–278.

Murphy, G. Self-injurious behaviour in the mentally handicapped: an update. *Association of Child Psychology and Psychiatry Newsletter*, 1985; **7**:2, 2–11.

Murphy, G., Wilson, B. *Self-injurious behaviour*. Kidderminster: BIMH Publications, 1985.

Murphy, K., Byrne, D.J. Selection of optimal modalities as avenues of learning in deaf, blind, multiply disabled children. *In* Mencher, G.T., Gerber, S.E. (Eds.). *The Multiply Handicapped Hearing Impaired Child*. New York: Grune and Stratton, 1983, 355–395.

Murray, M.E. Modified time-out procedures for controlling tantrum behaviors in public places. *Behavior Therapy*, 1976; **7**, 412–413.

Nellhaus, G. Abnormal head movements of young children. *Developmental Medicine & Child Neurology*, 1983; **25**:3, 384–389.

Nunes, D.L., Murphy, R.J., Ruprecht, M.L. Reducing self-injurious behavior of severely retarded individuals through withdrawal of reinforcement procedures. *Behavior Modification*, 1977; **1**:4, 499–516.

O'Brien, M.A., Obrzut, J.E. Attention deficit disorder with hyperactivity: a review and implications for the classroom. *Journal of Special Education*, 1986; **20**:3, 281–297.

O'Leary, K.D. Pills or skills for hyperactive children. *Journal of Applied Behavior Analysis*, 1980; **13**:1, 191–204.

O'Leary, K.D. Behavior modification in the classrooms: a rejoinder to Winnett and Winkler. *Journal of Applied Behavior Analysis*, 1972; **5**, 505–511.

Oliver, B.E. Exclusion diets in mental handicap practice. *Mental Handicap*, 1986; **14**:3, 94–98.

Oliver, C., Murphy, G.H., Corbett, J.A. Self-injurious behaviour in people with mental handicap: a total population study. *Journal of Mental Deficiency Research*, 1987; **31**:2, 147–162.

O'Neil, P.M., White, J.L., King, C.R. Jr., Carek, D.J. Controlling childhood rumination through differential reinforcement of other behavior. *Behavior Modification*, 1979; **3**:3, 355–372.

Orton, D. Teaching a severely retarded child to wear shoes using a behavioural training programme. *Apex* , 1979; **7**:3, 80.

Ouvry, C. *Educating Children with Profound Learning Difficulties*. Kidderminster: BIMH Publications, 1988.

Pace, C.M., Ivancic, M.T., Edwards, G.L., Iwata, B.A., Page, T.J. Assessment of stimulus preference and reinforcer value with profoundly retarded individuals. *Journal of Applied Behavior Analysis*, 1985; **18**:3, 249–255.

Packham, H. Managing the violent patient. *Nursing Mirror*, 1978; June 22nd, 17–20.

Page, T.J., Finney, J.W., Parrish, J.M., Iwata, B.A. Assessment and reduction of food stealing in Prader-Willi children. *Applied Research in Mental Retardation*, 1983a, **4**:3, 219–228.

Page, T.J., Stanley, A.E., Richman, G.S., Deal, R.M., Iwata, B.A. Reduction of food theft and long-term maintenance of weight loss in a Prader-Willi adult. *Journal of Behavior Therapy and Experimental Psychiatry*, 1983b, **14**:3, 261–268.

Palmer, S., Horn, S. Feeding problems in children. *In* Palmer, S., Ekval, S. (Eds.). *Pediatric Nutrition in Developmental Disorders*. Springfield, Ill.: Charles C. Thomas, 1978, 107–129.

Palmer, S., Thompson, R.J. Jnr., Linscheid, T.R. Applied behavior analysis in the treatment of childhood feeding problems. *Developmental Medicine and Child Neurology*, 1975; **17**, 333–339.

Parrish, J.M., Iwata, B.A., Dorsey, M.F., Bunck, T.J., Slifer, K.J. Behavior analysis, program development, and transfer of control in the treatment of self-injury. *Journal of Behavior Therapy and Experimental Psychiatry*, 1985; **16**:2, 159–168.

Partridge, K., Chisholm, N., Levy, B. Generalisation and maintenance of ward programmes: some thoughts on organisational factors. *Mental Handicap*, 1985; **13**:1, 26–29.

Patterson, P.M. Making a plastazote helmet – its use and mini case history to outline both. *British Journal of Occupational Therapy*, 1982; **45**:4, 131–133.

Peck, C.L. Desensitisation for the treatment of fear in the high level adult retardate. *Behaviour Research and Therapy*, 1977; **15**, 137–148.

Perkins, E.A., Taylor, P.D., Capie, A.C.M. *Helping the Retarded: a Systematic Behavioural Approach (2nd Edn.)*. Kidderminster: BIMH Publications, 1980a.

Perkins, E.A., Taylor, P.D., Capie, A.C.M. *Developmental Checklist, 2nd Edn*. Kidderminster: BIMH Publications, 1980b.

Phibbs, J., Wells, M. The treatment of nocturnal enuresis in institutionalized retarded adults. *Journal of Behavior Therapy and Experimental Psychiatry*, 1982; **13**:3, 245–249.

Pickering, D., Morgan, S.B. Parental ratings of treatment of self-injurious behavior. *Journal of Autism and Developmental Disorders*, 1985; **15**:3, 303–314.

Pihl, R.O. Hyperactivity in children. Is there a treatment of choice? *Psychology in the Schools*, 1980; **17**:4, 500–508.

Podboy, J.W., Mallory, W.A. Caffeine reduction and behavior change in the severely retarded. *Mental Retardation*, 1977; **15**:6, 40.

Poling, A., Ryan, C. Differential-reinforcement-of-other-behavior schedules: therapeutic applications. *Behavior Modification*, 1982; **6**:1, 3–21.

Porterfield, J. *Positive Monitoring: a Method of Supporting Staff and Improving Services for People with Learning Disabilities.* Kidderminster: BIMH Publications, 1987.

Premack, D. Towards empirical behaviour laws: I. Positive reinforcement. *Psychological Review*, 1959; **66**:4, 219–233.

Premack, D. Catching up with commonsense or two sides of a generalisation: reinforcement and punishment. *In* Glaser, R. (Ed.). *The Nature of Reinforcement.* New York: Academic Press, 1971.

Presland, J.L. Behaviour modification in ESN(S) schools. *British Psychological Society Division of Educational and Child Psychology Occasional Papers*, 1981b, **5**:2, 25–32.

Presland, J.L. Modifying behaviour long-term and sideways. *AEP Journal*, 1981a, **5**:6, 27–30.

Presland, J.L. *Paths to Mobility in "Special Care": a Guide to Teaching Gross Motor Skills to Very Handicapped Children (2nd Edn.).* Kidderminster: BIMH Publications, 1989a.

Presland, J.L. *The Paths to Mobility Checklist: Objectives for Teaching Gross Motor Skills to "Special Care" Children (2nd Edn.).* Kidderminster: BIMH Publications, 1989b.

Presland, J., Farren, A. Working with Jasper: applying the concepts of an aims and objectives workshop. *Mental Handicap*, 1984; **11**:1, 32–34.

Presland, J., Roberts, G. Aims, objectives and ESN(S) children. *Special Education: Forward Trends*, 1980; **7**:2, 29–31.

Prior, M.R., Griffin, M.W. *Hyperactivity: Diagnosis and Management.* London: Heinemann, 1985.

Pulman, R.M., Pook, R.B., Singh, N.N. Prevalence of drug therapy for institutionalized mentally retarded children. *Australian Journal of Mental Retardation*, 1979; **5**, 212–214.

Quine, L. Behaviour problems in severely mentally handicapped children. *Psychological Medicine*, 1986; **16**:4, 895–907.

Ralph, A., Birnbrauer, J.S. The potential of correspondence training for facilitating generalisation of social skills. *Applied Research in Mental Retardation*, 1986; **7**:4, 415–429.

Rapp, D. Drool control: long-term follow-up. *Developmental Medicine and Child Neurology*, 1980; **22**:4, 448–453.

Rapp, D.L., Bowers, P.M. Meldreth Dribble Control Project. *Child: Care, Health and Development*, 1979; **5**:2, 143–149.

Rapoff, M.A., Altman, K., Christophersen, D.R. Elimination of a retarded blind child's self-hitting by response-contingent brief restraint. *Education and Treatment of Children*, 1980; **3**:3, 231–236.

Rast, J., Johnston, J.M., Allen, J.E., Drum, C. Effects of nutritional and mechanical properties of food on ruminative behavior. *Journal of Experimental Analysis of Behavior*, 1985; **44**:2, 195–206.

Rast, J., Johnston, J.M., Drum, C., Conrin, J. The relation of food quantity to rumination behavior. *Journal of Applied Behavior Analysis*, 1981; **14**:2, 121–130.

Ray, S.A., Bundy, A.C., Nelson, D.L. Decreasing drooling through techniques to facilitate mouth closure. *American Journal of Occupational Therapy*, 1983; **37**:11, 749–753.

Rectory Paddock School. *In Search of a Curriculum, 2nd Edn.* Sidcup: Robin Wren Publications, 1983.

Reid, A.H. Psychiatry and mental handicap. *In* Craft, M., Bicknell, J., Hollins, S. (Eds.) *Mental Handicap: A Multidisciplinary Approach.* London: Ballière-Tindall, 1985, 317–332.

Reid, A.H., Ballinger, B.R., Heather, B.B., Melvin, S.J. The natural history of behavioral symptoms among severely and profoundly mentally retarded patients. *British Journal of Psychiatry*, 1984; **145**, 289–293.

Repp, A.C., Barton, L.E., Brulle, A.R. A comparison of two procedures for programming the differential reinforcement of other behaviors. *Journal of Applied Behavior Analysis*, 1983; **16**:4, 435–445.

Repp, A.C., Felce, D., de Kock, U. Observational studies of staff working with mentally retarded persons: a review. *Research in Developmental Disabilities*, 1987; **8**:2, 331–350.

Richmond, G., Rugh, J.D., Dolfi, R., Wasilewsky, J.W. Survey of bruxism in an institutionalised mentally retarded population. *American Journal of Mental Deficiency*, 1984; **88**:4, 418–421.

Richter, N.C. The efficacy of relaxation training with children. *Journal of Abnormal Child Psychology*, 1984; **12**:2, 319–344.

Rincover, A. *How to Use Sensory Extinction.* Lawrence, Kansas: H & H Enterprises, 1981.

Rincover, A., Cook, R., Peoples, A., Packard, D. Sensory extinction and sensory reinforcement principles for programming multiple adaptive behavior change. *Journal of Applied Behavior Analysis*, 1979; **12**:2, 221–233.

Rojahn, J. Self-injurious and stereotypic behavior of noninstitutionalized mentally retarded people: prevalence and classification. *American Journal of Mental Deficiency*, 1986; **91**:3, 268–276.

Rolider, A., Van Houten, R. Movement suppression time-out for undesirable behavior in psychotic and severely developmentally delayed children. *Journal of Applied Behavior Analysis*, 1985; **18**:4, 275–288.

Roos, P. Human rights and behavior modification. *Mental Retardation*, 1974; **12**:1, 3–6.

Rotatori, A.F., Switzky, H.N., Fox, R. Obesity in mentally retarded, psychiatric and non-handicapped individuals: a learning and biological disability. *In* Gadow, K.D., Bialer, I. (Eds.). *Advances in Learning and Behavioral Disabilities, Volume 2.* Greenwich Conn: JAI Press, 1983, 135–178.

Rotatori, A.F., Switzky, H., Green, H., Fox, R. Teachers as agents of behavioral change for severely retarded students. *Psychological Reports*, 1980; **47**:3, part 2, 1215–1220.

Royal College of Psychiatrists, Royal College of Nursing, and British Psychological Society. *Behaviour Modification: Report of a Joint Working Party to Formulate Ethical Guidelines for the Conduct of Programmes of Behaviour Modification in the National Health Service: a Consultative Document with Suggested Guidelines.* London: HMSO, 1980.

Runyan, M.C., Stevens, D.H., Reeves, R. Reduction of avoidance behavior of institutionalized mentally retarded adults through contact desensitization. *American Journal of Mental Deficiency*, 1985; **90**:2, 222–225.

Russo, D.C., Cataldo, M.F., Cushing, P.J. Compliance training and behavioral covariation in the treatment in multiple behavior problems. *Journal of Applied Behavior Analysis*, 1981; **14**:3, 209–222.

Sacks, B.I. Epilepsy. *In* Simon G.B. (Ed.) *The Modern Management of Mental Handicap.* Lancaster: MTP Press, 1980, 95–120.

Sandler, A.C., Thurman, S.K., Meddock, T.B., Du Cette, J.P. Effects of environmental modification on the behaviour of persons with severe handicaps. *Journal of the Association for Persons with Severe Handicap*, 1985; **10**:3, 157–163.

Schalock, R.L., Foley, J.W., Toulouse, A., Stark, J.A. Medication and programming in controlling the behavior of mentally retarded individuals in community settings. *American Journal of Mental Deficiency*, 1985; **89**:5, 503–509.

Schoen, S.F. The status of compliance technology: implications for programming. *Journal of Special Education*, 1983; **17**:4, 483–496.

Schoen, S.F. Assistance procedures to facilitate the transfer of stimulus control: review and analysis. *Education and Training of the Mentally Retarded*, 1986; **21**:1, 62–74.

Schroeder, S.R. Drug-behavior interactions with self-injurious behavior. *In* Ashman, A.F., Laura, R.S. (Eds.). *The Education and Training of the Mentally Retarded: Recent Advances.* London: Croom Helm, 1985, 107–143.

Schroeder, S.R., Mulick, J.A., Rojahn, J. The definition, taxonomy, epidemiology, and ecology of self-injurious behavior. *Journal of Autism and Developmental Disorders*, 1980a; **10**:4, 417–432.

Schroeder, S.R., Schroeder, C.S., Rojahn, J., Mulick, J.A. Self-injurious behavior: an analysis of behavior management techniques. *In* Matson, J.L., McCartney, J.R. (Eds.). *Handbook of Behavior Modification with the Mentally Retarded.* New York, Plenum Press, 1980b, 61–115.

Schworm, R.W. Hyperkinesis: myth, mystery and matter. *Journal of Special Education,* 1982; **16**:2, 129–148.

Sebba, J. *A System for Assessment and Intervention for Pre-School Profoundly Multiply Handicapped Children.* London: Barnardos, 1980.

Shackleton-Bailey, M.J., Hampshire Social Services. *Hampshire Assessment for Living with Others.* Winchester: Hampshire County Council, 1980a.

Shackleton-Bailey, M.J., Hampshire Social Services. *Hampshire New Curriculum.* Winchester: Hampshire County Council, 1980b.

Silverman, K., Watanabe, K., Marshall, A.M., Baer, D.M. Reducing self-injury and corresponding self-restraint through the strategic use of protective clothing. *Journal of Applied Behavior Analysis,* 1984; **17**:4, 545–552.

Simon, G.B. *The Next Step on the Ladder: Assessment and Management of the Multi-Handicapped Child (4th Edn.).* Kidderminster: BIMH Publications, 1986.

Singer, G.S., Irvin, L.K. Human rights review of intrusive behavioral treatments for students with severe handicaps. *Exceptional Children,* 1987; **54**:1, 46–52.

Singh, N.N. Bakker, L.W. Suppression of pica by overcorrection and physical restraint: a comparative analysis. *Journal of Autism and Developmental Disorders,* 1984; **14**:3, 331–341.

Singh, N.N., Millichamp, C.J. Pharmacological treatment of self-injurious behavior in mentally retarded persons. *Journal of Autism and Developmental Disorders,* 1985; **15**:3, 257–267.

Singh, N.N., Winton, A.S.W. Behavioural monitoring of pharmacological interventions for self-injury. *Applied Research in Mental Retardation,* 1984; **5**:1, 161–170.

Singh, N.N., Winton, A.S.W. Controlling pica by components of an overcorrection procedure. *American Journal of Mental Deficiency,* 1985; **90**:1, 40–45.

Singh, N.N., Winton, A.S.W., Ball, P.M. Effects of physical restraint on the behavior of hyperactive mentally retarded persons. *American Journal of Mental Deficiency,* 1984; **89**:1, 16–22.

Sininger, L.S., Yarnall, G.D. Teaching a mentally retarded, deaf-blind adult to follow commands in his living environment. *Visual Impairment and Blindness,* 1981; **75**:1, 17–19.

Smith, A.L. Jr., Piersel, W.C., Philbeck, R.W., Gross, E.J. The elimination of mealtime food stealing and scavenging behavior in an institutionalised severely mentally retarded adult. *Mental Retardation,* 1983; **21**:6, 255–259.

Smith, L.J. Training severely and profoundly mentally handicapped nocturnal enuretics. *Behaviour Research and Therapy,* 1981; **19**, 67–74.

Smith, M.D. Use of similar sensory stimuli in the community-based treatment of self-stimulatory behavior in an adult disabled by autism. *Journal of Behavior Therapy and Experimental Psychiatry,* 1986; **17**:2, 121–125.

Smith, P.S. The dark incontinent: a general introduction to toilet training. *Apex,* 1976; **4**:2, 9–12.

Smith, P.S. A comparison of different methods of toilet training the mentally handicapped. *Behaviour Research and Therapy,* 1979; **17**:1, 33–43.

Smith, P.S., Britton, P.G., Johnson, M., Thomas, D.A. Problems involved in toilet-training profoundly mentally handicapped adults. *Behaviour Research and Therapy,* 1975; **13**, 301–307.

Smith, P.S., Smith, L.J. *Continence and Incontinence : Psychological Approaches to Development and Treatment.* London: Croom Helm, 1987.

Solnick, J.V., Rincover, A., Peterson, C.R. Some determinants of the reinforcing and punishing effects of timeout. *Journal of Applied Behavior Analysis,* 1977; **10**:3, 415–424.

Sorce, J.S., Emde, R.N. The meaning of infant emotional expressions: regularities in caregiving responses in normal and Down's syndrome infants. *Journal of Child Psychology and Psychiatry,* 1982; **23**:2, 145–158.

Spain, B., Hart, S.A., Corbett, J. The use of appliances in the treatment of severe self-injurious behaviour. *British Journal of Occupational Therapy*, 1984; **47**, 353–357.

Spangler, P.F., Marshall, A.M. The unit play manager as facilitator of purposeful activities among institutionalised profoundly and severely retarded boys. *Journal of Applied Behavior Analysis*, 1983; **16**:3, 345–349.

Spreat, S., Lipinski, D., Hill, J., Halpin, M.E. Safety indices associated with the use of contingent restraint procedures. *Applied Research in Mental Retardation*, 1986; **7**:4, 475–481.

Spreat, S., Piper, T., Deaton, S., Savoy-Paff, D., Brantner, J., Lipinski, D., Dorsey, M., Baker-Potts, J.C. The impact of supervisory feedback on staff and client behavior. *Education and Training of the Mentally Retarded*, 1985; **20**:3, 196–203.

Starin, S.P., Fuqua, R.W. Rumination and vomiting in the developmentally disabled: a critical review of the behavioral, medical and psychiatric treatment research. *Research in Developmental Disabilities*, 1987; **8**:4, 575–605.

STEP. *Life Planning Manual (2nd Edn.)*. Southsea: STEP Publications, 1985a.

STEP. *Community Living Skills Assessment (2nd Edn.)*. Southsea: STEP Publications, 1985b.

Stunkard, A.J., Stellar, E. *Eating and its Disorders*. New York: Raven Press, 1984.

Sturmey, P., Carlsen, A., Crisp, A.G., Newton, J.T. A functional analysis of multiple aberrant responses: a refinement and extension of Iwata *et al's* methodology. *Journal of Mental Deficiency Research*, 1988; **32**:1, 31–46.

Sturmey, P., Crisp, T., Dearden, B. Room management with profoundly handicapped young adults by nurses in a hospital adult training unit. *Mental Handicap*, 1983; **11**:3, 118–119.

Tait, T., Brookes, M., Firth, H. Sleep problems in mental subnormality. *Nursing Mirror*, 1976; **143**, 69–70.

Thelen, E. Rhythmical behavior in infancy: an ethological perspective. *Developmental Psychology*, 1981; **17**:3, 237–257.

Thurber, T., Walker, C.E. Medication and hyperactivity: a meta-analysis. *Journal of General Psychology*, 1983; **108**:1, 79–86.

Tierney, D., Jackson, H.J. Psychosocial treatments of rumination disorder: a review of the literature. *Australia and New Zealand Journal of Developmental Disabilities*, 1984; **10**:2, 81–112.

Tomporowski, P.D. Training an autistic client: the effect of brief restraint on disruptive behavior. *Journal of Behavior Therapy and Experimental Psychiatry*, 1983; **14**:2, 169–173.

Topping, K.J. *Parents as Educators: Training Parents to Teach their Children*. London: Croom Helm, 1986.

Touchette, P.E., MacDonald, R.F., Langer, S.N. A scatter plot for identifying stimulus control of problem behavior. *Journal of Applied Behavior Analysis*, 1985; **18**:4, 343–351.

Toy, B.B., Hawthorne, G.G. *Parent Workshops: the Link Between Home and School*. No publisher noted, 1978.

Trott, M.C., Maechtlen, A.D. The use of overcorrection as a means to control drooling. *American Journal of Occupational Therapy*, 1986; **40**:10, 702–704.

Utley, B.L., Holvoet, J.F., Barnes, K. Handling, positioning, and feeding the physically handicapped. *In* Sontag, E. (Ed.) *Educational Programming for the Severely and Profoundly Handicapped*. Reston, Virginia: Council for Exceptional Children, 1977, 279–299.

Van Dijk, J. *Rubella Handicapped Children: the effects of bilateral cataract and/or hearing impairment of behavior and learning*. Lisse, The Netherlands: Swets and Zeitlinger BV, 1982.

Van Houten, R. *How to Use Reprimands*. Lawrence, Kansas: H & H Enterprises, 1980.

Van Houten, R., Rolider, A. Recreating the scene: an effective way to provide delayed punishment for inappropriate motor behavior. *Journal of Applied Behavior Analysis*, 1988; **21**:2, 187–192.

Van Wagenen, R.K., Meyerson, L., Kerr, N.J., Mahoney, K. Field trials of a new procedure for toilet training. *Journal of Experimental Child Psychology*, 1969; **8**, 147–159.

Varley, C.K., Trupin, E.W. Double-blind administration of methylphenidate to mentally retarded children with attention deficit disorder: a preliminary study. *American Journal of Mental Deficiency*, 1982; **85**:6, 560–566.

Volkmar, F.R., Cohen, D.J. A hierarchical analysis of patterns of non-compliance in autistic and behavior-disturbed children. *Journal of Autism and Developmental Disorders*, 1982; **12**:1, 35–42.

Volkmar, F.R., Hoder, E.L., Cohen, D.J. Compliance, "negativism", and the effects of treatment structure in autism: a naturalistic behavioral study. *Journal of Child Psychology and Psychiatry*, 1985; **26**:6, 865–877.

Wacker, D.P., Berg, W.K., Wiggins, B., Muldoon, M., Cavanaugh, J. Evaluation of reinforcer preferences for profoundly handicapped students. *Journal of Applied Behavior Analysis*, 1985; **18**:2, 173–178.

Waranch, H.R., Iwata, B.A., Wohl, N.K., Nidiffer, F.D. Treatment of a retarded adult's mannequin phobia through *in vivo* desensitisation and shaping approach responses. *Journal of Behavior Therapy and Experimental Psychiatry*, 1981; **12**:4, 359–362.

Warner, J. *Feeding Check List.* Buckingham: Winslow Press, 1981a.

Warner, J. *Helping the Handicapped Child with Early Feeding.* Buckingham: Winslow Press, 1981b.

Watkins, K.M., Konarski, E.A., Jr. Effect of mentally retarded persons' level of stereotypy on their learning. *American Journal of Mental Deficiency*, 1987; **91**:4, 361–365.

Watters, R.G., Watters, W.E. Decreasing self-stimulatory behaviors with physical exercise in a group of autistic children. *Journal of Autism and Developmental Disorders*, 1980; **10**:4, 379–387.

Wehman, P., McLaughlin, P.J. Teachers' perceptions of behavior problems with severely and profoundly handicapped students. *Mental Retardation*, 1979; **17**:1, 20–21.

Weiher, R.G., Harman, R.E. The use of omission training to reduce self-injurious behavior in a retarded child. *Behavior Therapy*, 1975; **6**, 261–268.

Weisberg, P., Passman, R.H., Russell, J.E. Development of verbal control over bizarre gestures of retardates through imitative and non-imitative reinforcement procedures. *Journal of Applied Behavior Analysis*, 1973; **6**:3, 487–495.

Westmacott, E.V.S., Cameron, R.J. *Behaviour Can Change.* Basingstoke: Globe Education, 1981.

Whelan, E., Lancashire Social Services. *The Personal Record System.* Manchester: Copewell Publications, 1980.

Whelan, E., Schlesinger, H. *Work Skills Rating Scale.* Manchester: Copewell Publications, 1980.

Whelan, E., Speake, B. *Learning to Cope.* London: Souvenir Press, 1979.

Whelan, E., Speak, B.R. *Scale for Assessing Coping Skills.* Manchester: Copewell Publications, 1980.

Whelan, E., Speake, B. *Getting to Work.* London: Souvenir Press, 1981.

Wheldall, K., Merrett, F. *Positive Teaching: the Behavioural Approach.* London: Unwin, 1985.

White, M., East, K. *The Wessex Revised Portage Language Checklist.* Windsor: NFER-Nelson, 1983.

Whitehead, W.E., Drescher, V.M., Morrill-Corbin, E., Cataldo, M.S. Rumination syndrome in children treated by increased holding. *Journal of Paediatric Gastroenterology and Nutrition*, 1985; **4**, 550–556.

Whitman, T.L., Scibak, J.W., Reid, D.H. *Behavior Modification with the Severely and Profoundly Retarded.* New York: Academic Press, 1983.

Wickings, S., Jenkins, J., Carr, J., Corbett, J. Modification of behaviour using a shaping procedure. *Apex*, 1974; **2**:2, 6.

Wiener, R., Crosby, I. *Handling Violence and Aggression: Adolescents Project Training Paper.* London: National Council for Voluntary Care Organisations, 1986.

Wieseler, N.A., Hanson, R.H., Chamberlain, T.P., Thompson, T. Functional taxonomy of stereotypic and self-injurious behavior. *Mental Retardation,* 1985; **23**:5, 230–234.

Williams, C.A., Forehand, R. An examination of predictor variables for child compliance and noncompliance. *Journal of Abnormal Child Psychology,* 1984; **12**:3, 491–504.

Williamson, D.A., Coon, R.C., Lemoine, R.L., Cohen, C.R. A practical application of sensory extinction for reducing the disruptive classroom behavior of a profoundly retarded child. *Schools Psychology Review,* 1983; **12**:2, 205–211.

Wilson, B. Toilet training. *In* Yule, W., Carr, J. (Eds.) *Behaviour Modification and the Mentally Handicapped.* London: Croom Helm, 1980, 133–150.

Wolf, M.C., Cohen, K.R., Rosenfeld, J.G. School-based interventions for obesity: current approaches and future prospects. *Psychology in the Schools,* 1985; **22**:2, 187–200.

Woodmansey, A.C. Emotion and the motions: an enquiry into the causes and prevention of functional disorders of defecation. *British Journal of Medical Psychology,* 1967; **40**; 207–223.

Woods, P.A., Cullen, C. Determinants of staff behaviour in long-term care. *Behavioural Psychotherapy,* 1983; **11**:1, 4–17.

Wurtele, S.K., King, A.C., Drabman, R.S. Treatment package to reduce SIB in a Lesch-Nyhan patient. *Journal of Mental Deficiency Research,* 1984; **28**:3, 227–234.

Wynn-Jones, A. (Ed.) *Emotional Responses of Mentally Handicapped People.* Taunton: MENCAP, 1983.

Yarnall, G.D., Dodgion-Ensor, B. Identifying effective reinforcers for a multiply handicapped student. *Education of the Visually Handicapped,* 1980; **12**:1, 11–20.

Yule, W., Carr, J. (Eds.). *Behaviour Modification for the Mentally Handicapped (2nd Edn.).* London: Croom Helm, 1987.

Zarkowska, E., Clements, J. *Problem Behaviour in People with Severe Learning Disabilities: A practical Guide to a Constructional Approach.* London: Croom Helm, 1988.

Index

┬